# Usability Engineering

## Process, Products, and Examples

## LAURA M. LEVENTHAL
Bowling Green State University

## JULIE A. BARNES
Bowling Green State University

PEARSON
Prentice
Hall

Upper Saddle River, New Jersey

**Library of Congress Cataloging-in-Publication Data**

Leventhal, Laura M.
  Usability engineering : process, products, and examples / Laura M. Leventhal, Julie A. Barnes.
    p. cm.
  Includes bibliographical references and index.
  ISBN-13: 978-0-13-157008-5
  ISBN-10: 0-13-157008-0
  1. User interfaces (Computer systems) 2. Computer software—Development. 3. System design. I. Barnes,
Julie A. II. Title.
  QA76.9.U83L49 2007
  004.6—dc22                                                                        2007007126

**Vice President and Editorial Director, ECS:**
  *Marcia J. Horton*
**Executive Editor:** *Tracy Dunkelberger*
**Associate Editor:** *Carole Snyder*
**Editorial Assistant:** *Christianna Lee*
**Director of Team-Based Project Management:**
  *Vince O'Brien*
**Managing Editor:** *Camille Trentacoste*
**Production Editor:** *Karen Ettinger*
**Director of Creative Services:** *Christy Mahon*
**Associate Director of Creative Services:** *Leslie Osher*
**Creative Director:** *Juan Lopez*
**Art Director, Cover:** *Heather Scott*

**Cover Designer:** *Tamara Newnam*
**Cover Image:** *Hannah Gal, Photodisc/Getty Images*
**Managing Editor, AV Management
  and Production:** *Patricia Burns*
**Art Editor:** *Gregory Dulles*
**Director, Image Resource Center:** *Melinda Reo*
**Manager, Rights and Permissions:** *Zina Arabia*
**Manager, Visual Research:** *Beth Brenzel*
**Manager, Cover Visual Research and Permissions:**
  *Karen Sanatar*
**Manufacturing Manager, ESM:** *Alexis Heydt-Long*
**Manufacturing Buyer:** *Lisa McDowell*
**Marketing Assistant:** *Mack Patterson*

© 2008 Pearson Education, Inc.
Pearson Prentice Hall
Pearson Education, Inc.
Upper Saddle River, NJ 07458

**Pearson Prentice Hall**® is a trademark of Pearson Education, Inc.

Printed in the United States of America

10 9 8 7 6 5 4 3 2 1
ISBN 13: 978-0-13-157008-5
ISBN 10:     0-13-157008-0

Pearson Education Ltd., *London*
Pearson Education Singapore, Pte. Ltd.
Pearson Education Canada, Inc., *Toronto*
Pearson Education—Japan, *Tokyo*
Pearson Education, Inc., *Upper Saddle River, New Jersey*

Pearson Education Australia Pty. Ltd., *Sydney*
Pearson Education North Asia Ltd., *Hong Kong*
Pearson Educación de Mexico, S.A. de C.V.
Pearson Education Malaysia, Pte. Ltd.

*We dedicate this book to*
*The loving memory of Roger L. Barnes*
*Alan, Brian, and Sam—endless sources of joy*
*And to our mothers, who have always been there for us*

# Contents

# Part 4   Designing a User Interface to Match the User's Needs

## Part 7  Context, Constraints, and Responsibilities for User Interface Design

## 14  The Human in Human–Computer Interaction   267

# Preface

## Introduction

In the last twenty-five years, the issues of usability in computer systems and software have become of increasing importance to software developers. What the consumer sees as the software product is the user interface. If the interface does not satisfy the user's needs, the functionality of the package is not likely to meet the user's needs. As computer science educators, we have come to acknowledge the need to give our students some knowledge in usability engineering before they join the workforce of software practitioners. Also, as experienced educators and practitioners, we know that most of our students learn concepts better by doing rather than reading.

Hence, this textbook was written for an introductory, one-semester course in usability engineering. At Bowling Green State University (BGSU), this course is a required, junior-level offering in our curriculum. Our course is project based and encourages the active learning process that many of our students prefer. To that end, this text is focused on the process and the stages of development of a usability engineering project. Throughout the text we will use examples from a typical class project to illustrate the user interface development process.

This text is not an encyclopedia of usability engineering concepts, nor is it an in-depth research treatise. We cover the entire usability engineering life cycle while emphasizing certain techniques and methodologies. We do not cover all methodologies in depth, and in many cases we follow simplified strategies. We do this because we want our students to understand the activities and goals in the usability engineering process rather than a particular methodology. Also, we do not use a specific programming language or development environment in this text, as we have used a variety of development environments in our course for projects.

## Content

The text is intended to support a project-based course with emphasis on the development process. As such it addresses the following questions about usability and the process of user interface development:

- *What is usability?* We discuss some of the commonly accepted definitions of usability. We compare these to establish their common components. We define the terms *task, user, user interface,* and *system.*
- *What is a user interface?* Many of the devices and tools that we use in everyday life have user interfaces. We discuss some of the issues presented in Norman's *The Psychology of Everyday Things* (Norman 1988) and explore reasons why some common interfaces have developed.
- *How can software engineers incorporate usability into their projects?* We introduce the software development life cycle and the corresponding user interface development life cycle. We discuss the parallels between the two and how to incorporate usability engineering into

software engineering processes. We discuss the major misconceptions related to software and interface development.

- *Where does a usability engineer start?*   Usually at this point in their computer science education, our students have equated computer science with programming. They do not realize that software development of any kind involves a number of tasks in addition to programming. In most programming courses, we as teachers diligently define the problem for students. We often restrict students' design choices so that we can cover specific techniques. In this text, we discuss the importance of some of these other activities including *context setting, defining the problem, designing a solution,* and *assessment.*

- *How does one design a user interaction?*   What are the common interaction styles? To design usable interfaces, designers first need to design the interaction, and to do this they need to be familiar with their choices. In this text, we define a number of interaction styles, as well as their advantages and disadvantages, and the types of situations for which they are appropriate.

- *What can we learn from other people's design experiences?*   We discuss issues of visual design. We discuss standards and guidelines in the context of design, illustrating each with real-world examples. We also show a design example and discuss how a designer might make a predictive assessment of the usability of a design.

- *How does one differentiate between good and bad software design?*   In nearly all usability engineering situations, the user interface is part of a larger software engineering effort. In the text we discuss the process of software engineering and the use of the Universal Modeling Language as a notational tool to describe design components. We discuss some basic concepts of quality design from software engineering, including *cohesion, coupling,* and *reuse,* and we present some ideas of how one might evaluate the quality of a software design.

- *How does the usability engineer know that an interface is usable?*   We define and discuss evaluation concepts and the process of usability assessment.

- *How can one use iteration in the user interface design process?*   We define and discuss basic prototyping techniques, such as storyboards, demonstrations, and version 0 prototypes.

- *What basis is there for determining what is usable?*   We introduce some fundamental concepts from cognitive psychology. We develop a model of cognition that is analogous to the subsystems of a computer (I/O, storage, and processing) and relate that to the human sensory, memory, and cognitive processes.

- *What is universal usability?*   Why is it important? What can a designer do to improve usability for everyone? We introduce the concept of universal usability and how to design user interfaces to include special and diverse audiences.

During the discussion of the process of usability engineering, we have included in the text a medium-scale development example. This example is of the same magnitude as a term project that we have used in our class. We have tried to include enough detail in the example so that if you are developing a project in your class or teaching a class with a project, you will be able to use it as a model for your own class projects. We have also included a number of chapter exercises to solidify the points of the chapters.

We hope that you enjoy our book. We have written it in the conversational style of our teaching, so we hope that it keeps you engaged.

## Why Choose Our Book?

In the last few years, a number of fine usability engineering textbooks have been published. So, you may be wondering why you might select this book for your class or, if you are a student, why your teacher may have selected this book over one of the other choices. We feel our book has a number of features that you may find compelling:

- A number of excellent books on user interface topics are really survey textbooks. While our field has more than enough material and ideas to justify a shelf full of survey books, we felt that our students wanted a book that was more detailed and specific. While we acknowledge that our book does not have the breadth of many of the survey texts, we feel that the trade-offs are justified for our students.

- A number of the best books on the market are really intended for graduate students. Over the years, we have found the materials in these books to be too high level, too advanced, and missing too many details for our undergraduate students. This book was developed for undergraduates after teaching this material to undergraduates for many years.

- Unlike a number of survey books, our book integrates a project, similar to the group project that our students actually do, into the material. This project is an amalgam of the many projects that we have assigned over the years and includes what we think are key elements of a project of this type. The project in this book allows us to show detailed examples and to have continuity from chapter to chapter.

- Unlike a number of newer books, the examples in our book for the most part *are not* Web based and do not necessarily reflect Web technology. We think that this is a strength, not a weakness. Usability engineers develop user interfaces for many kinds of settings and technologies. We have tried to provide examples that apply to a number of settings, including the Web.

- Unlike other books, we introduce early those factors that can really impact how usable an interface is. Then, throughout the rest of the process of usability engineering, we show how these factors can be considered as we understand the tasks that the user interface is to support, can be used to influence design decisions, and can be used in usability evaluation. In particular, we emphasize the impact that situational characteristics can have on the ultimate usability of an interface and how to understand and utilize the situational characteristics throughout the development process.

- Most real usability engineering projects take place in the context of a larger software engineering effort. In our book we tie the activities in the usability engineering life cycle back into the bigger process of software engineering.

## Notes to Students

This text and its earlier iterations were pilot tested by several generations of Bowling Green State University students. Where our students encountered problems in understanding concepts, we have tended to add extra explanations. We hope that these embellishments will help you to understand these concepts as well.

*A comment about definitions.* One of the things that our students have found difficult in our usability engineering course is just the sheer volume of material to learn. Yes, a lot of terms must be learned, and realistically most of us hate to learn terms and definitions. However, the terms and definitions that we present are the basis of the language of usability engineering; to understand or to work in this field, a person really does have to be able to speak and understand the language. So learning the terms and definitions is worth the effort. Our students report to us that this ability to "speak the language" is a really important skill to have, both during interviews and in the workforce.

*A comment about the process.* It is likely that the emphasis in your previous classes was on the product or outcome that you were to produce. For example, in your programming courses you were graded on your ability to construct a program using certain programming language elements. Now, in your usability engineering course, you may feel that the rules have changed! Instead of just being evaluated on the final product that you build, we are asking you to focus on *how* you build your product. It turns out that the better you follow the process, the better your final product will be. In truth, when you are in the workforce the particulars of the technologies you use will change, but what will remain constant are the activities of the process, at least in the abstract.

*A comment on your intuition.* No doubt you have experienced many user interfaces for software, and you probably have a pretty good idea of what you like. One of the really tough things to understand about usability engineering is that you are not your user! Consequently, using your intuition or even your own preferences as you build an interaction and an interface can lead to disaster. So what you like or think is an obvious choice may not be the right choice for your user. Throughout this book, we show you ways to better understand what your user wants and needs and how to design a user interaction for the situation at hand.

*A comment about the project.* In our classes, our students complete projects that are similar to the Audio Catalog project shown throughout this book. Our students complete the project as a team, following the steps we show them. Our students tend to find the project challenging. The sheer size of the project, working in a group, and following a development process all contribute to this challenge. So why do we bother? First, working in teams is a reality in much of the computing industry, and the employers who hire our students like to see that the students have experience working on a team. Second, real development efforts involve much more than just programming, so once again, the employers that hire our students are happy to see that the students have practiced a number of steps in the development process. Finally, we encourage each of our students to keep a neat copy of the project to take on job interviews as a portfolio project. Our students have found that employers are really impressed to see the level and quality of work they can produce. We think you will benefit from doing a project in much the same way as our students do.

## Notes to Teachers

We assume that you are using our book for an undergraduate course. We encourage you to incorporate a term project into that course. It may seem like a lot of work, but we find that our students really learn the material by doing the project, and they accrue some valuable lessons about the challenges of group work.

Feedback from previous students indicates that they consider our usability engineering course to be one of their most valuable, both in getting a job and after they enter the workplace. The course is an introduction to usability engineering, and for most students it is also an introduction to software engineering. Under the proposed *Computing Curricula 2001: Computer Science* (Joint Task Force on Computing Curricula 2001), students are to have 8 core hours of human–computer interaction and 31 core hours of software engineering. We believe that by introducing concepts of both in a usability engineering course, students can see software engineering concepts in context. See Barnes and Leventhal (2001) for more details.

## What Our Book Is Not

We have learned in the course of writing this book that you just cannot include everything. We have made some specific choices of topics to leave out or to save until the end of this book for the sake of clarity and, hopefully, for improved pedagogy. We have opted to focus on a project and on development for a user interface that is much like a traditional graphical user interface (GUI), rather than focusing on some newer technologies. Our experience in our own classes is that it is most important for our students to learn about the process of usability engineering; using an interaction model that is very familiar seems to allow them to focus on process and to understand that even in what they think is a familiar setting, significant design choices and evaluations must be made. Second, although in practice, usability engineers would typically make extensive use of prototyping, we have on purpose delayed a discussion of the topic until later in the book. Once again, with our students we have found that it is helpful to force them to go through a more traditional development cycle in order for them to understand what the differences are among the various development activities. Third, while we discuss a variety of user audiences, for the most part we have focused on the *one user model*. We do recognize that user interfaces are designed more and more often to support collaborative work, but we have found that this type of user audience introduces a level of difficulty that many of our students are not ready to manage. Fourth, we present a strategy for specifying an interaction that uses a mix of scenarios, use cases and hierarchical task analysis (cf. Leventhal, Barnes, and Chao 2004). The technique that we present is intended first and foremost to teach a way of building a specification. We are in no way offering this technique for industrial practice, although we believe that understanding our technique will enable a student to use any of a number of industrial-strength techniques. Finally, this book is not a handbook for practitioners, nor is it intended to serve as a reference book. We hope that you will keep it on your shelf for the long term, but our primary goal is to teach you, the students, the process of usability engineering that you can apply throughout your careers. Hopefully, even as technologies and development methodologies change, you will be able to look back at what you have learned from our book and be able to apply it to those new situations.

## About the Authors

**Laura Leventhal,** Ph.D., is a Professor of Computer Science at Bowling Green State University. She holds a Ph.D. and M.S. in Computer and Communication Sciences from the University of Michigan and a B.S. in Information and Computer Science from the Georgia Institute of Technology. Her specialization within computer science is human–computer interaction, with emphasis on applied cognitive psychology and research methods. Dr. Leventhal is on the editorial board of *Behaviour and Information Technology,* is the author of numerous articles in the field and has been an active member of Special Interest Group on Computer Human Interaction (SIGCHI) and other human–computer interaction (HCI) organizations for many years.

**Julie Barnes,** Ph.D., is a Professor of Computer Science at Bowling Green State University and former department chair. She holds a Ph.D. in Computer Science from the Ohio State University, as well as an M.S. degree in Computer Science and M.A. and B.S. degrees in Mathematics from Bowling Green State University. Dr. Barnes is the author of several papers and co-author of *The Integrated Chameleon Architecture: Translating Electronic Documents with Style* with Sandra Mamrak and Conleth O'Connell. She was the 1992 College of Arts and Sciences recipient of the Faculty Excellence Award from the Undergraduate Student Government. In addition to being a college professor, she has taught high school mathematics and Spanish.

## Acknowledgments

The authors would like to thank our many students who have given us feedback on earlier iterations of this book. We would also like to thank the BGSU Office of the Provost for granting Laura Leventhal a sabbatical to work on this text. We would like to thank the reviewers of our book for their numerous and insightful comments and useful guidance from David Gilmore, Elizabeth Churchill, and Keith Instone. We especially would like to thank the dedicated teachers of HCI that we have met through the years for their enthusiasm and support for the teaching of this critical topic. In addition, we would like to thank Donald Leventhal for his detailed and thoughtful review of the mechanics of producing this book. We would like to thank the many people at or affiliated with Pearson Prentice Hall including: Tracy, Christianna, Karen, Marcia, Robin, and Heath, who kept us on task. Finally we would like to thank Deborah Hix, Rex Hartson, and Barbee Teasley for providing models for how to teach engineering processes to undergraduates—their books and visions remain an inspiration to us.

# Part 1

# Introduction to Usability

# 1

# What Is a User Interface?

## Motivation

Welcome to your usability engineering class. You are probably wondering what you will be studying here. What does this class have to do with computer science or information technology? What new programming language or software will you learn? What kind of software project will you develop? What is a user interface? What is a bad user interface? For that matter, what does it mean to be a good user interface?

This book is intended as an introduction to *usability engineering,* a term that fifteen, or even ten, years ago you would never have seen in a computer science curriculum. Our discipline has gone through sweeping changes, reinventing itself as markets and technologies have changed. Usability engineering is now central to what many computer scientists and information technology professionals do. We hope that this book will help you as you prepare to enter our field.

But what do we mean by *usability engineering* or any of the other names that have been loosely applied to the topics that you will study in this book? At the core, we will study the user interface: how to engineer an interface, how to evaluate the quality of an interface, how and why people react the ways that they do to an interface, and what kinds of tools are needed to build an interface. However, before we can start with the how-tos and the whys, we really have to step back and try to understand what we mean in general by the notion of *user interface.* We need to understand how different people can look at the same computer system and "see" different interfaces. We need to understand that the setting in which a system is used can have a tremendous

3

effect on whether an interface is useful or not. Finally, we need to understand that the historical context in which we build interfaces can impact our expectations of the interface.

In this chapter, we will focus on defining *user interface* and the attributes of user interfaces. You may be surprised to see that we talk about other kinds of systems in addition to computer systems as we try to grasp what we mean by an *interface*. When you are finished with this chapter, you should be able to do the following:

- Look at an object or a system that you have in your home and separate the functional components of that system from the user interface of the system.
- Analyze a user interface of a simple device for specific characteristics that may impact usability.
- Understand how the characteristics of a user interface, even for a simple device, can make it more or less usable.

## 1.1 Introduction

What is a user interface? If you look up the term *interface* in a dictionary, you will find a definition similar to this one:

Main Entry: ¹in·ter·face

Pronunciation: ′in-t&r-″fAs

Function: *noun*

Date: 1882

1 : a surface forming a common boundary of two bodies, spaces, or phases <an oil-water *interface*>

2a : the place at which independent and often unrelated systems meet and act on or communicate with each other <the man-machine *interface*> b : the means by which *interaction* or communication is achieved at an interface

Source: Reprinted from the *Merriam-Webster's Online Dictionary*, Copyright 2007, with permission from Merriam-Webster, Incorporated (www.Merriam_Webster.com).

An interface is a boundary between two things. In a computer system, the user interface is the boundary between the user and the functioning part of the system. The interface may greatly disguise the inner workings of the system. It may use metaphors to express the kinds of tasks that someone can do with the system. A familiar example is found in operating systems that do jobs such as scheduling the execution of programs and controlling the retention of files. When users turn on their personal computer systems, they typically do not see the assembly language or binary instructions of the operating system needed to perform these tasks. They generally do not even see any text that describes these operations in the detail that is involved. Instead, they see a visual representation of a desktop metaphor. By manipulating menus and the visible objects on the virtual desktop, they are actually issuing instructions to the operating system. The desktop interface is the boundary between the user and the operating system. Trained computer scientists who use these systems understand the relationship between the metaphor and the operating system. They are aware of both the interface and the internal workings of the system. To a new or novice user, on the other hand, the desktop *is* their system. The user interface defines the experience to them.

Computer systems are not the only systems with these characteristics. Consider a thermostat. The thermostat in my house looks something like Figure 1.1.

I do not know a lot about heating systems. So from my perspective, this interface *is* the heating system for my house. When my furnace fails and the plumbing and heating repair people come over, they see the thermostat interface. However, they also see and understand the fans and pilot lights that make the furnace function correctly. For them it is essential to understand how the functioning part of the furnace works and how it is tied to the thermostat. For me, however, it is enough to know how to operate the thermostat and what the expected outcome of my operations should be.

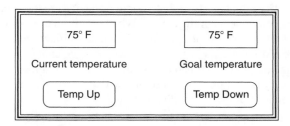

Figure 1.1    Thermostat.

Of course sometimes we understand neither the interface nor the underlying system. We have all heard jokes about people who cannot program their VCRs. As we develop more electronic devices, some people feel overwhelmed by the number of interfaces they have to learn to use everyday appliances.

## 1.2 Common Objects and What We Can Learn from Them

As computer scientists who will be developing user interfaces, we can learn a lot by studying the interfaces of noncomputer systems. Don Norman has written a book and a number of articles in which he discusses the Psychology of Everyday Things. This concept is sometimes referred to as POET, which stands for the **P**sychology **of E**veryday **T**hings (Norman 1988).

Norman's book and his other writings contain many different examples of poorly designed everyday objects. The book also discusses how the design process could be altered to ensure a better design. In Norman's works, he describes some principles that will help us understand why we can or cannot use everyday objects easily. We discuss some of his ideas in this section.

By studying everyday objects, we can learn some objects simply cannot be operated. Norman (1988) uses the work of the artist Jacques Carelman to illustrate a number of functional but nonoperational or barely operational everyday objects (Carelman 1994). For example, Carelman presents a "hatchet with two handles" in which the hatchet blade has two handles, pointed in opposite directions out of the blunt end of the blade. While the blade could cut, as a means of chopping, the device is essentially unusable because the two operators would be trying to swing the hatchet at the same time (Carelman 1994, 11). On the other hand, many objects are functional but not always easy to use. Consider this thought from Norman: "If I were placed in the cockpit of a modern day jet airliner my inability to perform gracefully and smoothly would neither surprise nor bother me. But I shouldn't have trouble with doors and switches, taps and cookers" (Norman 1988, 2). ("Taps" and "cookers" refer to faucets and stoves.) How many times have you walked up to an "automated" washbasin in a public restroom and tried to figure out how to get the water to come out of the faucet?

Many products have not benefited from investment in the design of their interfaces. This is not all that surprising. If the device does not function (i.e., does not do what it is designed to do), the interface is not important. People will not purchase a product that does not work no matter how easy it is to use. However, if you cannot use the product because of a poorly designed interface, it might as well not function!

The first step in building or designing a user interface for a device or system is to be able to separate or at least identify which parts of that system or device are the user interface and which parts are the functional components of the device. Whether it is an everyday object or a computer system, we can divide the object into its user interface and its functional components (the parts that do the work). Users often see these two components as the same. A user interface designer appreciates that we can have well-designed user interfaces with marginal functional components, or that we can have a very robust functional product with a poorly designed interface, or that we can have other combinations of usability and functionality.

Here is an exercise to test yourself. You have just been given three objects: a stapler, a stuffed animal, and a software package. Can you distinguish between the functional elements and the interfaces of these everyday objects? Can you identify what parts belong to the interfaces? Can you find which parts of the object do the work (i.e., the functional parts)? Do you know how you interact with the object? As you answer, focus on the primary purpose or objective of each object.

Here are the answers:

**Manual stapler:**
- *Objective*—To connect several pieces of paper by inserting a wire brad.
- *Interface*—Top surface where you push.
- *Functional part*—Slot where the staples come out.
- *How do you interact? What do you do with the stapler?*—Push on the top.

**Stuffed animal:**
- *Objective*—To give enjoyment to the user by permitting petting and hugging.
- *Interface*—The stuffed animal's "skin."
- *Functional part*—Same as the interface because the "skin" is where the user pets and hugs the animal.
- *How do you interact? What do you do with the toy?*—Pet, touch, and hug.

**Software:**
- *Objective*—Once installed, to perform some useful function.
- *Interface*—If the package has a visual interface, the interface consists of the windows, menus, buttons, and dialog boxes that the user uses to enter commands.
- *Functional part*—Software often gives the impression that the interface is the functional part, but actually the algorithms and modules that execute the commands accessed from the interface are the functional parts.

- *How do you interact? What do you do?*—Because software comes with so many different types of interface components, it is impossible to say what actions the user must perform with the interface without a specific example!

How did you do? For some objects, like the stuffed animal, this is not an easy task. People respond and react to user interfaces. Their ability to use a device is directly related to their ability to understand the intended functionality of the user interface components. When they misunderstand the relationship between the interface and the outcome of using the device, they have a poor chance of using the device as they wish.

## 1.3  How Do Users Know What to Do with an Interface?

User interface components can help us understand what they are intended for if they are well designed. Otherwise they can mislead us (cf. Norman 1988). How are we able to use everyday objects? These objects provide subtle perceptual cues that are most often visual and they tell us the following:

- What part of the object to operate (i.e., what is the interface)?
- What we are supposed to do with the interface?
- How our interaction is constrained by the interface and the interface's relationship to us?
- What is supposed to happen when we operate the interface?

Through experience, we learn to recognize these cues. For familiar objects we do not even have to think consciously about what to do. We recognize the cue and we operate. So the next time that you go to the mall, watch yourself open the door. How is it that you know to pull to go in and push to go out? Long experience with doors that meet modern fire codes has trained you on this pattern. How do you know which side of the door to push? As Norman (1988) has pointed out, subtle visual cues like crash bars, handle locations, door knobs, and the locations of hinges give us clues about how to use doors. Take away these cues or construct them out of clear plastic and even a routine task such as opening a door becomes difficult.

Here is a great story about knowing what to do with the user interface. I (LML) was recently traveling in Portugal. I found an ATM and was trying to withdraw money because I was broke. I do not speak or read Portuguese, so I was forced to use only the visual, displayed cues on the ATM. On the screen was a picture of a keyboard. After I scanned my money card, the ATM gave me some instructions in Portuguese, which I thought said, "Enter your personal ID code." The screen was flat and the picture of the keyboard was detailed and simulated a three-dimensional image. I thought the screen was a touchpad, so I entered my ID by touching numbers for my PIN on the keypad on the screen. Nothing happened, and my session timed out after a few more tries. By now, a number of people were watching me, which was making me really nervous, considering that I was holding my bank card and wallet in my hand. I tried again. The same thing happened. I was about to leave when I noticed a physical keyboard not right underneath but some distance from the screen, which I had not noticed. When I tried the ATM again using the physical keypad, everything worked. The lessons learned? (1) The pictured keypad was realistic enough to catch my attention. I did not look elsewhere for another keypad. I was misled by the interface cues. (2) The screen had the flat look and feel of a touchpad. Being a usability expert, it made sense to me that this bank would offer a touchpad. Experience helped me to believe that the image on the screen was a touchpad. (3) Since I could not read the instructions, I was forced to rely on the visual cues that I misinterpreted.

Erik Wegweiser maintains a Web site called the Gallery of the Absurd v2.0 that has numerous examples of visual images in which the cues from the image are mismatched with the intended function or usage. Figure 1.2 provides an ATM example from his collection. Wegweiser comments that "Obviously this system was programmed by folks who weren't told that some of their ATM machines have keyboards off to the side instead of below the screen."

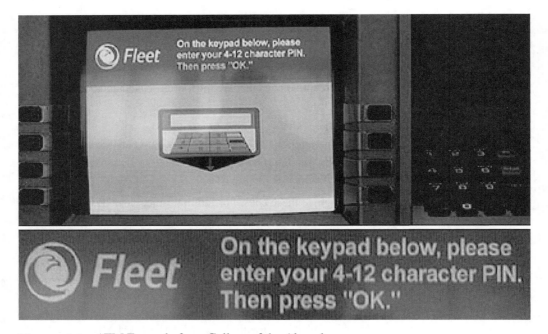

**Figure 1.2**    ATM Example from Gallery of the Absurd.
Source: Gallery of the Absurd, v2.0. "Logan Airport ATM—2000-05-13." Retrieved November 30, 2006, at http://www.ichizen.com/goat/goat_ergonomics. (Photo courtesy E. Wegweiser.)

### 1.3.1 Perceptibility of Salient Cues from the Interface

For us to perceive subtle clues about an interface, the important parts must be perceptible. For simple objects, the important parts of the interface typically must be visible, and they must convey the correct message. We call this property of the interface *perceptibility* of salient cues.[1] To be perceptible, the interface must provide the appropriate information for achieving relevant tasks. For an example of perceptibility, consider the plastic salt and pepper shakers that you often

---

1.  Norman calls this property of interfaces *visibility*. Perceptible cues in the user interfaces of everyday objects typically are visual. However, in user interfaces for software, perception of other types of information may be useful and important, so we have selected the more general term of *perceptiblity*.

see in fast food restaurants. A user would need to determine which shaker contains salt and which contains pepper. Generally, the shakers give us a visible cue as to which one is salt and which one is pepper—the color of the shaker. Usually, the salt shaker is white and the pepper shaker is a different color.

This example contains some subtle hints about what it means to be *perceptible*. First, most of us rely on the visual, perceptible cue of color to identify which shaker is which. If both of the shakers were identical with no perceptible cues as to the difference, a user might need to shake both onto a napkin to decide which was which. Second, to use the visual cue, the user needs to understand what cue to look for and how to interpret it. If a person has no expertise or experience with these kinds of shakers, they might not even notice the color difference, and even if they did, they might not understand the intended meaning. Finally, perceptible cues do not always need to be visual, even though they generally are for simple objects. In the case of the shakers, suppose that a voice announced either "Salt" or "Pepper" when the user picked up the shaker. This would be a perceptible cue, but it would be auditory rather than visual. As we will show later in this book, in some situations it is effective to deliver perceptible cues using modalities other than vision.

### 1.3.2 User Models of Devices

Each time we are called upon to use a device, we process the information from the device through whatever existing internal mental model we have about this kind of device. The new or situational information allows us to build a model of how this specific device will work in the current context. This mental model that we build is based on the subtle clues that we have picked up or perceived from the device. It includes our notions of how the device should be operated, some notion of how the device operates and what the outcome of the operation will be. Sometimes designers also provide an external model of the behavior of the interface, called a *conceptual model*. This model is external to both the person and the system in question. Good conceptual models can also help us understand the operation and behavior of the interface (cf. Mayer 1989).

Remember the notion of perceptibility (i.e., the notion that an object offers subtle perceptible cues about its use). We build our mental models of devices based on at least three pieces of information from the visual structure of the object.

- What do you perceive you can do with the user interface?
- What are the limitations of the user interface?
- What is supposed to happen when we operate the interface?

Norman (1995, 194) makes this point:

> In general, if a simple piece of equipment such as a door or a kitchen stove requires labeling, that need is sign of design failure. Wonderful capabilities become meaningless if they are hard to discover and use.

### What Do You Perceive You Can Do with the User Interface?

When we confront an interface, one essential piece of information we must extract is what we can do with the user interface. For simple user interfaces involving buttons and handles, we typically can push, grab, and grasp the interface directly. If we encounter a user interface element that is a button, for example, we usually perceive that we need to push the button.

However, if we see a button and perceive that we are to pull it, we probably will have little success using the button.[2]

### What Are the Limitations of a User Interface?

What we perceive from the structure of an object may tell us how its operation is limited. Norman (1988) has called this characteristic of an interface a *constraint.* When you look at a keyboard, you can see that typical operation is limited to individuals with fingers, hands, or some mechanism to deliver force to the keys. The keyboard also has other constraints. For example, the operator's hand strength in relation to the amount of force needed to operate keys is a potential constraint. It is useful to note that how a user interface is constrained is directly related to the features of the user interface that are most closely associated with characteristics of the user. The limitations or constraints of a user interface limit the number of users who can successfully use the system or device.

### What Happens when We Operate the Interface?

What we perceive from the structure of an object may tell us how the user's input to the interface is related to the expected function. Our perceptions of this issue give us some notion of how the device functions and explains what the relationships are between actions at the interface (inputs) and actions of the device (outputs). Norman has called this interface characteristic *mapping.*

Most of the time when we use devices, we are concerned with the outcome of our use. From the perspective of the interface, what is important here is to have some idea of how our actions at the interface will lead to an outcome from the device. Mapping is the relationship of the operations of the interface to the action or outcome of the device. Push the power button (interface input) on your TV's remote control and the TV turns on (outcome). The mapping in this situation is that the push of the button on the remote control causes the TV to turn on. More specifically, pushing the power button on the remote causes the TV to change states because the TV turns off if it is already on.

Mappings are not limited to buttons and discrete events. For example, when I am riding a bicycle and I turn the handlebars to the right (interface action) the tires turn right (outcome). This mapping is the relationship between the handlebars interface and the action of the tires.

Part of our mental model is based on our perception of clues for how things work. Again, these clues come from the visible structure of the device. If we misinterpret any of these pieces of information, it is unlikely that the device will work in the way we expect.

### An Example: A Jar Lid

This example shows how we might analyze the user interface for a jar lid, based on the content of the previous section.

- What is the user interface of the jar lid?

    The outer rim of the lid is the user interface.

---

2.   Norman calls this characteristic of an interface its *affordances.* According to Norman (1995) affordances are "an intuitive indication" of what you can do with an object. In other words, the affordances of an object are what you can do or perceive you can do with an interface. The notion of affordances is based on an older notion in psychology that comes from British psychologist James Gibson. He characterized an affordance as a characteristic of the environment that conveyed information about its use (Gibson, 1979).

- What does the outer rim of the lid permit us to do?

   The user interface permits us to grasp the object.

- How does the user interface *constrain* what we can do with it?

   The size of the jar lid constrains our use of the interface. If the size of the lid is very large, a person with small hands may not be able to put their hands around the lid.

- How does the device work? What is the *mapping* between operating the user interface and the outcome when we operate the interface?

   Grasping the jar lid connects the user to the lid, although obviously there is more to the use of this interface. Revisiting the question, we see that we not only *grasp* the user interface but also *twist* the lid. If we add *twisting* to the set of user actions, we have another user-to-interface mapping: twisting to move the jar lid. How is twisting potentially constrained? The user must have sufficient hand strength to twist effectively.

What can we say about this user interface and how it might succeed or fail? Key to success or failure is how well users can perceive the salient information from the user interface and then integrate this information into their mental models and put this knowledge into action. So when users see the jar lid—and if they perceive where to put their hands, if they know which way to twist, and if they are strong enough to twist off the lid without a jar-opening aid—they may have good success with the user interface.

### 1.3.3 Designing Aggravating Interfaces

A surefire way to build an interface that is aggravating and annoying to use is to build one in which the user cannot build an effective mental model. This can be accomplished in at least three easy ways.

First, you can build an interface containing no clues as to how to use it. Suppose that I build a remote control system for a stereo system based on shaking. One shake means power on or off. Two shakes means raise the volume. Three shakes means lower the volume. Consider the remote control for a stereo system shown in Figure 1.3. Suppose I want to change the volume. There is no perceptible clue as to what I am to do with this device. A slight improvement is illustrated in Figure 1.4. Now at least the interface conveys the idea of shaking.

Figure 1.3   Stereo Remote—Box Model.      Figure 1.4   Stereo Remote—Rattle Model.

Second, we can confuse the user about the constraints of the remote. Consider our shaker remote. We could further frustrate our user by giving no clue as to how its interface is constrained.

Our remote looks like a baby's rattle, a device that is usually very robust. If we build our device so that a strong shake causes the device to fall apart, we have given misleading information as to how it is constrained.

Third, we can mislead the user as to the mapping between the inputs to the interface and the outcomes of the system. Considering our shaker remote again, we could really frustrate our user when they try to guess how the actions of this device are mapped onto the action of the stereo. Suppose we use one shake to turn the stereo on or off. The user may begin to feel in charge. If two shakes mean full volume, the user is likely to be pretty dissatisfied.

### 1.3.4 How Do We Know that Our Mental Model Fits the Device?

When we try to use an interface, we evaluate and expand our mental model by the *feedback* (or lack of feedback) we receive from the device. When we receive feedback shortly after an interface action, we assume that there is a causal relationship. A well-designed device sends information back to the user about what action has been accomplished. This feedback may take many forms. For example, when someone dials a rotary phone, they receive tactile (touch) feedback in the sense that the dial takes longer to return to the base point after dialing a nine than dialing a one. A user does not get this kind of feedback when using a touchpad interface to a phone, but may get different feedback such as different tones for different digits or from the directions in which their fingers move.

In summary, if a device leads the user to develop a good and usable mental model, the device is likely to be more usable than one that does not lead to such a model. The extent to which cues from the device and its interface can be extracted impacts the quality of the user's mental model. For everyday things, the mental models are usually simple and well understood. They do not have to be complex. When a user's mental model is incorrect or inadequate, the user may have problems using the device. The closer the mapping is between the control and its function, the more accurate the user's mental model will be.

## Conclusions

Everyday devices have an interface or connection with users. Everyday devices can be designed well or designed poorly for the user and the task. We cannot evaluate the design of the device and its usability independently of either the user or the task.

Everyday devices have an interface, or boundary, between the device and the user that can be good, okay, or terrible. As we will learn, software interfaces, like the interfaces of everyday devices, also can be good, okay, or terrible. Principles that assist in the design of usable everyday objects are useful to consider when designing software interfaces. Heightened awareness of good versus poor design of everyday devices can make us better evaluators of software interfaces. The distinction between the interface and the functional components can be very important! For example, my uncle (JB) uses only the beverage button on the microwave oven. If his food or beverage isn't warm enough after the first cycle, he just uses the beverage button again rather than programming the oven to warm the food appropriately the first time. He doesn't need to understand the functional components of the microwave to warm his coffee. In fact, he doesn't have to understand most of the interface either.

The dimensions for evaluating the usability of everyday objects are *perceptibility, mappings, feedback, affordances,* and *constraints.* When evaluating the usability of an everyday device, you should consider these dimensions. Two user interfaces might both *map* to the functionality of a piece of software, but the two interfaces may not be of equal quality.

## Exercises

1. Define the following terms: user interface, constraint, mapping, perceptibility, feedback, and mental model.

2. In this chapter, we discussed how a user's mental model of everyday things is affected by at least three characteristics of the object's user interface:
   - What can a person do with the interface? For an everyday object, this might involve gripping or pushing the interface.
   - How is a person's interaction potentially constrained by the interface? For an everyday object, this might involve the size or the resistance of moving parts of the object.
   - How do a person's actions at the interface translate to an action of the object?

   We have also considered some specific examples and discussed these three characteristics for the interfaces.

   For this exercise, pick a *simple* device. Answer the following questions about your everyday object:

   a. Name and describe the device and its intended function. Feel free to provide measurements of the device.
   b. Draw a detailed picture of your device. Circle and label the user interface.
   c. Who are the intended users of this device?
   d. What does one do with the interface?
   e. How is the operation of the interface potentially constrained?
   f. Describe the ways that the actions at the user interface are mapped onto the outcome or function of the device.
   g. Consider your answers to the previous questions. Are there ways that a user might form an incorrect or misleading mental model of how to operate this device? What would be the source of this confusion?

3. Think of an everyday device that you believe has *too much perceptibility or visibility*. In other words, think of a device whose user interface seems to be providing too many perceptible cues as to how to use it. Of these many perceptible cues, could you remove some of them and still be able to use the device?

4. Think of an everyday device that you have used with less than perfect success—for example, household appliances or tools. Identify the user interface. Using the framework from this chapter, analyze why the interface made this object difficult for you to use. In other words, does the user interface have features that might lead a user to construct an incorrect mental model of how to operate this device?

5. Consider an everyday device that you have had difficulty operating. How did the design of the device's interface disrupt your mental model of its use? Did it mislead you about how to operate it? Was there a problem with how the interface was constrained? Did your input to the device result in a response that you did not anticipate?

# 2

# What Do We Mean by Human–Computer Interaction, Usability, and User Interfaces?

## Motivation

Now we are ready to define some of the key terms in usability engineering. By define we mean more than just giving you a dictionary definition. When you are finished with this chapter, you should be able to do the following:

- Discuss the terms *HCI* and *usability*. What are some of the common perceptions that do not accurately reflect what HCI is? What types of problems are difficult to resolve?
- Identify some factors that pushed the emergence of HCI onto the main stage of computer science.
- View a technology in a magazine, in real life, or in a museum and reflect on where that technology fell in the historical development of similar technologies. When the particular technology was released or marketed, how many resources did the developers spend on making the device usable? Were the intended users of the device already such experts that they could use the technology whether resources had been dedicated to usability or not? Were the intended users trainees who needed to "come up to speed" fast?

## 2.1 What Do We Mean by Human–Computer Interaction?

When you picked up this book, perhaps you noticed that keyword topic areas were listed as *HCI* or may be *CHI*. Both these terms are acronyms: HCI stands for **Human–Computer** Interaction, and CHI stands for **Computer–Human** Interaction. The terms are generally used interchangeably.

According to Hewett et al. (1992), "Human-computer interaction is the discipline concerned with the design, evaluation and implementation of interactive computing systems for human use and with the study of the major phenomena surrounding them."

Another common acronym you may see in conjunction with HCI is *UI*, which is just short for User Interface and refers to the user interface artifact. Another term you are likely to encounter is *usability*. For most HCI practitioners, usability is the goal of the work that they do. For our purposes we can say that an interface is usable if it is appropriate for the users and for the task being performed. We will expand on usability later.

Many people have confused the field of HCI and the goals of usability with the term *user-friendly*. You even may have seen products advertised that claim to be user-friendly. More than twenty years ago, Stevens (1983) recognized that HCI professionals, such as usability engineers, generally are not trying to build interfaces that are user-friendly. For a number of reasons, user-friendly interfaces are not the goal of usability engineering. For one thing, *user-friendly* is an anthropomorphic term, meaning that we are assigning human attributes to an interface. Taken literally, *user-friendly* would mean that a computer would have human characteristics and would respond to the user in a friendly manner. ☺ In general, users do not wish to be friends with their computers, so this term is somewhat misleading. A second problem with the term is that it is a binary concept. A system either is friendly or is not. As we will see, assessment of interfaces is usually much more complex and cannot be summarized by a yes-or-no characterization.

## 2.2 What Factors Influence the Success of a User Interface?

Many factors influence the success of an interface. It is not just a simple matter of deciding whether to use a menu or a command-line type of interface. The success of an interface is usually determined by a broader perspective. A number of factors influence us in regard to using a computer and our eventual success or failure.

Some broader issues might include these:

- Type of user
- Type of task
- Hardware constraints
- Social and cultural limitations

These factors, together with the user interface, contribute to a user's overall experience. The interplay among these issues and the usability of a system are discussed throughout the rest of this book.

## 2.3 Who Is Qualified to Participate in Human–Computer Interaction?

The field of HCI is very broad, and many fields have made contributions. Of course, computer scientists have contributed by building computer systems. Many other fields have left their marks on HCI. Human-factors experts, ergonomicists, and psychologists have developed methodologies for assessing interfaces and studying how users actually interact with interfaces. Contributors from other fields of social science, such as sociology and anthropology, have also modified the research methods of their fields to make contributions to the study of interfaces. Experts in cognitive science and artificial intelligence have contributed to both the development of intelligent interfaces and the construction of models of human behavior. Also, thousands of HCI practitioners, who we call usability engineers, build and design interfaces with usability as a goal.

In your computer science curriculum, it is likely that the emphasis up to now has been on learning a programming language, possibly two, and how to design and debug a computer program. You may have had opportunities to design a software system or to work on a software development team. As you read this book and learn about becoming a usability engineer, we are going to challenge you to widen your view of what computer science is. In this book, we are going to work through an interface development project. We hope that you learn that lots of other things in addition to programming are involved in the development of an interface. We are going to ask you to "think outside the box" because that is what usability engineering is all about. We remind you what Myers (1998, 52) and a number of other HCI professionals have noted:

> If students do not know about user interfaces, they will not serve industry needs. It seems that only through Computer Science does HCI research disseminate to products.

## 2.4 Why Is There Interest in Usability and User Interfaces Now?

In the early years of computer science, few were thinking about usability. What a different situation we have now. Today, in many markets it is difficult to sell computing products that are not usable and, in fact, computer and software manufacturers often make claims of good usability as an advertising tactic. In years gone by, no courses focused on HCI. As recently as ten years ago, very few universities were offering courses in this topic area for graduate students, and even fewer programs were offering HCI courses to undergraduates. Now HCI is considered a core topic in an undergraduate computer science curriculum (Joint Task Force on Computing Curricula 2001). Why did this change occur? What factors have influenced the discipline of computer science to the point that HCI, once unknown outside the ranks of a few psychologists and industrial engineers, is now considered important enough to require all computer science students to have some exposure to it?

A number of excellent articles detailing the development of HCI and usability concerns have appeared, including Gaines (1984), Baecker and Buxton (1987), and Myers (1998). These articles make a clear case that interest in interactive and user-oriented computing did not just appear in the last ten years but that the basis for today's user interfaces were set in the 1950s, 1960s, and even earlier. Interest in interactive and real-time computing dates as far back as the Whirlwind project, which started in 1944. The Whirlwind computer initially was intended as a flight simulation system, sponsored by the United States Navy. The project continued for almost a decade and evolved into an effort to develop a system that responded to real-time, user-initiated events (National Research Council 1999). In the mid-1960s, IBM introduced point-of-sale terminals in some industries. These terminals also responded to user-initiated, real-time events (cf. Waldrop 2001). In another example, in 1963 Ivan Sutherland developed Sketchpad. This was a system in which the user could manipulate pictures rather than text (Sutherland 1963).

Even with these early innovations, no one could claim that the computing industry valued usability fifty years ago. So how did we get from the big mainframe computers of the 1950s and 1960s, when little thought was given to usability, to today's proliferation of personal computers and increased emphasis on usability? We suggest that at least three factors over the last forty years have pushed us in this direction:

- Changes in hardware environments
- Diversification of users
- Diversification of applications

In the next three sections, we explore an overview of some changes in these three key dimensions of the computing industry that are related to the increasing interest in usability.

### 2.4.1 Changes in Hardware Environments

From the 1940s through the 1960s, hardware was the primary cost factor in computing endeavors. Mynatt (1990) suggests that hardware costs were as high as 80 percent of the total cost of a project. With hardware as the significant source of cost in a computing system, developers focused on hardware development and were much less concerned with software development. User interfaces were given almost no consideration at this time. According to Mynatt (1990), the ratio of hardware to software costs began to change dramatically in the 1960s. She indicates that hardware costs had dropped to 60 percent of total costs and that by the 1990s hardware costs were down to 20 percent of the total cost of a project. (See also Boehm 1983 and Pressman 1992.)

In the early days of computing, a single user would load a single program into a computer's memory and execute that program. Peripherals were minimal, so there was little need for an operating system (OS) to control scheduling or allocation of resources. A "good" program was one that maximized use of the hardware. In those days the user interface was pretty minimal and may have consisted of the programmer entering a program directly via switches or on a stored media, such as paper tape. So in spite of the programmer spending his or her time painfully loading a program into the computer, the cost of building and testing the program was still much less than the cost of the hardware.

The single-user/single-program strategy of the early days of computing had a number of drawbacks relative to the utilization of the hardware. Perhaps the most obvious was that the expensive hardware sat idly at least some of the time while the programmer set up for the next job. In part to address this hardware down time, in the 1950s and 1960s the importance of the OS increased. The OS controlled the scheduling of resources such that the hardware utilization became more efficient. OSs began to use a batch processing approach. As jobs were submitted, the OS would analyze what resources (applications, compilers, etc.) were needed to process each job. Jobs that needed the same resources (such as the FORTRAN compiler) were grouped together to be run at the same time. The idea was that the FORTRAN compiler would be loaded into memory once and would process all jobs that required it at the same time. This would lead to more jobs being processed in a given time period because the needed resources had already been loaded into memory and hence reduced the setup time per job. Because jobs were not processed immediately, users often had to wait, sometimes for hours, before getting their output. Access was restricted to expert users who knew the arcane job control language that specified the necessary job resources to the OS.

During the 1960s and 1970s, hardware costs for components such as memory began to drop. It became possible to have larger memory units and potentially more than one program loaded in memory at once. At the same time, OS concepts became more sophisticated and began to include time-sharing and multiprogramming environments. In both time-sharing and multiprogramming systems, the OS schedules the processor to move from job to job. Jobs are not scheduled to run to completion as in a batch system. A job can be interrupted to serve another request. In multi-programming, multiple jobs or parts of multiple jobs could be loaded into memory at the same time. The central processing unit (CPU) would then be shared across several jobs over the same time period. For example, suppose that job 1 and job 2 are both loaded in memory. Job 1 starts to run on the CPU. After executing for a period of time, job 1 needs a data input from the user. While job 1 is busy waiting for input, job 2 can jump in and use the CPU. In time-sharing, jobs would receive a timer interrupt and then share the CPU with another job.

Both multiprogramming and time-sharing systems helped lead to the emergence of interactive systems in which multiple users could log on to a computer at the same time, type in commands, and get "immediate" responses from the computer. This change in interaction occurred because the management of interactive sessions is itself a programming problem. Only in a computing environment that permits sharing of resources is this kind of user interaction really feasible. With the emergence of more interactivity, users had to learn a fundamental set of interactive commands to access files and applications from the command line. Users were still primarily experts, but the technology had been proven to be beneficial to organizations, and the number of users was increasing.

Into the 1970s, user interface hardware may have included interactive terminals, such as teletypes or CRTs. These primitive display user interfaces made sense particularly with time-sharing strategies because they allowed users to see the status of their jobs, among other functions. Also during this period, the cost of hardware was declining and minicomputers were being introduced as affordable computing options for smaller organizations, and the spread of computing facilities into small businesses led to the need for more trained computing professionals.

During the 1970s and 1980s, hardware prices dropped even more significantly. The first microcomputers were developed. Individuals who worked on larger computers at work could afford to purchase a microcomputer for the home. The types of computer applications changed and grew. Payroll and scheduling, word processing, spreadsheet, and personal finance software applications were added, as were computer games and other entertainment programs. More people were introduced to the functionality of computers, and, because of the dramatic reductions in cost, more people could afford them. This increased the number of users, many of whom had never had formal computer training.

Continuing today, we see a number of hardware trends that have driven usability concerns to the forefront of the computing market:

- Ever-increasing power at the user's work unit, which may be a desktop computer, cell phone, mobile device, gaming station, or other information appliance
- High-quality displays
- Alternative input and output devices, including the mouse, speech recognition systems, gesture recognition software, and immersive devices

These improvements in hardware have enabled users of various skill levels to have access to computing. Without the advances in hardware that facilitated the processing of a number of computing jobs at once, it is likely that programming would still be done by one person, entering the program at a bank of switches.

In summary, we can say three things about hardware changes in the last forty years that have increased the need for usability in our computing systems:

- The hardware has become much more powerful in terms of processing speed, storage capabilities, and output characteristics. This has permitted the development of more sophisticated user interfaces, such as graphical user interfaces.

- The hardware that the user interacts with directly (peripherals) has become more diversified. This has also contributed to the development of different user interfaces.

- The hardware has become more accessible to a wider range of users primarily due to the decreasing costs. This large group of diverse users has demanded a greater number of ways to interact with the technology.

---

## Programming in the Early 1970s: A Personal Perspective

During winter quarter of 1973, I took my first programming course, CS 101, at Bowling Green State University. At that time, we typed our programs on punch cards, while sitting in a large room full of keypunch machines in the Math–Science Building. We typed our FORTRAN programs with one line of code per card. We also typed JCL (IBM 360 job control language) statements, one to a card, which gave commands to the operating system, regarding the compilation, loading, and execution of our programs.

We took our cards over to a card reader and fed them into it. The program that we submitted was by definition in the order of the punched cards. Because our programs were compiled and executed in batch mode, we then waited and waited (sometimes for an hour or more) for our results. Most of the time, we sat and waited on the floor of the main hallway of the Math–Science building. It was not the most comfortable surroundings, but the atmosphere was pretty social, since it was likely that most of the people in your class were waiting on the floor also.

Once the results were done, they were printed on green bar line printer paper. We would pick up our listings to see our results. Because we typically had such a long turnaround between job runs, most of us put a lot of effort into correcting our errors before we submitted again. We did quite a lot of desk checking of our code because most of us did not have the time for multiple runs of our programs.

—J. Barnes, BGSU, Class of 1976

---

### 2.4.2 Changes in User Characteristics

Back in the early days of computer science, the only users of computers were computing professionals. These professionals had knowledge of the computer languages that were necessary to operate the systems of the 1950s and 1960s. They "spoke" languages such as FORTRAN, IBM 360 Assembler Language, and JCL (IBM 360 Job Control Language) when they interacted with computers. These professionals used computers for software development and probably only rarely for personal work or entertainment. There really was no group who could be called "discretionary users." Since the middle to late 1980s, the number and diversity of nonprofessional computer users have increased dramatically to the point that they clearly outnumber the professional computer scientists. Many of these nonprofessional computer users are quite savvy and expect sophisticated interfaces with low error rates and fast responses.

In summary, we can say two aspects of the diversification of users in the last forty years that have increased the need for usability in our computing systems:

- The proportion of professional computer scientists to discretionary users has changed dramatically, with a great many more discretionary users than professional computer scientists today.
- Novice users have sophisticated expectations about the computer systems that they use. They expect systems that are easy to use and robust.

### 2.4.3 Changes in Software Environments and Applications

At the same time that available hardware and the pool of computer users was changing, software environments and their applications were diversifying. In the 1950s and 1960s, most software was designed to support computations for banks, corporations, governments, and the military. Such software included operating systems, database management systems, compilers, and large programming systems. By the 1970s, software was becoming available to support the needs of small businesses. In the 1980s, we started to see visual or graphical interfaces for a variety of software. Hypertext and multimedia applications started to emerge. Of course by the 1990s, many home and personal computer applications, such as spreadsheets and word processors, were widely available. Browsers and software for Internet and networked applications are now standard software on most personal computers. With this diversification of applications, the cost of software has dropped dramatically in many cases.

In summary, two aspects of software diversification in the last forty years have increased the need for usability in our computing systems:

- The characteristics of software and hardware are equally critical in the marketing and sales of computers. When buying a new computer, users need to consider the software they want to use and choose hardware that will support it.
- The software applications that the user interacts with directly have become more and more diversified. Some of the activities users perform today with the aid of their computers include shopping, paying bills, balancing checkbooks, watching videos, recording music, and playing games.

### 2.4.4 More History of Human–Computer Interaction

Myers (1998) points to a number of innovations in the 1960s and 1970s that provided the essential groundwork for today's user interfaces, including text editing, the mouse, multiple windows, and hypertext. These and many other innovations occurred at a time when computer science was dominated by large mainframe computers running FORTRAN, COBOL, and assembly language programs. Much of the research underlying these developments took place in universities and research labs. Much of this research was not focused on developing commercial products per se but instead was exploratory. The following are some of the specific innovations developed in research labs that changed the way people interacted with computers (Myers 1998):

- *Direct manipulation of graphical objects.*  Myers points to Sketchpad (Sutherland 1963) as the first example of direct manipulation of graphical or visual objects. Myers gives additional examples from the mid to late 1960s of research projects that involved early forms of icons, and points to the Xerox Star and the Apple Lisa as the first commercial systems to include direct manipulation, circa 1981 and 1982, respectively.

- *Mouse.*   The mouse was developed initially in 1965 as an alternative for the light pens that had been used in CAD systems for at least ten years. The mouse appeared commercially with the Xerox Star and the Apple Lisa in the early 1980s.

- *Windows.*   Systems with multiple windows were developed in the same project as the mouse, around 1968. Overlapping windows were demonstrated by Alan Kay's Smalltalk system in 1974 and appeared commercially as early as 1979 in LISP machines.

Some novel applications came from research labs, including these (Myers 1998):

- *Video games.*   The first graphical video game was developed around 1962 at MIT. An early commercially successful video game, Pong, was marketed by Sears around 1976.

- *Drawing programs.*   Drawing programs preceded the development of the mouse in such products as Sketchpad, and at least two drawing programs were developed for the Xerox Alto during the 1970s. Early commercially successful drawing programs for the Macintosh included MacPaint and MacDraw.

- *Text editing.*   Text editing, with a mouse or light pen, was developed as early as 1968. The Xerox Star and Apple Lisa were both delivered with what we would probably consider contemporary text editors.

- *Spreadsheets.*   The first spreadsheet, VisiCalc, was developed for the Apple II around 1978.

- *Hypertext.*   The notion of hypertext or nonlinear text has a long history. The Talmud, dating back 2,000 years, is an excellent example of a nonlinear text. (See Schühlein 2006 for a description of the Talmud.) Computerized hypertexts have been around since the mid 1960s. Early uses of hypertext included prototype online journals and patient medical records. The most visible commercial example of hypertext is the World Wide Web, with the initial browsers released in the early 1990s. Nielsen (1995) gives an in-depth overview of hypertext.

## 2.5 Human–Computer Interaction Grows Within the Computer Science Field

Early in this century, psychologists and human factors experts recognized that characteristics of one's work environment could have a profound impact on worker productivity. Early studies, called *man–machine studies,* focused on production of mechanical objects on assembly lines. To find the most efficient way to do a job, time-and-motion studies analyzed how workers did their jobs, taking into account that many factory workers of the time were not skilled, educated, or literate and may not have spoken the language of management, which generally was English in the United States. During World War II, numerous scientific studies of workspace design occurred with an emphasis on sensory motor and routine tasks. The idea of scientific evaluation of computer interfaces was not a far-fetched idea! As early as 1967, Grant and Sackman (1967) published a comparison of batch processing versus time-sharing computer use. In 1971, Gerald Weinberg published *The Psychology of Computer Programming,* which discusses programming in both an individual and social context. James Martin's 1973 book, *Design of Man-Computer Dialogues,* brought some awareness of interface design issues to computing professionals.

By the late 1970s HCI was beginning to receive serious attention within the computer science discipline. In 1977, Thomas Green and others begin to publish a series of empirical studies of programmers. These studies by Green were influential in laying the groundwork for an area that is still called *empirical studies of programmers,* or *ESP* (see Katz, Petrie, and Leventhal 2001). The work of Green and others was important because it established the notion that empirical and scientific research could be applied to questions about user interfaces. At the time, the work focused on programmers because the primary users of computers were computer programmers.

In 1980, Ben Shneiderman published his book *Software Psychology,* which was written to disseminate some of the known HCI results to practitioners. For example, the text included guidelines for designing the command-line interfaces prevalent at that time. Now in its third printing, this book continues to be a useful source of information for user interface and software designers.

At what point did "enough HCI" suggest that we had reached some sort of maturity, relative to usability in the computing industry? One key indication is the emergence of HCI conferences during which competing theoretical models of usability were shared. As interest in the HCI field grew in the 1980s, a number of conferences and organizations emerged. One notable event was the 1982 Gaithersburg Conference on Computer-Human Interaction, which occurred in Gaithersburg, Maryland, and is considered to be the first Association for Computing Machinery Special Interest Group on Computer-Human Interaction (ACM SIGCHI) conference. The 1984 INTERACT'84 conference in London was also a landmark event. Annual versions of these and other conferences today draw large crowds of social scientists, computer scientists, usability engineers, and managers. The subject matter of these conferences is as diverse as contemporary interfaces and user groups, and they often spotlight new technologies for inputs and outputs, while also exploring the needs of children and seniors as users. The conferences provide excellent opportunities to see the application of traditional experimental methods to questions in HCI, as well as a variety of qualitative and field study methodologies.

## 2.6  The Context of Human–Computer Interaction

In his 1989 *SIGCHI Bulletin* article, Baecker presents a framework for the HCI discipline. His model is multilevel and indicates that HCI includes individuals, groups, and communities. Where does this broad discipline leave its practitioners? In other words, what is it that we do? We perform systems and interface design. We do this based on observation, experimentation, and theory. What systems are we actually designing? We design software interfaces in the context of user support, the physical environment, and the sociopolitical environment. How do we do these things? We rely on the theories, methods and tools that emerge from HCI research and practice. Clearly no one person is an expert in all these endeavors. In practice, usability engineers and HCI professionals work with other professionals whose skills span this broad framework.

## 2.7  The Process of Usability Engineering

Usability is a lot more than just the user interface that comes out with the product at the end of the development process. Usable systems do not emerge by accident. They typically are the result of a careful process called *usability engineering.* To build a good interface, you must follow a nonchaotic development cycle. Hix and Hartson (1993) indicate that usability engineers must master elements of the user interface product itself, as well as the process of development. In their view, the product involves the content of the user interface, human factors issues, design guidelines, and interaction styles. The product is a specific artifact, or artifacts, that includes mice, graphical user interfaces, manuals, and such. By contrast, the process is the strategy for developing the product and involves methods, techniques, and tools for development and assessment. It goes without saying that the process of usability engineering usually happens as a team. Your team may have members from many different kinds of technical and professional backgrounds.

Does this make sense to you? For most of you, your computer science courses have focused on a product: a written program. This course may be your first exposure to the idea that a big part of computer science involves the *process* of development. In a usability engineering course, your instructor may actually give more points on your projects for your process performance than for your final result. As HCI professionals, we are concerned with both.

## 2.8 Why Is Usability Engineering Difficult?

Okay. You are convinced. Good usability engineering is difficult to do. But why should it be any more difficult than any other area of computer science? Myers (1994) points out that "user interfaces are hard to design" because the required detailed application knowledge is hard to obtain. A common HCI proverb is "Know your user for they are not you." Unfortunately, really knowing the users and their tasks is time intensive and may require the designers to change their worldviews. The tasks required are increasingly complex, and good user interface designs may have a number of conflicting requirements. For example, they may require adherence to industry standards for commercial products but at the same time need to meet the stated requirements of the user. User interfaces are increasingly called upon to guarantee accessibility to users with a wide variety of skills, needs, and expectations. Users expect fast response and complex graphical layouts at the same time. As Myers (1994) mentions, just as there is "no silver bullet" for the difficulties of software engineering, there is no "magic solution" to the problems of usability engineering. (The reference to "no silver bullet" refers to the article by Brooks [1987] that makes the point that there is no magic solution to the productivity problems faced by the software industry.)

Can we ignore usability when we build software products? Beyond the fact that it is tough to sell a product that is not perceived as usable, Brad Myers has stated, "There is substantial empirical evidence that attention to usability dramatically decreases costs and increases productivity" (Myers 1994). Chrusch (2000) extends that thought further: "Industry data show that each dollar spent on user studies during product design saves $10 on problem fixes during product development, or $100 or more in rework after product release." He further notes, "It's estimated that 80% of maintenance costs are spent on unforeseen user requirements, while only 20% are due to bugs."

### 2.8.1 How Do We Guarantee Usability?

One thing we seem to have learned over the years is that no one formula guarantees usability every time. There are no easy ways to always build a good user interface. We know that relying on a designer's intuition usually is risky. We know that evaluation of interfaces is critical. However, we also know that markets change quickly and that it is important to get a good product out the door. Usability engineers may not have the luxury of long-term, large-scale evaluation efforts.

In an article in *interactions* magazine, Chrusch (2000) discusses seven myths of usability. Many computer professionals will swear that these myths are, in fact, true. Here are four of them:

- Good user interfaces are just appealing graphics.
- Usability is an outcome of common sense.
- Guidelines, applied to user interface problems, will lead to usability.
- Usability problems can be solved with help/training/documentation.

Buy into these myths and you are in trouble. Usability is anything but common sense. If it were, we would not have the plethora of unusable and bad interfaces that we see in applications and on the Web today.

## 2.9  Where Are We Going?

In a 1991 film, one of the characters makes a toast to the future, referring to it as the "undiscovered country." Another character in the scene cites the reference as coming from William Shakespeare's *Hamlet.* The actual quotation (Act 3, Scene 1) is

> But that the dread of something after death,
> The undiscover'd country from whose bourn
> No traveller returns

While fans of the film debated whether the "undiscovered country" referred to death or the future, we prefer the more optimistic viewpoint. What will we find in the future or undiscovered country of HCI? Here are a few guesses as to what we think will be the focus of HCI in the future. (If you still have this book in ten years, please send us an e-mail to let us know what we were right and wrong about!)

- *Universal usability*   (cf. Shneiderman 2001; Brown, Heller, Jorge, and Tremaine 2001). Usable interfaces should be for everyone, even if people have differing needs. For example, most contemporary user interfaces are designed for healthy, young adults. What about senior citizens who may have failing health and a lack of familiarity with technology? Effectively designed interfaces can bring "everyday" computing, as well as rehabilitation services, to these people, keeping them functional, independent, and connected with others.
- *Gesture recognition and gestural devices.*   Dix, Finlay, Abowd, and Beale (1998) define *gesture recognition* as a technique of giving instructions that do not use commands in the keyboard or mouse-click sense. For example, an interface that can recognize pen strokes is a gesture recognition system. Myers (1998) notes that Sketchpad from 1963 supported light pen gesture recognition.
- *Speech and natural language interaction.*   Speech has a number of advantages as an interaction style. Speech is a more "natural" way for the user to convey commands to the computer. It is mobile and hands free. Coupled with natural language interaction, users would not need to learn a language of interaction but could "speak" with the user interface in their own languages.
- *Multimedia and multimodal interfaces.*   As you navigate on the World Wide Web, you are frequently faced with *multimedia* interfaces. These are interfaces that display information in a variety of representative forms, including text, still pictures, animation, sound, realistic video, and virtual reality. Multimodal interfaces react to and interact with a variety of human modalities,

including gaze and gestures. For example, attentive user interface systems monitor users through sensing via computer vision and speech recognition (cf. Oviatt and Cohen 2000).

- *Virtual worlds and immersive environments.* A virtual world is usually one in which the user sees and experiences three-dimensional characteristics of real settings. A virtual world has a characteristic level of immersiveness. The level of immersiveness can range from the user being an outside observer to the user being an active participant of the virtual world. A world that is highly immersive is one in which users wear some kind of device, such as a head-mounted display, to cut them off from the real world and make them part of the virtual world.
- *Virtual communities and cooperative work.* Few human endeavors happen in single-person mode. Introductory programming is one of the few exceptions. Clearly technology can facilitate the ability of individuals to work together and form communities, even over great physical distances.
- *Mobile devices and computing on the go.* In recent years, we have seen more and more computing applications delivered on mobile devices or in settings that are mobile. Applications that are usable on mobile devices are not necessarily simply miniaturizations of desktop computing applications.

In Chapter 8, we discuss some of these issues in greater detail.

## Conclusions

Concerns for software usability evolved in the context of computing technology and usage patterns. As computer hardware became less expensive, computer users became more diverse and applications changed from primarily scientific and business computations to more popular applications, such as word processing and computer games.

Building usable interfaces is not easy. The development process and the elements that make up the final product have an influence on usability. Building usable interfaces is not just common sense.

## Exercises

1. Define the following terms: *HCI, usability,* and *user interface.*
2. Pick a particular type of computer peripheral, such as an input or output device. Trace the evolution in this device in terms of changes in both user interface characteristics and breadth of choices.
3. Think of an activity in which you participate. Distinguish between *product* and *process* in the context of that activity. What difference does having your focus on the product or on the process make in your behavior?
4. The first typewriter with a QWERTY keyboard was placed into mass production in 1873. Research the emergence of the typewriter and the various user interfaces that have been used with it. Based on your research, discuss the relationship between concerns with usability and changes in the typewriter (cf. McLean 2003).

# 3

# Defining Usability and Models of Usability

## Motivation

Now we are ready to define *usability* in more detail. By this, we mean more than just giving you a dictionary definition. Usability is really the goal of the interfaces that we hope to build. When you are finished with this chapter, you should be able to do the following:

- Explain what it means to have a *model of usability.*
- Recognize that different authors have defined usability differently.
- Understand why it is useful to set usability in a context.
- Understand why it is important to be able to *operationalize* various aspects of usability.
- Understand that the identification, measurement, and interpretation of variables that impact usability should be an integral part of usability engineering.
- Understand how to realize if we have achieved usability.
- Think about measurements and causality in the context of usability.
- Recognize that there are trade-offs to consider as you design for usability.

## 3.1 Introduction: What Exactly Does Usability Mean?

We have seen what HCI is not (i.e., user-friendly). We have learned that a major goal of well-engineered interfaces is usability. In this chapter we want to define *usability* in detail. As we continue through this book, we will use our detailed definition to justify our user interface development process and to help evaluate interfaces for usability.

The international standard ISO 9241-11 defines usability like this:

Usability: the extent to which a product can be used by specified users to achieve specified goals with effectiveness, efficiency and satisfaction in a specified context of use.

Note that this definition is still not detailed enough to evaluate whether a system is usable or not, although it certainly indicates what some characteristics of a usable system might be. (See Serco 2001 for a discussion of this definition.) How can we extend a definition like this into something that could actually be used to evaluate usability? Many authors have defined *models of usability*. A model not only states the characteristics of a usable interface but also indicates how those characteristics fit together, what they mean, and how they contribute to usability.

Let's examine three popular models of usability. Each puts usability in a context and gives us some idea of the factors that contribute to the usability of an interface. The three models have some common features, but they are also unique. We will also consider our hybrid model, which we will use in later chapters as a foundation for specification, design, and assessment of user interfaces.

## 3.2 Shackel's Model of Usability

The first model that we will examine was developed by Brian Shackel (Shackel 1986). Figure 3.1 shows some of the elements of the Shackel model. In the model, four dimensions are important to usability: *effectiveness, learnability, flexibility,* and *attitude*. The Shackel model is a practical one. For each of the four usability dimensions, Shackel gives some sense of how one might measure or specify the dimension. In other words, the elements of the Shackel model relate abstract usability concepts, such as *effectiveness,* to measurement strategies. Shackel does not weight the dimensions, recognizing that the importance of each of these may vary from project to project.

Let's consider an example of how a usability engineer might use the Shackel model of usability. Suppose that Alice and Darius are developing a product for Woodrow Wilson High School. The

---

Effectiveness
- Better than some required level of performance
- By some required percentage of the specified target range of users
- Within some required proportion of the range of usage environments

Learnability
- Within some specified time from installation and start of user training
- Based on some specified amount of training and user support
- Within some specified re-learning time each time for intermittent users

Flexibility
- Allowing adaptation to some specified percentage variation in tasks and/or environments beyond those first specified

Attitude
- Within acceptable levels of human cost in terms of tiredness, discomfort, frustration, and personal effort

---

**Figure 3.1** Shackel's Operational Model of Usability.
Source: Shackel 1986. Copyright Cambridge University Press.

product is called *Señores y Señoritas* and is intended to help high school Spanish students with vocabulary drills. The contractors for the product are the teachers at Woodrow Wilson High School.

These teachers are most concerned with the package being easy to learn. Alice and Darius note that one way to define learnability in the Shackel model is for users to have learned a defined set of skills *within some specified time from installation and start of user training.* So, in the contract for the system, the contractors (the teachers) and the developers (Alice and Darius) agree that users of the system will become competent with the system within one hour of use. They define "competent" to be less than 10 incorrect keystrokes per 100. The two parties agree that they will measure competence with Señora Jones's class of twenty-four students at Woodrow Wilson High School. If all twenty-four students in this class are competent within one hour of using the package, this aspect of the contract will be met and both parties will agree that the system is usable.

## 3.3 Nielsen's Model of Usability

The next model of usability was developed by Jakob Nielsen (1993a). In the Nielsen model, usability is embedded into such other system concerns as *usefulness.* System concerns, including utility, usefulness, practical acceptability, and social acceptability, all contribute to system acceptability.

Like Shackel, Nielsen identifies a number of dimensions that contribute to usability. Figure 3.2 shows some of the elements of the Nielsen model (1993a, 25). In the model, five dimensions are important to usability: *easy to learn, efficient to use, easy to remember, few errors,* and *subjectively pleasing.* Like Shackel, Nielsen gives some sense of how one might measure or specify these dimensions. For example, Nielsen suggests that to measure *easy to learn,* one should select some users new to the system and measure how long it takes them to reach some preselected proficiency level (Nielsen 1993a, 29). Like Shackel, Nielsen does not weight the dimensions, recognizing that the importance of each of these may vary from project to project.

An important aspect of Nielsen's model is that it places usability in a larger context of software engineering concerns. In Nielsen's view usability is part of usefulness. If a system is not

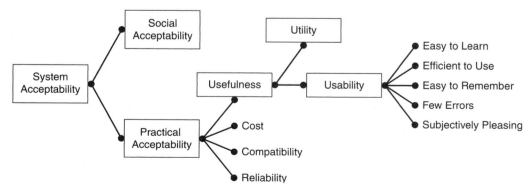

**Figure 3.2**   Nielsen's Model of the Attributes of System Acceptability. Usability is an attribute of system acceptability.
Source: Reprinted from *Usability Engineering,* Jakob Nielsen, p. 25, Copyright 1993, with permission from Elsevier.

useful (i.e., it does not meet the specified needs of the user or customer), it really does not matter if it is usable or not because the user or customer will not accept it. Other performance features, such as reliability, which is often defined as mean time between failures, can similarly impact whether a system is accepted or not.

In summary, usability is a limited concern in Nielsen's model when compared to the larger issue of system acceptability, which deals with whether the system is good enough to satisfy all the needs and requirements of users and other stakeholders (users, clients, and managers). System acceptability is defined as the sum of social acceptability, practical acceptability, and usability. In this sense, usability is just one of the characteristics of a software-engineered system. Others might be reliability and cost. Nielsen provides five dimensions that contribute to usability. Like Shackel, Nielsen gives us some idea of how one might measure these dimensions, and the two models share many of the same concepts. Usability is influenced by *learnability* in Shackel's terms, which is *easy to learn* and *easy to remember* in Nielsen's terms. *Effectiveness* in Shackel's terms is *efficient to use* and *few errors* in Nielsen's terms, and *attitude* in Shackel's model is *subjectively pleasing* in Nielsen's model.

## 3.4 Eason's Model of Usability

Eason's model is the third model of usability that we will consider (Eason 1984). Kenneth Eason has an industrial engineering background and published his model in an early issue of *Behaviour and Information Technology*. His framework for usability was based on his field study of factors that he observed to influence usability. In his model, the interaction of the *system* under consideration, characteristics of the *user*, and characteristics of the target *task* determine the usability of a system. In other words, the usability of the system is set into the context of the purpose for which it is being used and who the users are. Each of these three aspects—system, user, and task—is defined by several inputs or independent variables. As these inputs interact with each other and as we vary the inputs, the usability outcome will change. In the Eason model, the major indicator of usability is whether the system or facility is used. This position is based on this notion: if the system is not used, then it is not usable. In the positive usability outcome, the system is used and in the negative usability outcome, there is limited or no use of the system. Eason's model is shown in Figure 3.3 (Eason 1984, 138).

The lesson from Eason's model is that you cannot measure usability without considering users and their target tasks. These environmental features provide essential contextual information and can influence usability as much as the characteristics of the user interface itself. Now let's look at the specifics of the Eason model.

### 3.4.1 System (User Interface) Characteristics

The first set of dimensions is the characteristics of the interface itself. Eason indicates that *ease of use, ease of learning,* and *task match* of the interface are significant determinants of usability. In this framework, *ease of learning* means the effort required to understand and to operate an unfamiliar system. *Ease of use* means the effort that is required to operate a system once it has been understood and mastered by the user. These notions are different. For example, a system that is easy to learn, via a dialogue that guides the user through the tasks, may be difficult to use because the dialogue is actually in the way. Or a system that is difficult to learn initially, because it has many commands to memorize, may be easy to use once the user has memorized the

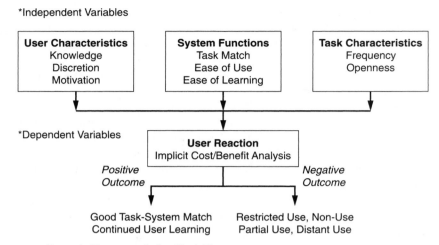

**Figure 3.3**  Eason's Framework for Usability.
Source: Reprinted from Towards the experimental study of usability, K. D. Eason, Behaviour and Information Technology, Copyright 1984, with permission from Taylor & Francis Ltd, (http://www.tandf.co.uk/journals).

commands. You probably have noticed that these two issues, *ease of use* and *ease of learning,* are also important characteristics in the usability models of Shackel and Nielsen.

*Task match* means the extent to which information and functions that a system provides match the needs of the user for the given task. Consider this: if I have poor task match, the device is not usable regardless of the quality of the user interface. For example, gaming systems may have wonderful interfaces, but if I wish to use the interface for word processing, then the system has poor task match with my needs. The system is probably not usable by me because of poor task match. User interfaces that support the user's tasks, but do so in obscure or unpredictable ways, may also have poor task match and consequently will have a negative usability outcome.

Eason (1984) makes the point that the variables of the system (user interface) often are the easiest to measure and certainly the easiest to change. As we will see, the variables of the task and the user are usually the setting or context for our work. As such, we will be trying to work within these variables, not trying to change them.

### 3.4.2  Task Characteristics

What does Eason mean by *task?* The task is what you *do* with the device and may be more or less independent of the specific system. Suppose the system is a broom. The tasks that one might do with a broom include sweeping the floor, knocking down cobwebs, chasing away mice, and flying. Eason specifies two characteristics of task in his framework: *frequency* and *openness*. *Frequency* means the number of times a task is performed by a user. *Openness* refers to the number of options that an interface offers for a task. Specifically Eason states (1984, 138), "If the task is open-ended, the options may have to be much greater." In other words, is the task extremely mechanical or is it flexible?

Consider the broom system and the task of sweeping the floor. Many of us sweep the floor daily, making sweeping a frequently performed task as household tasks go. As to openness, the task is not particularly modifiable and therefore is not very open.

Notice that these dimensions of task, frequency, and openness are related but are not opposites. Each influences our expectations of the system and the user interface. For example, consider frequency: if a task is routine (not open) and done frequently (frequent), users probably want speed and efficiency. If the task is infrequently done (not frequent), the user may want guidance from the user interface.

You have probably already guessed that if you take the task and the system together, you influence usability. Suppose that I am using my word processor to mail merge, which is an infrequent task for me. If my system is easy to use (I have already learned the system and now I am using it), I should be able to mail merge effectively even if the task is performed infrequently. However if the system is not easy to use, I will need to go back and relearn much of what I probably knew at one time, and I will likely experience a negative usability outcome.

### 3.4.3 User Characteristics

Users bring many characteristics into the picture when they use an interface. Eason has identified three of these characteristics that seem to have a major influence on usability. His first user characteristic is *knowledge*. This means the knowledge that the user applies to the task. The knowledge may be appropriate or inappropriate. For example, the skills and experiences that you have collected in learning to drive a car may not be transferable when learning to pilot a boat.

A second user characteristic is *motivation*. If users have a high degree of motivation, they are likely to put more energy into overcoming problems and misunderstandings with the system. In a usability engineering course, you may use a prototyping tool to create a user interface. Some students are more motivated to get an A than other classmates and will spend more time learning to use the prototyping tool.

A final user characteristic is *discretion*. Discretion refers to the user's ability to choose to use (or not use) some part of the system at hand. An example would be using the many features in a popular word processing package. I can take the time to learn how to define my own formatting styles, or I can use other tools in the package that will give me the same result.

Clearly, users bring many characteristics with them, beyond the three in the Eason model. Some other characteristics that might be important include learning style, problem solving skills, age as it influences experience, physical characteristics, and skills.

### 3.4.4 An Illustration of Eason's Model

The following example may help you better understand Eason's model of usability. Suppose I am asked to evaluate the usability of the Omnia Gallia X.17 World Winning Word Processor. In the X.17 user interface is a computerized wizard named Julius. Users specify to Julius whether they are entering data or editing existing data, and the wizard then leads them through the appropriate steps to accomplish the task in the user interface (the system in Eason's model). To understand the factors that contribute to the usability of this system, I would need to consider the user interface of Omnia Gallia, characteristics of the person using the word processor, and the task for which they were using this system.

In the example of Omnia Gallia, the characteristics of the user and task may vary, as shown in the following two scenarios. In scenario 1, the user is a beginner to word processing, so he or she does not know much about word processing as a task, independent of the user interface. The scenario 1 user is planning to use the word processor for the task of repetitively entering data; the repetitive and highly structured nature of this task makes it not open. So far, we know that the user has relatively little knowledge of the task and that the task has little variation in how it can be completed (the task is not open). Now, consider the user interface (the system). Because the wizard Julius leads the user through a set sequence of steps, the user has to make few to no decisions. Even though the user is a novice, because the sequence of steps through the interface is set, the user is not required to have deep knowledge of the task to map into the interface. It seems likely that the system will be easy to learn and easy to use, even for the novice user. So long as the task sequence in the user interface matches the sequence of the real task, the task match should be good also. With the information that we have so far about the user interface for Omnia Gallia, it seems as if the system may match the user's characteristics and task very well and that the system should produce a positive usability outcome.

The usability outcome is likely to be different in scenario 2. In scenario 2, the user is very knowledgeable about word processing and therefore has a high level of knowledge about the tasks in word processing. In this scenario the task is to prepare a professional travel brochure, with many choices along the way, so the task is very open. Once again, the user interface presents a sequence of steps led by Julius. Remember that the user has a good understanding of the task itself and, likely, has a mental representation of the steps that he or she wants to follow to complete the task. Because the sequence of steps that Julius presents probably will not match the steps the user has in mind or the steps for the open-ended task, the user interface will likely have poor task match and will be difficult and awkward to use. In this scenario, the user interface characteristics are likely to impair ease of use for the experienced user on the less rigidly defined task. The usability outcome is more likely to be negative as compared to scenario 1.

### 3.4.5 Does Any Evidence Support the Eason Model?
Eason's model is compelling and reasonable. Maybe it even seems like common sense. But is there any scientific evidence to suggest that his model is valid, beyond what is offered in Eason's original paper? Trumbly, Arnett, and Martin (1993) put part of Eason's model to the test. In their experiment, they tested the notion that a relationship existed between an interface's match to the user's knowledge and the user's performance with the interface. What they found was that when the characteristics of the interface had a good match with the user's knowledge level, performance was significantly improved.

## 3.5 A Note About Causality and Usability Models
The three models (Shackel, Nielsen, and Eason) suggest that certain properties of the interface and, in the case of Eason, properties of the situation have a *causal* influence on usability. This is particularly clear from Eason's model. According to Eason, the three dimensions of user, system, and task characteristics are *independent variables*. In an experiment, the goal of the experimenter is to provide support for a hypothesized causality. The independent variables are those variables that the experimenter manipulates. In other words, we can think of independent variables as inputs or as causes of outcome. The level or setting of the independent variable should be *independent* of the settings of any other variables. The dependent variable is an indicator of outcome. In most experiments, you would measure the level of the dependent variable for each setting of the independent variable to determine the impact of the independent variable on the dependent variable.

A simple example may clarify these terms for you. Many of you have, no doubt, participated in a science fair. Here is an outline of a science project that earned a grade of "Superior" at the 2001 Ohio State Science Day, sponsored by the Ohio Academy of Science (Jaffee 2001). The experiment was entitled "How High Will it Go? The Effect of Mass on the Height of Model Rocket Flight" and was presented by Sam Jaffee. In this study, Jaffee was interested in exploring Newton's second law of motion: *Force = mass × acceleration.* He knew that acceleration and height were related, so using model rockets in which the engines exert a known impulse (related to force), he made predictions that the more mass a rocket carried, the lower its height would be. For his experiment, his *independent* variable was the mass of the rocket and his *dependent* variable was the height of the flight. Jaffee had three levels of rocket mass: rocket + 1 penny, rocket + 2 pennies, and rocket + 3 pennies. He made direct observational measurements of the rocket flights under each of the three experimental conditions. Using some trigonometry, he was able to determine the height of the rocket flight for each condition. Typical of an experiment, he repeated each condition and measurement several times and held factors other than mass constant, so that they would not be incidental independent variables. These other factors included the type of rocket and engine, placement of the pennies in the rockets, and the weather conditions and site for the launch. Jaffee found that his measured outcome was similar to his predicted outcome.

Now back to usability models. The three usability models also suggest at least implicitly that if the designer were to vary characteristics of the user interface (the independent variables), the variations of the system characteristics could influence the usability outcome (dependent variable). Unlike an experiment, however, when we use usability models we are not testing causality; rather, we are using the suggested causality of the model to help us to better understand the factors that can influence the usability outcome. So what can we learn from the rocket study that applies to usability? First of all, in the rocket study, Jaffee started with two concepts: mass and height. He operationalized these abstract constructs into something that he could measure. In particular, he chose ways to measure mass and height. When usability engineers use usability models, they too must operationalize their abstract concepts. If the designer and the customer have determined that a variable like *ease of use* is a key component for usability, they will still have to define what *ease of use* really means for the product and how it will be measured.

In Jaffee's rocket study, he set up his experiment so that he could determine if a causal relationship existed between mass and height. He controlled potentially independent variables so that they could not contribute to the outcome. He also limited the number of independent variables that he was manipulating in his experiment to a small number so that he would have confidence if a causal reaction was found that it was due to his experimental manipulations. The usability engineer in general will not be trying to establish that the factors from one of the models have a causal relationship with the usability outcome. However, the developer will often decide that one of the variables is more important to the usability outcome for his or her user interface. For example, the developer and the customer may determine that *ease of use* is more essential than *ease of learning* and will focus more on one factor than another. Once again, without a model and its implications about the causal effect of different user interfaces and possibly situational features, the usability engineer would be guessing as to what factors potentially influence usability.

## 3.6 Our Model of Usability

The three models of usability tell us much about those factors that contribute to usability. In this section, we integrate some elements of the three models into our own model of usability. Our model is an attempt to put together the most important features of the three models that we have considered and to show you how you might use the model.

Following the structure of the three models we have looked at, the structure of our model is also implicitly causal. In our model, we assume that a number of variables that taken together will determine whether the interface is usable. Following Eason's model we will identify a set of user interface and situational variables that taken together can influence usability. We will discuss some ways that various levels of these variables may make different demands on the user interface vis-à-vis usability. In conclusion, we will show an example that illustrates some ways that a usability engineer might apply our model.

### 3.6.1 Situational Variables: Task

Like the Eason model, our model recognizes that key situational variables include key aspects of the task and of the user. In this section we discuss our task variables. From Eason we include *frequency* as a task variable. We also include two additional variables: *rigidness* and *situational constraints*. Rigidness is similar to Eason's concept of openness in the sense that it deals with options; however, we have tried to make the concept more specific and easier to operationalize and evaluate. Situational constraints are a catchall category of variables that may also impact usability.

#### Frequency

Eason recognized that the frequency of a task could influence the ultimate usability of an interface. Tasks that are performed frequently are likely to include well-learned sequences of user actions; the particulars of the sequences may vary, of course. Therefore an interface that supports a frequent task should recognize that the user has good knowledge of the task sequences. On the other hand, for an infrequently performed task, the user is less likely to know the sequences needed to complete the task and may require extensive prompting through the task.

#### Rigidness

Eason's original definition of openness states that a task that is more open will have more options; in our definition of *rigidness,* we try to specify what it means to have options. We note that *options* can refer both to the number of choices as well as to the number of ways that the choices may be sequenced as the user completes the task. We define *rigidness* in terms of two issues: (1) the number of paths through the task and (2) the number of options that are available along the paths through the task. Thus, a task with few options and only one or two sequences of options through the task is very rigid, and a task with many options and a myriad of paths through the task is not rigid. How can the rigidness of a task interact with interface characteristics to influence usability? If a task is very rigid, the number of options is small and the number of sequences through the task is minimal. An interface that leads the user through a corresponding sequence may be more usable than one that has an unclear sequence.

#### Situational Constraints

The dimension of situational constraints is not found specifically in any of the models previously discussed, but situational constraints address some issues that can potentially influence usability. Some examples of situational constraints include answers to the following questions:

- Is the task ever done collaboratively?
- Is the task done for entertainment?
- Does the task have any security restrictions?
- Does the task have any unusual scheduling characteristics?

- Is the task conducted in a hands-free setting or in some other way limited in terms of the user's modes of interaction?
- Is the task conducted in a setting with low bandwidth limitations, limited display characteristics, or slow or intermittent processing speed behind the interactions?
- Is the task such that it is better accomplished if information is presented in multiple formats? For example, some instructional tasks may benefit from presenting the instructions in both a verbal and a visual format.

The variables of situational constraints represent task variables that may be critical to the success or failure of an interface. For example, if a task is to be completed for entertainment purposes, as would be the case for a game, the design of the interface might be improved if it included hidden or tricky information. On the other hand, if the task was not for entertainment, then the hidden information could be a serious impediment to the usability of the interface.

### 3.6.2 Situational Variables: User

Like Eason, we also include user characteristics as potentially key factors that influence usability. We identify two primary user characteristics: (1) *user expertise* incorporating Eason's variables of user knowledge and discretion and (2) *user motivation.*

### User Expertise

In Chapter 14, we discuss some factors of *expertise* in detail. For now, it is probably sufficient to note that expert users generally experience situations within their domains of expertise differently than occasional or novice users do. Experts have much greater knowledge of the task and the context. In Chapter 1, we learned that someone's ability to perceive information from a user interface is key to a person's ability to use that interface. Experts generally perceive different information and form different mental representations of the situation than less expert users. Consequently, their experience with a given interface for a task is likely to be much different from that of less expert users. Expert users often need the freedom and flexibility to apply their own mental model of the solution to the user interface, rather than just following a set sequence from the designer. Following Eason's variable of discretion, experts generally can sort out those actions that they really need to make to accomplish a particular task, rather than blindly following a series of programmed steps. Because experts typically understand the task very well, their performance and ultimate satisfaction may be hampered by interactions with numerous prompts and confirmations of steps that they already know.

By contrast, novice users generally have a very limited mental model of the task and its execution. This group may often benefit from prompts and reminders. Finally, the occasional user, who is somewhere between an expert and a novice, may have a pretty good idea in the abstract as to how to accomplish a task but may have forgotten the precise details. For this expertise level, an interface that provides a clear task structure but also supports some user choices may lead to higher usability.

### User Motivation

As Eason noted, user motivation in using an interface may also influence the eventual usability outcome. He noted that users with high motivation might be more willing to put effort into the completion of a task, even when the user interface is difficult. User motivation can be high or low or somewhere in between. Strong motivation may be intrinsic to the situation or may be due to external factors, such as money. When users are highly motivated, especially if the motivation is intrinsic, the users may be more persistent in their use and more tolerant of an interface than users with lower motivation are. For example, the typical game player enjoys mastering the intricacies of a game. This user is willing to tolerate difficulties in completing the game. On the other hand, most of us do not like doing our income taxes. Many of us just want the process to be over as quickly as possible. Understanding the user's level and type of motivation may help the developer to achieve a positive usability outcome.

### 3.6.3 User Interface (System) Variables

Eason, Shackel, and Nielsen have all recognized that several user interface characteristics can potentially influence usability. In our model, we have included (1) *ease of learning,* (2) *ease of use,* (3) *ease of relearning,* (4) *task match,* (5) *flexibility,* and (6) *satisfaction.* Figure 3.4 illustrates our model.

### Ease of Learning, Ease of Use, and Ease of Relearning

Shackel, Nielsen, and Eason have all included *ease of learning,* or how easy the interface is for new users to learn, and *ease of use,* or how easy the interface is to operate for experienced users to use on a continuing basis, in their models of usability. Nielsen has a variable called *ease of remembering*, which we will call of *ease of relearning. Ease of relearning* refers to how easy a user interface is to use when it has once been learned but, because it has not been used recently, has to be at least partially relearned. Note that these variables refer to the learning, use, and relearning, of the user interface and not to the task itself. For a novice user who is also a novice to the task, a system that supports good ease of learning, use, and relearning will provide a lot of support for the task and the steps to complete the task. For a user who already has a good understanding of the task, an interface with good ease of learning, use, and relearning will emphasize the match between the real task and the user interface support for the task.

### Task Match

Eason included *task match* as a variable of the interface that influences usability, and it is a factor in our model as well. Good task match between the user interface and the real task can aid

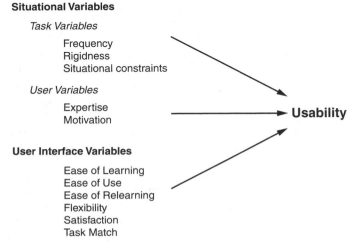

**Figure 3.4** Our Model of Usability.

expert users in mapping their understanding of the real task to the interface. Good task match can help a novice user develop a better understanding of the real task and of the steps necessary to complete the task with the user interface.

### Flexibility

Shackel noted that the *flexibility* of a user interface might influence usability. *Flexibility* refers to the capability of the interface to support unanticipated usage patterns. If I were designing a cash register system and it was not possible for the clerk to override the system-defined price, as might be the case for a closeout item, then the interface would not be flexible.

### Satisfaction

Both Nielsen and Shackel included the variable *user satisfaction* in their models, and we include it in ours. A user interface that is highly satisfying may be highly usable, even if it is less successful in terms of the other user interface variables. An interface that is easy to use and learn is likely to be very satisfying.

## 3.7 What Do You Do with a Model of Usability?

Once we have a definition of usability, we would like to do something with the model! We could use the model for a number of things, including these:

- Evaluate an existing system and user interface for usability.
- Utilize customer demands for usability characteristics, together with information from situational variables to drive a design toward a usable interaction and interface.
- Monitor and evaluate usability during the development of our own user interface.
- Critique a final product.

For each of these activities, the usability engineer and the customer will likely agree on a set of variables that will influence or have a causal influence on usability for a particular product or development effort. Once the customer and the usability engineer have identified the variables of interest, they will want to incorporate the variables into one or more of the activities in the preceding list. Like the rocket experiment that we discussed, the customer and developer will need to operationalize the variables into a set of measurements and understand how the measurements might be interpreted. For example, suppose the developer determines for a particular product that a particular task is performed once per month. Is that a frequently performed task? Only by understanding the measurement in the context of the project could one know the answer to this question.

In Chapters 5 and 6, we demonstrate how the usability engineer can collect information about tasks, users, and requirements for user interface characteristics. In Chapters 7 and 8, we discuss how information about situational variables and requirements for user interface characteristics can help drive design. In Chapter 11, we describe the evaluation process and how the variables of our usability model can be used in the assessment and evaluation of a computer application.

Here we address measurement and the variables of the model. Measurements do not always have to be numeric. In some situations, qualitative data that can be interpreted can also serve as a type of measurement. For the sake of simplicity, we simply refer here to measurements. For the variables of ease of learning, ease of use, and ease of relearning, performance variables of accuracy, speed, and error rate may be key measurements. For variables of task match and the flexibility of the user interface to support new tasks, the opinions of experts, given either quantitatively using measurement scales or qualitatively, may be useful. Expertise can often be measured by assessing the user's knowledge, experience, or response to situations. Motivation can also be measured in terms of a user's response to situations. Finally, satisfaction may be measured in terms of rating scales.

The following are some typical usability measurements that could be operationalizations for several of the variables we have discussed:

- User's self-assessment on a scale.
- User's years of training or number of courses taken.
- User's score on a comprehension test. Test is given after learning the system.
- Number of errors on a standard task.
- Time to complete a standard task.
- Number of standard tasks completed in a set time period.
- Number of features used.

## 3.8  Applying Our Model: An Audio Catalog

In this section, we give a brief overview of how we might use our usability model to collect information about the situation and the user's interface expectations with respect to usability. Our expectation is that once we understand the variables of interest in the usability model, we can design and build a product that will lead us to (cause) a positive usability outcome. We could also use the information from applying our usability model to assess an existing product.

For the rest of this text, we will use the sample project of building an audio catalog. For the moment, you can consider an *audio catalog* to be a collection of recordings with such information as recording artist and format. In later chapters, we discuss more of the details of this project. For now, you have been asked to build the user interface for a computerized audio catalog. Suppose that in the current system the user has some kind of paper catalog in which she or he keeps the information for the audio catalog. You and your customer have agreed that you want to have a good chance of building a usable system, so you are going to operationalize, measure, and interpret values for the situational variables and establish user interface expectations for your project.

### 3.8.1  Assessing Task Characteristics

One task in the audio catalog that will ultimately be supported in the user interface is *adding items to the catalog*. (In subsequent chapters we clarify what we mean by items.) In the current paper setup, *adding items to the catalog* involves the following sequence of steps:

- Find catalog.
- Find the right place in the catalog for the new item. Let's assume that the items are stored in some sort of order and that it is obvious where the new item would go.
- Place the new item in the catalog.
- Put the catalog away.

In terms of task variables, we need to assess the frequency, rigidness, and situational constraints for this task.

## Frequency

To measure frequency, you would need to know how often the task occurs over some set time period. You can ask a group of experts to specify, on average, how often they would put new items in the audio catalog during a one-month time period. You and your customer may agree that if the typical user performs this task more than twenty times per month, then the task is frequently performed, and if the frequency is less than two times per month, then the task is infrequently performed.

## Rigidness

On the surface, it appears that our task is relatively rigid in terms of sequence and that the only option available is that the different items may fit into different places in the sorted order. To determine rigidness for sure, you need to assess how many options and how many sequences occur throughout the task. You might give your group of audio catalog experts $1 for every idea about how this task might really vary, especially in terms of sequences of steps. You and your customer agree that if you find that you are handing out less than $3 on average, then you have a good idea that the task is relatively rigid.

## Situational Constraints

In our usability model, we have identified seven situational constraints that ultimately may impact usability:

- Is the task ever done collaboratively?
- Is the task done for entertainment?
- Does the task have any security restrictions?
- Does the task have any unusual scheduling characteristics?
- Is the task conducted in a hands-free setting or in some other way limited in terms of the user's modes of interaction?
- Is the task conducted in a setting with low bandwidth limitations, limited display characteristics, or slow or intermittent processing speed behind the interactions?
- Is the task such that it is better accomplished if information is presented in multiple formats?

Once again, you and your customer may consult a group of experts. For each of these questions, the experts might answer a rating question. For example, the expert might answer the following question to determine a rating for "Is the task ever done for entertainment?" and then justify the answer:

On a scale from 1 to 5, rate how often this task is done for fun.

1 = never    2 = rarely    3 = a moderate number of times    4 = often    5 = very often

Perhaps you and your customer agree that if the average answer to this question is 4 or higher, then entertainment is a key constraint on the task that will need to be taken into account in the user interface.

### 3.8.2 Assessing User Characteristics

To learn about user characteristics, you might want to learn more about individuals who are most likely to use this device. You and your customer would assess users of a paper audio catalog and potential users of the computerized audio catalog. Your assessment of expertise and motivation could be for an individual task or for the use of the entire audio catalog.

### User Motivation

Our goal here is to measure how motivated a person would be to use a computerized audio catalog. To evaluate this variable, you could ask the user to make a self-assessment of his or her motivation. The following might be a sample question:

> On a scale from 1 to 5, indicate how important it is to you to use a computerized audio catalog.
> 1 = not very important   2 = minimally important   3 = important
> 4 = very important         5 = urgently important

Another measurement would be to see how willing someone is to use the computerized audio catalog under conditions of adversity. The following might be a sample question:

> Suppose that you are using the computerized audio catalog while you are watching your favorite television program. You are trying to put a new item in the catalog right at the most exciting part of your show. On a scale from 1 to 5, indicate how motivated you would be to put the new item in the catalog, even if it means that you miss part of your program.
> 1 = not motivated     2 = minimally motivated   3 = motivated
> 4 = very motivated   5 = highly motivated

### User Expertise

For this variable, you are interested in the user's expertise in using paper audio catalogs, so you might ask users to self-assess their ability to use audio catalogs:

> Indicate your assessment of your own expertise in the use of audio catalogs.
> 1 = none   2 = low   3 = average   4 = high   5 = very high

You might also assess the knowledge of your potential users. You could give your potential users a test. For example, you might ask them some questions about the steps necessary to complete tasks using an audio catalog.

### 3.8.3 Assessing User Interface Characteristics

In our model of usability, we have identified six variables that are potential characteristics of a user interface. At the beginning of your development effort, it is very useful to agree with your customer, on a task-by-task basis, about how you will assess your eventual product based on these variables and how relatively important these variables are to usability. If you are assessing an existing product, you and your customer will still want to agree about how to assess these variables and what their relative importance is for usability.

### Ease of Learning

The intent of *ease of learning* is to get an idea of how easy or difficult it is for a user to go from no experience with your user interface to some level of proficiency. Ease of learning typically does not refer to the user's expertise related to the task that the user brings to the user interface. Common ways to measure ease of learning are to take a time or error count measurement. To do this, you and your customer would select a standard task and measure performance over some learning time period. You and your customer should agree about what a particular measurement might mean. For example, for the audio catalog we have already identified a standard task: *adding items to the catalog.* To assess ease of learning, we might measure how long it takes a beginner to do this task in the computerized system. We might give the user ten practice exercises that require adding new items. Then we might ask the user to add an eleventh item and measure his or her performance time.

Another option could be to pick a target time that would be considered good for a user to add a new item to the computerized catalog. You could measure the time, the number of practice exercises, or the total number of errors made until the user is at this level of proficiency for the standard task.

Another option would be to pick a target number of errors that would be considered acceptable. Again, you could measure the time, the number of practice exercises, or the total number of errors made until the user is at this level of proficiency for the standard task.

### Ease of Use
*Ease of use* refers to the user's ability to use the system, once she or he is proficient. You could use measurement strategies for ease of use similar to those you would for ease of learning. However, your user would have to be trained to an acceptable proficiency level with the user interface before you could assess performance.

### Ease of Relearning
*Ease of relearning* refers to the user's ability to use the system, once he or she is proficient but after spending some time away from the system. You could use measurement strategies for ease of use similar to those you use for ease of learning. However, your users would need to have an acceptable level of proficiency with the user interface and some time would have to elapse after training before performing the assessment.

### Task Match
*Task match* refers to the extent to which the sequence of steps through the real task is supported and similar to the steps provided in the user interface. Once again, you might interview a panel of experts to provide numerical assessments of this. A sample question might be this:

On a scale of 1 to 5, indicate how well this user interface will support the task of adding a new item to the audio catalog.

1 = not at all    2 = marginally    3 = okay    4 = pretty well    5 = excellent

You and your customer would evaluate the data from these measurements and determine an acceptable average value for task match of the system.

### Flexibility
*Flexibility* refers to the extent to which the user interface is able to support new or unexpected twists on tasks. You might interview a panel of experts again to provide numerical assessments of this. Perhaps you could pay $1 for every idea that your experts produce about new uses of the existing user interface.

You and your customer would evaluate the data from these measurements and determine how much money paid out would represent the appropriate level of flexibility for the system.

### Satisfaction

*Satisfaction* refers to the emotional or affective response of users to your user interface for individual tasks and for the entire user interface. One way that you might evaluate satisfaction is to ask the following question for each type of task supported in the interface:

On a scale of 1 to 5, indicate how satisfying this user interface will be in supporting the task of adding a new item to the catalog.

1 = not at all    2 = marginally    3 = okay    4 = pretty good    5 = excellent

### 3.8.4 Now What?

Once we have our data from our usability assessment, we should take this information into account as we design our user interface. We also could use this information as a basis for our subsequent assessment of the product that we build. Suppose we find that most of our users are experienced and highly expert so they really understand the tasks associated with the audio catalog. We can probably conclude that the users of the computerized catalog will be long-term users and that ease of use is going to be a key predictor of usability. Perhaps from our analysis, we will find that speed of completing a task is the definition of ease of use that makes the most sense. In design, we might select an interaction in which the user does not experience long sequences of prompts through the task for each execution of the task or long confirmation sequences.

Suppose the situation changes and we learn that, at least for some tasks, such as *adding items to the catalog,* it is necessary to have a high level of security (perhaps the item includes credit card information). The need to maintain security often requires more steps, and this may increase the amount of time required to complete the task. Situational constraints (security) may conflict with previously agreed upon usability requirements (ease of use when it is operationalized as completing the task quickly).

## 3.9 Conclusions About Measurements

Some concepts are easier to *operationalize* than others. For example, you may define ease of use in terms of the number of errors on a standardized task. You may define user knowledge as the number of computer science courses that a user has completed. Other concepts are difficult to operationalize. It can be difficult to create meaningful measures for rigidness of a task and flexibility of a system.

We have made several references to a *standard task.* In an experiment, the task that the user performs is one of the variables in the experiment. By creating standard tasks for the user to perform, we hold the task constant. All users perform the same standard tasks. In the preceding example *adding items to the catalog* was a standard task.

The example measures that we have described in this chapter yield numerical or quantifiable data. As we will see in Chapter 11, we also can use qualitative data for these characteristics.

## 3.10 What Parts of the System Have to Be Usable?

Often we think that we are only concerned with the usability of user software (the user interface), but usability really should be applied to all facets of a product and aspects of the user experience: manuals, installation, online help, training, hotline support, maintenance, and such. These areas are receiving more attention within the HCI community than in the past. However, we focus primarily on the user interface.

## 3.11 Usability Characteristics and the User Interface

In Chapter 1, we noted that everyday objects have several characteristics that are related to their usability. Two characteristics are key:

- The user must be able to perceive the noticeable clues as to what parts of the interface are important and how these parts will be used. The perceptible information, in combination with the user's knowledge will contribute to the user's mental model of the interface, including what and how to use in the interface.
- The interface should provide feedback for user actions. Feedback from user actions at the interface can reinforce accurate user understanding of the interface or help the user to adjust an inaccurate model.

What do these characteristics have to do with user interface characteristics such as ease of learning, ease of use, and ease of relearning? Clearly the issues from Chapter 1 and the user interface characteristics address features of an interface at very different levels. However, it seems worth noting that interfaces that contain perceptible, noticeable cues and offer feedback are more likely to support ease of use and ease of learning than those that do not. In fact, the presence of perceptible, noticeable cues and feedback could be used to define higher-level user interface characteristics.

### Conclusions

What can we conclude about usability models? Clearly no one definition or answer is right. The four models that we have looked at indicate that a number of factors contribute to usability and may be measurable. Common to all four models are the variables of *ease of use* and *ease of learning* in the interface itself. Nielsen's model places usability in the larger context of system acceptability. Eason's model is clearly causal and indicates that usability is driven by three different categories of variables: user interface (system) characteristics and the contextual variables of user and task characteristics. All four models suggest that the characteristics of usability can be measured. Table 3.1 summarizes the main ideas of the Shackel, Nielsen, and Eason models. Our usability model is a hybrid of the three and thus does not appear in Table 3.1.

In his article, Eason (1984) makes the case that as designers we have the most control over system characteristics. A usable interface will be one that emphasizes ease of learning, ease of use, and good task match while understanding the context of use. Eason also suggests the notion that the usability of a system (user interface) is an outcome of the interaction of the situation and the user interface. Because the usability engineer usually cannot control or change the situation, the best chance for a highly usable interface is to make design decisions that take the variables of the situation into account. No single design can possibly fit every situation.

Table 3.1    Summary of Usability Models.

|  | Shackel | Nielsen | Eason |
|---|---|---|---|
| **System Characteristics** | | | |
| Easy to learn initially | Learnability | Easy to learn | Easy to learn |
| Ease of relearning for intermittent users | Learnability | Easy to remember | |
| Matches target performance level | Effectiveness | Efficient to use | Easy to use |
| Low error rate and recoverability | | Errors | |
| Pleasing to users | Attitude | Subjectively pleasing | |
| Adaptable | Flexibility | | |
| Match between system function and task | | | Task match |
| **User Characteristics** | | | |
| Knowledge | | | Knowledge |
| Motivation | | | Motivation |
| Discretion | | | Discretion |
| **Task Characteristics** | | | |
| Openness | | | Openness |
| Frequency | | | Frequency |

## Exercises

1. Define the following terms: *ease of learning, ease of use, ease of relearning, frequency, satisfaction, user expertise, user motivation, discretion, task match, openness, flexibility, rigidness,* and *situational constraints.*

2. The objective of this exercise is to become more familiar with our model of usability and to understand how we might apply it to an existing user interface.
   - Suppose that you have been asked by your boss to evaluate the user interface for a *hand mixer* or a *steam iron.* You are to base your evaluation on our model of usability.
   - Describe the user inputs and actions that initiate functions from this device. Explain how the user inputs result in actions from the device (*mappings* from Chapter 1). You may wish to draw a picture to accompany your text description.
   - Now, *identify measurements* for the hand mixer *or* steam iron for each of two user characteristics, two user interface characteristics, and two task characteristics. You are not supposed to make the measurements. You are to describe how you would make the measurement and what the measurement is. For each measurement, explain which characteristic your measurement relates to and why the measurement is appropriate for that characteristic. You should be able to answer the following questions about your characteristic measurements:

     What are you measuring?

     How does your measurement relate to a variable of our usability model?

     How are you going to measure it? If your measurement involves your user engaging in a standard task, also explain what the task is.

Why is this an appropriate way to measure this? In other words, why does your measurement make sense for the variable that you are measuring?

How will you interpret your measurement in terms of the particular measure that you are considering? For example, if you measure the number of times per month that someone performs a task and find that they perform the task four times per month, you must decide and explain if that means that the task is frequent, infrequent, and so on.

Hints:

- Tasks are sometimes difficult to identify. Concentrate on the *task* that you would *normally* do with the device.
- Do not just modify the examples that were presented in this chapter. They may not be appropriate for the system that you are analyzing. Try to think of some modifications that make sense for the system you choose and its use.
- Do not just write "Standard task." Describe it.

# Part 2

# The Process of Usability Engineering

# 4

# The Process
# of Usability
# Engineering

## Motivation

At this point, we hope you agree that building high-quality user interfaces is necessary. From the usability models, you probably already have some ideas of factors that can influence the quality of a user interface. In the next several chapters, we discuss how to build a quality user interface and how the building process fits into the larger process of software development. At the end of this chapter, you should be able to do the following:

- Describe the distinct activities that occur in a software engineering project.
- Explain why software development may move in a linear progression or may be iterative in nature.
- Explain how developing a user interface is part of the larger problem of developing software.
- Explain why the principles of usability engineering are not random, not obvious, and not intuitive.
- Explain why the principles of user interface development are not applied as often as they should be.

## 4.1 User Interface and Software Development

Building a user interface rarely happens by itself, and the user interface does not stand alone. Usually, a user interface is built as part of a larger software system. Before we consider the process of usability engineering, it is useful to understand the process of software engineering and how the development of a user interface changes the process of software engineering.

Examine the software industry. What are you likely to see? Continually falling costs for software increases potential markets. Demand is increasing for more diverse software functionality. At the same time, the size and complexity of software always seem to be increasing. In other words, the demand for software seems to be ever increasing, and the software that is demanded seems to be of ever-increasing complexity and type. But software takes a long time to develop. Development costs apparently remain high. Software is regularly delivered with errors. Many authors have called this situation a "software crisis." According to Pressman (2001, 11), this is not an acute crisis but a "chronic affliction" of our industry. Software takes a long time to develop and often has errors, but in spite of some technological improvements, such as *computer-aided software engineering (CASE) tools,* we are not enormously faster at development. This syndrome has held true since the 1970s, if not earlier, and it is still true. Software engineering methodologies and tools may help. Code reusability also may help. Even better training of computing professionals may help some, but the bottom line is that software is still hard to build. Remember the concept of "no silver bullet"? This idea suggests that no new tool or development methodology will miraculously make software development easy (cf. Brooks 1987). Software is simply difficult to develop.

Rittel and Webber (1984) developed the term *wicked problem* to describe problems that they had observed in their studies of social planning. In their work they observed that for some kinds of problems, solving the problem often revealed more problems or more complexity. For example, they noticed that when neighborhoods with poor housing were rebuilt, the problems of the poor housing went away but social and community networks may have been inadvertently destroyed as well. In other words, by solving the one problem of inadequate housing, other problems cropped up. Rittel and Webber identified ten defining characteristics of *wicked problems,* for example:

- Wicked problems do not have a stopping rule.
- Wicked problems do not have criteria to evaluate if a design is a solution to the problem.

Both of these characteristics suggest that it is difficult to determine if a design will yield a solution or if a "solution" truly solves the problem. Software projects often have problems in determining when they are complete. How often have you worked on a program for which you think of one more thing to make it better? You can always add one more thing to a software project.

Here is another feature of a wicked problem:

- Wicked problems do not have a set or a known list of well-defined solutions.

In other words, the solver of a wicked problem does not have a set of well-defined solutions from which to choose. Consider the problem of building a bridge. You could select from several types of bridges, such as cantilever and suspension bridges. The properties of the different types are well-known as are the different conditions for which each of the designs is appropriate. This is not the case with most software projects.

Building software has been identified as a wicked problem (cf. Budgen 1994). In building software, it is rarely clear what the stopping criteria are. Nor is a set of potential solutions typically available.

In summary, developing software is not easy because the problems that are addressed are complex and not easily solved. The development process may be improved by following an organized approach and by using tools, but the process will remain difficult, complicated, and challenging.

## 4.2 User Interface and Special Challenges to Software Development

Development of any software system with a significant user interface raises all the same challenges as traditional software development does, plus a few more. Does that really matter? You bet it does! In many software systems, 50 percent or more of the total code is related to the user interface. In some applications, the percentage is actually much higher.

Myers (1994) describes a number of reasons that explain why developing a user interface is difficult. We have already looked at these issues in Chapter 2. To review, Myers explains that to really understand a user's problem, the usability engineer must have significant domain knowledge; in other words, the developer must have or develop some expertise in the user's area of expertise. This is usually very difficult to do. He also mentions that having a piece of software with a significant user interface may introduce inherent conflicts into the requirements. Some examples of potential conflicts may be between interface standards and user needs. As we will see in Chapter 5, it is difficult to thoroughly specify an interface for all but the simplest of user tasks.

Myers makes the additional point that user tasks are often complex. You may be asking "So what?" since software itself is complex. In other words, software is difficult enough to develop! But imagine that you are building complex software for the WG Satellite Shield Security Corporation (WG). The software that WG needs requires extensive reliability and security, as well as lots of data handling. Typical tasks for the WG product are three-dimensional data modeling tasks. Now you start to think about the users of this software. Suppose they include engineers who will be using three-dimensional data modeling to study what-if questions for WG. No simple question-and-answer interface is going to support their complex task needs. In this example, the user interface would likely need to support a variety of informational presentations including text, graphics, and animations. So the software package for WG will need to support a complex user interface and be secure and reliable. Clearly, the demands of the user interface in this example add complexity to an already difficult software development problem.

The conclusion is that—once again—building software is difficult. Experience has shown that when you add the user interface, software development is just that much harder. Many applications do not have significant user interface components. When they do, the interface adds special challenges. According to Myers (1994), a user interface adds to the complexity of software in special ways for a number of additional reasons.

When we build software for systems or database management work, our target environment is often a single operating system or database management system. User interfaces, on the other hand, regularly support a number of input and output devices. It is generally not enough for our interface to support just one kind of input or output device. For example, many windows-based visual interfaces permit users to input data via a keyboard and a mouse. A keyboard can provide both textual and navigational inputs. A mouse similarly can provide a variety of types of input. The user interface must be able to correctly interpret and sequence these inputs, which by definition are asynchronous and user driven. Add joysticks and light pens, and the handling of user inputs becomes even more complex. The user interface similarly drives the output devices, such as displays and audio outputs.

In software systems with significant user interfaces, users may wish to extend or tailor the interface to their own specifications. Some of these tailoring steps seem simple enough; for example, in a word processing system, a user may wish to set the default first page number. When the interface permits the user to redefine the meanings of physical inputs or to integrate macros into an interface, the problem is obviously more difficult. Because personalizations can be accomplished in numerous ways, the user probably will not choose from a short list of alternatives.

Finally, the essence of user interfaces used to be one-user, stand-alone systems. Now, more and more user interfaces are called upon to support *computer-supported cooperative work* (CSCW) and connectivity (via the Internet, for example). Under this usage pattern, the interface supports simultaneous use by more than one person. For example, an interface may support live, virtual meetings. What would be required for such a meeting? The synchronization and security issues are daunting to think about, let alone to implement. Now think about the kind of information that needs to be exchanged in a virtual meeting. The spoken, verbal information may be the easy part. In a real, face-to-face meeting, lots of nonverbal cues are exchanged among participants. For example, meeting participants may communicate via facial gestures or even by where they sit in the room. Software to support virtual meetings should preserve and distribute this nonverbal information. Development of user interfaces for cooperative work is an ongoing challenge, and instant messaging and chat systems simply do not meet the need.

## 4.3 The Process of Development

In a typical programming course, your teacher gives you an assignment and you are to write a program to solve the problem that he or she has stated. Your teacher may even outline for you how the program is to be constructed and may give you some data to verify that your solution will work.

Not so in the real world! In the real world, the software developer will take on some of those jobs that your programming instructor has done for you in the past: specify the problem that you are to solve, deconstruct the solution into modules, specify the data structures or classes, provide test data, and so on. Computer scientists who work in this broader scenario are called *software engineers* because they engineer a project from its earliest conception until its ultimate completion or retirement.

This simple scenario illustrates the process of development. Suppose that Julie's cats, BC, Boo, and Snickers, need cat food, but Julie does not have time to go to the store to pick it up. Laura volunteers to get the food. The first thing that Laura *does not* do is to go to the store. She has never had a cat and knows nothing about cats. First she has to understand a little about the environment in which she will be working and to determine if it is feasible for her to get the food. She has to find out approximately how much money cat food will cost and which store carries cat food. Is the store on the way to work? Does Laura have enough money in her wallet? Next Laura needs to understand the problem better. Because Laura is not an expert on Julie's cats, she will need to consult with Julie to get a better handle on the problem. She will need to learn about what the cats' specific nutritional needs are. Do the cats have hairballs and need hairball food? Are the cats overweight so that they eat special diet food? So Laura asks Julie a few of these questions to better understand the problem she is supposed to solve. Of course, Julie now may tell Laura things about the cats that are totally irrelevant to the problem at hand. Together they will need to sort out precisely what problem Laura is supposed to solve and develop a problem description.

Next they will design a solution to this problem. The design might include identifying the specific store, type of cat food, and size of bag. Next is the easy part; Laura goes to the store and buys the food. Finally, Laura turns the food over to Julie, but the process is really not finished until Julie actually tests out the food by feeding it to the cats to see if it is adequate.

Developing engineered software is something like the process that Laura and Julie went through. In their scenario, going to the store was the easy part. In software engineering, actually writing the code may take less time than the other parts of the process.

Let's review the cat food scenario and identify the steps that Laura and Julie went through:

- Learning about the environment and checking for feasibility
- Understanding the problem
- Designing a solution
- Implementing the solution
- Testing the solution

These are precisely the phases that well-engineered software goes through. As in the cat food scenario, in which Laura did not rush off to the store immediately, software engineers do not rush to write program code right away.

## 4.4 Software Life Cycle

More than thirty years ago, a number of computer scientists recognized that a software development project was more likely to succeed if the development effort were disciplined and followed a timeline. It is now widely accepted that software development should go through a number of phases. The phases are summarized in the Waterfall Model that was first proposed by Royce (1987). Figure 4.1 shows one version of the Waterfall Model of software development. As you can see, the Waterfall Model suggests a systematic, sequential approach to software development.

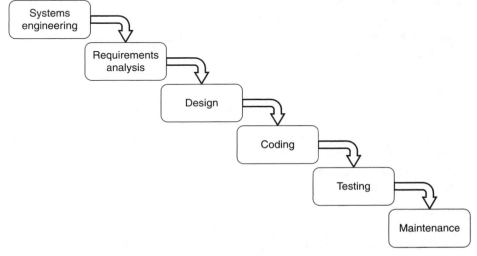

Figure 4.1   Classic Waterfall Model of Software Development.

The model begins at the environmental, contextual systems level and progresses through a series of phases. Output of one phase is input to the next phase. The process continues in one direction with the completion of one phase indicating the start of the next phase. In this section, we describe the different phases of the software life cycle in detail.

### 4.4.1 Systems Engineering and Analysis

The purpose of this phase is to gather information about the context and environment of the proposed software. A typical question that a software engineer might ask would be "What other software, hardware, people, procedures, and such, will the software interface?" The software engineer and customer may also consider the feasibility of the project, especially if cost estimates are available.

### 4.4.2 Software Requirements Analysis and Specification

This phase, in which the developer is defining and understanding the problem to be solved, is probably the most critical to the eventual success or failure of any problem. The developer has to get a clear picture of the customer's requirements; in other words, the developer must *analyze* the customer's problem in such a way as to understand it in enough detail to design a solution. The goals of this phase are to understand the nature and functionality of the program(s) to be built. In addition, the developer must understand the problem domain and how the domain influences the problem. Finally, understanding the problem may involve more than understanding the problem per se; the customer may have special nonfunctional requirements, such as software performance, (software) interfacing constraints, the target run environment, and characteristics of the user interface. It is not enough for the developer to understand the problem personally, but he or she must also document an understanding of the problem. The output of the requirements analysis phase is usually a *software specification document.* This specification serves as a contract (often a legal contract) between the developer and the customer because it gives a precise statement of the problem to be solved. This phase is often challenging to the developer because, going into the project the developer may not understand the customer's situation at the level of detail necessary for the final specification document. In this phase, the developer probably will engage in extensive data gathering from the customer.

To complete this phase in development, the analysis and resulting specification document must have these traits (Fairley 1985):

- *Complete:*   All relevant aspects of the problem to be solved must be included. Like many problems, the challenge to completeness is in the details. To be complete, the specification document should be so detailed that designers who receive the document do not have to fill in any details themselves.
- *Consistent and unambiguous:*   The different parts of the analysis and resulting specification should not be in conflict. Designers should not have to make choices or inferences because the specification is inconsistent or ambiguous.
- *Correct:*   The analysis and specification should describe the *right* problem.

### 4.4.3 Software Design

In this phase, the developer is designing a solution to address the problem that was specified in the requirements phase. This phase is usually conducted as a multistep process that focuses on four distinct attributes of the program(s): data structures and software objects, software architectures, procedural details (for example, algorithms), and (software) interface characteristics. The output of this phase is usually a *software design document.* The design document should be detailed enough so that the implementers are not forced to make design decisions.

### 4.4.4 Coding
In this phase, the developer will translate the design into machine-readable and executable form. The output of this phase is the *program code,* as well as the *program documentation.*

### 4.4.5 Testing
As code is generated, the developer will begin testing. Testing focuses on (1) logical internals and code flows through the software and (2) functional externals and how well the software meets the specifications. The output from this phase is a *testing report.* Often, boundary cases and interesting situations will be discovered during the requirements analysis phase. Interestingly, several software engineering strategies encourage the design and development of testing strategies and software during the software design stage.

### 4.4.6 Maintenance
Most development is not finished even after the product is shipped out. Software often undergoes changes after it is delivered or marketed. Software changes result because of errors, external changes in the environment, or the requirements change. Maintenance uses a mini form of the life cycle for its changes. Maintenance activities include correcting errors, adding features, and updating software to accommodate environmental changes such as a new operating system. If development takes one year, maintenance could go on for ten years. The ratio of maintenance costs to the development costs of a system has increased significantly over the years (cf. Pfleeger 2001).

### 4.4.7 Guessing Game
Now we are going to play a guessing game to see how much you know about software development.

**QUESTION 1.** *If my total development effort, before maintenance, is 100 units, how many units are devoted to* **testing?**

**ANSWER 1.** You might be surprised to find that: up to 50 percent or more of development effort may be spent on testing (Myers 1979). This means that only 50 percent of your total effort goes into defining the problem, designing a solution, and implementing your design.

**QUESTION 2.** *If my total development effort before maintenance is 100 units, how many units are devoted to specification and design? How many units to coding?*

**ANSWER 2.** According to Gilbert (1983) 30 to 40 units will be spent on specification and design and 14 to 20 units will be spent on coding.

**QUESTION 3.** *If it costs $1 to find and fix an error during requirements, how much will it cost to fix during testing? After delivery?*

**ANSWER 3.** Boehm and Papaccio (1988) suggest that the error may cost $20 to find and fix during testing and up to $200 to find and fix after delivery.

How did you do? The most common mistake that students make on this exercise is to underestimate the time that developers spend on testing and, by inference, overestimate the amount of time that goes into coding. This is not a surprise. In your programming courses, most of your effort has been focused on coding.

### 4.4.8 Issues for the Waterfall Model

The Waterfall Model is the oldest and most widely used description for the process of software engineering. A number of methodologies and CASE tools are built around this model of software development. For the developer, following a methodology based on the Waterfall Model imposes discipline on the software development process. In our discussion so far, we have referred to a single person as a developer. In reality, most development efforts involve teams. Individuals on these teams may work on only one or two parts of the development effort. In large teams, following a disciplined approach to development is essential to success.

Large software development projects involve lots of planning so that the developer will know how much the project will cost, over what time period it will extend, how many people are needed, and so on. Following the phases of the Waterfall Model facilitates cost and resource estimations; thus, software developers can specify a timetable for their development project.

### 4.4.9 Some Problems with the Waterfall Model

It may have occurred to you that it might make sense to move back and forth between the stages of the Waterfall Model. This is called *iteration*. An example from our cat food scenario might be if Laura had gone to the store and found two cat food brands that fit Julie's needs. The one that they had selected for Laura to buy was not on sale, but an exact competitor was. Laura might call Julie from the store and ask her if she wants to go with an alternative solution, that is, the cheaper cat food. In other words, Laura would be going back to the requirements and making changes even though she was in the implementation stage.

Here is the story on software development. Real problems rarely follow the sequential flow that the Waterfall Model suggests. Iteration always occurs or wants to occur and creates problems in the application of the strict Waterfall paradigm. Trade-offs always occur when following a methodology that follows a strict Waterfall Model as opposed to a model that supports iteration. While no methodology leads to perfect scheduling calculations, resources for models that support iteration are notoriously difficult to predict in advance.

On the other hand, a methodology based on the strict forward Waterfall Model depends on the customer having a precise vision of the final product. Realistically, it is often difficult for the customer to state all requirements explicitly at the beginning of a project. The classic life cycle has difficulty accommodating the natural uncertainty that exists at the beginning of many projects. Customer expectations may change as they learn more about what is possible. Adding to this difficulty is the observation that the customer and developer usually do not speak the same language, especially at the beginning of a project. What customers say they want and what the developer "hears" may be different. Finally, in a strictly forward development, the customer must have patience. A working version of the software will not be available until late in the life cycle. The customer will not have a product to look at until the end of the project.

A number of authors have offered modifications to the Waterfall Model that support iteration. One strategy is to use prototyping and the assessment of prototypes to drive iteration. What is a prototype, you may ask? A prototype is a model of something. In software engineering, it is usually a partial representation of a system or some aspect of a system. Prototypes may be detailed or sketchy, done with paper, demonstration technologies, or real implementation tools. Prototypes may be thrown away, or they may migrate to full systems. Prototypes, their types, and the tools to build them for usability engineering are discussed more fully in Chapter 10.

Prototypes can be used for a number of purposes, depending upon where the developer is in the development cycle. Early on, the developer can show the user the prototype as an example of his or her understanding of the problem. Later the prototype can be used to demonstrate system features or behaviors. Prototypes facilitate evaluation of the product under development at multiple points instead of only at the end of the project.

## 4.5 Building a Model That Includes Usability Engineering

Problems with the Waterfall Model are especially significant when developing a user interface. In this section, we explore how we could modify the Waterfall Model to make it more appropriate for a project that includes a significant user interface.

### 4.5.1 What Activities Are Necessary for Usability Engineering?

Recall that we identified these activities as necessary for good software engineering:

- Defining the context and checking for feasibility
- Understanding the problem
- Designing the solution
- Implementing the solution
- Evaluating the implementation (against the problem definition and the design definition)

These activities, at an abstract level, are similar for engineering a user interface, and we expect to conduct these activities in some form for usability engineering.

We note in our model that at a more detailed level, some key differences arise between software engineering and usability engineering activities. In summary, these are the differences:

- *Understanding the "problem."* In software engineering, the problem involves some kind of system or process that requires a computerized solution. In usability engineering, the *problem* is to understand the user's tasks that must be supported by the user interface, in the context of the user and task characteristics. In other words, the variables that influence usability for a given project need to be identified.
- *Designing a solution.* In software engineering, the *design* is defined in terms of algorithms, objects, and so on. In usability engineering, the *design* is defined in terms of both the design of the interaction (the user's look and feel) and the design of the software that supports the interaction. Two design activities are taking place: (1) design of what the user will see and (2) design of the software to present the user interface.
- *Evaluating the implementation.* In software engineering, we test the code for logic errors and for mismatches with the problem and design documents. In usability engineering, we test the code in the same way. In addition, we evaluate our interaction for usability and to ensure that it satisfies our usability needs. Again, we identify two activities: (1) the usual software testing and (2) user evaluation to confirm that the user interface meets the usability criteria.

Experience suggests that, in the real world, it is tough to have a noniterative development effort. Even traditional software engineering projects often benefit from iteration and reevaluation.

We now present a variation on the Waterfall Model that integrates the phases of software and user-interface development. As can be seen in Figure 4.2, our model supports iteration and indicates

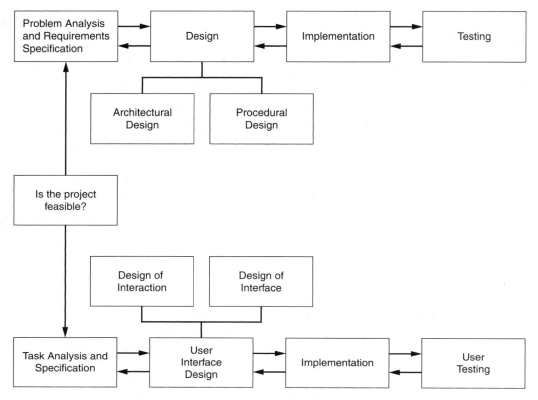

**Figure 4.2** Parallel Software Engineering and User Interface Development Activities.
*Source:* Barnes and Leventhal, 2001.

the parallel activities in software engineering and the development of the user interface. In our model, user interface development has to happen in the context of a larger software engineering effort unless the only goal is to build an interface prototype. We give a brief description of the parallel activities of software engineering and usability engineering. In later chapters we give more detailed presentations of the usability engineering activities.

Table 4.1 describes some of the activities that take place in each of the phases of the parallel paradigm. Remember that many of these activities happen away from the computer. As you can see from Table 4.1, each phase in the software development life cycle has a companion set of activities for user interface development. While the specific artifacts produced by the software development activities differ from those that are produced in user interface development, the activities that produce these artifacts are similar.

Problem analysis or task analysis is the phase in which the developer gains a better understanding of the problem to be solved. The goal of these context-setting activities is to understand the environment in which the product—software or user interface—will eventually function, as well as to identify need and feasibility. During analysis, the activity is to understand the problem to be solved, whether it is the software package or the user interface.

Table 4.1    Parallel Software Engineering and User Interface Development Activities

| Activity | Sample Software Engineering Activities | Sample Usability Engineering Activities | |
| --- | --- | --- | --- |
| Context Setting | Systems Engineering, including feasibility studies, project planning, resource scheduling | Establishing need for interface, feasibility, overall usability expectations, project planning, resource scheduling | |
| Requirements Analysis and Specification (understanding and documenting the problem) | Identify what the proposed system should do and how it is constrained Generate data flow descriptions; use case and scenario descriptions | Identify precisely what tasks the user will accomplish with the interface Understand the nature of these tasks Identify user's specific usability requirements Identify the critical user characteristics Identify other relevant situational characteristics Generate scenarios; use case diagrams, task analysis and specifications, user profiles | |
| Design—High-level | Architectural design of software Design of communication among modules, subsystems, or classes Distribution of work and services between clients and servers | Design of interaction; design of overall layouts and style of interaction | Architectural design of software to support interaction |
| Design—Detailed | Design of algorithms, modules, and data structures | Design of individual screens or individual interactions | Design of algorithms, modules, and data structures to support interaction |
| Implementation | Implementation | Implementation | |
| Evaluation | Testing of logical flow (against design) and function (against specification) | Evaluation by experts, analysis or testing by users of interface against specification and for usability | Testing of logical flow and function of software to support interaction |

Design is the act of generating a solution to a defined problem. Design starts with a high-level or nondetailed solution. In software, the high-level design may describe the arrangement of software modules or subsystems, the distribution of services among clients and servers, or the data and control flows between modules or subsystems. The low-level design selects algorithms and data structures to support the high-level design. In usability engineering, design is concerned with both the design of the user's interaction with the system and the software to run the interaction. So the design activities for the interface software precisely match those for a conventional software development project. For the interaction, the high-level activity corresponds to the selection of an interaction style, such as a command-line interface, and the overall style of presentation. The low-level design corresponds to the design of individual interactions, such as screens.

Implementation is implementation! If you have written more than one computer program, you know what is involved and we won't elaborate any further.

Evaluation of a software project typically involves testing the software logic and testing the software against the specification. Customers often are involved in the final phases of software testing. Evaluation of a usability-engineering project once again has two parts: testing the interface software and user evaluation. Testing the interface software is much like testing any other software project. User evaluation may involve evaluation by experts and testing by users; the goals of the evaluation typically are to determine if the user interface solved the problem that was identified in the specification and if the interface is usable for the target audience.

## 4.6 Methodologies, Models, Notations, and Mechanics

So far our description of the software development and user interface development processes has been somewhat generic. In Chapters 5 through 12, we discuss some specific techniques for usability engineering. At this point, it is important to distinguish some of the components of this process.

### 4.6.1 Methodologies

About thirty years ago, some experts within the software development community noticed that the process of software engineering would go much better if some kind of integrated approach covered the software life cycle. The idea was that whatever method was used to develop a requirement specification would then feed into the method for design, and so on. In essence, a system would be in place to support the phases in the Waterfall Model.

One of the earliest methodologies was the *structured analysis and structured design methodology* or SA/SD (see DeMarco 1979, Gane and Sarson 1979, Yourdan and Constantine 1979). In this methodology, the developer builds a description of the requirements in terms of data flows through the proposed system. These data flows illustrate the necessary transformations for data from input to output, from the perspective of the customer. The transformations occur within processes. These data flows are illustrated in a hierarchical set of *data flow diagrams* (DFDs). The DFDs begin as an abstract version and are refined into more detailed versions. The information in a DFD is enhanced with a *data dictionary* containing all process and data flow names and definitions. Other information in the specification includes detailed descriptions of the processes and data stores, as well as the specification of nonfunctional requirements.

In SA/SD, once the customer has approved the specification, the software developer begins to generate a design specification. The data dictionary from the requirements is the starting point for the data dictionary of the design. The designer translates the DFDs from the requirements into a software architecture. The process descriptions are translated and enhanced to form module specifications in the design.

In other words, in SA/SD the artifacts that are produced at the various stages of development are linked together. SA/SD consists of *methods* for each stage of the life cycle linked together to form a *methodology*.

A number of other software development methodologies and variations exist. The Jackson-System Design Methodology is a popular approach that emphasizes data structures (cf. Jackson 1975). Also, the Unified Software Development Process is an integrated and object-oriented approach (cf. Jacobson, Booch, and Rumbaugh 1999). The Unified Process is based on an iterative process for software development rather than the linear Waterfall Model. Like many other development methodologies, the focus of the Unified Process is on the development of models.

A number of authors have suggested specific usability engineering methodologies as well. For example, Mayhew (1999) presents a very detailed usability engineering methodology that includes notational structures and strategies for each stage of the life cycle. Rosson and Carroll (2002), Rosson, Carroll, and Rodi (2004), and Carroll (2000) describe a usability engineering methodology called *scenario-based development* or SBD. The emphasis of the SBD methodology is on the development and evolution of scenarios from problem description to eventual design. In SBD, the problem and the designs are presented as scenarios, unlike a number of other usability engineering methodologies in which the problem definition evolves into a design using a variety of alternative notational forms. Both the Mayhew and the Rosson and Carroll approaches are by nature iterative. The methodology that we present in Chapters 5 through 12 is presented as if the developer would perform each of the activities in each phase only once. In reality, the developer who uses our methodology would also follow an iterative strategy, an issue that we discuss in more detail in Chapter 10.

### 4.6.2 Models
Pick up almost any software engineering textbook, and you will see references to models. Models in this sense are simply descriptions of something. Different software engineering methods and methodologies will have characteristic models. So SA/SD includes DFDs as models of data flow through a system. The Unified Process includes many different types of models for showing data relations, functions, and flows.

### 4.6.3 Notation
A notation is different from a methodology. A notation is simply a way of specifying or illustrating a model within a methodology. Within the Unified Process methodology, the notation is UML (universal modeling language). You can think of notation as the syntax of a methodology and the methodology as the rules for forming meaning with the syntax. Once you start usability or software engineering, you may feel like what you are using is just the notation, but it is important to remember that the notation is just a way of executing the methodology. So if you start generating case diagrams using UML notation, hopefully it will be in the context of an object-oriented development methodology.

### 4.6.4 Mechanics
We noted that a number of methodologies are supported by CASE tools. These tools guide the developer through the methodology and provide support for compliance with the methodology. CASE tools can make the mechanics of generating diagrams, models, and other components of the methodology easier, better looking, and more internally consistent.

## 4.7 The Development Team
Here is a fact of life: as a computer science practitioner, you will probably do your work as a member of a team. The job of building a good interface has to be taken on by the team that designs the product as a whole. Formation of development teams is rarely as random as in your computer science classes. It takes some thought in assigning the right people to a team.

During job interviews, students are often surprised to hear questions about their team skills, such as these:

- "When you are in a group, what role do you normally take? Are you a leader, a follower, or what?"
- "Describe some of your leadership experiences."

In preparing for employment interviews, you should think about this type of question. You should also be prepared to discuss what kind of role you would like on a development team: designer, tester, user-interface specialist, technical writer, or some other role.

### 4.7.1 Team Structure

Before the start of the project, the team needs to be assigned to or needs to agree to a command and communication structure. Two distinct structures have emerged:

- Chief-programmer team
- Ego-less programming

In *chief-programmer teams,* all communication goes through a team leader, the chief programmer, so the number of potential communication paths is limited. Non-chiefs do not typically communicate, except through the chief. This can create extra costs related to increased communication. An *ego-less programming* situation, by contrast, has no chief programmer. The leadership style is more democratic. Communication is direct among team members. (See Pfleeger 2001 for more details.)

Which design team structure is best? It depends on the group dynamic and the type of problem. Typically programmers spend a great deal of time interacting with their team members. McCue (1978) studied programmers at IBM and found that 50 percent of a typical programmer's time was spent on interactions with team members (30 percent working alone and 20 percent working on activities not directly tied to productivity, such as travel). This high percentage of interaction suggests that the ability of personnel to work together is critical to the success of the team. Work by Leavitt (1951), Porter and Lawler (1965), and Shaw (1971) suggests that the size and structure of the team can impact the success of a group. Their work indicates that, when possible, smaller groups with democratic leadership may be the best choice.

Problem type also influences the choice of team structure. Exploratory problems may work better with an ego-less programming team structure. On the other hand, familiar, well-structured problems may be better with a chief programmer who has created similar solutions and knows the problem domain well.

## 4.8 How Involved Are the Users?

In most software engineering efforts, the software engineers guide the process. Users and customers provide information about the problem to be solved and give feedback on the design and implementation. Normally designers gather information from users and filter that information into their designs. Usually, the designer is not the user. Subsequent usability depends on how well the designers have interpreted the information that the users have provided.

An alternative model has been suggested. This alternative is usually called *participatory design.* As indicated in the previous paragraph, we have been assuming a split between the roles of designers and users. This has been the traditional mode of operation for many usability engineering situations. In participatory design, users are members of the development team and work closely with the designers. Advocates of participatory design stress that the participatory aspect leads to greater buy-in from users and hence higher user satisfaction (cf. Blomberg and Henderson 1990).

## Conclusions

Usability and software engineering always follow a process. In the past, the process was chaos. Several models have been suggested to structure the software development process, one of the earliest being the Waterfall Model. Usability engineering often takes place in the larger context of software engineering. Your choice of usability process model is very important in determining the overall success or failure of your project. Use of a development methodology does not guarantee that your interface will be usable. However, failure to follow some kind of methodology almost invariably dooms a project to failure.

## Exercises

1. Define the following terms: *software engineering, CASE tools, computer-supported cooperative work, Waterfall Model, iteration, chief-programmer team, ego-less programming team, participatory design, methodology, model,* and *notation.*
2. Name and describe the different phases of the Waterfall Model for software development. What products or documents are created during each of the phases? Approximately what percentage of time in a project is spent in each of the phases?
3. Think about making a cake or building a model airplane. Identify the Waterfall Model activities that occur in these activities.
4. This is a good exercise to do in a group. Many of you have worked as summer interns or in jobs in industries that follow a methodology with a well-defined process. Some examples of such industries are the software industry, of course, but also the construction industry and the manufacturing of engineered products industry. Thinking about your experiences, what was the life cycle that you followed in your job? Was it formally specified or informal?

# Part 3

## Defining and Documenting the User's Needs

# 5

# Understanding and Documenting the User Interface

## Motivation

In Chapter 4, we introduced the idea of a *process* of usability engineering, which by necessity, is embedded into a process of software engineering for most projects. The idea is that development goes through a series of phases. The flow of activity among these phases may be in a strictly forward direction. More often the flow of activities between phases is forward and backward, especially for user interface development.

In Chapter 4, we also saw that the early phases of the usability engineering process involve context setting and feasibility assessment, as well as understanding and documenting the problem. The "problem" to understand and document in usability engineering is to identify the user tasks that will be supported by the user interface in the context of the situation. In this chapter we explore these issues further. By the end of the chapter you should be able to:

- Describe the different aspects of context setting and feasibility assessment.
- Understand and document a problem using the simple task analysis and specification technique presented in this chapter.
- Describe techniques to collect information about users.

We assume that you will be doing some analysis and specification activities as part of a class project when you finish this chapter. These activities will give you a chance to practice what you have learned. We have found that the most difficult of these activities is task specification, so we focus on that process. In our class, we normally provide the context and user analysis information as part of the project description. Your instructor may opt for you to perform all three of these activities. Chapter 6 illustrates in detail these activities for a large-scale project, the audio catalog.

Good luck with the activities presented in this chapter. So far, most of you have written programs that were based on your teacher's well-planned specifications and timetables. If you complete a large-scale specification activity with this chapter, you will have begun to acquire an important and marketable skill.

## 5.1 Introduction

For the developer, understanding the target problem is critical. Otherwise, he or she may solve the *wrong* problem! Thinking back to our model of usability in Chapter 3, you may recall that the factors that influence the ultimate user reaction and usability of a system are situational characteristics, user characteristics, and characteristics of the user interface. The developer has control over the user interface characteristics, but the user and situational characteristics are essentially determined by the user and the situation.

Ask yourself what you need to know to understand a problem, and you will probably conclude that the issues from our usability model are precisely what you need. Understanding the user's characteristics, the tasks, and the setting that your user interface needs to address can go a long way toward specifying the problem you need to solve.

In this chapter and later ones, we banter about two terms, *analysis* and *specification*. A quick definition is in order. *Analysis* is the activity of understanding and breaking down a problem, so *task analysis* means understanding the user's tasks at both a high and a detailed level. *Specification* means "documenting" or "describing in detail," so a *task specification* is the documentation of your understanding of the user's tasks. It is not enough to understand without documenting, and vice versa.

## 5.2 Context Setting and Context Specification

Suppose you are the CEO and only employee of your own user interface development consulting firm. A potential customer calls you with a project that they would like you to do. Take a few minutes to think of some questions you would need to answer before investing resources in this customer's project, then continue reading this text.

You probably came up with some questions like these:

- What kind of platform and programming language will I be using?
- What is the customer's time frame for the project?
- Where will I be working: at the customer's site, at my site, or somewhere else?
- How much money does the customer want to spend on this project?

The answers to such questions set the context for your work. They give you, the developer, an idea of the feasibility of a project before you jump into the middle of a large effort. For example, if the customer is expecting you to deliver a project on a platform that you know nothing about and is not willing to pay for your training, the project may not be feasible for you.

Your context analysis and specification minimally should explore and document at least three pieces of information:

- Usability expectations
- Needs
- Feasibility

### Usability Expectations

Users may wish you to develop an overview document in which they establish their general usability expectations for the proposed user interface. Such a *usability expectation specification* might include:

- *Overriding usability goals.* If the user expects that overall the user interface will be easy to learn, easy to use, fun to use and so on, it is important to document *exactly what the user means by this.* This document should specify as carefully and in as much detail as possible how you will operationalize and assess these goals.

### Needs

Some authors have suggested that the usability engineer should analyze the *need* for the new system before continuing with the rest of the usability lifecycle (cf. Hix and Hartson 1993). A *needs specification* might include:

- *A rationale* to establish and document that a new user interface is needed.
- *A statement* of the goals and expected use of the proposed user interface.
- *A feature list* of the proposed product. These features might specify operational characteristics of the system, platform information, and so on. In other words, the feature list could spell out what specific things a user could do with this proposed user interface and in what environment the interface will be used. The feature list could also describe particular attributes of the proposed interface. For example, the feature list might specify that the interface supports automatic backups or provides "undo" mechanisms.

Sometimes the developer will define the need for the customer. For example, the developer may make a proposal for the features of a proposed project in order to convince the customer that they need to pay for the development effort.

### Feasibility

A *feasibility specification* might include:

- Costs and resources needed to build the user interface.
- Potential constraints and underlying assumptions for the proposed user interface. For example, you might specify the target platform as an assumption or constraint for this project.

Regardless of whether or not you conduct and document a formal needs analysis, an informal assessment of feasibility, a statement of context, or an overview of the project's expectations, it is critical to identify *a process* for context setting and to produce a context specification. In your programming classes, your teacher decides feasibility and features of your final product. The assumption with a class project is that it is feasible. This is a dangerous assumption on a real project!

## 5.3 Understanding Users' Problems by Understanding Their Tasks

Once the context for a user interface has been established and the project is known to be feasible, the usability engineer must develop a detailed understanding of the user's problem. What does it mean in the context of a user interface to "understand" the user's problem? For the most part it means developing a specification model or models of the tasks that the user plans to do with the interface. A number of strategies have been suggested to analyze the user's problem and to produce a description of the tasks that the user or customer will do with the interface. In the following subsections, we briefly describe three methods for analyzing and specifying user tasks, then we present our simplified and modified strategy of task analysis and specification. Please note that our specification strategy is intended to show some of the essential concepts of task modeling and, as such, takes elements from a number of industrial methods. It is our goal to teach you about the specification process by using a simplified approach rather than making you an expert in a particular specification methodology.

### 5.3.1 Strategy 1: Use Case Analysis

Within the Unified Software Development Process, one element of requirements specification involves the construction of *use case models*. *Use cases* describe the expected functionality of a target system. A use case model documents how the target system will interact with people and systems that are outside the target system.

A use case is a representation of how external actors, such as users, will use the system under development. The idea in use case analysis is that the software engineer understands the problem in terms of how the target system will interact with external systems. Then he or she documents the problem by building a visual model that shows the ways that external actors use the system, with an "actor" fulfilling an actual role that an external agent will play with the system. The use case model may then be decomposed for more detail using any of a number of other modeling techniques within the Unified Process. For example, a use case model may be expanded into a step-by-step description of how the task is to be done using *sequence diagrams*. The workflow necessary to accomplish the use case could be shown with an *activity diagram* (cf. Artim 2001; Jacobson et al. 1992; Jacobson, Booch, and Rumbaugh 1999; Constantine and Lockwood 2001; Kruchten, Ahlqvist, and Bylund 2001).

Use case analysis and modeling have some advantages as a task analysis and as a specification tool. For example, use case models and the models that follow emphasize sequencing and workflows, which force the software engineer to understand these issues. Use case models also facilitate a fairly seamless transition to an object-oriented design for the interface itself. Finally, a number of excellent commercial CASE (computer-aided software engineering) products exist to support use case modeling and the Unified Software Development process. However, use case analysis and modeling also have some disadvantages as a task analysis and specification tool. Since use cases are intended to show the functionality of a target system, rather than to describe the tasks that a user will perform with the system, a use case analysis can easily become system centered rather than user centered. For example, a use case model of an iron might focus on the iron's function (e.g., produce heat) rather than what a user would do with the iron (e.g., make a cheese sandwich). As we will see in some later examples, in our view, use case models alone do not seem to be sufficient for describing user tasks but appear to be useful in combination with other techniques.

### 5.3.2 Strategy 2: Analysis Using Scenarios

Rosson and Carroll (2002), Rosson, Carroll, and Rodi (2004), and Carroll (2000) describe the usability engineering methodology called *scenario-based development* (SBD). The emphasis of the SBD methodology is on the development and evolution of scenarios from problem description to eventual design. In the analysis phase of SBD, the usability engineer collects problem scenarios from the relevant stakeholders in the problem. Rather than translating these scenarios to another specification format, the scenarios themselves form the specification. The SBD methodology is highly iterative, and developers continue to refine and modify the problem scenarios at the same time as they are developing scenarios of the design. Developers also practice "claims analysis" as a way to identify emphasis points and resolve apparent differences among scenarios.

According to Rosson and Carroll (2002), SBD and the use of scenarios have a number of advantages. First, in SBD, scenarios are stories that are detailed and contain descriptions of the user's plans and goals, as well as descriptions of the tasks they will accomplish. Because they are story based, scenarios are flexible and can contain both concrete and abstract ideas and information. Second, scenarios can be collected and evolved through the perspective of multiple persons. Third, problem scenarios describe the behavior of users in the problem domain. As such, the scenarios may reveal characteristics of the work environment, user interactions, or the problem itself that will impact the eventual success or failure of the design.

### 5.3.3 Strategy 3: Hierarchical Task Analysis

Another way of describing a user's tasks is in terms of the hierarchical relationships among them. Some authors have called this activity *hierarchical task analysis* because the outcome is a hierarchical breakdown of tasks (cf. Dix, Finlay, Abowd, and Beale 1998). Mayhew (1999) calls her variation on this approach *contextual task analysis* because it evaluates the user's tasks in the setting in which the user performs the tasks. For our purposes, we call the understanding activity *task analysis* and the documentation the *task specification*.

The idea of task analysis is to understand the user's tasks by decomposing them into the detailed subtasks that define them. By developing a hierarchical breakdown, the usability engineer can understand the user's tasks in both an abstract and detailed way simultaneously. The usability engineer can also understand detailed and low-level tasks in context. The task analysis is done completely from the user's perspective and does not describe system sequencing or workflow. During and after the process of understanding the problem via task analysis, the usability engineer documents his or her findings in a *task specification*. The specification details the hierarchical task structure, as well as details of the tasks.

### 5.3.4 Which Approach to Use?

The three techniques that we have mentioned, use case analysis and modeling, scenario-based development, and task analysis and specification are not mutually exclusive. In fact, Rosson and Carroll show an example of a hierarchical task analysis and diagrams as support for their scenario-based design (2002, 59). Use cases may be derived from scenario descriptions, and step-by-step scenario descriptions may be used to expand use cases. Unified Software Development Process sequence diagrams may show a kind of task decomposition, similar to what might result from a hierarchical task analysis. For our purposes, we focus on a simple method for analyzing and specifying user tasks and use a combination of scenario descriptions and use cases for illustrating tasks at a high level. We then turn to a hierarchical task analysis and specification technique (derived from Hix and Hartson, 1993) to identify and specify details of the tasks. While our approach potentially limits the richness of user inputs and does not resolve conflicting points of view among users, we feel that it is a good way to get started. We hope that you agree!

Some authors (cf. Schmuller 2002) have explained that use cases are really a collection of scenarios of how the system will work. Specifically, in Schmuller's vision, these scenarios describe step-by-step sequences of events. Schmuller's description of scenarios is different from the Rosson and Carroll (2002) vision, in which the scenarios contain context information and may or may not contain step-by-step descriptions. In our technique, the use case models and scenarios that we discuss are high level and are insufficient unless a hierarchical task breakdown specifies requirements in a complete way.

In addition, while the methodology we use involves scenarios, we use them in a way that is different from SBD. Like SBD we use scenarios as a starting point for information about the problem. However unlike SBD, we do not evolve the scenarios as a dynamic repository or set of descriptors of the problem description or design. We use scenarios as one source of information about the problem, and we analyze scenarios, as well as other forms of information, into the hierarchical task format that we present.

This simplified task analysis and specification technique produces a detailed document that can then be used to drive a design. This document describes in detail how the users will use the system that the usability engineer is eventually going to build. The document does not specify how the designer will build the eventual system, it does not show the look and feel of the eventual system, and it does not describe the flow of system activities necessary to accomplish the tasks. The focus of this effort is on understanding and providing enough detail about only the user's problem (the tasks) that you as the designer can solve. The document that is produced should be so detailed and specific that it leads directly to a design. Don't forget that understanding the user's tasks may be the most critical stage in the eventual success or failure of a user interface development project! *Failure to spend enough time and resources on this activity will only cost you later.*

A CASE tool can help you develop use case models and the task specification. Alternatively, you can generate your specification with drawing and word processing tools.

### 5.3.5 Our Analysis and Specification Strategy: How to Do It

What kind of information do we need to understand a user's problem? It would be useful to know what tasks the user planned to accomplish with the proposed interface. In other words, we would like to know what roles the user will play with the interface. It would also be helpful if the user described the problem at different levels of detail. An abstract description would help us to understand "the big picture" of the problem. Detailed descriptions of the components of the problem would help us with a design that exactly satisfies the problem. In addition, it would be nice if we could get some ideas of the usability-related characteristics of the task as suggested by the Eason model, such as frequency and openness.

First we start with analysis. We need to understand what tasks the user wants to support in the user interface. We will start with some high-level scenarios that acquaint us with how the target user interface will be used. Based on these, we will identify the user roles and a number of use cases relative to the interface. We will keep track of what we have learned about the problem by using the notational techniques of UML and loosely following the methodological approach of the Unified Process. The use cases that we identify will help us to translate the scenarios, which describe specific situations, into more abstract descriptions of user tasks. Based on our use cases, we will work with the user to understand the hierarchical breakdown of the task, so that we can understand the task at both a conceptual and a detailed level. At the top level of the hierarchy we will have an abstract description of the big task. We will then decompose this task into subtasks, each with more detail than the top-level description.

Next we do the specification. What do we document? The short answer is *everything*. We will draw pictures of our use cases that we derive from our scenarios. We will draw hierarchical decomposition diagrams for each task and subtask. And, because we will learn much more about the task as we proceed, for each task and subtask we will generate a detailed, point-by-point specification of the task in narrative form.

Another specification issue is: When do we document? The short answer is *constantly*. We keep track of every part of our understanding of the problem as we go. We document everything that we learn as we go. So while we are doing the analysis activity mentally and in a group discussion form, we generate specification documents as we learn. We can always change or enhance the documentation we have, but if we have nothing written down, our best understanding of the problem may be lost.

Our goal from the analysis activity is to produce a document that we can use as the task specification. The document should reflect the user's understanding of the problem, but it should also be written in terms that a user interface designer can use. We will assume that this is a final version of the document although, as we see in Chapter 10, we probably will use a more iterative process. The document will contain the following:

- A title page and table of contents.
- A high-level narrative description of the user's tasks.
- A set of scenarios of specific examples of the user's tasks along with an informal use case model of each scenario. If the user has told us anything about relevant data or data structures, we document that as well.
- A high-level use case model created from a consolidation of the information from the scenarios, the informal use cases, and the high-level narrative description of the user tasks.
- A description of the primary entities and their attributes, based on the information in the use case diagrams, scenarios, and the high-level narrative description.
- A hierarchical description of the user's tasks in pictorial form. We will call this the *task analysis diagram* because it is an externalization of our understanding of the problem. At the top levels of the task analysis diagram, we should have clear correspondence between the diagram tasks and the use cases that we have identified. Each task and subtask will be specified by a name in a box. The picture will give us a clear idea of how the task has been decomposed. Since the structure is hierarchical, we can use structure or organization charts. For real problems, one or two levels of breakdown rarely provide enough detail to fully describe the problem and to drive design. Many drawing tools support this type of diagram. The tasks in the diagram should be numbered following a hierarchical numbering strategy. The hierarchy of tasks starts with general tasks and breaks them down into very specific tasks. Typically each "box" in the hierarchy corresponds to a task that the user will perform with the interface.

- A text description of each task in the diagram. We will likely learn many details from our user that we want to include in our specification. These details are difficult to include in a hierarchical diagram, so the text description will help us keep track of the details. We can use a word processing tool to develop this part of the task analysis.

In brief, our task analysis and specification process will proceed as follows:

**STEP 1.** We will start with a narrative description of the tasks that the user wishes to accomplish with the proposed user interface. This description will likely be incomplete.

**STEP 2.** Following the narrative description, we will look at a number of scenarios describing specific tasks that someone might do with our interface.

**STEP 3.** For each scenario, we will build an informal use case diagram.

**STEP 4.** From the collection of informal use case diagrams, we will extract what seem to be the "things" that our users are operating on. As much as possible, we will try to identify what the attributes of these "things" are. Stiller and LeBlanc (2002) call these "things" *primary classes.* We will call them *primary entities.*

**STEP 5.** With our informal use case diagrams and models of primary entities, we will consolidate to form a high-level use case diagram that shows what tasks a user might perform with the interface. We will use the primary entities to form the terminology of the use case diagram.

**STEP 6.** For each use case, we will perform hierarchical task decomposition (hierarchical task analysis).

**STEP 7.** For each task in each task decomposition, we will develop a multipoint descriptive narrative.

**STEP 8.** For each task, we will consider any other information that the user has shared, perhaps about the structure of data or any details of the functionality, and incorporate this information into the task decompositions and descriptive narratives.

### 5.3.6 Task Analysis and Specification Process Example

Our starting point in our analysis and specification process will be to build a very high-level description of how the user will use the proposed system. In other words, we want to show at a very high level the task or tasks that the user wishes to perform with the system. If the user can play multiple roles or if multiple outside influences affect our proposed system, we would like to show them as well. Our first three steps will be to identify the high-level tasks and who is doing them.

**STEP 1.** Develop a narrative description of the tasks that the user wishes to accomplish.
The task: A BGSU graduate student is going to bake a cake using kitchen supplies.

**STEP 2.** Collect specific scenarios of specific tasks that someone will do.
Here are several scenarios:
Scenario 1: Sepideh is going to bake a cake. To do this she starts by cleaning the kitchen and gathering ingredients. For example, she gathers flour, eggs, sugar, butter, baking powder, salt, and vanilla extract.

Scenario 2: Following the recipe, Daryl mixes the ingredients. He sifts the dry in-gredients and mixes up the wet ingredients and then combines the wet and dry mixtures.

Scenario 3: Brian pours the batter into a greased pan to cook the cake.

Before going to step 3, we need a little more information about use case diagrams. The goal of the use case diagram is to illustrate the relationship between *actors* outside of the system (in our case, the user interface) and the tasks or uses that they will make of the system. Each of the interactions be-tween actors or task that can be achieved by the system can be considered to be a use case. Actors are anything external to the system that interacts with the system. Each actor indicates a possible role in which someone or something could engage. For example, in user interfaces, the actors outside of system are the users of the interface. The icons for the use case diagram are simple: a stick person for an actor, a line for a relationship, and an oval for each of the use cases (see Table 5.1).

Table 5.1   Summary of Use Case Icons and Their Meanings

| Use Case Icon | Use Case Entity | Meaning |
|---|---|---|
| (stick figure) | Actor | A person or external entity involved in the task. For our example, a user would be an actor. |
| (line) | Relationship | An unnamed association between the use case and the actor. |
| (oval) | Use case | A task to be accomplished through use of the system. |

STEP 3. For each scenario, identify graphically what the task is and who is doing it using informal use case diagrams.

The use case diagrams can be seen in Figures 5.1, 5.2, and 5.3.

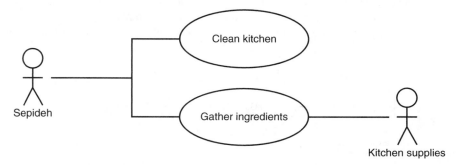

Figure 5.1   Use Case for Scenario 1 of "Bake a Cake" Example.

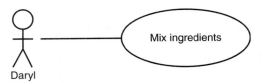

**Figure 5.2**    Use Case for Scenario 2 of "Bake a Cake" Example.

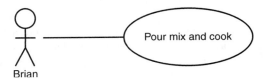

**Figure 5.3**    Use Case for Scenario 3 of "Bake a Cake" Example.

**STEP 4.** Identify the *primary entities* or "things" in the tasks.

First let's consider our actors: Sepideh, Daryl, and Brian. From the information that we have, we know that their structure is identical. Each actor has the following attribute of interest: *graduate student name.* However, except for different values for this attribute, the actors are identical. We reason that each of our actors are just instances of a class: *Graduate Student Cake Baker.* Based on the narrative and the scenarios, nothing distinguishes one graduate student from another except their names. None seem to have any unique characteristics. *Kitchen supplies* is a repository.

How about "things" that are acted upon? It seems at least two things are acted upon: *Kitchen* and *Ingredients. Kitchen* does not seem to have any particular attributes as there seems to be only one instance of this. *Ingredients,* on the other hand, has attributes of *Ingredient Kind* and *Wet or Dry.* We also seem to have a thing called *Pan,* which needs to be *Greased.* Finally we have the *Recipe.* Let us assume that *Recipe* follows a conventional format for which amounts of ingredients are listed followed by the instructions to assemble the cake. By looking at the "things" that we have and their attributes, we may be able to identify some potential user tasks.

**STEP 5.** Consolidate the information from the high-level narrative scenarios, informal use cases, and primary entities into a set of use case diagrams.

At the highest level, our use case diagram looks like the diagram in Figure 5.4.

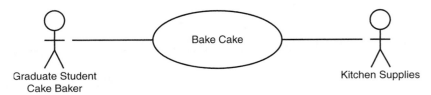

**Figure 5.4**    High-Level Use Case Diagram for "Bake a Cake" Example.

What information can we consolidate? The first use case shows two different functions, and they seem to us to be at a more detailed level than the use cases for the other scenarios. So we will combine and compress the informal use case diagrams into the diagram in Figure 5.5.

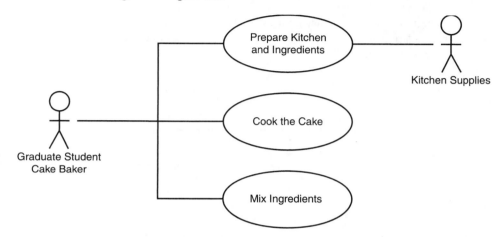

**Figure 5.5**   Consolidated Use Case Diagram for "Bake a Cake" Example.

The use case diagram is just one strategy that the Unified Process uses to capture and thoroughly specify system requirements. Even the simple diagrams that we showed in Figures 5.1 through 5.5 would have to be supplemented with textual descriptions for each of the use cases if they were serving as requirements specifications.

For our purposes, we will simply use the use case diagram as a link between our scenarios and the task analysis. In Chapter 13, we will use the use case diagram to link our task analyses to other UML-specified design documents.

**STEP 6.** Break down the tasks hierarchically (task analysis).

Now we are going to practice breaking a task down hierarchically. This is important because we need to understand the task at a detailed level so that we may be able to check our understanding against that of the user.

Our use case diagram had one high-level task with three subtasks. On that basis, we have the task breakdown in Figure 5.6 for the first two levels of the task analysis.

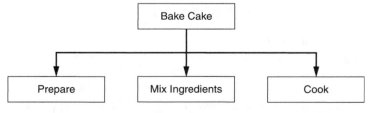

**Figure 5.6**   High-Level Task Analysis for "Bake a Cake" Example.

Now let's expand the task analysis to provide a little more detail. Assume that our details are either coming from the work that we have already done or from additional input from a user. We will get a diagram similar to the one in Figure 5.7.

As you look at the diagram in Figure 5.7, note how important it was for us to have thought about the primary entities. As we start the process of hierarchical task decomposition, having a good idea of the key objects of interest will help us understand the tasks at a detailed level.

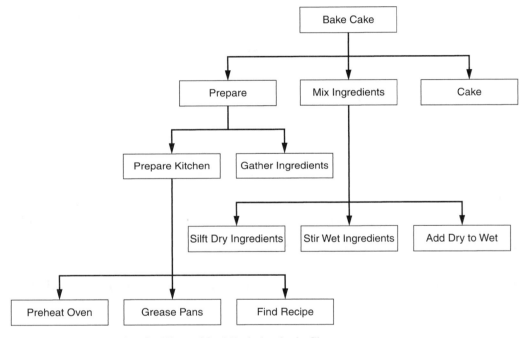

**Figure 5.7**   Example of a Hierarchical Task Analysis Chart.

### 5.3.7 Completing the Specification

Obviously this is only a partial solution. We did not include many details, but we should notice some things in Figure 5.7. Time order is not necessarily from left to right. Does it really matter if you grease the pans first or preheat the oven? Also, note that since subtasks shown are *activities,* most boxes begin with a *verb.* For the most part, the "things" in the tasks are the primary entities that we already have identified. In a larger problem, the user may also tell us about some of the key "things" to take into account.

Now let's take one of the subtasks in the diagram and provide some additional text information about the subtask. We pose this additional information as a series of questions followed by answers about the task. While the questions may seem as if they could be answered in a word or two, the more detail in the answer the better. In their work on user interface representations, Hartson, Siochi, and Hix (1990) and Hix and Hartson (1993) have indicated that we need at least the following information about each subtask, and we have elaborated on these concepts and developed the following set of questions in Leventhal, Barnes, and Chao (2004):

- What is the goal of this task?
- Is this task a subtask of a larger task?
- What subtasks define this task? Where is the task in the graph?
- What noninterface functions does this task require? This question refers to the software that runs behind the user interface. For example, will your subtask require a sorting algorithm or some database management activity? In general, high-level tasks will have no noninterface functions, but low-level functions that need to sort and access data will have a number of non-interface functions.
- What kinds of inputs or actions does this task require from the user?
- What kinds of outputs or results occur by virtue of performing this task?
- What automatic actions does this task expect from the system? An alarm might be an example of an automatic action. An automatic action is something that occurs without user input. Another example of an automatic action might be if the user interface updates a date and time display automatically.
- What special characteristics of this task should we record? The user might make some special requests.

As Hartson, Siochi, and Hix (1990) and Hix and Hartson (1993) note, tasks may have some required sequencing, so we add the following two questions about sequencing to the list:

- In this subtree, is there a task that must come before this one?
- In this subtree, is there a task for which this one is the immediate predecessor or is there a task that can co-occur?

We also add the following question about primary entities to the list:

- Which, if any, entities (or things) are involved in this subtask?

Because tasks are not always completed, we ask this question:

- How can this task fail (or end in noncompletion)? The answer may be that failure can occur due to outside (of the interface) conditions or it may be because another task or subtask was not included. Or it simply may fail due to user input error. At this point we probably should assume that any task could fail due to user input error, but it may be helpful to document the nature of the user error. We are trying to indicate other potential problems as well.

Finally, during analysis and specification, we try to get as much information as we can about the task and usability characteristics, as suggested by our model of usability:

- How frequently is this task performed?
- How rigid is this task, especially in terms of its sequence or input options?
- Are there unusual situational constraints to consider? Recall from Chapter 3 that these included constraints involving expectations for fun, collaboration, security, and unusual scheduling requirements.

- What, if any, are the specific usability expectations (e.g., ease of use, ease of learning, ease of relearning, task match, flexibility, and satisfaction) for this task, and how do we anticipate determining if we have satisfied the expectations?

Let's try to fill in the answers to these questions for the task *Grease Pans.*

- What is the goal of this task?

  The goal of *Grease Pans* is to put enough grease on the pans so that (1) the cakes do not stick to the pans while they are cooking and (2) we can easily remove the cakes from the pans once the cake is done.

- Is this task a subtask of a larger task?

  Yes. This task is part of *Prepare Kitchen.*

- What subtasks define this task?

  None. This task is at the bottom of the hierarchy.

- What nonuser interface functions does this task require?

  None. (*Note:* For the current system, this question may not seem to make sense because there is no software interface. With a software user interface, any actions outside of the user interface software that are involved in completing this task should be documented. For example, if the task required a binary search, that activity would be recorded here.)

- What kinds of inputs or actions does this task require from the user?

  The user must decide whether to use a solid or spray shortening to apply the grease to the pans. (*Note:* In a computer system, if a task required a value or input from the user, the answer to this question would be the kind of user input necessary to complete the task.)

- What kinds of outputs or results occur by virtue of performing this task?

  Here the result is that the pans are greased.

- What automatic actions does this task expect from the system?

  Suppose that an alarm went off when the user had applied too much grease to the pan. That would be an example of an automatic system action. In our original use case diagram, we indicated that the kitchen supplies are external actors to the task of baking a cake. Here you might note that the kitchen supply "grease" is used.

- What special characteristics of this task should we record?

  Suppose that the person who will eat your cake is allergic to dairy products. For the task *Gather Ingredients,* you may note to use olive oil instead of butter. Nonstick pans or the use of cupcake liners do not require this task to be completed.

- Is there a subtask that must come immediately before?

  The task *Find Recipe* should occur before the tasks *Preheat Oven* and *Grease Pans.* The recipe will contain information on the required temperature for the oven and the type of pan appropriate for the cake.

- In this subtree, is there a task for which *Grease Pans* is the immediate predecessor or a task that can co-occur?

  No, although technically you can grease the pans while the oven is heating to the required temperature.

- Which, if any, primary entities (things) are involved in this subtask?

  The primary entities are Pan and Grease. (Note: Are these listed as primary entities from the use case analysis?)

- How can this task fail?

  If I cannot find a pan or grease, then the task cannot be completed. In other words, this task can fail only if I fail to collect these objects. (*Note:* By thinking about how the task can fail, I may discover that I have not included other user tasks. For example, here I would go back to the user and ask if he or she had a task for collecting missing baking objects?)

- How frequently is this task performed?

  In the context of baking one cake, the task is performed once per pan.

- How rigid is this task?

  The task of greasing pans is relatively constrained in the sense that grease must go into the space of the pan and nowhere else. On the other hand, the choice of type of grease and how it is applied might have a number of alternatives, including shortening applied with a paper towel, olive oil applied with a pastry brush, and so on.

- Are there any situational constraints?

  None.

- What, if any, are the specific usability expectations (e.g., ease of use, ease of learning, ease of relearning, task match, flexibility, and satisfaction) for this task, and how do we anticipate determining if we have satisfied the expectations?

  We might reasonably expect ease of use to be measured as the time to complete the task *Grease Pans* being less than 10 percent of the total time to complete the entire cake construction task.

In addition to these points, you may wish to include the following information in your narrative description of the task:

- Other error handling concerns.
- Additional assumptions about context, user skills, and so on.

We were able to develop this hierarchical task analysis and specification ourselves because most of us are familiar with the process of baking a cake. If you did not know anything about the domain of baking, you might have interviewed a number of student bakers, particularly if you were unsure of the meanings of terms or sequencing constraints. Perhaps they would describe scenarios for baking a chocolate cake, cupcakes, or a birthday cake.

### 5.3.8 Task Analysis "Do's and Don'ts"

Here are some hints that will help you to analyze tasks and document your analysis.

**Do:**

- Use verbs to describe user actions. Use of verbs in the names of your tasks and subtasks will help to convey the idea of actions.
- Give *details, details, details.* The more details you can include in your task analysis, the more completely you will have specified your problem. The more complete your specification, the more likely it is that you will design and implement a solution for the problem that the user had in mind.
- Keep your hierarchical diagram neat and organized. We encourage our students to assign hierarchical identifiers to each task and to show the identifiers on all diagrams and narrative descriptions. In the "Bake a Cake" example, the task *Prepare* could have been numbered 1. The tasks below could have been numbered 1.1 *(Prepare Kitchen)* and 1.2 *(Gather Ingredients).*

The tasks below *Prepare Kitchen* could have been numbered 1.1.1 *(Preheat Oven)*, 1.1.2 *(Grease Pans)*, and 1.1.3 *(Find Recipe)*. Having these numbers will help you to verify that your diagrams and narrative descriptions are internally consistent. In addition, you can carry your numbering forward into your design to ensure that your design supports the tasks from your specification. In the larger example in Chapter 6, we will use hierarchical numbering.

**Don't:**

• Impose your own task understanding onto the user. Do not assume that your understanding of the situation before analysis is the same as the user's understanding. Remember that the purpose of the task analysis activity is to gain an understanding of the task from the user's perspective. Some software engineering methodologies (e.g., Unified Process, cf. Quatrani 2000) assume that the final interface will be *windows based* and have a graphical user interface (GUI). We feel that even this assumption is a mistake, unless it is imposed by the user. As we will see in Chapters 7 and 8, there are many choices for interaction styles, and a GUI may not always be your best choice.

• Impose artificial sequencing on the user. Do record essential sequencing information, but do not impose a sequence of tasks on your user. Imposing artificial sequencing is especially easy if you already have an interface design in your head.

• Reproduce a hierarchical menu design. Suppose that you are specifying some file management tasks for a user. You might come up with an analysis similar to Figure 5.8:

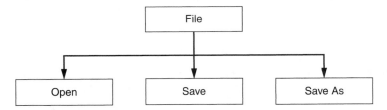

**Figure 5.8**   Draft File Management Task Analysis.

These are typical options in a standard file menu in many applications. However the terminology is very system oriented, and in this context the term *File* is a noun and not a verb. A better hierarchical breakdown, from the user's perspective, might be the one in Figure 5.9:

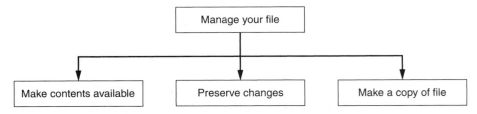

**Figure 5.9**   A Better File Management Task Analysis.

### 5.3.9 Task Analysis Challenges

Task analysis is hard, even for a task as relatively simple as baking a cake. The following are some challenges you are likely to face:

- You might like to know if your analysis is complete and correct. While some techniques for formal proofs of correctness exist, especially for software requirements, these proofs are often difficult to perform.
- It is sometimes tough to know how simple is simple enough for the subtasks at the bottom of your chart. For example, in the case of baking a cake, should you have a different task for sifting salt into the flour than sifting baking powder into the flour? The answer can depend on how similar the tasks are and whether you can document the variations in the narrative.
- Many task analysis methods assume that the user will not make errors. Under this strategy your specification may not deal with errors, but experience suggests that error handling constitutes a large part of the activity in many user interfaces. If error processing involves user actions or feedback, that should be noted in the analysis. In the cake example, we have not shown what the user will do if the recipe cannot be found or if the oven catches on fire, yet we know from our own experiences that these problems could arise.

### 5.3.10 Task Analysis and Specification Errors

The following are some typical errors to avoid as you conduct your task analysis and prepare your specification:

- Avoid inconsistencies between the items in the chart and your written descriptions. In particular, be careful to use the same spelling conventions for the names of your subtasks in both your chart and text description and make sure your task numbers in the chart and narratives match.
- Avoid tasks that appear only in the chart or only in the written description.
- Avoid spelling and grammar errors. Such errors make your work appear unprofessional at best and may be misleading at worst.
- Avoid describing the task as if you were doing it. Your description of the task should be from the perspective of the user, not yourself. When in doubt, ask the user how to describe the task, rather than guessing about it.
- Avoid analyses with insufficient detail. When in doubt provide more detail, not less. If some of the information is redundant or not necessary, it will disappear in the design phase.

### 5.3.11 Tasks Versus Implementation

As we have already said, task analysis is not implementation. Unfortunately, it is really tempting to jump into implementation, even unwittingly. An example of confusing implementation with task analysis can be found in the trap of *multiple inheritance.*

### The Trap of Multiple Inheritance

Suppose you are specifying an interface. The user wants to be able to *cut* and *paste* information from two different data entities (say, text and a graphic). The user may even use the terms *cut text, cut graphic, paste text,* and *paste graphic* while describing these tasks to you. The trap of multiple inheritance would be to describe the tasks as shown in Figure 5.10.

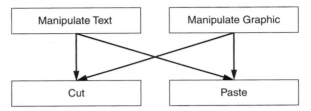

**Figure 5.10**   The Trap of Multiple Inheritance.

While both of the tasks are "cut" and "paste" tasks, they are potentially different tasks because the context is different and may mean radically different things to the user. It is imperative to show that these two types of cut and paste are different and thus preserve the contextual information that your user provided. Avoiding multiple inheritance in the task analysis does not necessarily mean that you will have different screens for the operation in your eventual implementation. It simply means that you have preserved contextual information received from the user.

Make no assumptions at this stage about the eventual interface. It is probably a mistake to conduct your task analysis with the mind-set that users will be using a particular interface to accomplish their tasks unless your user has already selected an interaction style and specified it in the context-setting documentation. As you have seen in most office productivity software, the interface often has only one set of cut and paste commands. This is an implementation decision. Do not assume that you can merge the different cut and paste tasks during the task analysis. It is important to maintain the context information at this point in case the tasks cannot be merged in the implementation stage.

### 5.3.12 Task Analysis and Specification Summary
For many of you, the task analysis activity may be the most conceptually difficult activity that you do as a computer scientist. Give yourself lots of time to complete the analysis and specification. In our experience, students generally underestimate the amount of work they will do during this process. Remember to do the following:

- Start with a narrative description of the problem.
- Review usage scenarios and derive from them informal use case diagrams.
- Generate a use case diagram that shows the interactions among the external actors and the interface at a very high level and in terms of the tasks that the actors will perform with the system.
- Generate a list of primary entities. To the best of your ability, identify attributes of those entities.
- Generate a hierarchical task analysis diagram. The purpose of this diagram is to force you and the user to develop a detailed description of tasks by describing them both abstractly and in a detailed way.
- For each task in the task hierarchy, generate a written description of the task. The written description includes a statement of where the task falls in the task breakdown, connections to noninterface and automatic services, a description of sequencing concerns, information about relevant primary entities, information about how the task can fail, task characteristic information (frequency, openness), and expectations for usability.

• For each task, consider any other information that you have from the user (the structure of data or details of functionality) and incorporate this information into your task decompositions and descriptive narratives.

### 5.3.13 Additional or Missing Information Relevant to the Specification

Information may be presented in other forms outside of scenarios. For example, users may give a list of functionality that is to be included in a task. In addition, your users may be able to tell you about some of the entities and their attributes that come into play related to their tasks. Another helpful source of information may be a database if your interface has to interact with one. In the use case diagram that we showed in our "Bake a Cake" example, we imply a database of kitchen supplies. In a real database, we would include not only the database entities but also their relationships.

It may have occurred to you that our analysis technique may be missing some information in our effort to show you a simple analysis technique. For example, we have not focused on understanding and documenting trade-offs. Other techniques, such as scenario-based development, do include this kind of information.

### 5.3.14 Eliciting Task Information from Users

Where and how do you get the necessary information from users? A number of techniques can be used to get information about tasks, including user interviews, user surveys, direct observation, and ethnographic techniques. We discuss these strategies in more detail in Chapter 11 in the context of assessment. Users may describe typical scenarios of use, expected functionality, or expected data entities and their attributes. You may have existing software available as a guide, or you may be able to observe users in naturalistic settings.

In the example presented previously, we used scenarios to provide detailed and contextual information. The following are a few suggestions as to how to get useful scenarios from users. When users describe scenarios, be sure to get as much detailed information from them as possible. The scenarios should be concrete and describe things with real values rather than abstractions. In this way, the scenario may reveal hidden relationships and restrictions. The scenario may contain significant task decomposition and sequencing information. Recall that several users may describe the same scenario from a different perspective, weighing different aspects of the scenario differently. When you can, ask users to describe their scenarios in terms of step-by-step actions. Whatever the sources of information, your job as the usability engineer is to analyze and distill the information into a coherent specification.

One advantage of scenarios is that the tasks initially can be described informally and with minimal detail. Later they can be expanded to any level of detail to build your specification or to resolve apparent inconsistencies among user viewpoints. If you are basing your specification on scenarios, it is usually a good idea to get a variety of descriptions that vary in detail and perspective.

The scenario descriptions that you collect can then serve as the basis for standard tests of functionality for your design. Many potential angles of a problem are only clear when users describe not only the systems that they want but also how they will use them.

In summary, you can solicit a variety of different types of information from the user, and you can present it in a range of ways. If you focus on the listing of tasks in the hierarchical task analysis style, then your product is going to be somewhat abstract but also very complete. If you use a collection of representative task scenarios as the basis of your design, your task analysis will be very specific. In practice, you probably want to capture both types of information in your specification.

Finally, your task specification, is not right until your user agrees that it is. During the process of task specification, and certainly at the end, you should plan to have a checkoff session with your user. By presenting your specification both graphically and in narrative form, you hope to have enough detail that your user can adequately evaluate whether or not you have captured a description of his or her task.

## 5.4 Developing User Profiles

We have spent a lot of time describing how to identify the task characteristics for our system. We also must identify user characteristics, particularly those that potentially will impact the usability of our user interface. To get a good interface, you have to figure out who is going to use it and what they are going to do with it. Our usability model suggests that user expertise and motivation impact the usability of a user interface. A more extensive list of issues to explore includes (1) background issues about users, (2) user feedback about job functions, (3) how this interface would impact a user's job, and (4) organizational and workflow considerations. This information is not abstract; the answers to questions about these issues should reflect the variables and goals that are relevant to the current task and situation. We would like to have detailed understanding of potential users, recognizing that our users may be from different groups with different needs. Certain groups of users—for example, children—may have different needs and requirements. It also may be useful to know if your system has a social impact: Does your system displace workers? How does this influence the attitude of future users of your system? Will your system have regular users and/or incidental users? Many authors have called the document that results from this process a *user profile document* (see Mayhew 1999).

### 5.4.1 How User Characteristics May Impact Your Final System

Is it really that important in the problem definition stage to identify characteristics of your users? You bet it is. Mynatt (1990) discusses how knowing one user characteristic—computer system knowledge—can help developers design and build interfaces that are appropriate and usable. She identifies three categories of users, based on their computer knowledge: novice user, knowledgeable intermittent user, and frequent user. *Novice users* have little or no knowledge of using computer systems. Intermittent users have used a number of different systems but on a sporadic basis. *Frequent users* can be considered to be experts or "power" users, are completely familiar with a given system or systems, and use them on an ongoing and regular basis. These categories are based on an earlier classification from Shneiderman (1992).

Mynatt (1990) describes interface characteristics for each of these user groups. For novice users, she suggests interfaces with a small number of commands or actions and reducing of error as much as possible, even if it means limiting some advanced capabilities. Intermittent users can handle many more commands or actions, but consistency and simplicity of commands are still critical for this group. Intermittent users should be offered the opportunity for safe but educational exploration. Experts want fast response and shortcuts, and they may consider all but the most minimal feedback to be cumbersome.

What should you do if your user profiles indicate combinations of user types? Mynatt (1990) suggests that you may want to provide a layered interface, in which each group can "find" its layer.

### 5.4.2 Where to Start Building User Profiles

As with task analysis, a number of techniques can be used to get information about future users, including interviews, surveys, direct observation, and ethnographic techniques. In your data gathering, you will likely be trying to collect information about the usability model variables (described in Chapter 3) of user expertise (including language, skills, and background) and user motivation. You may wish to identify the users' level of computer knowledge as suggested by Mynatt (1990). You might also want to learn about the users' ages and cultures. A large number of today's interfaces are developed for people who are twenty to forty years old. People outside of this group may have different needs than those in it. You might want to learn about your users' reactions to similar interfaces or to your set of features. In your data gathering, be sure to document who provided information, how these people were chosen, how you collected the data, and how you obtained permission from the users to collect information about them.

It is important to remember this: The individuals and groups that provide data know more about what they want than you do. They or their bosses are paying you to do work for them. It is risky to assume that you know what your users want. In addition, it is important to inform your users of your goals when you collect data. It is unimaginable, and nearly always unethical, to collect information from users without their knowledge. Users should be informed of the purpose of your data gathering and should give their explicit consent to the process. We will discuss this issue more in later chapters.

### 5.4.3 Structure of a User Profile Document

Hix and Hartson (1993) have suggested that at least three types of information are important to put into the user profile document. These types of information include user characteristics (such as age), user skills, and a description of how users will use this interface. Mayhew (1999) expands the list to include psychological characteristics (such as motivation, knowledge, and experience), job and task characteristics (such as frequency of use), and the users' physical characteristics, including physical handicaps. Mayhew further emphasizes the need for user profiles for each category of user. Eason and our usability models suggest including information about user expertise and motivation.

## 5.5 Other Specification Documents and Information

Your user may require some additional specification documents. You may wish to include a number of other types of information in your specification because they will ultimately help you better understand the problem. For example, in our simplified task analysis strategy, we have assigned equal importance to all the tasks shown and have assumed that all subtasks will take place each time the whole task is performed. Clearly this assumption does not always hold true. Dix, Finlay, Abowd, and Beale (1998) suggest an extension to the type of task analysis that we have shown in which the task analysis is documented with "plans" that illustrate different combinations of subtasks. These plans can also be weighted with the more popular combinations receiving higher weightings.

Other methodologies may include other specification documents. For example, a task model developed under the Unified Process may include state diagrams or sequence models to define the specific objects and timing of events in the user tasks (cf. Schmuller 2002).

## Conclusions

At this point, we have described two documents to help you specify the problem that you will eventually be solving with your interface: task specification and user profiles. You may also generate documentation about the context and feasibility of your project. These documents justify the need for your project, describe the tasks that will be done with the interface, and describe the users.

In Chapter 6, we present a large-scale project that includes a task analysis document. Your instructor may wish to introduce other specification techniques at this point or move on to design. If you are doing a class project with a task analysis, we suggest that you read through this example.

Our presentation of task specification has assumed that you are building an interface for a new project, rather than developing a replacement. Should you be developing a replacement interface, you would still create the documents that we have described. However, in addition to user inputs, you also would have the legacy system as a source of task information.

### Exercises

1. Define the following terms: *analysis, specification, context setting, context specification, usability expectation specification, needs specification, feasibility specification, task analysis, task specification, use case, hierarchical task analysis, primary entities, multiple inheritance,* and *user profile.*

2. Imagine that you are throwing a pizza/(insert name of your favorite television show) party. Develop a task analysis for the subtasks that would be involved in preparing for the party. (We suggest that you work on this problem in a group so that you will have multiple perspectives of the task.)

3. Consider the following scenario: As part of its services, the Match Maker Dating Service would like to help its clients to create the perfect dating experience. So far, the service has decided to include the following activities as part of this online service:
   - Selecting a restaurant for dinner with price options of expensive, moderate, and cheap.
   - Selecting an activity with options of movie, ballgame, or athletic activity, such as hiking, tennis, or ice-skating.
   - Selecting a day of the week and the choice of afternoon or evening.

   Generate a hierarchical task analysis chart for the tasks in "Create a Perfect Date." Your chart should have at least three levels of decomposition for some tasks. It is not necessary to write text descriptions for the tasks.

4. Here is another problem you can work on in a group. Suppose you have been asked to design a game for children ages three to five. These are some of the possible titles for your game:
   Land of the Lilies
   Stuffville
   Sharpen Your Shovels
   The Forest

   It is up to you to pick a title and perform and build a task analysis and specification for your game. Remember that parents of three- to five-year-olds are the people who buy games for this audience and will not buy anything that is violent or in any other way inappropriate. Be creative as to the tasks involved in the game!

5. Consider a remote control device for your automatic washing machine. Generate a user profile for this device. Include at least three categories of user characteristics.

# 6

# Large-Scale Example of Analysis and Specification of User Context, Tasks, and Characteristics

## Motivation

In Chapter 5 we described how to analyze the context setting, tasks, and user profiles and how to document each of these. This chapter illustrates a large-scale project similar to one that you might do as a class project. We include excerpts of specification documents for context setting, task analysis, and user profiles. By the end of this chapter you should be able to:

- Perform a task analysis for a user interface project and create a task specification document.
- Perform a context-setting analysis and create a context specification document.
- Perform a user profile analysis and create a user profile document.

## 6.1 Introduction

We are now going to analyze and derive a specification for a project that is similar in complexity to a class project. The sample project is to specify and build a user interface for an audio catalog system. Because we are describing this project, there are no users to interview or observe. All information about the project is contained within the description.

How might users describe the interface that they would like you to build? They may give you (1) a set of specific scenarios to illustrate how the interface might be used, (2) a list of tasks and their expected functionality, or (3) some description of the data entities that are involved. Our sample project includes all three types of information. In real life, you might observe your potential users, survey their user characteristics, analyze an existing user interface, or study the users' work environment to help you build documentation of the context, tasks, and user profiles. Usually, no single presentation of information provides enough data to develop a full specification.

To help you get started on the sample project, we have made some simplifications. We describe a piece of software that we would like to have. We present the information in three forms, but we have separated these to some extent. In real life, the information might be more jumbled together. On a real project, your job would be to analyze this information and to produce your specification documentation. For this example, the information contained herein will serve as the customer's request for software. The needs of the user are described in this chapter.

Please note that we have specifically given you only one perspective of the desired functionality. In a real setting, you would likely have a number of users, all with their individual priorities and conflicting story lines.

Let's review the steps in our specification process. First, we are given the narrative description of the tasks that users wish to accomplish with this interface. From this we move on to the hierarchical task analysis. We describe eight usage scenarios along with the informal use case diagram equivalents. Next, we abstract the use case diagrams and refine them to lead us to a high-level breakdown of tasks. From the high-level task breakdown, we build a document showing a detailed task breakdown, along with detailed, written descriptions of the tasks that the user interface must support. As we are building our hierarchical task specification, we will incorporate the task functionality and entity descriptions that were provided. With that information, we develop a minimal context-setting analysis and a user profile description.

### 6.1.1 Steps for Our Analysis and Specification

In our example, we start with the task analysis and specification. For this example, the steps in our analysis of the tasks follow the steps from Chapter 5.

**STEP 1.** We will start with a narrative description of the tasks that the user wishes to accomplish with the proposed user interface. This description will likely be incomplete.

**STEP 2.** Following the narrative description, we will look at a number of scenarios describing specific tasks that someone might do with the interface.

**STEP 3.** For each scenario, we will build an informal use case diagram. Ultimately these informal use case diagrams will help us to understand the user's tasks and assist us in forming our analysis.

**STEP 4.** From the collection of informal use case diagrams, we will extract what seem to be the primary entities upon which our users are operating. As much as possible, we will try to identify what the attributes of the primary entities are.

**STEP 5.** With our informal use case diagrams and models of primary entities, we will consolidate to form a high-level use case diagram that shows what tasks a user might perform with the interface. We will use the primary entities to form the terminology of the use case diagram.

**STEP 6.** For each use case, we will perform hierarchical task decomposition and analysis. We will document the task structure visually.

**STEP 7.** For each task in the task decomposition, we will develop a multipoint descriptive narrative.

**STEP 8.** For each task, we will consider any other information that the user has shared with us and incorporate this information into your task decompositions and descriptive narratives.

Once we have completed the example task analysis and specification, we will show examples of a user profile and a context-setting analysis.

## 6.2 Task Analysis and Specification for the Audio Catalog

### 6.2.1 Task Narrative Description for the Audio Catalog

We are going to design a user interface for a catalog system to manage an audio library that we will call an *audio catalog.* On my hard drive, I have a large number of songs digitized. In some cases, I have whole CDs digitized. In other cases, I only have single songs. I currently have a paper catalog of my collection that contains entries for songs and CDs. I would like to have a computerized catalog. Your job is to build the interface for this new computerized catalog.

### 6.2.2 Typical Scenarios for the Audio Catalog

The following scenarios describe how I use the paper catalog and how I would like to use the computerized catalog.

### Scenario 1

It's time for a party, and I want to find some great songs from my collection to make a CD. I get my catalog of favorite songs and open it. I look through the table of contents and look for the song, "Highland Howliday." I am hoping to find out what the name of the original album was and when it was first released. I also would like to see what the original album cover looked like. However, I have difficulty finding it because the table of contents is organized by categories of songs (reggae, heavy metal, classical, and so forth). So I start to page through my catalog, but I cannot find the song. So I go to the alphabetical index for my catalog and notice some of the pages are dog-eared and some pages have information about extra songs clipped to them. That reminds me that I put a sticky note on the description of "Highland Howliday." I open the catalog to the sticky note and find the entry for the song. (*Hint:* At least four search strategies that you should include in your task analysis are implied here.)

The following was attached to the entry in Figure 6.1:

Review from http://www.animal_arts.com

*Highland Howliday* is the best representation of Maggie D's artistic talents yet. The lilting melody of the title track, "Highland Howliday," is a counterpoint to the haunting tone poem "Heaven Is a Grassy Meadow."

Song: Highland Howliday
Album: Highland Howliday
Artist: Maggie and the Shelties
Original Release Date: 2001
1. He Ain't Nothin' but a Sheepdog
2. Fetcher in the Rye
3. My Puppy Love
4. Dog House Rock
5. Highland Howliday
6. Little Lamb of Mine
7. Heaven Is a Grassy Meadow
8. Shetland Island Getaway

**Figure 6.1**    Sample Entry in My Audio Catalog.
(Photo by L. Leventhal)

### Informal Use Case 1

Scenario 1 has two outside actors or roles, relative to the audio catalog. Scenario 1 refers to (1) the CD maker and (2) the audio collection (see Figure 6.2). The interactions with the system involve searching for songs and for CDs.

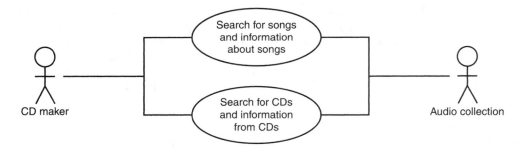

**Figure 6.2**    Use Case for Scenario 1.

### Scenario 2

I am still working on the CD for my party. I want to include the BCT (Barnes Cat Trio) song "Black Cat Blues." I look through my catalog and notice that I had annotated the entry for this song to say that I had downloaded it from http://www.fauna_musica.com. Seeing this title made me remember that I wanted to buy a BCT and some other CDs. I start a shopping list: BG Music and Video, which I call BGMV. Unfortunately, I only wrote down "BCT" before I was distracted by a phone call. When I return, I can't find the shopping list immediately, but eventually I retrieve it from the other papers on the kitchen table. (*Hints:* What does this scenario tell you about the attributes and the entities in the catalog? What did you learn about the entity shopping list? Can there be more than one shopping list?)

### Informal Use Case 2

In this scenario, three actor roles are mentioned: (1) the CD maker, (2) the shopper, and (3) the audio collection. Each of these roles interacts with the audio catalog in some way (see Figure 6.3).

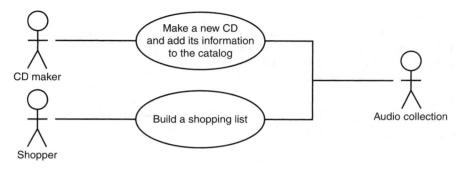

**Figure 6.3**   Use Case for Scenario 2.

### Scenario 3

I go shopping and buy some CDs including *Simon Carlson: Greatest Hits.* I add the songs and the CD to my catalog. I make a note in the catalog entry for this CD that I want to skip "Your UI Is So Plain" when I listen. (*Hint:* What does the scenario tell you about modifying entities in the catalog?) I notice that the song "Ten O'Clock Jump" is listed as "Tin O'Clock Jump" in my paper catalog. I correct the spelling of the title. (*Hint:* What does the scenario tell you about modifying attributes in the catalog?)

In my collection on another CD, I also notice that the song "Stars and Stripes" is in the category "Rock." I decide that I would like it to be in the "Patriotic" category, so I write down "Patriotic" next to the song. This is the first instance of a song in the "Patriotic" category. (*Hint:* What does the scenario tell you about adding categories?)

### Informal Use Case 3

In this scenario, two actor roles are mentioned: (1) the audio catalog user and (2) the audio collection (see Figure 6.4).

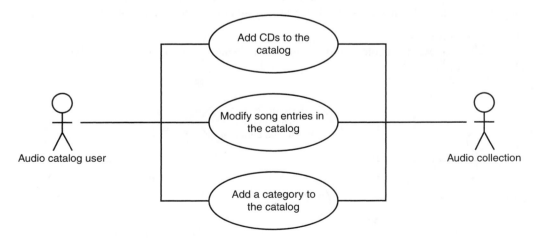

**Figure 6.4**   Use Case for Scenario 3.

### Scenario 4

I finish my CD for the party and call it *Super Party Hits.* As I skim through my paper catalog to find a place to put the new CD entry, I notice an entry for the album *A. Hogg: The Sty's the Limit.* I take a pen and mark a large X through the entry. (*Hint:* What does this scenario tell you about what you can do with catalog entries?)

### Informal Use Case 4

In this scenario, three actor roles are mentioned: (1) the CD maker, (2) the audio catalog user, and (3) the audio collection (see Figure 6.5).

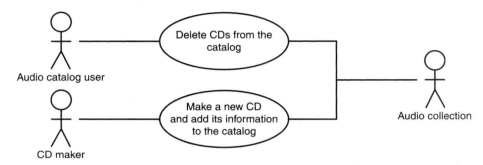

**Figure 6.5**    Use Case for Scenario 4.

### Scenario 5

Next week, we are having a euchre party. We plan to make a CD of show music for the party. One of our guests cannot stand any songs by Esther Mermaid. With a paper catalog, I can physically browse through my collection to see if I have any CDs by Esther Mermaid; sometimes I keep the collection in order by CD or song. If I had a computerized catalog, I would be able to generate a list (REPORT) of all the songs in my collection that were show music and not by Esther Mermaid. (*Hints:* How might I find the information and generate a report? How about browsing through my catalog? What are some different ways that I might navigate through the catalog?)

### Informal Use Case 5

In this scenario, two actor roles are mentioned: (1) the audio catalog user and (2) the audio collection (see Figure 6.6).

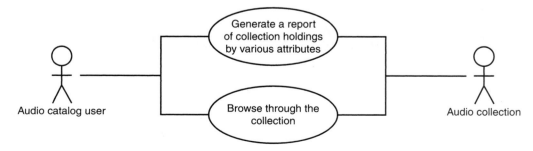

**Figure 6.6**    Use Case for Scenario 5.

## Scenario 6

I want to listen to some elevator music made before 1965. I wish I could ask (QUERY) my catalog to list all songs whose category is "Elevator" and that were made before 1965. In "computerese," the query might look like:

Give all songs where category == elevator AND date < 1965

I want to save the question as "Craving Elevator" so that I can use it later. If I had a computerized CD catalog, I could ask my question, and the catalog might respond with a list of ten songs. I could save the response in a list (REPORT) that I could call "Craving Elevator Report" with the title *Elevator* on top of the report. The name of the report is how I will refer to the report in my CD catalog, and the title is an internal feature of the report itself.

I notice that one of the songs in the report is a tango. I edit the report to delete the tango. I save the revised report. I print the report today and will reprint it every time that I crave elevator music.

## Informal Use Case 6

In this scenario, two actor roles are mentioned: (1) the audio catalog user and (2) the audio collection (see Figure 6.7).

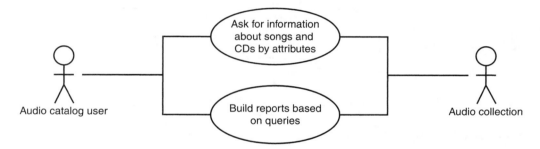

**Figure 6.7**   Use Case for Scenario 6.

## Scenario 7

I am donating a CD to the Humane Society. I want to put a sticky label with the songs on the label. I sure wish I could get my computerized catalog to help me do this.

## Informal Use Case 7

In this scenario, two actor roles are mentioned: (1) the audio catalog user and (2) the audio collection (see Figure 6.8).

**Figure 6.8**   Use Case for Scenario 7.

*Scenario 8*
I want to make a CD called *Cat House Blues* in honor of Fat Cat Felinoux. My CD would contain different recordings of the song "Bayou Fishing for You." Numerous artists have recorded this song. I search my collection of CDs for all instances of it. I build a new CD that contains this song in all its variations. Later I decide that the title I chose is too obscure, so I change the title to *Bayou Fishing for You.*

*Informal Use Case 8*
In this scenario, three actor roles are mentioned: (1) the CD maker, (2) the audio catalog user, and (3) the audio collection (see Figure 6.9).

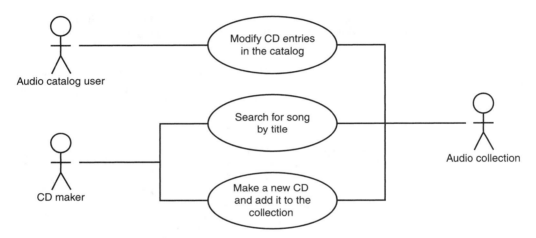

**Figure 6.9**   Use Case for Scenario 8.

### 6.2.3 Identifying Primary Entities: Who and What Are the Important Players and "Things"?

So far we have read eight scenarios describing various ways that our audio catalog could be used. The descriptions were fairly informal and usually were in terms of specific examples. For each scenario, we abstracted the described function into the use case diagram. Now we would like to identify the primary entities that seem to be involved in the scenarios.

First, who are the actors or the roles that occur outside of the interface? Looking at the use case diagrams so far, several roles outside of the interface have emerged, including (1) an actor representing the collection itself, (2) an actor who constructs new CDs, (3) an actor who modifies the contents of the catalog, and (4) an actor who wants to create a shopping list using the information in the collection. The last actor uses the information in the collection to search, browse, generate reports, query, add, modify, or delete either attributes or whole entities in the collection. However, all these actors are in fact users of the audio catalog with little to distinguish them beyond the specific scenario in which they appear. We will combine them into a single external entity called *audio catalog user.* We also have an external entity, *audio collection,* that is involved in each informal use case.

Next we want to identify the key *things* or *primary entities* that are being operated on, as indicated by the narrative description and by the scenarios and our informal use case diagrams. The primary entities that keep appearing seem to be (1) CDs, (2) songs, (3) shopping lists, (4) reports, (5) queries, (6) labels, (7) categories, and (8) the catalog itself.

We will assume that this constitutes the data that we want to keep in the catalog. We know that some of the entities will have *many-to-many* relationships based on the scenarios. For example, in Scenario 8, we know that there is a many-to-many relationship between CDs and songs. One CD contains many songs, and a song may appear on several different CDs.

To be able to search for entities in the catalog, each entity will have to have an identifier. In Table 6.1, we have marked some attributes with (\*\*) because they are the primary identifying information (i.e., primary keys) for that particular entity. The primary key information is required for each entity. Many of the attributes listed in the table are discussed in the scenarios that have been presented.

Why bother with this information now? The structure of the data accessible by the audio catalog is important to the problem. As we can see from the use case diagram, we will be entering

**Table 6.1**   Entities and Their Attributes for the Audio Catalog.

| Entities | Attributes | |
| --- | --- | --- |
| **Songs** | song title\*\* | digital format on my hard drive |
| | CD titles (up to 10) | date of song |
| | artists names (up to 10) | notes |
| | musical categories (up to 5) | other related songs |
| **CDs** | CD title\*\* | digital format on my hard drive |
| | song titles (up to 20) | date CD made or published |
| | artists names (up to 10) | notes |
| | musical categories (up to 5) | |
| **Shopping lists** | shopping list name\*\* | artists names (up to 10) |
| | CD titles | musical categories (up to 5) |
| | song titles | notes |
| **Reports** | report name\*\* | musical categories (up to 5) |
| | report title | digital format on my hard drive |
| | song title | notes |
| | CD album titles (up to 10) | other related songs |
| | artists (up to 10) | associated query names |
| **Queries** | query name\*\* | query content (fields, values, |
| | query results | operators) |
| **Labels** | label name\*\* | label notes |
| **Categories** | category name\*\* | category notes |
| **Catalog** | songs | queries |
| | CDs | labels |
| | shopping lists | categories |
| | reports | |

\*\*Primary identifying information.

and retrieving various kinds of detailed data in the interface. If we are able to specify the data, then we should at this time.

You might notice that we did not explicitly include *artist* as its own entity. From the scenarios, *artist* is referred to in the context of songs and CDs but does not seem to stand on its own.

### 6.2.4 Use Cases and Scenarios

The use cases that we have described in the diagrams in previous sections imply that the interface must support the following user tasks:

- Adding new CDs to the collection
- Removing CDs from the collection
- Changing the contents of CDs
- Searching for specific CDs
- Sorting CDs
- Browsing through the CDs in the collection
- Adding new songs to the collection
- Removing songs from the collection
- Changing characteristics of songs
- Changing characteristics of CDs
- Searching for specific songs
- Sorting songs
- Browsing through the songs in the collection
- Making a shopping list

You may have noticed that the tasks for CDs and songs seem really similar, and you may be wondering why we did not just group them together under some heading called "collection element." The list would be shorter if we had done that! The reason that we have not is that the scenarios contain references to both CDs and songs—just look at our list of primary classes. We have to assume that from the user's perspective, at least for now, there are differences between the tasks involving CDs and those involving songs. In our eventual design, we may end up treating CDs and songs as subclasses of something called "collection element," but for now the indication is that the user sees them as different.

The other thing to notice from the list of tasks and the scenarios is that they seem to be interrelated. None of the tasks listed are necessarily independent of any others. For example, the person who needs a shopping list may also need to search through the collection by CD. The roles of CD maker, shopper, and audio catalog user potentially could be combined into an audio collection user. The collection itself continues to be an entity outside of the interface. So we really have only two actors outside of the interface: the audio catalog user and the audio collection itself.

With each of the entities, the audio catalog user was doing a number of tasks. For example with CDs, the audio collection user may add CDs to the collection, modify existing CDs, delete CDs from the collection, search for CDs, sort CDs, or browse the collection. In other words, the interface must support the user's task of managing his or her CDs within the catalog. So far, our general use case diagram would look like Figure 6.10.

**Figure 6.10**   Use Case for Audio Catalog.

From the scenarios, it is clear that the interface should also support the management of these other entities, such as songs, shopping lists, reports, queries, labels, and the catalog itself. Further examination of Scenarios 3 and 6 indicates that *categories* is a *primary entity* of interest. So our high-level use case diagram might look like Figure 6.11.

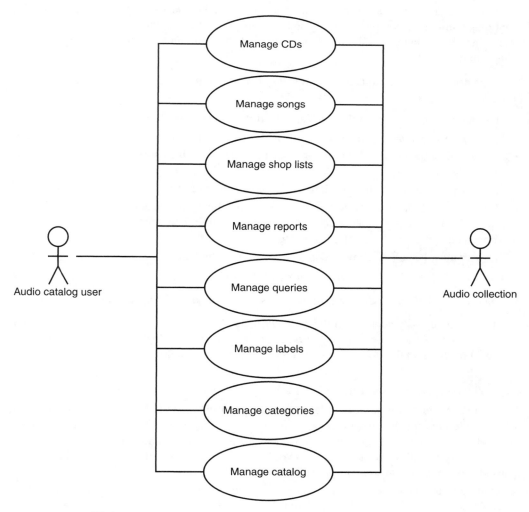

**Figure 6.11**   High-Level Use Case for Audio Catalog.

### 6.2.5 More Information from Users

As your customer, I am relatively satisfied that I have told you the tasks that I want to perform with my new computerized audio catalog. However, I think of a few more:

- The user must be able to search using named or unnamed queries. The queries are constructed by specifying a field or fields with a test (filter) for one of the following: *less than, less than or equal to, equal to, greater than, greater than or equal to, begins with, contains.* Filters for more than one field can be connected in the same query with the operators *and* and *or* or modified by *not.*
- I would like some predefined choices of musical categories, including at least *reggae, rock and roll, metal, classical, country, show, patriotic,* and *elevator.*
- The user must be able to delete music categories.
- I really liked the pictures that were in my paper catalog, but I have changed my mind about including them in the computer catalog. Did you already include management of pictures in the task list? Sorry, but you will have to take that out. It is not unusual for customers to change their minds!

I have decided on some specific features that I want regardless of how you organize the user tasks:

- The user must be able to set the fonts and the order of attributes for reports and labels.
- The user must be able to print reports and labels on a variety of commercially available papers.
- The user must be able to define the print characteristics, such as portrait or landscape, zoom, etc.
- The user must be able to preview a report or label before printing.
- The user must be able to make a new catalog, open an existing catalog, automatically save changes to the catalog, make a copy of the catalog with a new name, print the catalog as a whole, and exit the audio catalog application.
- The user must be able to copy, cut, and paste text information.
- The user must be able to get help on how to use the catalog.

I have decided on this usability expectation as part of my overall expectations:

- After six hours of practice with the new system, I should be as fast at entering information about a new CD as I am with my current paper catalog. (*Implication:* The developer must know how long it takes to perform this task with the paper catalog.)

## 6.3 Analyzing the User Tasks

As you read through this somewhat lengthy description of the tasks that someone will do with the user interface for the audio catalog, you should see that a lot of information is presented. Some of it is very detailed, and some is abstract. The presentation is not orderly enough to serve as a task analysis without some work from you! Now we are going to decompose all the tasks requested, from the most abstract to the most detailed.

Reading through the presented information you should see several ways to organize the user's tasks. At the topmost level, we have Figure 6.12.

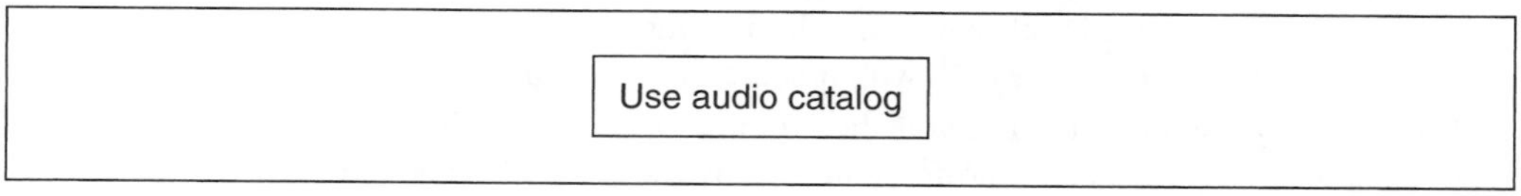

Use audio catalog

**Figure 6.12**   Top Level of Task Analysis for Audio Catalog.

How were we told that one would be using the audio catalog? One vision would be by functionality, using the catalog to add and delete different entities. Another vision would be to think about the tasks that are performed with the primary entities in the description. Let's explore this strategy first. How would we find these primary entities? We were fortunate that our user provided a list of entities believed to be relevant and their structures. Based on that list of primary entities, we see that we need to include at least seven primary entities in the catalog: *songs, CDs, categories, shopping lists, reports, queries,* and *labels.* Now let's look at the scenarios to see if we can find any more primary entities. The introduction to the scenarios mentions the catalog. Scenarios 1 through 4 discuss CDs, songs, shopping lists, and the catalog. Scenario 5 introduces the primary entities of categories and reports. Scenario 6 tells us about the primary entity query, and Scenario 7 mentions labels.

We are fortunate that the list of entities appears to match the scenarios. For example, Scenario 1 mentions a sticky note on a CD entry. CDs have an attribute, called *notes,* which would seem to include the sticky note.

The following is a list of some of the functionality of the user interface, organized by entity that seems to be described in the scenarios:

**Songs**
- The user must title a song entity because the title is the primary key and several of the scenarios refer to songs by title. (Scenarios 1, 2, 3, 8)
- The user must be able to add, modify, or remove any song in the catalog. (Scenarios 1, 2, 3, 8)
- The user must be able to add, modify, or remove data in any of the attribute fields of a song. The user must be able to make changes to individual attributes of a song without having to delete and recreate the entire song entity. (Scenario 3)
- Individual entries for song attributes may be incomplete. For example, songs in the scenarios were often referred to by title only with no other information specified. (Scenarios 2, 3, 8)
- Thinking about songs and CDs, you should think of CDs as collections of songs. These collections may be produced by professionals or by the user. CDs contain many songs. A song can be on many CDs. In other words, there is a many-to-many relationship between CDs and songs. (Scenario 8)

**CDs**
- The user must title CDs because the title is the primary key and several of the scenarios refer to CDs by title. (Scenarios 1, 3, 4, 8)
- The user must be able to add, modify, or remove CDs in the catalog. (Scenarios 1, 4, 8)
- The user must be able to add, modify, or remove data in any of the attribute fields of a CD. The user must be able to make changes to individual attributes of CDs without having to delete and recreate the entire CD entity. (Scenario 8)

- Individual entries for CD attributes may be incomplete. For example CDs in the scenarios were often referred to by title only with no other information specified. (Scenarios 3, 4, 8)
- Thinking about songs and CDs, you should think of CDs as collections of songs. These collections may be produced by professionals or by the user. CDs contain many songs. A song can be on many CDs. In other words, there is a many-to-many relationship between CDs and songs. (Scenario 8)

### Shopping Lists
- The user must name shopping lists because the name is the primary key. (Scenario 2)
- The user must be able to add, modify, or remove data in any of the attribute fields of a shopping list. (Scenario 2)

### Reports
- The user must name a report because the name is the primary key. (Scenario 6)
- The user must be able to select a report by name or by browsing. (Scenarios 5, 6)
- The user must be able to print a report. (Scenarios 5, 6)
- The user must be able to add a title to a report. (Scenario 6)
- The user must be able to edit a report. The user must be able to add, modify, or remove data in any of the attribute fields contained in a report. The user must be able to make changes to individual attributes of a report without having to delete and recreate the entire report. (Scenarios 5, 6)

### Queries
- The user must name a query because the name is the primary key. (Scenario 6)
- The user must be able to select a query by name or by browsing. (Scenarios 5, 6)
- The user must be able to print the results of a query. (Scenarios 5, 6)
- The user must be able to add or remove a query. (Scenario 5, 6)
- The user must be able to edit a query. The user must be able to add, modify, or remove values in any of the attribute fields of a query. The user must be able to make changes to individual attributes of queries without having to delete and recreate the entire query. (Scenarios 5, 6)
- The user must be able to select a query as a filter for the catalog. The user must be able to generate a report containing the results of a query. (Scenarios 5, 6)
- The user must be able to set the content (fields, values, operators) of a query. The system should provide some default settings for this task. (Scenario 6)

### Labels
- The user must name a label because the name is the primary key. (Scenario 7)
- The user must be able to select a label by name or by browsing. (Scenario 7)
- The user must be able to print a label. (Scenario 7)
- The user must be able to edit a label. (Scenario 6)

### Categories
- The user must name a category because the name is the primary key. (Scenario 3)

- The user must be able to add or remove a category. (Scenario 3)
- The user must be able to edit a category. (Scenario 3)

Catalog

- The user should be able to browse the catalog entities for songs and CDs by name or category or by using any of the other fields in the catalog. (Scenarios 1, 2, 3, 4)
- The user should be able to browse a portion of the catalog that satisfies a query. (Scenarios 5, 6)
- The user should be able to browse alphabetically. (Scenarios 1, 2, 3, 4)
- The user should be able to mark (dog-ear) and retrieve entities. (Scenarios 1, 2, 3, 4)
- The user should be able to browse the catalog sequentially by moving from one entity to the next or previous entity. (Scenario 1, 2, 3, 4)
- The user should be able to sort the catalog using any field in either increasing or decreasing order. (Scenario 5)
- From the user's perspective, the catalog is a collection of separate entities. How they are actually derived and stored is an implementation issue.

Typical file operations, such as open and save, should also be included. Finally, in the description of general functionality, we find mention of some kind of help facility.

We can envision that the tasks users will do with these primary entities all involve management. Using the verb *manage,* the first two levels of the task analysis would look something like Figure 6.13.

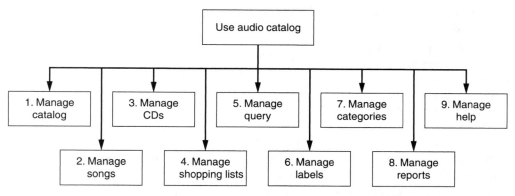

**Figure 6.13** First Two Levels of Object-Based Hierarchical Task Breakdown.

This breakdown is not finished! We have lots more information in our description of what we can do with the primary entities. Let's consider the primary entity CD. What can we do with CDs? We show the actions that we can take with CDs that constitute managing CDs in Figure 6.14.

We often find it useful to use a hierarchical numbering system to identify tasks. Using such a numbering system, we would number *Manage CDs* as Task 3. The tasks *Add a new CD to catalog* and *Change an existing CD* would be numbered as 3.1 and 3.2, respectively. These numbers are use-

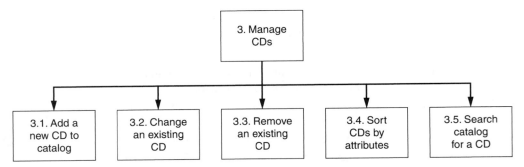

**Figure 6.14**    Hierarchical Breakdown of *Task 3: Manage CDs*.

ful later in matching more detailed narrative descriptions of the tasks with the location of the tasks in the hierarchical charts. Also, as we design interactions to support the tasks in the hierarchy, we can use the numbers to match the tasks and the interactions.

We still need to complete the text description for each of the tasks that we have identified so far. Let's fill in a text description for the task *Manage CDs* in Figure 6.14. The format of the narrative description was given in Chapter 5.

### Description of Task 3: Manage CDs
- What is the goal of this task?
  The goal of Manage CDs is to allow the user to add, modify, delete, and search for CDs in the audio catalog.
- Is this task a subtask of a larger task?
  This task is a subtask of *Use audio catalog* (root task).
- What subtasks define this task?
  3.1: *Add a new CD to catalog.*
  3.2: *Change an existing CD.*
  3.3: *Remove an existing CD.*
  3.4: *Sort CDs by attributes.*
  3.5: *Search catalog for a CD.*
- What noninterface functions does this task require?
  This task does not require noninterface functions. Some of its subtasks will require access to the database that contains the CD entities.
- What kinds of inputs or actions does this task require from the user?
  The user will need to choose this activity from among several other tasks for managing entities.
- What kinds of outputs or results occur by virtue of performing this task?
  Users will receive some feedback from the system to guide them as to which CD activity they wish to engage in.
- What automatic actions does this task expect from the system?
  Any changes to the audio catalog that result from one of the subtasks should be automatically saved.

- What special characteristics or special requests from the user of this task should we record? None.
- Sequencing constraints: In this subtree, is there a task that must come before this one? In this subtree, is there a task for which this one is the immediate predecessor or that can co-occur?

  The user may choose to perform the tasks in *Manage CDs* in any order relative to the other tasks.
- Which, if any, primary entities are involved in this subtask?

  The primary entity is CD.
- How can this task fail or end in noncompletion?

  This task cannot fail.
- How frequently is this task performed?

  Because CDs are at the heart of the audio catalog, this task will be performed frequently.
- How rigid is this task, especially in terms of its sequence or inputs?

  The task is not very rigid. *Manage* incorporates many activities, which could be performed in a variety of different orders and with a potentially infinite number of inputs.
- What are the situational constraints on this task?

  None.
- What if any are the specific usability expectations for this task, and how do we anticipate determining if we have satisfied the expectations?

  Some of the subtasks may have specific usability constraints. Overall, we expect that the use of the interface for *Manage CDs* will be satisfying. Specifically, we define satisfaction for this task like this: After a group of users has been using this system for ten hours, so that they are proficient, we will ask them to rate their satisfaction on the following scale to each of the tasks that corresponds to the subtasks of *Manage CDs*. We expect that the average rating should be 4 or above. This is a sample question:

  On a scale of 1 to 5, indicate how satisfying this user interface will support the subtask of *Fill in subtask*.

  **1 = not at all   2 = marginally   3 = OK   4 = pretty good   5 = excellent**
- Assumptions

  We are dividing the tasks that can change CDs into those that add a new CD, change an existing CD, or remove an existing CD from the catalog.

  From the user's perspective, a CD might contain many songs or the same song by many artists. In *Manage a CD,* we may need to show multiple songs or multiple iterations of the same song. This notion is not really clear from the scenarios but follows from the descriptions of the data entities.

Am I finished with the breakdown of *Manage CDs*? We would argue that the answer is "no." Let's consider a couple of the tasks that make up *Manage CD*. First, let's look at the task of *Add a new CD to catalog*. Reading through the information, we get the idea that adding a CD means adding a new CD to the catalog by adding a new CD title. So a breakdown of *Add a new CD to catalog* might look like Figure 6.15.

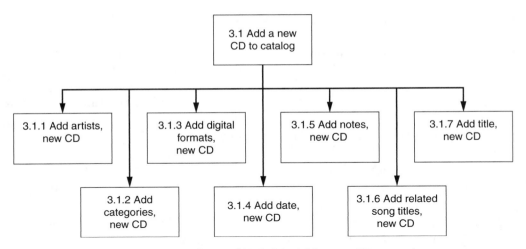

**Figure 6.15**    Hierarchical Breakdown of *Task 3.1: Add a new CD to catalog.*

**Description of Task 3.1: Add a new CD to catalog**

- What is the goal of this task?
  The goal of *Add a new CD to catalog* is to allow the user to add a new CD entity to the catalog by entering the CD title and other attributes.
- Is this task a subtask of a larger task?
  This is a subtask of Task 3: *Manage CDs.*
- What subtasks define this task?
  3.1.1: *Add artists, new CD*
  3.1.2: *Add categories, new CD*
  3.1.3: *Add digital formats, new CD*
  3.1.4: *Add date, new CD*
  3.1.5: *Add notes, new CD*
  3.1.6: *Add related song titles, new CD*
  3.1.7: *Add title, new CD*
- What noninterface functions does this task require?
  This task does not require noninterface functions. Some of its subtasks will require access to the database that contains the CD entities.
- What kinds of inputs or actions does this task require from the user?
  The user will need to choose this activity from several for managing CDs.
- What kinds of outputs or results occur by virtue of performing this task?
  The user will receive some feedback from the system to guide them as to which attributes they wish to add.
- What automatic actions does this task expect from the system?
  Save state information.
- What special characteristics or special requests from the user of this task should we record?

The CD title is the primary key for this type of entity, so the user interface must ensure that the user enters at least a title. The other information is discretionary.

- Sequencing constraints: Is there an order in which the tasks must be performed?
  There is no mandatory sequence to the tasks for entering a new CD. Because the user must enter at least a CD title, a possible sequencing constraint is to make sure that the task *Add title, new CD* is performed first.

  The paper version of the catalog had several required steps before the user could enter data (*Find catalog, Find location*). These steps are not required in the automated version. By choosing this task, the user has already "found" the audio catalog. Because the entities can be sorted by the application, it is not necessary to find a specific location.
- Which, if any, primary entities are involved in this subtask?
  The primary entities are CDs, songs, and categories.
- How can this task fail?
  This task cannot be completed unless the subtask *Add title, new CD* is completed. The user is not required to perform any of the other subtasks.
- How frequently is this task performed?
  The typical user purchases or creates two CDs per month. This will be a relatively frequent task. (In a real project, you would define a measurement and interpretation and then verify the measure.)
- How rigid is this task, especially in terms of its sequence or inputs?
  The task of entering data pertaining to a specific CD is not very rigid. The user should only be required to enter a title and may enter other data in any order.
- What are the situational constraints?
  None.
- What if any are the specific usability expectations for this task, and how do we determine if we have satisfied the expectations?
  Ease of use could be measured by timing how long it takes a user to enter the data for a new CD after being trained. The criteria might be that the user can complete the task in two minutes or less. Ease of learning could be measured by having a new user do ten training exercises in which new CD data are entered. We would then time how long it took the user to add another item. The criteria might be that the user can complete the task in two minutes or less.
- Assumptions
  1. From the user's perspective, a CD may contain many songs or the same song by many artists. In adding a CD, we may need to show multiple songs or multiple versions of the same song.
  2. An assumption is that when the user adds a CD, the user must eventually add a CD title, as this is the primary key for a CD.
  3. A hidden assumption is that the songs or categories for a CD may not already exist in the catalog. A song or category that is added to a CD that does not exist in the catalog should be automatically added to the catalog.

### Description of Task 3.2: Change an existing CD

This task involves editing attributes as well as managing the tools for cut, copy, and paste of CDs. Its breakdown can be seen in Figure 6.16.

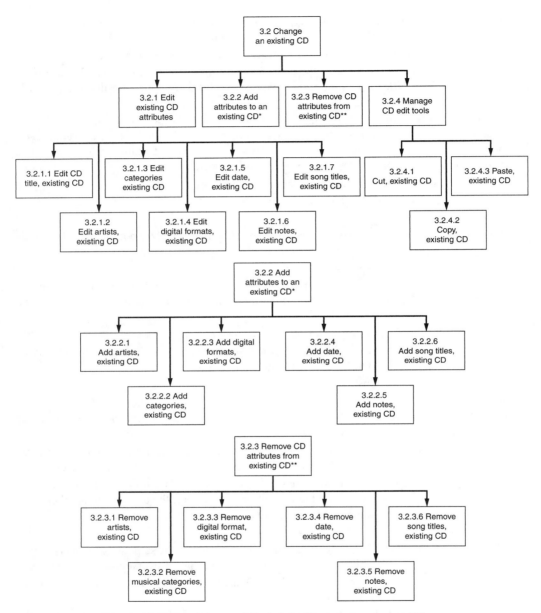

**Figure 6.16**   Hierarchical Breakdown of Task 3.2: *Change an existing CD.*
Note: Due to space limitations, this diagram has been broken into three parts. The asterisk (*) on Task 3.2.2 indicates the connection between the node directly under Task 3.2 and the subtree with Task 3.2.2 as root. The double asterisk (**) on Task 3.2.3 indicates the connection between the node directly under Task 3.2 and the subtree with Task 3.2.3 as root.

This task has three major subtasks:

3.2.2: *Add attributes to an existing CD*
3.2.1: *Edit existing CD attributes*
3.2.3: *Remove CD attributes from existing CD*

These three tasks may seem the same but they are not. Task 3.2.2: *Add attributes to an existing CD* adds values to fields that were previously empty. Task 3.2.1: *Edit existing CD attributes* changes existing values in fields. Task 3.2.3: *Remove CD attributes from existing CD* removes values and does not replace them with alternative values. It may be that all three tasks are reflected identically in the implementation of the user interface, but conceptually they are potentially different because the contexts are different. Hence, it is critical in the task analysis to preserve the difference.

The following is a sample text description for Task 3.2.2: *Add attributes to an existing CD*, which is at the middle of the hierarchy, built using our outline of essential information.

### Description of Task 3.2.2: Add attributes to an existing CD

- What is the goal of this task?
  The goal of *Add attributes to an existing CD* is to allow the user to add new values for CD attributes that were previously empty.
- Is this task a subtask of a larger task?
  This is a subtask of Task 3.2: *Change an existing CD.*
- What subtasks define this task?
  3.2.2.1: *Add artists, existing CD*
  3.2.2.2: *Add categories, existing CD*
  3.2.2.3: *Add digital formats, existing CD*
  3.2.2.4: *Add date, existing CD*
  3.2.2.5: *Add notes, existing CD*
  3.2.2.6: *Add song titles, existing CD*
- What noninterface functions does this task require?
  This task requires access to the database that contains the CD entities.
- What kinds of inputs or actions does this task require from the user?
  The user will need to choose this activity from several for modifying CD entities.
- What kinds of outputs or results occur by virtue of performing this task?
  The user will receive some feedback from the system to guide them as to which attributes they wish to add and to indicate that the values have been successfully added.
- What automatic actions does this task expect from the system?
  Save state information.
- What special characteristics of this task should we record?
  None.
- Sequencing constraints: Is there an order in which the tasks must be performed?
  From the user's perspective, the user may choose to perform this task in any order relative to the subtasks in the subtree at this level.

- Which, if any, primary entities are involved in this subtask?
  The primary entities are CDs, songs, and categories.
- How can this task fail?
  This task cannot be completed unless the CD actually exists.
- Assumptions
  The user can add any attributes to an existing CD, except for the CD title. By necessity, the CD title already has been set so that the CD entity exists.

For the remaining questions, we currently do not have enough information and would need to go back to the user.

- How frequently is this task performed?
- How rigid is this task, especially in terms of its sequence or inputs?
- What are the situational constraints?
- What, if any, are the specific usability expectations for this task, and how do we anticipate determining if we have satisfied the expectations?

The following is a sample text description for the subtask *Paste existing CD,* which is at the bottom of the hierarchy.

### Description of Task 3.2.4.3: Paste, existing CD

- What is the goal of this task?
  The goal of *paste existing CD* is to allow the user to place cut or copied text or pictures into one of the attribute fields.
- Is this task a subtask of a larger task?
  This is a subtask of Task 3.2.4: *Manage CD edit tools.*
- What subtasks define this task?
  None. This task is at the bottom of the hierarchical breakdown.
- What noninterface functions does this task require?
  This task requires access to the data structure that the system is using to store cut or copied information.
- What kinds of inputs or actions does this task require from the user?
  The user will need to indicate where (by cursor position) he or she wants to place the pasted information.
- What kinds of outputs or results occur by virtue of performing this task?
  The user should see the result of pasting by seeing the new information in place.
- What automatic actions does this task expect from the system?
  The cut or copied information will be retained by the system.
- What special characteristics of this task should we record?
  None.
- Sequencing constraints: Is there an order in which the tasks must be performed?
  None.
- Which, if any, primary entities are involved in this subtask?
  None.

- How can this task fail?
  This task cannot be completed if the user has not cut or copied before this task.
- How frequently is this task performed?
  This task will be performed frequently.
- How rigid is this task, especially in terms of its sequence or inputs?
  Paste involves selecting the location of the paste and then performing the paste operation, so the task has a set sequence and is very rigid.
- What are the situational constraints?
  None.
- What if any are the specific usability expectations for this task, and how do we determine if we have satisfied the expectations?
  Ease of use might be important here. Users may expect this task to lend itself to minimal errors and minimal keystrokes, especially in the selection of the spot of the paste. Minimal errors might be 10 errors in 100 tries. Minimal keystrokes might be less than five keystrokes per paste. Note that minimizing keystrokes may improve usability if the task is performed frequently.
- Assumptions
  The task applies to both text and pictures. However, it appears from the description that *Paste* is not concerned with preserving the particular appearance (format) of the text or the picture. In a real project, the developer would go back to the user and clarify this issue.

We finish this section by presenting the hierarchical breakdowns of some of the other tasks in Figure 6.14. Task 3.3: *Remove an existing CD* involves removing the CD from the catalog. Minimally, to remove a CD from the catalog would mean deleting the CD title. The hierarchical breakdown for Task 3.3 can be seen in Figure 6.17. Sorting the CDs in the catalog involves sorting by attribute. Sorting on any attribute could mean increasing or decreasing order. The hierarchical breakdown for Task 3.4: *Sort CDs by attributes* can be seen in Figure 6.18.

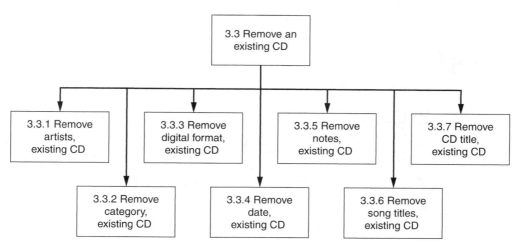

**Figure 6.17**   Hierarchical Breakdown of Task 3.3: *Remove an existing CD.*

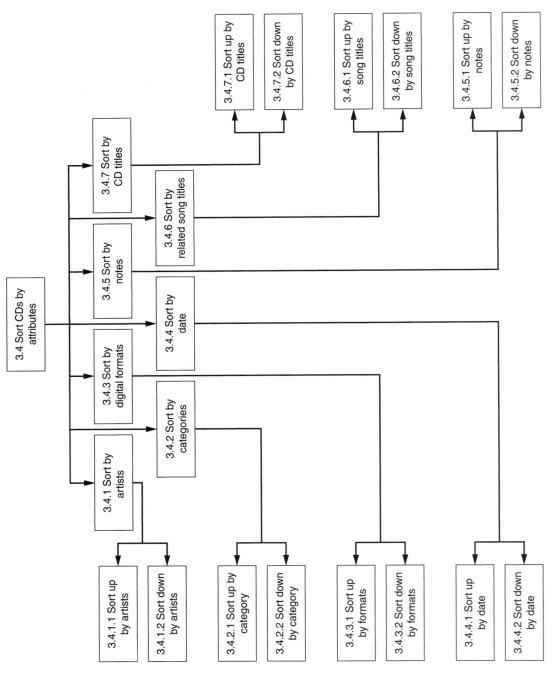

Figure 6.18    Hierarchical Breakdown of Task 3.4: *Sort CDs by attributes.*

Finally, consider the action of searching for a CD in the catalog. Scenario 1 suggests that I could search for an individual CD using a table of contents. Scenario 1 also indicates that I could search by an alphabetic index or by bookmarks ("pages are dog-eared"). Scenario 1 also mentions that I could search by categories. Finally, Scenario 6 suggests that I could search by query. In the description of functionality, it is stated that the user should be able to search by a primary entity attribute; however, reflection on this should suggest that searching by one or more attributes is really just a query as described in Scenario 6. Because there is specific mention of searching by category, we have left that as a specific task, even though category could be an attribute of a CD. The resulting hierarchical breakdown for Task 3.5: *Search catalog for CD* might look like Figure 6.19.

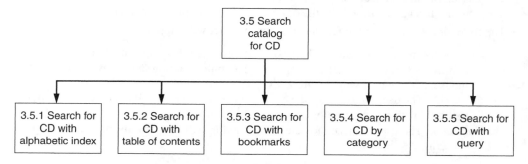

**Figure 6.19**   Hierarchical Breakdown of Task 3.5: *Search catalog for CD.*

## 6.4 User Profiles

Another part of the analysis and specification process is the collection of user profiles. Typical issues addressed in the user profile include these:

- User expertise for the task.
- User motivation.
- User knowledge of computer skills.
- User age and cultural issues, if relevant.

The following is a sample user profile for the audio catalog.

*User expertise for the task of using the audio catalog.*   The typical user is fairly expert at the common tasks that one would do with the paper catalog, especially the adding of new CDs to the library. The typical user edits and deletes entries for CDs only on an irregular basis. Any other tasks, such as manipulating records about songs or artists, are new to the user. However, as long as the procedures to perform these tasks are similar to the procedures for CDs, the user should be relatively familiar.

*User motivation.*   The typical user is highly motivated to use the computerized audio catalog, and they are interested in musical CDs.

*User knowledge of computer skills.*   The typical user is computer literate and familiar with the visual environment of most personal computers.

*User age and cultural issues, if relevant.*   The typical user is between the ages of nineteen and twenty-six and is not interested in CDs with questionable content.

In Chapter 3, we discussed measurement and interpretation of user characteristics. At this point, in a real project we might have done a much more extensive analysis of our users for the audio catalog.

## 6.5 Context Setting

Normally, we would have completed the context setting activities *before* starting the analysis and specification of the user interface. Since this chapter is just an example, we will show you some brief contextual information for this project.

- There is an established need for this product: I want it! This product is viable and feasible, and the customer has agreed to pay for the cost of development plus 10 percent.
- The following are some of the features that this product will support:

    *Feature 1.* The user interface is housed inside software that will run on an operating system that supports a visual environment. The only pointing device available will be a mouse, and the user will also have a keyboard available.

    *Feature 2.* The user interface for the audio catalog will support all the tasks that I can normally do with a paper catalog.

    *Feature 3.* The user interface for the audio catalog will support advanced searching and reporting.

## 6.6 Some Notes About Groups and Tools

Major development efforts rarely are completed by an individual person. Most likely, a development team or teams will work together on a project. Developing a task analysis of a project with the complexity of the audio catalog is a lot of work and may be done in a group.

We have deliberately picked a low-tech approach to task analysis so that you can focus on task analysis and not on learning a specific tool. Many different CASE tools or graphics programs may be used to generate the hierarchical diagrams. A word processor can be used to generate the text descriptions, but a number of CASE tools include tools to link a text description to each box in the chart. If you use a CASE tool for both the chart and the text description, your tool will likely check your work for spelling inconsistencies, and it also might build a data dictionary of all the elements in your solution.

## Conclusions

In this chapter we have looked at some detailed elements of analysis and specification for the user interface for the audio catalog project. In subsequent chapters, we discuss the design of the interaction to support these requirements.

## Exercises

1. The task analysis for the audio catalog is not complete. Task analyses for most of our class projects usually consist of 70 to 120 tasks. Form a group of three or four classmates and finish the hierarchical decomposition for the audio catalog. Write the text descriptions for each of the tasks in your hierarchical decomposition.
2. Discuss the advantages of developing a detailed task analysis specification.

# Part 4

---

# Designing a User Interface to Match the User's Needs

# Designing the Interaction and a Solution

## Motivation

At this point, you should be starting to feel comfortable with the idea that much of usability engineering is involved with understanding users' problems. To understand those problems, you must have a detailed description of the tasks users wish to accomplish, their characteristics, and what features they hope to find in the interaction and user interface that you will eventually build. Your description should be unambiguous and include information, such as the sequencing of interaction activities, so that you can hand it off to a coding specialist. Finally, your design should include specific information about how the interaction's look and feel are connected to the rest of the software system.

In design, you can follow either a system-centered approach or a user-centered approach. *System-centered design* means that the design is created around system characteristics. For example, if your eventual product will be running on a given platform, you would build the design to optimize and fit that platform. *User-centered design* was first suggested by Norman and Draper (1986). In this case, the design is created to best address the user's needs and tasks as stated in your requirements documents. In user-centered design, you may actually sacrifice some system efficiency to better address the user's needs in the interaction and the interface that you build.

Now we are getting to the point where we are ready to design a solution. At the end of this set of chapters (Chapters 7 through 9) you should be able to:

- Explain the difference between interaction design and interface design.
- Describe the characteristics and guidelines of different interaction styles. When is each style appropriate? What guidelines apply to interaction design regardless of the interaction style?

- Design a user interaction that is appropriate for the user's problem. What are the steps you need to complete in order to design and build the interaction?
- Describe and apply various guidelines, external standards, and principles of visual design that can be used to improve an interaction design.

It is our assumption that you will be doing some design activities when you finish this chapter. These activities will give you a chance to practice what you have learned.

## 7.1 Introduction

In Chapter 4, we learned that within the usability engineering life cycle are two design activities: interaction design and interface design. *Interaction design* is concerned with the design of the overall look and feel of the user interface, as well as the design of individual interactions. *Interface design* means the design of the actual software that will drive the interaction.

Both the interaction design and the interface design have high- and low-level design activities. For the interaction design, the high-level activities focus on the selection of an interaction style and the selection of the general pattern of interaction. Low-level activities involve the design of individual interactions. Examples of low-level design decisions include choosing the content and arrangement of menu options, selecting button types, selecting background colors, and such. Designing the interface is really a software design problem. At a high level, the designer will select overall architecture for the software; this means that the designer will select an overall pattern of procedure calls, assignment of workload, and distribution of communication. At a low level, the designer will be concerned with the design of classes, member functions, data structures, data members, and other modules.

## 7.2 Design of Interaction

The term *interaction style* refers to how a user interacts with a computer system from the user's point of view. An *interaction* not only includes the interface itself and the devices through which the user communicates with the system but also the application objects that the system provides to the user. Some people would characterize the interaction style as a key element of the *look and feel* of the interface; an interaction style is made up of what the user perceives, how the style is controlled, and the manner in which the user receives feedback. The concept of style is central to our ability to characterize and understand the diversity of interactive systems.

(*A note on terminology:* A lot of "I" words are floating around in this chapter. When we refer to *interaction* or *interaction style,* we are referring to how the user interacts with the interface from the user's perspective. When we talk about an *interface,* we mean a specific implementation on paper or a computer system that includes one or more interaction styles.)

The choice of interaction style is critical to the eventual success of your interface. As we have already learned from Eason (1984), user reaction is driven by the characteristics of user and task. Not surprisingly, the choice of interaction style should depend on the type of user or the type of task. Other variables also influence the choice of interaction style. Hardware, such as the user's input devices, have a major impact on the type of interaction style that is a practical choice. For example, when a user has only a keyboard for input, the programmer may define the arrow keys as navigational or "pointing" tools, but this style of pointing is primitive compared to a mouse or gestural device. Given that setting, the designer may develop an interaction with minimal pointing and maximal textual input. Screens with minimal screen area, such as personal digital assistants and cell phones, may also limit the type of interaction.

Sometimes real-world concerns become dominant forces in the choice of interaction styles. For example, the designer may feel that a graphical interaction is the best solution for the user and the task. However, the user only has a cell phone with a keypad and a text-based display for the interface. If this cell phone has no capability to display or respond to graphical interaction, the designer will be forced to choose another interaction style.

When you design an interaction, you potentially have many different interaction styles from which to choose. You are probably familiar with the idea of different interaction styles from your own experiences. No doubt you have noticed that your interaction differs depending on whether you are playing a video game, placing an online order, or reading your e-mail via a terminal application. It may surprise you to learn that some underlying design principles seem to hold across interaction styles. *Consistency* is an example of a design guideline that is often emphasized, regardless of the interaction style. However, what it means to be *consistent* may vary across styles.

For many people, the selection of interaction style (e.g., menu versus command-line) and the eventual implementation *is* usability engineering. Some usability engineers have a favorite interaction style (such as graphical user interfaces, or GUIs). In this chapter we discuss different interaction styles and when to use them. You may be surprised to learn that for some user and task combinations, graphical user interfaces and menu-based interactions may *not* be the best choice. For example, if your users have a high level of expertise and demand extreme speed in their interactions, some kind of command-line interaction may be their best choice. Once you have chosen a particular interaction style, a lot of design work still remains to be done. For example, if you have decided to use buttons in your interaction, you still need to decide where to put the buttons, what size to make them, and what kind of labels to associate with them. These design activities are part of *interaction design.* Selection and detailed design of interaction are critical to your eventual success.

## 7.3 Overview: Interaction Styles

Many interaction styles are available to choose from, and it is often not a simple matter to assign a specific interface to only one interaction style. Categories of interactions are defined primarily by the ways that the user provides input and receives information back from the interaction. We can loosely separate the styles into three groups: those based on manipulations of visual objects, those based on manipulations of conversational objects, and those that are tied to nonvisual and combination manipulations. In Section 7.4, we further categorize interaction styles within these groups.

Styles based on manipulating visual objects are those in which the user provides input to the system by selecting a visual or graphical object in the interface presentation. Many times the user's inputs are accomplished by using a pointing device, such as a mouse. Changes in the visual representations of the objects provide output information to the user. Examples of visual manipulation interactions may include menu-based interactions, windows-based interactions, form fill-in interactions, and direct manipulation interactions.

Styles based on manipulations of conversational objects are those in which the user interacts with the system in a conversational way using verbal symbols such as words or wordlike symbols. In this style of interaction, both inputs and outputs tend to be in verbal or textual forms. The common input device to support these interactions is the keyboard. Conversational interactions usually involve an exchange, using verbal symbols, between the interaction and the user. In such interactions, the user bears considerable responsibility for knowing the "language" used in the conversation. Command-line interactions are examples of conversational interactions.

This classification of interaction styles may seem artificial to you. In fact, you may have noted that many specific interfaces that are familiar to you include a number of different interaction styles. For example, the familiar graphical user interfaces (GUIs) popular on contemporary personal computers may offer combinations of visual manipulation and conversational elements. Even within an individual interaction style, the specific interface itself may be a combination of visual, verbal, or neither. Consider the menu, shown in Figure 7.1. GUIs use pull-down menus to convey the commands available to the user at any given time. The user interacts with the menu by using a pointing device. In this sense the user is a manipulating a visual element in the interface. However, most menus are lists of words, and frequently used commands have keyboard accelerators. In this way, menus in GUIs also have a conversational aspect. Our reasoning for considering this interaction to be primarily visual is that the user manipulates visual objects (word strings) in making choices.

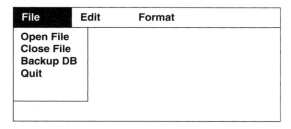

**Figure 7.1**   A Simple Visual Menu Example.

On the other hand, menus were a recognized interaction style long before GUIs became commonplace. A command-line interface, which is a verbal interaction, also may include menus. An example can be seen in Figure 7.2, which is also a menu. However, the command-line interaction in which it is embedded is a verbal interaction because it uses a conversational style between the user and the interface. (See Hutchins et al. 1986 for a more detailed discussion of the dichotomy between visual and verbal interaction styles.)

> \>> Enter a choice of actions.  Choices are O *filename* for open, C for close, B for backup and Q for quit.
> \>> *User selects from the menu of choices by typing a verbal response.*

**Figure 7.2**   A Simple Verbal Menu Example.

In this chapter, we briefly discuss a third category of interaction style that does not involve the manipulation of visual elements in the familiar sense of GUIs and is not verbal like command-line interactions. Some of these interactions involve nonvisual manipulations, and others are combinations of the first two categories of styles. What makes these interactions interesting is their use of manipulative devices or mixed interactions that do not rely exclusively on vision or exclusively on conversation. Compared to a typical system today, you might consider them to be unconventional in terms of the input and output venues. An example of this type of interaction might be an interface that permitted parallel input of information by a pen on a graphical object and by speech, or an interface in which the user interacts by touch (cf. Oviatt 1999). As with the delineation of visual and verbal, we acknowledge that the distinction between interactions driven primarily by manipulations of visual elements and interactions that focus on nonvisual elements may be tricky and is artificial in some cases. For example, an interaction may have manipulable visual elements that provide both visual and tactile feedback. We will treat this as an example of the third category of interactions, acknowledging that many of the design strategies that are appropriate for manipulable visual interactions may apply here as well.

Among the lessons to be learned here is that as soon as we define a given interface and its interaction to be in a specific category, we will probably find embedded elements that are exceptions. In our discussion, remember that interaction styles may be combined or modified in a specific application.

Also, in our discussion of the different interaction styles we assume that the user is interacting with a conventional computing system with a keyboard and a mouse (or its equivalent). This may be an oversimplification in many cases. For example, in using a cellular telephone, some user interactions with an application could be by voice commands (speech recognition). Such a voice interaction could be precisely designed and structured following much the same design rules as a conversational interaction that uses typed commands.

Hopefully, you will be able to generalize the discussion in this chapter to venues other than the standard personal computer. For a specific problem, you should consider all the reasonable interaction styles. Don't be afraid to mix and match!

## 7.4 Major Categories of Interaction Styles: Quick Descriptions

As much as possible, we have tried to categorize interactions independently of the "usual" interface implementations. Remember that you will be able to find exceptions to our list, but our goal is to provide a general framework.

### 7.4.1 Manipulation of Visual Elements

In this category of interaction styles, the user inputs commands by manipulating visual objects that are presented in the interface. The system supplies feedback to the user by modifying the visual object or modifying some other visual aspect of the interface.

*Menus or menu-based interactions:* Commands or expected user responses are explicitly presented to the user. The alternatives are presented as a list of visual objects. (We will consider a box containing a text string to be a visual object.) The user selects his or her choice from the list of alternatives. Inputs often involve the use of a pointing device or a key press.

*Windowed interaction:* The user's output display is divided into a number of possibly overlapping rectangular areas. Each window handles a specific function or is a "virtual terminal."

The windows may themselves contain other interaction styles and accept input from both keyboard and pointing devices.

*Form fill-in interaction:*    Users are presented with a form on the display where the blanks in the form are visual objects. The UI form is analogous to the common paper form and users input information by filling in the blanks. Users typically navigate around the form with a pointing device or key press.

*Direct manipulation interaction:*    The user manipulates "objects" presented in the interaction to accomplish tasks. Direct manipulation systems strive for a "feeling" of reality, in the sense that the actions within the interaction seem to be continuous. Many would argue that GUIs are also direct manipulation interactions.

### 7.4.2  Conversational Interactions

In this category of interaction styles, the user "converses" with the system by inputting text strings. The system responds and supplies feedback to the user by presenting text strings.

*Command-line interaction:*    To initiate actions, users enter verbal symbols, often in the form of text commands. The vocabulary and the syntax of the command language are formally defined. The UNIX operating system supports a command-line interaction (The Open Group 1995–2006).

*Natural language interaction:*    This can be considered a special instance of a command-line interaction. The vocabulary is a significant, well-defined subset of some natural language, such as English. The user may type responses as is commonly done in command-line interactions, or the system may have a speech-recognition component.

*Question-and-answer interaction:*    The application solicits information from the user by asking a series of questions. The user may type answers or select answers from menus.

### 7.4.3  Manipulable and Combination Interaction Styles

In these interaction styles, user inputs and outputs involve manipulations but not necessarily manipulations of visual objects. Manipulations may be via other modalities and/or may involve multiple styles of interactions, acting in parallel.

*Haptic interactions:*    Users can feel and manipulate objects in the interface. The user interacts via tactile and/or positional feedback. An example is computer-assisted surgical systems.

*Multimedia and multimodal interactions:*    In multimedia interactions, output to the user is presented in many different media, such as text, graphics, and sounds. Conversely, in multimodal interactions, input to the system can be provided by the user in verbal, visual, or other forms, using a diverse set of devices, such as keyboards, microphones, pointing devices, light pens, and so on. In some regard, multimedia interactions are examples of multimodal interactions. In multimodal interactions, the user has a number of ways that he or she can interact. For example, users may interact with objects by using a pen or speech; in this example, the speech and pen interactions would occur in parallel, and the choice of interaction would be at the discretion of the user. Multimodal interactions hold great promise for users who find more conventional interactions an encumbrance.

*Virtual reality and virtual worlds:*   The web site Whatis.com defines virtual reality as "the simulation of a real or imagined environment that can be experienced visually in three dimensions of width, height, and depth and that may additionally provide an interactive experience visually in full real-time motion with sound and possibly with tactile and other forms of feedback" (whatis.com 2004–2006). Virtual reality systems have different levels of *immersion* based on how involved the user becomes with the virtual world. Virtual worlds can be presented on a typical computer display, but other devices, such as head-mounted displays, can also be used. The virtual world typically contains visual objects with which the user can interact.

*Video games:*   There are many varieties of video games and associated interactions. Interactions for video games involve the manipulation of visual objects, as well as tactile and multimedia interactions. Video games usually support a wide variety of input devices.

*Mobile and handheld device interactions:*   Interactions for small computing devices may be somewhat different than those for larger devices. Handheld devices often have limited keyboards and alternative pointing devices (stylus). Cellular phones have renewed the interest in designing text-based menu systems.

## 7.5  General Design Guidelines

In this section, we discuss guidelines that can be applied across interaction styles. For any interaction style, it is possible to design an excellent, usable interface. Similarly, it is possible to design an absolutely unusable interface. Before we discuss the details of specific interaction styles in Chapter 8, we review some general design principles. You should consider these principles to be tools for design. Following these principles should help you to design usable interfaces. Remember that Eason (1984), Nielsen (1993a), and Shackel (1986) all emphasized that usable interfaces are those that are easy to use, are easy to learn, and have good task match (are effective). Nielsen and Shackel also indicated that usable interfaces should minimize user errors and should be satisfying and efficient to use. In the following discussion, we relate the general design principles to some of the variables of usability. *A disclaimer:* While these guidelines have emerged from the work of many experts in usability engineering and HCI, actually determining if the guideline has been met in a specific interface requires a formal assessment. It is not enough for the designer to simply say that this interface is in compliance with the brand X guideline simply because he or she believes it to be so.

### 7.5.1  Guideline 1: Facilitate the Development
### and Use of Workable Mental Models

From the discussion of everyday objects in Chapter 1, we learned that users build a *mental model* of how the interface is supposed to function. They either bring this model to the experience or form it as they are learning about the interface. The user's mental model helps the user to, among other things, identify what he or she can do with the interface, how the interface is constrained, and how his or her actions map to the action of the device. As we learned in Chapter 1, a user's mental model can be enhanced when he or she receives feedback for his or her actions with the interface.

Users also have mental models of software user interfaces, which include the same kind of information as for an everyday device. It should be obvious that the better the interface either matches, or facilitates the development of, a workable mental model, the more it will aid in making the interface usable. For new users, being able to build a workable mental model enhances the ease of learning an interface. Being able to apply a workable mental model enhances ease of use, user satisfaction, and efficiency.

A *workable* mental model means that the behavior of the interface is close to the behavior predicted by the user's mental model. The user's mental model will often include information about the verbal, visual, and spatial characteristics of the interface. The mental model will permit the user to correctly interpret textual information, icons, objects, and navigational requirements through the interface.

You can do some things to help a user build and use workable mental models of your interface:

- Present the interaction consistently across actions and terminology. Consistency encourages maximum transfer of skill and understanding across tasks within an application. Consistency across applications may encourage maximum transfer as well. This concept sounds so obvious that you may wonder why we even include it. Well, while the idea seems obvious, putting it into practice may be difficult. The problem is to define what exactly you are going to make consistent. Do you consider your interface consistent if you use the same colors throughout? What about if the navigational strategy is the same throughout? Is that consistency? These issues can be so thorny that Grudin (1989) has even suggested that consistency is not always a great idea. At best, you should give careful thought to any aspects of your interface for which consistency is a potential issue.

- Allow the user to build a mental model of the system based on the tasks they actually perform with it rather than what the system actually does. Suppose, for example, that the city of Burbia has a subway system. The trains do not run on a rectilinear grid. However, to depict the subway for users, an approximation of a rectilinear grid is good enough. Maps of the Burbia Subway, like maps of other metropolitan subways, present the layout of the subway as if it were rectilinear. The model that users build of the subway is also rectilinear. Is this a problem for subway users? Probably not since their model is accurate enough for them to use.

A map of the Burbia Subway is shown in Figure 7.3. Using the map, riders of the subway can see that the Dotted Line can be used to get from the Central Business District (CBD) to the museum or that you have to transfer to the Dashed Line to get to East Station. As you can see the layout is essentially rectilinear.

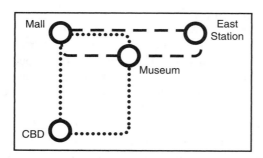

Figure 7.3   Map of the Burbia Subway System.

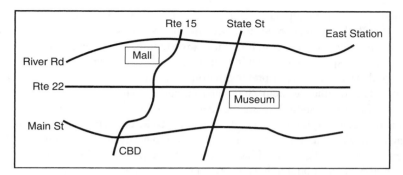

Figure 7.4   Map of Burbia.

Compare this picture to the map of Burbia shown in Figure 7.4. As you can see, the layout of Burbia is not as rectilinear as it is shown in the subway map. The point is that to use the subway, I do not have to know the exact layout of the train lines and, in fact, it might be confusing to have a true representation.

Here are some more suggestions that can help people to build and use mental models:

• Use terminology in your interface that matches the user's use of language. Many contemporary interfaces express user actions in *computerese*—jargon filled with technical terms. Building an interface with its own language, rather than in the language of the user, will limit the extent to which users, especially new users, can apply existing mental models of the task. Also, interfaces that use the user's terminology are more likely to increase and improve task match.

• Guide new users through normal and reasonable patterns of usage. Many novice users are building a mental model of the system that they are using as they are using it. The model that they build will be based solely on their experiences with the interface. The presentation of the interface and the order of presentation are critical factors in the eventual model that novices build.

• Support the mental model of experts. Experts often come to an interface with a thorough mental model of the interface and the underlying functionality. They can often take shortcuts and do not need the extra guidance that novices do.

• Use words and objects in the same way (consistently) throughout the interface. Thus, words need only be represented once in the user's mental model, and the designer can rely on the user's prior experience with language.

• Provide feedback. Interaction feedback can greatly influence a user's mental model. For example, suppose that every time a user types an incorrect input, the system feedback message is "Incorrect." Such a marginal feedback message leaves it to the user to identify how the input was incorrect. If the user adopts a strategy to generate "Correct" feedback messages, that strategy could easily be based on an incorrect understanding of why the original input was incorrect.

• Support wayfinding. Development of a mental model for a system often involves the development of a model of the spatial features of the interface, including landmarks, routes through different screens, and an overarching view. Clear landmarks and directions enhance *wayfinding* (spatial navigation) through the system. Many interfaces facilitate the use of individual screens but still allow users to get lost because the user was unable to form a model of the routes in the interface or an overarching view. (See Dillon, McKnight, and Richardson (1990) for a discussion of spatial navigation in user interfaces.) In the real world, Kaplan and Kaplan (1982) hypothesize that people prefer environments in which they can both apply existing mental models and enhance them. Such environments "make sense" and "are engaging." To make sense, the person should be able to identify key informational elements from the environment and understand them as a coherent whole. To be engaging, the environment must be sufficiently interesting and have hidden information to motivate the person to explore further. While few specific studies in HCI have applied the Kaplan and Kaplan model to user interfaces, we believe their model to have intriguing possibilities.

### 7.5.2 Guideline 2: Use Meaningful Analogies and Metaphors

How do people build mental models in new situations? Gentner and Gentner (1983) suggest that people may transfer some of what they know about another phenomenon to build a model in a new situation. In other words, we transfer and apply what we know from one setting to another one that seems to be similar. Humans tend to apply analogies to situations, whether the analogy is appropriate or not. How many times have you said to yourself, "This situation is like X, so I will respond like I did before"? This strategy can be effective so long as the analogy is meaningful in the new situation. If the analogy is misleading, then using it to guide actions and expectations can be disastrous. Use of meaningful analogies and metaphors in interface design can greatly enhance ease of learning and ease of use, as well as other usability variables.

*A note on language:* A *simile* uses "like" or "as" when comparing two things. An example is "as happy as a hog in a mud hole" to indicate bliss. A *metaphor* is an indirect comparison between two things. An example is "He was a bear of a man" to indicate an individual who was large, strong, and fierce. An *analogy* is similar to a metaphor in that it draws similarities between things that are different. In terms of user interface design, we use metaphor and analogy synonymously.

We are all familiar with the idea of metaphors in interfaces. After all, you probably spend a number of hours each day using a "desktop" metaphor. This metaphor uses familiar-looking "objects" like file folders and trash cans in place of directories and a command for delete. The idea is that anyone who has worked at a real desk should be able to apply their knowledge of how the real desktop works to the metaphorical desktop that they see on their computer screens. A real file folder holds files until they are thrown away. The same thing happens on the metaphorical desktop. The trick for the designer is to select meaningful analogies and metaphors. Wozny (1989) has suggested that as people gain more knowledge about computing systems, they will be able to apply analogies from one system to a new system.

Many designers of user interfaces have recognized that metaphors and analogies can be incorporated into an interface to improve the interface. For example, Apple Computer, Inc. (1992, 4) suggests:

> You can take advantage of people's knowledge of the world around them by using metaphors to convey concepts and features of your applications.

Some authors have offered ideas to improve the use of metaphors. The *Macintosh Human Interface Guidelines* (Apple Computer 1992) suggests the use of concrete and familiar ideas for metaphors. The document further suggests that it is important to achieve a balance between the implications of the metaphor's use and the ability of the software to support the interpretation of the metaphor.

Misleading analogies can be particularly problematic for novice users because novices may rely on the inferences from the analogy to guide their behavior. For example, users may carry the analogy farther than was intended in the interface. Users may not be aware of any restrictions not implied by the analogy. Halasz and Moran (1982) make the case that conceptual models or external representations of an interface that use abstraction rather than analogy may actually be useful in some circumstances.

Analogies can be used to familiarize users with an interface, or they can be used to help users extend their understanding of the interface. For example, the desktop metaphor uses familiar objects, such as a trash can and file folders, to help new users understand the operation of the interface. Metaphors that are not so familiar, but suggest new ways of using the interface, can be useful to those who already have some mastery of the interface (cf. Heckel and Clanton 1991). In summary, when choosing a metaphor, select one that is clearly related to the task and meaningful to the user.

### 7.5.3  Guideline 3: Avoid Anthropomorphism

The word *anthropomorphism* means "to assign human characteristics to an inanimate or nonhuman entity," and for our purposes, it is a special kind of analogy or metaphor. If you build an anthropomorphic interface, a reasonable interpretation by the user may be that the interface is saying, "I am an intelligent being. I am like you." The user may then expect the interface to respond in a number of human ways that are not supported. In general, anthropomorphism is confusing in an interface and should not be used (cf. Hix and Hartson, 1993).

### 7.5.4  Guideline 4: Minimize Modal Interactions

*Modality* is defined as a set of user actions that has a different outcome in one context than in another. For example, suppose that I am in screen 1. I triple click my mouse, and my screen background turns yellow. However, in screen 2 I triple click my mouse, and all files with modification dates greater than one month ago are deleted. These actions are modal, because the outcome is determined by the context in which they are performed (i.e., whether I am in screen 1 or screen 2).

Is modality ever acceptable? It would seem that under some circumstances it is nearly unavoidable. The biggest problem that modes introduce is that users may be unsure of where they are or how they got to where they are. In Chapter 1 we learned that an interface can fail if it does not convey information about the *mapping* of interface action to outcome. Modal interactions make it much more difficult for users to predict what the mapping is from the interface action to the outcome. Novices would seem to be particularly likely to become lost due to modes, but experts can be victimized also. For example, many text editors and word processors have both a text-insert mode and a text-replace mode. While I (JAB) was working on this manuscript, I somehow got into text-replace mode and had to use the help feature to return to text-insert mode. As you can see, modes can be confusing, especially if you can change modes inadvertently (cf. Hix and Hartson 1993).

### 7.5.5  Guideline 5: Reduce the Cognitive Workload of the User

When users develop mental models of systems, the characteristics of the interface can influence their *cognitive* (mental) *workload* in constructing the model. For example, expecting users to remember and reproduce apparently arbitrary strings of actions may result in a heavy cognitive workload. You can follow a number of strategies that should help to reduce the user's cognitive workload. Following these strategies should enhance ease of use and user satisfaction.

- Present options clearly and explicitly and avoid presentations that include multiple, reasonable interpretations. Surprisingly, a lengthy English language description of a user action may be ambiguous if it is nonspecific or uses elaborate and descriptive language.

- Avoid interface elements that attract the user's attention away from the meaningful elements. It is possible to mask the meaning or importance of interface elements by drawing the user's attention to superfluous interface elements. For example, humans are attracted to movement such as blinking and to incongruities such as mixed fonts. Is this the part of the interface that you wish users to be attracted to? If not, avoid such devices in your interface.

- Reduce strain on the user's working memory (more in Chapter 14 on this). As much as possible, allow users to use *semantic knowledge* (knowledge about the task), rather than the *syntactic knowledge* of the interface.

- Reduce strain on the user's working memory. Utilize *recognition* strategies as opposed to *recall* strategies. An example is the use of visual menus in which all options are displayed so that the user can identify the proper input; this strategy permits recognition. When users see a flashing prompt with no cues as to the proper input, the interaction relies on the user to remember the correct response; this would be an example of recall. With menus, the user recognizes the meanings (semantics) of the commands and does not have to remember the order of the different parts of the command (syntax).

- Reduce strain on the user's working memory. Utilize clear, closed, and—when possible— short sequences of user actions to accomplish a task. In this way, users will need to remember fewer specifics in their own memories.

- Reduce the number of cognitive transformations or translations from the interface to the user's mental model. Suppose that the user receives the following message from the interface:

    0001032 × The Red Planet is rising

Maybe the meaning of the message is that the file "The Red Planet" is about to be processed at 10:32 am. In any case, the burden for translating the meaning of the interface into something that the user can understand lies with the user. It should be the interface's responsibility to present messages that the user will easily understand.

Hix and Hartson (1993) have suggested that good interfaces support *cognitive directness*. This means that interfaces with minimal user transformations are more cognitively direct than those with lots of transformations. Making your interface cognitively direct can enhance the user's efficiency and satisfaction. This raises a number of considerations. An interface that seems direct to an expert may still be indirect to a novice user. An interface built around a metaphor may be cognitively indirect if the metaphor is inappropriate for the task and the user.

- Reduce the number of cognitive transformations or translations from the interface to the user's mental model by enforcing good task match between the interface and the user's task set.

- Recognize that the user's cognitive workload may be greatly influenced by his or her interactive modality. For example, while we discuss the design of menus as visual presentations, it is also possible to present audio menus. The demands to remember where one is in a menu hierarchy may be much different when users can see the menu hierarchy than when they hear it and have to remember it.

### 7.5.6 Guideline 6: Let the User Be in Charge

To the extent possible, users should be in control of their own experiences. This does not mean that they should necessarily have to ask for CPU scheduling, but when possible they should be able to make choices. Giving the user access to the maximum number of actions allows the user to explore the interaction and to build a more complete mental model. Expert users can use the system in ways that match their understanding and take advantage of shortcuts. Putting the user in control increases the likelihood of good task match and should add to user satisfaction. However, it is critical that the interface protect the user by providing warnings and reversible actions. The following are some strategies that should enhance the user's feeling of control:

- Allow users to accomplish tasks directly. While your interface should support exploration, where appropriate, it is also important to provide direct paths to the users' goals.
- Allow users to try again. If users make an error or take an unintended action, they should be able to go back and to try again.
- Provide appropriate feedback to users. You may recall from our discussion of everyday objects in Chapter 1 that users need feedback from their use of everyday interfaces. The same is true with software interfaces. The interface should provide immediate feedback that an action has been selected, is being performed, and is completed.

Feedback may be visual or verbal. For example, on a number of popular personal computer window systems, the feedback for disk copy is a dialog box with a visible gauge showing what portion of the disk has been copied. The gauge usually disappears on completion. These systems also use a clock or another shape with a moving dial to indicate that an operation is in progress.

System messages are an important source of verbal feedback. System messages can be system centered (stated in terms of system tasks) or user centered (stated in terms of user tasks), threatening or nonthreatening, nonsensical or meaningful. As an example, most of us would find the following message:

`>> File X has not been copied to File Y due to insufficient memory`

more useful than,

`>> stack overflow`

or even worse,

Hix and Hartson (1993) note that users need *articulatory feedback* or feedback to their motor inputs. For example, if a user clicks on an interface object, that object should somehow reflect that it has been clicked on. Hix and Hartson further note that users also need *semantic feedback,* which is feedback on the meaning of the user input. For example, if a user selects a menu option, he or she should see the result of that option in his or her environment.

- Be careful not to provide too much feedback, especially feedback requiring user input. A system that requires the user to click multiple buttons to confirm an action is annoying and can lead to user error.

- Encourage the user's perception that his or her interaction experience is stable. You might accomplish this by including stable reference points across changing displays. For example, consistent graphic elements, such as a menu bar or a list of all menu options (even what is not available), can increase the user's perception of stability. Another strategy to suggest stability is to provide defaults for interaction elements that are reasonable and sensible in relation to the task.

### 7.5.7 Conclusions About General Guidelines

Based on your experience, you probably think that interaction styles are very different from each other, and in many ways they are. However, certain common guidelines or "rules of thumb" seem to apply to just about all interaction styles. Remember that what the guidelines really mean may be different for different interaction styles. As you review the general guidelines presented, you may think that they appear to be just common sense. However, if guidelines were *just* common sense, why are they not followed more often?

Our guidelines are, at best, suggestions of strategies that should improve your designs. Adding a measurement strategy to determine if the guideline has been met will greatly increase your confidence in the usability of your design.

Remember that guidelines are often in conflict and may be applied differently to different applications. The user interface designer may have to make trade-offs in design decisions with respect to a set of guidelines being used in the interface development.

## 7.6 Beyond Guidelines: Relating Situational Variables to Interaction Design Decisions

As we come to the end of our list of general guidelines, once again we need to think about the relationship of the design situation to our design decisions. Eason's (1984) model of usability tells us that the usability outcome of any design is going to be determined by characteristics of the design (system characteristics) and characteristics of the situation in which we are working. Eason separates these situational characteristics into characteristics of the task and of the user, and in our usability model we have tried to expand and elaborate on this set of variables. As we define the problem (Chapters 5 and 6), we try to document these situational characteristics.

What is the relationship between design and these situational characteristics? For the most part, you get to do the creative work of design. Out of your design, you hope to build something that satisfies the user's usability goals for ease of use, ease of learning, and task match. Your design and its eventual success are for the most part constrained by the situational variables. Typically, the usability engineer cannot change the situational variables. You will need to take the task and user characteristics into account when you select and design the details of your interaction.

Our final set of heuristics for design is somewhat beyond guidelines because they attempt to provide some pointers in context. You will notice that these heuristics often overlap with the more general guidelines. By placing them in context, we hope to draw your attention to situations in which they are most important.

### 7.6.1 Relating Task Characteristics to Interaction Design Decisions

Our usability model reminds us that tasks have at least three critical characteristics relative to usability: frequency, rigidness, and situational constraints. Some guidelines for considering task characteristics in design are described in the following subsections.

### Frequently Performed Tasks

Frequently performed tasks are likely to be very familiar to the user. Some examples of user tasks that might be frequently performed include "Save a document" in a word processor or "Refresh a drawing" in a drawing program.

- Consider streamlined sequences of inputs/user actions.
- Consider minimizing the number of keystrokes.

### Infrequently Performed Tasks

Infrequently performed tasks are not as likely to be familiar to users. Even when users are experts in the task, they may have problems remembering the details of infrequently performed tasks.

- Provide cuing as to the sequence of possible reasonable user actions.

### Rigid Tasks

In rigid tasks, the sequence of inputs/user actions is usually known in advance.

- Limit user errors if the user cannot depart from the known sequence of inputs.

### Nonrigid Tasks

An example of a nonrigid task might be drawing a picture with a drawing program. Many sequences through this task are possible. For example, one artist might draw shapes first and then add color, print, rotate, and so on. Another artist might select different subtasks or impose a different order on the subtasks. An infinite number of user inputs or actions are possible.

- Your interaction should allow the user to input a variety of values or to use tools in a variety of sequences.
- Some tasks, such as data entry, may have a potentially infinite number of user inputs. However, user errors may be limited if the interface provides cueing about the format(s) expected or provides an explicit list of values that have already been accepted.

### Situational Constraints

In Chapter 3, we mentioned that tasks are sometimes shaped and constrained by the situation. For example, a task may be collaborative by nature. Decisions about interaction design for this situation should facilitate collaboration. While it is difficult to identify guidelines relative to situational constraints, it is useful to remember to keep situational constraints in mind during design.

- Your interaction should support the situational constraints.

### 7.6.2 Relating User Characteristics to Interaction Design Decisions

Eason (1984) reminds us that users have at least three critical characteristics relative to usability: knowledge, motivation, and discretion. In Chapter 3, our usability model limits this list to two critical characteristics: expertise and motivation. Many studies of usability suggest that user expertise is the more critical of the two. Some guidelines for different groups of users are described next.

### Novice Users

Novice users have minimal knowledge and understanding of the task and are typically unfamiliar with the user interface. They have incomplete mental models of the task and the interface. Within the user interface, feedback in response to their actions will help novice users build a more complete mental model of the interaction and the task. Because novices have incomplete understanding of the interface, it is likely that they will make errors, unless their set of action choices is limited. For example, providing the set of valid inputs, throughout the interaction, may help reduce errors. Also, errors can be reduced if sequences of user actions are kept short and clearly related to the task at hand.

### Occasional Users

Occasional users are those who have broad knowledge of the task but do not have or do not remember the operational details of the interaction. It is useful if occasional users can apply their knowledge of the task in meaningful ways to the interaction without being required to remember obscure operational details of the interaction. As for novices, feedback in response to their actions will help occasional users build a more complete mental model of the interaction.

### Expert Users

Expert users have a high level of expertise about the task and the interaction. In general, they know how to accomplish the task at hand and how to accomplish it within the interaction. Successful interactions for experts support the action sequences that their mental models suggest.

## Conclusions

Once the problem that you are to solve has been specified, your next job is to develop a design. The design process involves both the design of the interaction and the design of the interface. Both of these design activities possess high-level and low-level aspects.

You can choose from many interaction styles. Regardless of your choice, several guidelines may apply. As you peruse the guidelines, you will note that they center on the following themes:

- Facilitation and use of mental models.
- Intelligent consumption of user's cognitive resources.
- Support for task match.
- Facilitation of navigation and user control.

As we select interaction styles for a particular project, the guidelines will form the basis for our design rationale.

## Exercises

1. Define the following terms: *interaction design, interface design, system-centered design, user-centered design, congruency, anthropomorphism, cognitive directness, metaphor, modality, semantic knowledge, syntactic knowledge, windowed interaction, menu-based interaction, form fill-in interaction, direct manipulation interaction, command-line interaction, natural language interaction, haptic interaction, multimedia interaction,* and *multimodal interaction.*

2. Most people have experience with a library card catalog. Think of an interface application in which a card catalog would be a strong, appropriate metaphor for first-time users.

3. In Chapter 1, we learned about the importance of a person's mental model of an interface. In light of the guidelines that were discussed in this chapter, list and describe three ways to facilitate the development of a usable mental model.

4. For each of the following task situations and interfaces, identify the likely guideline or guideline that has been violated.

a. A user is using a word processor and wishes to print the current document. They must select "print" from the list of choices in the following menu:

```
Enter Choice: ____

SF (save file)
LPDS (load printer driver and spool)
RFD (remove file and delete)
ROS (return to operating system)
```

b. A user sees the following button choices in a print interaction:

```
OK          Cancel
```

Then the user sees the following button choices in an interaction to insert clip art:

```
Cancel          OK
```

5. For the following interaction, the user has selected "OK." How do you know that? What kind of feedback does this demonstrate (articulatory or semantic) and why? What would you need to do to add the other kind of feedback?

```
OK          Cancel
```

# 8

# Interaction Styles and How They Relate to Project Situations

## Motivation

In Chapter 7, we learned that user interface design involves the design of both the overall interaction and the design of individual interactions. In this chapter we discuss the characteristics and design decisions of the different interaction styles. At the end of this chapter you should be able to:

- Describe the differences among the various interaction styles.
- Select an interaction style based on the circumstances and the values of the different situational variables.
- Apply the guidelines for developing individual interactions within a given interaction style.

This is a long chapter with a lot of information. To help you better navigate the chapter, we have used a uniform presentation for each interaction style, emphasizing, where possible:

- Definition of the interaction style.
- Advantages and disadvantages of the interaction style.
- Pertinent design decisions.
- Variations.
- Selection and manipulation issues.
- Guidelines for the design of individual interactions.

## 8.1 Introduction

In Chapter 7, we learned that our first design task is the design of interaction. Colloquially this means that we need to design an overall look and feel for our user interface. There are many choices of interaction style and many ways to combine them. Once you have selected an interaction style or styles, your work is not done. Your next task will be to design the individual interactions to support the tasks that you identified in your task analysis.

In this chapter we discuss in detail the interaction styles that were introduced in Chapter 7. For each of these interaction styles, we discuss the circumstances and values of the situational variables of our usability model for which the style would be most appropriate.

## 8.2 Getting Started

How do you know that one interaction style would be more appropriate than another? This is a tough question. The Eason (1984) model of usability and our hybrid model give us a framework for that choice. These models suggest that it is the interaction of the user characteristics, task characteristics, and system (user interface) characteristics that drive usability. As usability engineers, we design and build the user interface characteristics, but most likely the task and user characteristics are given to us. The task and user characteristics define the circumstances or situations in which our user interface will reside. Our choice of interaction style should be based in part on the ability of the interaction style to support the situation. We can use the guidelines from Chapter 7 to help us narrow the match between an interaction style and the situation, as well as to help us improve our chances to achieve such usability outcomes as ease of learning, ease of use, and task match.

Once we have selected an interaction style, plenty of work remains ahead. Within our chosen interaction style, we still must design the overall look and feel of all the screens and interactions. Then we return to the tasks that we have identified in our task analysis. For each of the tasks we have identified, we must be sure that an interaction or interactions is available. Both design problems (overall look and feel and individual interactions) require design decisions. For each of the interaction styles that we discuss, we show some of the design options and guidelines that you can apply as you make design decisions.

We will continue to group the interaction styles as follows:

*Styles that are visual,* that is, those in which the user interacts by manipulating visual or graphical objects. In these styles, the user provides input via a visual or graphical object in the interface. Changes in visual objects provide output information to the user.

*Styles that are verbal* in which the user interacts through *conversation* using verbal symbols (words or wordlike symbols). In these styles of interaction, both inputs and outputs are in verbal or textual forms.

*Styles where the user interacts through nonvisual manipulations.* In these interactions, the user inputs may be from a variety of modalities, such as touch, and/or they may permit a combination of inputs, such as pen and speech, in parallel. Outputs may be in combinations of many formats, often in parallel.

## 8.3 Manipulation of Visual Elements Interaction Styles

A number of interaction styles are primarily visual and manipulable in some way. We discuss menus, windowed interactions, forms, virtual reality, video games, and graphical direct manipulation.

### 8.3.1 Menus or Menu-Based Interactions

We are all familiar with menus in restaurants and probably in software. A menu is simply a list of choices for the user. In restaurants, these choices are usually for food. In software, these choices are a list of things that the user can do, but they also could be choices of specific entities or objects. A menu may also include an identifier (title), help, or navigational information. The choices may be expressed as text, symbols, graphical images, or shortcuts.

You are probably familiar with the appearance and behavior of menus in Apple Macintosh and Microsoft Windows applications. You may be surprised to see that the designer potentially can choose from many other styles of menus.

### Advantages and Disadvantages of Menus

Menus appear to have advantages for novice users. First, menus and navigation via menus can tightly structure tasks and show clear paths to accomplish tasks. The traversal of menus and the specific choices of menu options can help the novice user build a user's mental model of the task. So one potential advantage of menus is that they can facilitate the development of user models (Chapter 7, Guideline 1).

Another advantage of menus, especially for novices, is that users do not have to remember all of their options; the options are explicitly presented to them. We can say that using a menu is a *recognition* task because the user is required to recognize the correct choice out of a set of explicitly presented alternatives. In usability engineering, we distinguish between *recognition* tasks and *recall* tasks. In a recall task, the user is asked to remember or recall their options. Numerous behavioral studies have indicated that recognition tasks are generally easier than recall tasks. You probably are aware of this already. In general, which kind of test do you find easier, assuming the test contains no trick questions?

Multiple-choice test (recognition)

Fill-in-the-blank test (recall)

You probably said that the multiple-choice test format is easier because all the choices for the answers are explicitly presented. With this format, you are only required to choose the best answer. With a fill-in-the-blank test, you need to select the right answer, *and* to recall it. Use of recognition, instead of recall, is one way to reduce the user's mental workload (Chapter 7, Guideline 5).

A final advantage of menus is that many user tasks involve a series of choices among alternatives. If the series of menu choices mimics the structure of the task, then menus can be constructed to preserve good task match to the user's task (Chapter 3, our usability model).

Well-built menus that provide shortcuts can be useful for experts. However, some menus can seem cumbersome to experts. Because experts understand the task very well, sometimes they recall the choices that they wish to make at a faster rate than the system can display and refresh a menu. In this situation, experts might perceive the menus to be slow, and their user satisfaction may be diminished. Also, experts generally have a rich mental model of the task at hand and may have a very clear sense of how to accomplish the task. If the menu structure does not support the same sequence of actions that the expert has in mind, the expert will have to "translate" the action sequence from his or her mental model to the action sequence in the interaction. This potentially increases the cognitive workload for the expert.

Menus alone are not well suited to very nonrigid tasks. Imagine that you are writing a poem. It would be awkward to write if you had to go through nothing but a series of menus to get the letters and would likely interfere with your "creative flow." Menus are best suited for tasks in which the steps and likely input values and combinations are predictable and rigid. While workable for nonrigid tasks, like poetry writing, a menu interaction may not be a good match.

Finally, menus may be useful for tasks that have a situational requirement for security or minimal input errors. Because the user is selecting from a limited set of choices in the menu, the user is less likely to make an input error than when he or she must enter the value or command by typing.

Table 8.1 summarizes some of the situational variables and guidelines that suggest the use of menus.

Table 8.1   Summary of Situations that May Call for Menus.

| User Characteristics | Task Characteristics | User Interface Variables Supported | Guideline Supported | Guideline Reference |
|---|---|---|---|---|
| User knowledge level—Novice | Rigid | Ease of learning | Facilitate the development and use of workable mental models | Guideline 1, Chapter 7. Facilitate the development and use of workable mental models. |
| | | | | Our model of usability. Because the user does not have to memorize user inputs, ease of learning should be enhanced. |
| User knowledge level—Novice | Rigid | Ease of learning | Reduce the cognitive (mental) workload of the user | Guideline 5, Chapter 7. Reduce the cognitive (mental) workload of the user. |
| | | | | Our model of usability. Because the user does not have to memorize user inputs, ease of learning should be enhanced. |
| User knowledge level—Occasional | Rigid | Ease of relearning | Reduce the cognitive (mental) workload of the user | Guideline 5, Chapter 7. Reduce the cognitive (mental) workload of the user. |

*(continued)*

Table 8.1   Summary of Situations that May Call for Menus. (*continued*)

| User Characteristics | Task Characteristics | User Interface Variables Supported | Guideline Supported | Guideline Reference |
|---|---|---|---|---|
| | | | | Our model of usability. The user once knew how to use the interaction. The values in the menus can cue the occasional user to the right choices in user inputs, thus enhancing ease of relearning. |
| User knowledge level—Novice | Rigid | Task match between the user interface and the user's tasks | Good task match | Our model of usability. Because the rigid task structure is reflected in the rigidity of the menu structure, the user interaction should have good task match. Good task match can contribute to high usability. |
| User knowledge level—Occasional, Expert | Infrequently performed | Ease of use Ease of relearning | Reduce the cognitive (mental) workload of the user | Guideline 5, Chapter 7. Reduce the cognitive (mental) workload of the user. |
| | | | | Because the task is done infrequently, the user probably understands the task at a high level but may not remember the low-level details. Menus can help to provide cues for these details, thus enhancing ease of relearning and ease of use. |

## Design Decisions for Menus

Many decisions must be made when designing menus for a software system. These decisions can be categorized as follows:

- Choice of menu architecture.
- Choice of specific content and layout of menu options.
- Choice of organization of the menu options, i.e., the content and structure of categories (what to group together).
- Choice of navigational structure of menus. Choices are single menus, linear navigation, tree navigation, or network (cyclic) (Shneiderman 1992).

- Choice of physical access to menus. Choice of style for selection (enter a number, point, use function keys). How does the user access the menu from the screen?
- Choice of type of menu (e.g., pull-down, pop-up, embedded [hypertext], pie).
- Strategies to provide support for experts.

**Menu Architecture**   When we think of menus, especially for complex tasks, we envision visiting a number of menus and choosing several options. The way you distribute these options across some number of menus is called the design of the *menu architecture*. The main design question here is how many items to put into one menu versus how many menus to have overall. Should you have many short menus or fewer long menus? For example, if you have 100 items to distribute in your menu structure, should you have one long menu of 100 items, two shorter menus of 50 items each, or 50 menus with two items each?

This issue is known as the *depth/breadth trade-off* (Miller 1981). Shneiderman (1992) has characterized this decision as a choice between breadth (number of items within a single level of the menu hierarchy) and depth (number of levels in the menu hierarchy). The terminology is slightly different from the question that we asked in the previous paragraph (how many menus, how many items per menu). In a typical GUI, the menu bar is the first level of the menu hierarchy. To increase the breadth of the menu structure would require putting more items in the menu bar (i.e., have more menus in the menu bar). In each of the pull-down menus, the breadth is the number of items in the menu. To get a sense of the depth of the menu hierarchy, you would have to pull down a menu and then see if any cascading menus are attached to it. Suppose that as I typed this paragraph, I examined the menu structure in my word processor. I notice that the *Insert Text* menu has a selection path of *Insert Letter Elements >> Insert Date Line >> Insert Today's Date,* so that the depth is four.

A number of studies have considered the issue of breadth versus depth. How does the designer choose? Some research suggests that limiting depth in favor of increasing breadth seems to lead to improved performance, although the size of the effect may taper as the breadth of the menu grows (Kiger 1984; Landauer and Nachbar 1985). This is a good rule of thumb:

When possible, limit the depth of menu structures. If a menu is so long that it requires scrolling or overruns the space available, it is definitely too long.

How does this guideline help us decide how to distribute the 100 items in a menu structure? It suggests that one menu with all 100 items is probably not the best design decision and that two menus containing 50 items each might be better. However, other issues must be considered when designing a menu structure.

Sometimes the designer will have a conflict between this rule and the general notion of good task match. For example, if the semantic structure of the menu choices suggests that the number of items per menu category is long, the designer will need to decide how to present the choices. Especially if the number of choices is greater than what can physically fit into a single menu, the designer will need to choose whether to artificially layer the choices or to have a menu that extends across more than one presentation. Consider this situation: I am building a menu structure for the Statistical Package for HCI Researchers. I decide to list my statistical tests as menu choices. Perhaps I am thinking that I will have one menu called "Tests" in which I group all the tests. This idea follows the semantics or meaning of the task, but it is likely that I will have many statistical tests in this single menu. So I might impose a categorization of the tests based on the test type and present the options in several menus. In this way, I can reduce the number of items in any one menu and still preserve some task match.

**Actual Content and Layout of Menus**     Menu titles, phrasing of items, and graphical layouts should strive for clarity and consistency (Teitelbaum and Granda 1983; Shneiderman 1992). Menu consistency can be improved by using a standard style of phrasing and a standard style of selection. For example, if some options are presented as verbs and selection is accomplished by typing the first letter of the option, this strategy should hold throughout. Titles should be placed in the same location on each menu, and similar indenting and justification should be used across menus.

In what order should the actual options in the menu be presented? When possible use a natural or temporal ordering. If it is not clear that such an order exists, other choices include an alphabetical or frequency-based ordering (cf. Shneiderman and Plaisant 2005).

**Semantic (Meaning-Based) Organization of Menu Options**     The semantic or meaning-based organization of a menu refers to the organization of different menu options. A good menu design is one in which the organization of menu options is meaningful in the context of the user's task. When you have a number of menu options, you will probably want to group them together to follow the user's task. The tough question is what to group together. What should the content and structure of categories be? Here are some suggestions:

- Groupings of items should not be arbitrary. When possible, the groups should reflect the groupings of the user's task. Liebelt, MacDonald, Stone, and Karat (1983) found that when users used meaning-based categories of menu options, their response times were much faster than when they used randomly or alphabetically categorized options.
- Categories should not overlap.
- Categories should not contain extraneous items.
- Following the organization of the task in menu organization is an excellent strategy to promote task match.

**Navigational Structure of Menus**     Most menu systems involve many menus. The designer will choose how the user will actually move through the menu structure. Shneiderman (1992) describes four ways that a user could navigate through a sequence of menus: The first way is navigating through a *single menu*. In this case, there would be no navigation through a menu structure. In the second case, the menu structure is linear. This means that the user sees the same sequence of menus no matter what choices he or she has made in a previous menu. An example of using a *linear menu* would be to collect responses to a series of survey questions. No matter how the user responds to an individual survey question, the next question would be the same.

Shneiderman's third menu navigation strategy is to design *tree-structured menus*. In a tree structure, the user traverses a hierarchical menu structure. At each menu, user decisions determine the next menu shown. To choose a different branch of the hierarchy, the user would need to go back to the top of the hierarchy and work down. If the user's task is very hierarchical, this structure will closely match the task structure. For example, suppose that you are constructing a menu structure for ordering items for a sporting goods store. Most of the goods that you will carry will fall into clear categories. Suppose you have the breakdown of your products that is illustrated in Figure 8.1.

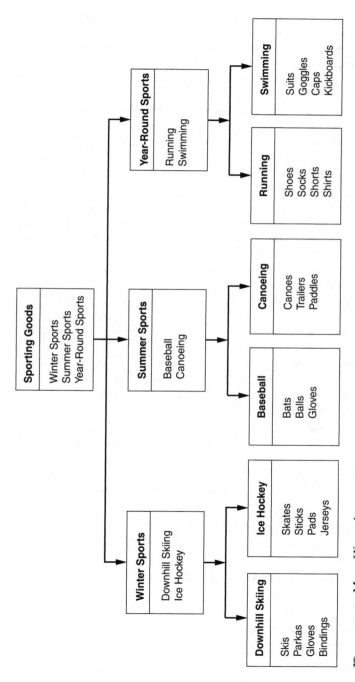

Figure 8.1   Menu Hierarchy.

You can probably imagine the hierarchical menu structure that you could construct for this sporting goods store. The menu structure would match the task structure, and the main menu would include the categories of winter sports, summer sports, and year-round sports. If you wanted to order kickboards, you would go through the logical hierarchy of menus of *Sporting Goods >> Year Round Sports >> Swimming >> Kickboards*. If you had ordered your kickboard and wanted to order a canoe, it would make sense in the context of the task to go back to the main menu and traverse down another set of menu branches.

Sometimes tasks are not as hierarchical as in the sporting goods store example. In that case, the designer may opt for a *menu network structure*. In the menu network, the user traverses the network menu structure by going up and down a particular menu and between different menus. Many popular applications, such as word processors, organize menus in this manner. Word processors support a task (writing) that usually is not rigid, and the user can cancel a task without completing it.

As a designer, how should you choose the menu structure? Choose a linear sequence of menus if the choice of one menu is independent of the next menu displayed. Tree-structured menus tightly structure the task and are appropriate for tasks with some sense of categories. Network structures are the most open and probably allow users to make the most choices as to how to structure their own interactions. However, within a network menu structure, users have the most chance to get lost or to forget how they got to where they are in the structure.

Another navigational issue for designers is to determine where and how users activate menus. For the menus of most contemporary desktop interactions, menus are typically activated by making a selection from a menu bar at the top of the screen or application window. The menu bar stays visible throughout most applications, and the user can always start over or reorient from the menu bar. Another activation strategy for menu options is to use embedded or hypertext options, similar to those found on the World Wide Web. For embedded menus, the menu options are presented in the context of a larger portion of text. Here the organization and presentation of options may not be as clear as in the more familiar menus from a menu bar, nor will users necessarily know where they are in the menu structure.

Users are uncomfortable when they get lost in an interaction and even more uncomfortable without a home base. Under some conditions, navigation may be improved with mapping assistance (Billingsley 1982); this is not uniformly true, however (Stanton, Taylor, and Tweedie 1992). In some of our work, we found that when people navigated an amorphous hypertext with no clear home base, performance and satisfaction degraded. If no home base is provided, users will invent their own base (Mynatt et al. 1992).

The following guidelines are related to navigating menus:

- Choose a menu structure that most closely matches the structure of the user's task (cf. Shneiderman 1992).
- Facilitate wayfinding through the menu structure. Provide a clear home base for the menu structure.
- Provide cues to users as to where they are in the menu structure. Use meaningful names for menu titles. For lengthy or complex traversals, especially those involving hypertext menus, consider providing a "map" of the most recent visits.

**Physical Access to Menus**     Another design issue is physical access to the menu structure. You may select from a number of choices for input devices for access, including touchscreens, mice, light pens, joysticks, gestural interfaces, gaze detectors, function keys, and alphanumeric keyboards. Touchscreens, mice, light pens, joysticks, gestural interfaces, and gaze detectors are pointing devices that allow the user to select an option by pointing at it. In a gestural interface, the user's hand movements are captured and digitally encoded; a stylus for a digital tablet is an example of a gestural interface. In a gaze detection interface, the user's eye movements are collected and digitally encoded. With function keys or alphanumeric keyboards, the user will use a series of keystrokes to select the menu option. For example, the user may type the displayed menu options to make a choice.

A number of issues must be considered when making this design decision. If your interface is to be used by users with low-level typing skills, you might opt for a pointing device. If your target hardware environment is already configured, you will need to work within the confines of the environment. Disabled users may find gaze-detecting devices to be useful for menu selection (cf. Jacob 1990). Finally, the operating environment may come into play. As Shneiderman (1992) points out, touchscreens are the only input devices to have survived at Disney's EPCOT center. Presumably the touchscreens were more durable than other devices in the face of thousands of sticky fingers making contact with the device. The pointing nature of touchscreens no doubt also improved their usage for non–English-speaking users.

Guidelines for selecting an access mechanism in a menu interaction include the following:

• Choose an access mechanism that is both feasible to your application and matches the skills of your user population. For example, for users with limited motor skills, precise pointing may not be appropriate.

• If your access mechanism involves typing, choose a consistent location on the screen for the actual input and display of the typed option.

**Support for Expert Users**   While we most often think of menus for novice and occasional users, menus can also be effective for expert users. If your target user population includes both experts and novices, or if your task includes infrequently performed tasks, you may opt for menus. As we mentioned previously, expert users are most often frustrated by menus for two reasons: they perceive lengthy menu traversal to be unnecessarily slow, and they find that menu traversals artificially impose a solution strategy that differs from their mental models. Including menu hot keys or shortcuts may help reduce the menu traversal time for experts. However, especially in a highly structured menu traversal pattern, experts will be limited and will not be able to define their own solution sequences.

## Menu Types

A major decision in menu design is to choose the type of menu to offer. In this section we visit some different menu types.

**Keyboard-Based Menus**   In a keyboard-based menu, one of the simplest menu styles, the user is typically presented a list of word options and is asked to enter the text or symbol of his or her choice by using the keyboard. This type of menu interaction was prevalent in systems before GUIs became popular. Keyboard-based menus do not require graphical capabilities and can be supported in a text-based system with a keyboard for input. Keyboard-based menus may be a good style choice when the platform does not support pointing devices or the display of sophisticated visual information. A keyboard-based menu may also be a good option when the user has access to limited bandwidth or has a slow connection; in such cases, it may simply be more practical to display and make menu selections with simple text. This may be the case with a text-based terminal, a cell phone, or another device with a small screen.

You may be wondering why we would consider keyboard-based menus to be an interaction involving manipulation of visual objects. On the one hand, in a keyboard-based menu the user makes a selection by entering text rather than by moving the text around the interaction. On the other hand, the user has the visual cuing of the presented options.

**Pull-Down Menus**    Pull-down menus are some of the most familiar types of menus in use today. These are the menus that are anchored to a fixed menu bar. The user pulls down the menu by activating the title of the menu in the menu bar. The menu options are listed underneath the title.

Pull-down menus seem to have many advantages. First, this style should be familiar to most users, who may recognize pull-down menus and their operations across platforms or applications. Secondly, the menu bar provides a home base for users, reminding them of where they are in the menu structures. Finally, the menu bars of pull-down menus do not use a lot of screen space, but the information contained is readily available. A potential disadvantage of pull-down menus may be that the user will have to hold down and manipulate the pointing device to find the appropriate selection. This can be a problem for users with limited motor skills. Figure 8.2 shows a sample pull-down menu from a menu bar.

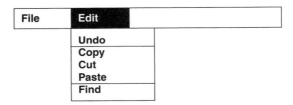

**Figure 8.2**    Example of a Pull-Down Menu.

The strategy of pull-down menus can be extended to provide context using *cascading menus*. In cascading menus, the user activates one menu from another menu. Figure 8.3 shows an example of a cascading menu. In this example, when the user chose the *Edit* menu and the menu item *Clear,* the attached menu with options *Picture* and *Text* was activated. The menu with the option *Clear* remains visible to provide context to the user.

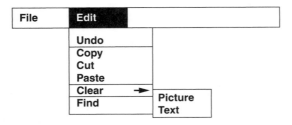

**Figure 8.3**    Example of a Cascading Menu.

Cascading menus have the advantage that the user can see how they arrived at their menu selection and where they can go. Cascading menus can be challenging from a motor-skill perspective. If a user is using a pointing device to select the menu option, the user has to select the first menu and its option and then the options from the cascaded menu. These multiple selections may involve more hand movements and more precision than would be necessary in a noncascading menu (Shneiderman 1992).

**Layered Context-Dependent (Lotus-Style) Menus**    *Layered context-dependent menus* present a restricted set of multiple layers from the menu structure. Typical implementations will present two levels of menu options. The option selected in the first level will determine the options that are displayed in the second level. The menu options may be presented horizontally or vertically.

An example of this kind of menu style is the menu style used in the version of Lotus 1-2-3 that ran on the DOS operating system. In fact, such menus are sometimes referred to as *Lotus-style* menus (cf. Powell 1990). Lotus 1-2-3 continues to be a popular integrated spreadsheet, database, and graphics package.

In Lotus-style menus, the selection on the top line determines the options that are presented in the second line. The user activates an item in the top menu and the corresponding choices under that choice appear in the second menu. The top line provides context for the second line, and the second line provides a glimpse ahead for the first line. In Lotus, these menus are navigated with arrow keys. In many regards, the menus from Lotus 1-2-3 resembled horizontal pull-down menus (cf. Grupe 1991). Figure 8.4a and 8.4b shows approximate examples of some Lotus-style menus.

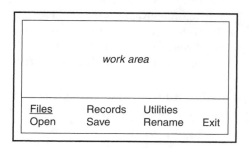

**Figure 8.4a**    Lotus-Style Menu Showing the Files Menu.

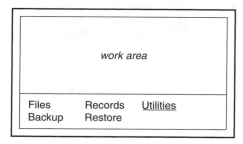

**Figure 8.4b**    Lotus-Style Menu Showing the Utilities Menu.

In Figure 8.4a, the Files choice is activated in the first level so the options in the second level are Open, Save, Rename and Exit. In Figure 8.4b, the Utilities choice is activated and the options are Backup and Restore. The menu could be navigated by using the arrow keys on the keyboard.

You might be thinking that layered context-dependent menus are historical. After all, they were popular more than fifteen years ago. However, we believe that for some applications the two-level menu style makes sense. If your menu tree is not particularly wide at any point, and you can fit all of the options for any choice in the second menu, you may wish to consider the layered style. This style of menu provides context and look-ahead without any additional keystrokes or mouse clicks. Users do not need to commit to a choice to see what would come next. For the audio catalog problem, we have had some students who successfully designed interfaces that used contextual menus. Those students presented the menus vertically and used a mouse to navigate. In their designs, the menu structures were at most two or three layers deep.

**Pop-Up Menus**    Pop-up menus appear when the user clicks somewhere in the interface, often in the work area, and a menu appears. Sometimes no clues indicate that the menu exists and the menu is not visible until it is activated. Which menu appears or whether a menu appears depends on the context in which the user is operating. Usually, pop-up menus require a multibutton mouse. For example, clicking on the right mouse button in many Microsoft Windows applications will activate a pop-up menu. Typical behavior has the pop-up menu appearing, the user selecting an option, and the menu disappearing.

Sometimes, pop-up windows can be anchored so that they do not disappear after the user selects an option. Typically an icon of a pushpin is used to indicate this capability. If the window is pinned, then the menu functions very much like a pull-down menu. The pushpin concept was used in some pop-up menus in windowed environments for UNIX, such as Sun's OpenWindows. A variation of the pushpin concept is used in Microsoft's Visual Studio to anchor or hide the Toolbox.

Figure 8.5 shows a stylized drawing of a pop-up menu that might appear in a text-editing application. The user has selected a section of text and then right-clicked on the selected text to reveal the *Edit* menu.

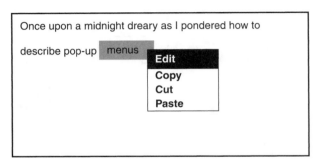

**Figure 8.5**    Example of a Pop-Up Menu in a Text Editor.

An advantage of pop-up menus is that the user does not have to go to the menu bar to activate the menu. Pop-up activation may be quicker than that of a pull-down menu. Also, pop-up menus are effective for data entry when the legal data items are from a closed set of responses. For example, many Web forms use a kind of pop-up menu to provide the name of a state for an address field.

Pop-up menus also have the advantage that they are located where the response is expected. They can be used as shortcut alternatives for experts, who can avoid the time necessary to access the menu bar. One of the potential challenges of pop-up menus is to make users aware of them. In addition, novice users may accidentally stumble over the pop-up menu with an inadvertent mouse click.

**Picture Menus**   Sometimes it makes sense to show your set of choices as pictures in *picture menus*. A typical picture menu displays a set of icons representing the menu choices. Toolbar menus have become a common application of picture menus. Picture menus are also useful when the user population may not be able to read menus easily when the options are specified as words. Such menus also may work well in software targeted for children or for the international market. Picture menus or palettes may have good task match for tasks involving graphical objects or in children's games.

A challenge to building picture menus is to make the meaning of the symbols clear. Successful use of this style of menu relies heavily on the user identifying the correct analogy between the symbol and the meaning. Some contemporary picture menus include textual (balloon) help to assist in this. If picture menus have more than one level, the challenges that we have seen with other menu styles hold, including enforcing task match, groupings of options, and navigation. Figure 8.6 shows an example of a picture menu.

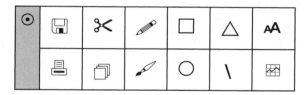

**Figure 8.6**   Example of a Picture Menu.

**Pie Menus**   Is there an alternative way of presenting the options that would speed up menu selection if you have only a small number of menu options? Callahan, Hopkins, Weiser, and Shneiderman (1988) have suggested that *pie menus* may offer just such an alternative. A pie menu is organized in a circle with the options laid out like pieces of pie. The user moves a mouse or pointing device to the menu choice and makes a selection. Callahan et al. indicate that when a menu has only a few choices, the selection of menu items may be faster than with more familiar menu styles. The options are close together and should reduce the time for mouse movement. Pie menus are best suited to menus with only a few choices. They are not well suited to menus with many choices or menu hierarchies with several levels. Also, pie menus may be unfamiliar to users, so their use may not be immediately obvious. Figure 8.7 shows a pie menu in the context of working in a text editor. The pie menu replaces the pop-up in Figure 8.5.

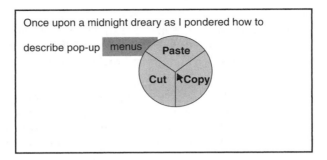

**Figure 8.7**    Example of a Pie Menu.

**Check Boxes (Multiple Selections)**    Menus can be used to allow users to make more than one selection at a time. Check box presentations are an effective way to present this idea. The sample shown in Figure 8.8 uses check boxes to let the user select zero, one, or many effects.

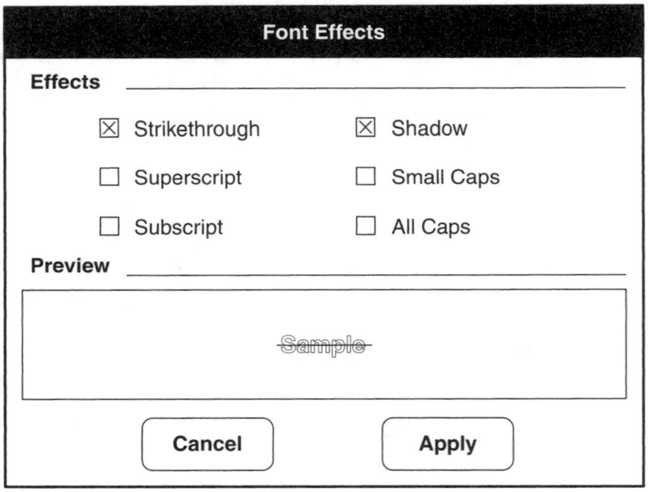

**Figure 8.8**    Example of a Check Box Menu.

### Selecting a Menu Type

With so many menu types to choose from, which should you choose? A number of factors should be taken into account. Consider the platform. Does it have a standard look and feel? What hardware constraints are present? Are there many options to include or just a few? What is the structure of the task, and can it be matched to a menu interaction? Will you have to accommodate any special characteristics of the user?

Remember that before making design choices concerning the types of menus for a project, the designer should check the customized and commercial style guidelines for the project. Whether the menu style is known or driven by a style guideline, the designer still must make numerous decisions.

### 8.3.2 Windowed Interactions

No doubt you are familiar with the windows that you see in many commercial visual interactions. You may be surprised to know that windows constitute a more general interaction style. You may be further surprised to find that not every interaction with visual elements is "windowed." By definition, windows simply divide the screen space into multiple displays, and a windowed interaction is one in which some part of the screen has a clear boundary or border. In windowed interactions, users can often interact with multiple windows at the same time, as if they had multiple output displays of different sizes. Windows may contain visual and/or textual outputs. Some windowed interactions follow a mixed model in which some windows contain text or command-line interactions and others present visual interactions. The specific appearance and behavior of windows are usually standardized across an application, while allowing the contents to vary.

Windowed interactions have two key advantages, regardless of user or task characteristics. First, multiple interactions can be separated and displayed essentially concurrently. Those interactions may be different representations of the same task. For example, if a user wants to access a database record, one window might contain the query and another window might contain a pictorial representation of the likely location of the record. Or if a task is situationally constrained by the necessity of collaboration, especially concurrent collaboration, windows provide a mechanism for each user to have a "space" to work in while simultaneously viewing the windows of their collaborators. If a user is working on a task that requires interactions with several different software systems, windows may permit that user to see the different software interactions concurrently. A user that is able to utilize multiple software systems at the same time likely has a high degree of expertise about both the task being worked on and about the interfaces and software being used. Whether supporting multiple views of the same software interaction or multiple views containing different software, Guideline 5 of Chapter 7, *Reduce the cognitive workload of the user,* must be supported. Users should not have to remember where information is and continually seek to find it.

A second advantage of windowed interactions is that windows are a visual mechanism to show groupings. If the designer has interaction elements that he or she wishes to group, a window can convey the grouping to the user.

Novice users may also benefit from windowed interactions. Compartmentalizing the task inside of a clear visual boundary may help the novice user recognize those parts of the interaction that apply only to what is in the window. For example, the designer may compartmentalize a keyboard-based menu inside of a window. This approach would support Guideline 5 of Chapter 7, *Reduce the cognitive workload of the user,* because users would have all relevant information in front of them in the window container even to the point of covering the entire screen with a single window. They would not necessarily have to search for the information that is relevant to their goals.

Displaying multiple windows can serve a number of purposes. A pop-up window may remind a user that a particular action is necessary, or it may confirm that an action has actually been requested. When a pop-up window appears, it may be modal, but because the primary window remains, the user still can see the primary context of the application window. A secondary window may even be used to help users keep track of information to use in the near but not immediate future. Also, different windows may set the mode of the interaction style in another window. For example, one subset of a command language may be used in one window and another subset in another window.

Table 8.2 summarizes some of the situational variables and guidelines that suggest the use of windowed interactions.

Table 8.2   Summary of Situations that May Call for Windowed Interactions.

| User Characteristics | Task Characteristics | User Interface Variables Supported | Guideline Supported | Guideline Reference |
|---|---|---|---|---|
| User knowledge level—Expert | Any task | Ease of use | User does not have to remember to keep reactivating different pieces of software to support the overall task. | Guideline 5, Chapter 7. Reduce the cognitive (mental) workload of the user. |
| | | | Reduce the cognitive (mental) workload of the user. | |
| User knowledge level—Novice | Any task | Task match between the user interaction and the user's tasks by establishing a clear boundary for each task within the interaction, especially if the window is just one of several visible interactions. | Good task match | Our model of usability. Good task match can contribute to high usability. |
| Any user | Situational constraint—must support collaboration. | Task match—each collaborator is given a bounded space in which to work. | Good task match | Our model of usability. Good task match can contribute to high usability. |

### Design Decisions for Windowed Interactions

A number of design issues are associated with the use of windows. As mentioned previously, typically the look and behavior of windows should be standardized across an application, so choosing those characteristics is important. For example, you may specify that all windows in an application have a title across the top, scroll bars on the right, and so on. You may also specify a default window size, determine if windows are movable across the display space, and determine a mechanism to alert the user as to which window is active. The designer will also have to decide what goes inside a particular window. Commercial user interfaces typically permit any application to reside in any window. This strategy is not the only option. It also is possible to build specialized windows for different applications. For example, if an interaction requires a reminder window, that window could have a default location on the screen.

Another issue to consider is the organization of multiple windows on a single screen. We once did a series of experiments about the usability of a hypertext encyclopedia about Sherlock Holmes. Our encyclopedia had a large number of information display types, including textual descriptions, story text, still pictures, and maps. Each of these, as well as navigational information, was housed in a separate window. We found that user accuracy and response time were improved on a question-and-answer task when the windows were tiled upon opening (i.e., laid out side by side as opposed to stacked on top of each other). We concluded that users could more readily see their options with the tiled presentation (Instone, Teasley, and Leventhal 1993). Bly and Rosenberg (1986) report that, especially for new users, overlapping windows may be more confusing than tiled windows because the users are manipulating the windows themselves, rather than operating inside the windows.

### 8.3.3 Form Fill-In Interactions

An interesting and useful interaction style is called *form fill-in*. Form fill-in interactions are modeled after paper forms in which the user fills information into a number of fields. Forms have the advantage that they can cue the user as to what inputs or data are required. However, unlike menus, the available options are much more open. Forms can be designed to provide guidance to the user about the expected content and format of the data to be entered. Because the fields for data are presented explicitly, the use of a form fill-in interaction is primarily a recognition task. Typically the only recall required is for the user to determine what data constitute legal values for a field and the actual data.

Forms are a familiar metaphor. As such, computerized form fill-in interactions have been available for a number of years, especially for office and data-entry applications. Today, the use of forms has become widespread, especially in e-commerce Web sites.

According to Mynatt (1990), form fill-in interactions are especially useful for occasional users who are generally familiar with the task at hand but need the cueing that the form can provide. For example, most of us only fill out federal income tax forms a few times per year. Computerized tax return packages use forms that are similar to the paper tax forms. Even with the infrequent use that most of us make of these forms, we can usually figure out how to fill in the forms. The cueing that is possible with forms, whether from the familiarity of the metaphor or from prior experience with the form, can help to reduce the user's cognitive workload (Guideline 5, Chapter 7).

Forms are useful and typically are associated with tasks with a lot of data entry. Data-entry tasks are often closed and tightly structured. In a data-entry task, the user has a number of data items to enter, but the template format of these data-entry items and the structure of the entry sequence are known in advance. A form can prompt the user as to the type and number of items to enter. What is not known in advance is the actual values of the data items. So, a form with set fields preserves the structure of the task quite well.

A form typically consists of a series of fields, identifiers, a title, and/or help text. A field consists of a space or box to fill in, an identifier to cue the input value, a text-entry prompt, help text, and information about the value to be entered into the field, such as its expected format. Many contemporary forms, especially those found on the Web, include embedded menus for fields with a limited set of options. In addition to these basic parts of a form, there may be controls to submit or to move on to another form. Typically, form filling is done on a screen with data entry via a keyboard and possibly a pointing device.

Table 8.3 summarizes some of the situational variables and guidelines that suggest the use of form fill-in interactions.

**Table 8.3**    Summary of Situations that May Call for Form Fill-In Interactions.

| User Characteristics | Task Characteristics | User Interface Variables Supported | Guideline Supported | Guideline Reference |
|---|---|---|---|---|
| User knowledge level—Occasional, Expert | Infrequent tasks.\n\nIf the task is performed infrequently, the form may prompt the user about appropriate responses and their formats. | Ease of learning | User does not have to relearn or remember the types of inputs or their sequence in the interface each time that they use it.\n\nReducing the cognitive (mental) workload of the user. | Guideline 5, Chapter 7. Reduce the cognitive (mental) workload of the user. |
| User knowledge level—Novice | The task resembles a paper form fill-in task. | Ease of learning | Users can apply their mental models of a paper form to the interaction.\n\nFacilitate the development and use of workable mental models. | Guideline 1, Chapter 7. Facilitate the development and use of workable mental models |
| User knowledge level—Novice, Occasional, Expert | Tasks where the type and the sequence of the responses are known and yet have open-ended values for the responses.\n\nData-entry tasks are well suited to form fill-in interactions. | Task match between the user interface and the user's tasks | Good task match | Our model of usability. Good task match can contribute to usability. |

## Design Decisions for Form Fill-In Interactions

The primary design decisions to consider for constructing effective form fill-in interactions include the following:

- Navigation across multiple forms.
- Distinguishing between data and commands.

- Organization, labeling, and contents of fields.
- Management of user feedback and handling errors.

**Navigation Across Multiple Forms**   Suppose that you have several forms. How do users navigate from one form to the next? Can they move forward and backward or only forward? How do they know where they are in the form structure? You can help users to navigate across multiple forms if you do the following:

- Provide navigational support if your interaction consists of multiple forms. It is usually a good idea to title or paginate your forms. For example, a notation at the bottom of the form that says "Form 1 of 10" tells users where they are and how many forms they will see (cf. Powell 1990).

How do users complete the form? It has become increasingly common to see a *Submit* button at the bottom of Web forms. We find that this practice can be confusing if not implemented properly. For example, when we want to reserve the university's computing laboratory for our usability engineering class, we go to the campus lab reservation form on the university's Web site. We fill out the required information and click on the *Submit* button. Guess what? Nothing seems to happen. The form is still displayed with our information in it. Was it submitted or not? What we usually do is click the *Submit* button a few more times and then reason that our request must have been submitted. In fact, it was submitted each time that the button was clicked. To avoid this problem:

- Provide meaningful feedback to your users when they submit their forms.

**Choosing Inputs for Data and Commands**   When using the keyboard for data entry, a number of the keys potentially could serve as data or as command keys. Two obvious examples are the enter (return) key and the tab key. As you may have noticed in filling out forms on the Web, the tab key is often used to move from field to field. If the user is typing a lengthy text entry into a field, the designer may opt to treat the return key as a data key. On the other hand, if the fields contain only short responses, then these keys may serve strictly as command (navigation) keys. What are the best rules for this decision?

- Make a choice and follow it throughout the form or forms. Do not make the use of these keys modal.

**Organization, Labeling, and Contents of Fields**   The organization and labeling of fields can give users a lot of clues as to what kind of information should go into various fields. Often users of forms are occasional users, so the groupings and labels of fields can provide memory cues.

Spacing of fields on a form can be important in several ways. First, the visual spacing of fields can provide clues about the groupings of fields. Second, when your form is likely to be more than one display long, you will want to use spacing to force related items onto the same display. Third, forms created with a lack of space will be difficult to read, and fields will be difficult to distinguish or find. Also, the spacing of fields can make your form visually appealing or horrifying. Consider the form in Figure 8.9, which shows some of what can go wrong when a form has poor spacing.

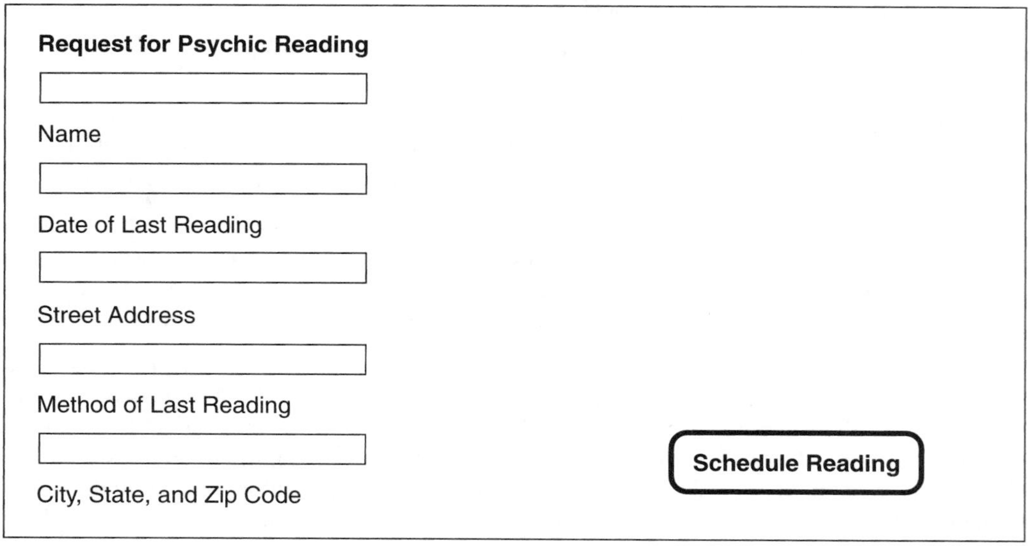

**Request for Psychic Reading**

[          ]

Name

[          ]

Date of Last Reading

[          ]

Street Address

[          ]

Method of Last Reading

[          ]                    ( **Schedule Reading** )

City, State, and Zip Code

Figure 8.9    Poorly Designed Form.

Several things are wrong with the spacing of this form. First, it looks funny because all the fields are pushed to the left. Also, the related fields are not grouped together. An alternative use of spacing can be seen in Figure 8.10.

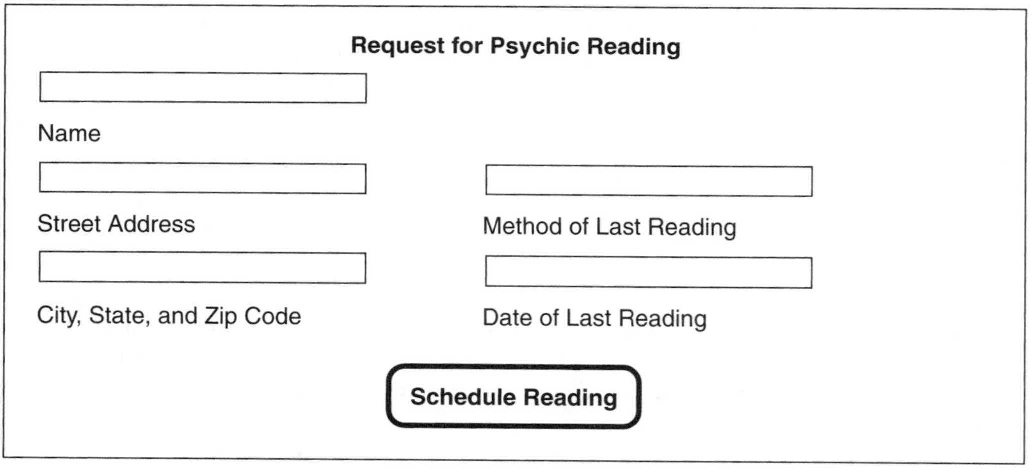

**Request for Psychic Reading**

[          ]

Name

[          ]                         [          ]

Street Address                      Method of Last Reading

[          ]                         [          ]

City, State, and Zip Code           Date of Last Reading

( **Schedule Reading** )

Figure 8.10    Improved Form Design.

In Figure 8.10, the fields are distributed across the space of the form. Related fields, such as those having to do with the user's last psychic reading are grouped together. The form in Figure 8.10 can still be improved. For example, the city, state, and zip code field could be reconfigured as three separate fields. This would reduce the possibility of input errors by the user.

Controlling the appearance of forms on the Web can be a true challenge. The default appearance of the form may vary with different browsers. Different browsers may place a different number of fields on the screen. Field contents that were designed to fit onto one screen may be off the screen in some browsers. The appearance of the fields themselves may be interpreted differently by different browsers. For example, some of our students designed a Web site for a local swim club. One of the features of the site was a form for parents to register their children to swim in particular meets. When parents had filled in the form, they submitted the form to the coach using the online submit feature. We had designed the form so that if a field was not completely filled out or if it was filled out erroneously, it was to be reshown with the bad fields marked in red. This worked fine in our development environment. Unfortunately, we found out later that some of the parents were using older versions of Web browsers. When the error information was displayed, the form was blank! The following are some rules of thumb for the visual design of forms:

- Use meaningful groupings of fields. The groupings should reflect the semantics of the task and thus yield enhanced task match (cf. Mayhew 1992).
- If your form will be displayed in a number of environments, design the appearance for the lowest common denominator.

**User Feedback and Management of Errors**   We have already seen some examples of ways to improve user feedback in forms. Providing feedback for user navigation is essential. User feedback can also aid in error correction. Consider again the swim meet registration form. Using colors to highlight errors can draw attention to user errors.

- Provide helpful error messages when unacceptable values are entered into a data field. A message such as "Invalid entry. Reenter value." is not a helpful message. A message such as "Social security numbers should have nine digits," is more helpful.

Forms also offer a number of opportunities for error prevention. Forms can be constructed so that the empty fields or the labels give indications of the type of data expected. For example, a field that has only a short list of allowed values can have an embedded menu. Figure 8.11 shows an example of an embedded menu, and Figure 8.12 shows the content of the embedded menu.

Figure 8.11   Form Field with Embedded Option Menu.

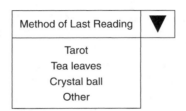

Figure 8.12   Form Field with Embedded Option Menu Expanded.

When possible, use underscores or other marks to indicate the number of characters required or the number of spaces available for the entry (cf. Shneiderman and Plaisant 2005). For example, many colleges and universities assign student ID numbers to students. Suppose that College AlphaBeta uses five-digit student ID numbers, preceded by "AB." Figure 8.13 illustrates a simple form for collecting that information.

```
┌─────────────────────────────────────────────┐
│                                             │
│           Welcome to College                │
│                AlphaBeta                    │
│          – Log in to Our Portal –           │
│                                             │
│                                             │
│           Enter your student ID:            │
│                                             │
│              AB _ _ _ _ _ _                 │
│                                             │
│       Enter your (optional) pledged gift:   │
│                                             │
│          $  [            .00 ]              │
│             ┌───────────────┐               │
│             │     Login     │               │
│             └───────────────┘               │
│                                             │
└─────────────────────────────────────────────┘
```

**Figure 8.13**   Form Field for a Fixed Number of Characters.

The field shown in Figure 8.13 contains clearly marked spaces for the five digits of the student ID. If the student ID for College AlphaBeta legally contains only numbers and the user types an ID with letters or special characters, the form might update to show which characters were filled in inadvertently. In addition, if a field is optional, as the gift field of Figure 8.13, it should be marked as such.

### 8.3.4 Graphical Direct Manipulation

Imagine riding a bicycle without handlebars, brake controls, or gearshifts on the handlebars; in place of the handlebars, you have only a keyboard for input. You could stop the bike by typing in a command like this:

*apply brake to front tire, do not apply brake to rear tire*

Are you thinking that stopping your bike would be difficult? What makes real bicycles easy to stop is the directness of their controls. In a real bicycle, each user interface on the handlebars is specially designed for controlling some function. Our theoretical computer bike has only one control: a keyboard. All the commands for controlling the bike come through this one interface and in some sense are translated by the user from actions into text strings.

Twenty or thirty years ago, software user interfaces were typically similar to the user interface for our hypothetical bicycle. Today, like the user interface for a bicycle, a large percentage of contemporary interactions have some degree of direct interaction or control. This style of interaction is called *direct manipulation* or *graphical direct manipulation,* in which the user sees a presentation of visual objects that usually represent the application's data items. The user manipulates those objects directly, via a pointing device, to achieve some action within the application.

Shneiderman has identified four defining features of direct manipulation interactions (Shneiderman 1992):

- Objects and actions are continuously represented.
- To manipulate objects and initiate actions, the user must engage in a physical action, such as pointing and clicking, as opposed to specifying a command string.
- The impact of a user's actions on objects is immediately visible. Minimal time elapses between the user's actions and the effect on objects.
- User actions should be reversible.

Please note that a number of contemporary commercial user interfaces include components that satisfy the rules for direct manipulation. Many video games include several or all of the features. Contemporary direct manipulation interfaces may include elements of other interaction styles, including windows, menus, forms, and so on. Typical Macintosh and Windows GUIs are built following a "widget construction" strategy, in which the basic widget set is fairly small and has some standardization of its look. Each widget has a predefined set of user actions to which it will respond, but the set of widgets is housed in an interaction that in many ways is a direct manipulation interaction.

Direct manipulation interfaces have a number of advantages. For example, some data suggest that graphical computer objects are easier to remember and use than keyed objects (Cunniff and Taylor 1987). By definition, actions are reversible, so that users can undo mistakes. Because the impact of a user's actions is immediately visible, users receive immediate feedback on their actions. Many direct manipulation interactions include metaphors; well-constructed metaphors can help users, especially novice users, to build accurate conceptual models of interactions.

Direct manipulation interactions also have some disadvantages. For example, since they often include metaphors, poorly constructed metaphors can lead users, especially novice users, to form misleading conceptual models. Direct manipulation interactions may be very rich and offer numerous alternatives. While this feature may be good in the sense that users can learn by exploration, it may be difficult for new users to identify the right step-by-step sequences to solve their problems. Further, while the richness of a direct manipulation interaction may support multiple ways of solving the same problem, new users may find it difficult to find a single way through the interaction (cf. Hutchins, Hollan, and Norman 1986).

Table 8.4 summarizes some situational variables that would call for a direct manipulation interaction.

### Examples of Direct Manipulation

Contemporary systems provide many examples of direct manipulation interactions. One type is document preparation, most of which is done today with WYSIWYG (What You See Is What You Get) word processors. In such word processors, the user enters and edits text in what appears to be a paper document. The results of the user actions are immediately displayed. User actions such as

Table 8.4    Summary of Situations that May Call for Graphical Direct Manipulation Interactions.

| User Characteristics | Task Characteristics | User Interface Variables Supported | Guideline Supported | Guideline Reference |
|---|---|---|---|---|
| User knowledge level—Novice | Task is not rigid and often has multiple paths to the solution. | Task match between the nonrigid nature of the task and the nonrigid nature of direct manipulation. User Satisfaction—the interaction allows the novice to discover sequences through the interaction in a "safe" setting since actions can be undone. | Good task match | Our model of usability. Good task match and high user satisfaction can contribute to high usability. |

boldfacing of text are easy to reverse. This direct manipulation style of editing is different from the indirect style of command-oriented (markup) document preparation. In markup systems, the user would insert tags into the document to indicate the formatting of text. For example, in UNIX troff (text processing), a .B tag at the beginning of a line before a string means that the string is to be boldfaced. With these markup systems, users could not see the results of their editing until the document was processed by an interpreter and printed.

Other familiar examples of applications that include direct manipulation interactions are spreadsheet applications and video games. For the most part, these applications have no syntax and few error messages and provide immediate feedback.

Where did the idea of direct manipulation user interfaces come from? Dix, Finlay, Abowd, and Beale (1998) credit Ben Shneiderman for inventing the term (Shneiderman 1982). The influences and philosophies for direct manipulation were greatly influenced by the user interface for the Xerox Star. The Xerox 8010 Star Information system was introduced in 1981 and was a combination of software, network support, and hardware. The user interface for the Star included a familiar conceptual model: the desktop. The user could see interface objects and could point rather than needing to remember commands and type. The interface included windows and icons, supported by a mouse and bitmapped graphics. Applications used universal commands such as *Move, Copy,* and *Delete* instead of application-specific commands.

As you may already know, the Star failed in marketplace. The timing of the Star was probably premature; most users at the time were still professional programmers who did not appreciate the interface. The cost of $16,500 was high, especially for an audience who had not really accepted the idea of a personal computer. Few applications could be run on the Star, and third-party vendors could not write software for it. (See Johnson et al., 1989, for a detailed description of the development, history, and features of the Star.)

Still, as we know, the direct manipulation interface of the Star has had far-reaching effects on the computing world. Apple Computer released the Lisa in 1982. It was modeled after some of the prototypes from Xerox but was less expensive at $10,000. Even this price tag was high, especially after the introduction of the Macintosh, which was considerably cheaper. The interface of the Lisa was similar to that of later Macintoshes. (See the San Diego Computer Museum Web site, http://www.computerhalloffame.org, for a picture of the Lisa.) The Lisa product line ended in 1986 after some attempts to retrofit it as the Macintosh XL (Bellis 2006).

### Direct Manipulation Design Decisions and Guidelines

Some of the challenges to designing good direct manipulation interactions involve the following:

- Providing feedback.
- Choice of graphical representation and physical actions.
- Support for expert users.
- Role of text.

**Providing Feedback**    One defining feature of direct manipulation interfaces is that the impact of user actions is immediately visible. The implication of this feature is that users receive immediate feedback for their actions. Hix and Hartson (1993) suggest that users need both articulatory and semantic feedback. *Articulatory feedback* tells users that their hands made the choice or action that the users thought they did. For example, suppose that I am playing a video chess game. I click on a knight icon, and the icon becomes bold. In other words, I received an indication from the interface that my hand did something, which is articulatory feedback. However, just because a user picked an icon does not mean that it is the right icon for the task. *Semantic feedback* tells the user that the action was right for the context. Continuing the example, if I pick the knight icon and several squares on the presented chessboard become bold, I know that I can legally move my knight. In other words, my choice made sense in the context of the task, which is semantic feedback. Based on Mayhew (1992), Mandel (1997), and Brown and Cunningham (1989), the following is a guideline for providing feedback in direct manipulation interactions:

- Provide feedback in your direct manipulation interactions that matches the user's expectations and is consistent with the task as portrayed in the direct manipulation interaction.

**Choice of Graphical Representation and Physical Actions**    The particular graphical representation should be both appropriate and meaningful. This means that the metaphors that you choose should be tied to the task in such a way that users can take advantage of existing conceptual models. Metaphors should also be culturally acceptable and appropriate.

- Choose graphical representations that are both appropriate and meaningful.
- Choose less arbitrary rather than more arbitrary metaphors.
- Symbols are not always meaningful to all and may be open to different interpretations.

We have heard arguments that only the objects that can be manipulated in a context should be displayed. We argue cautiously against this thinking. Displaying objects, active and inactive, provides a contextual overview that users, especially novices, may find helpful.

Because a direct manipulation interaction involves the movement of "objects" in "space" across time, a rule must be set for the relationships among these variables, or what one might call the "physics" of the interaction to define the physical actions of objects in the interface. It is not essential that this physics match the physics of the real world. Indeed, many successful cartoons follow a kind of "cartoon physics" that differs from the physics of the real world. In a cartoon an object may fall up, two objects may fall at different rates, or two objects may pass though each other. These differences make sense in the cartoon world. So what choice of physical actions makes sense? Barring other guidelines from the problem definition, a specification of physical actions that supports good task match would seem to be the best choice.

**Support for Expert Users**    When expert users have a good grasp of the tasks that they wish to perform, they may be frustrated by the movement and manipulation of objects and the requisite screen refresh issues in a direct manipulation interaction. They may also want to add new actions that could have been included in the interactions. Designers may wish to consider indirect manipulation alternatives to common commands.

**Role of Text**    One question you might ask about building a direct manipulation interface concerns the role of text. Should your layout lean as much toward the visual as possible? We do not think so. We have completed a number of studies about the roles of multiple representation styles and have concluded that, where possible, the designer is better suited to choose a *dual* presentation. This means that the same information is presented in both a text and a visual style. For example, a study (Leventhal 2001; Zimmerman, Barnes, and Leventhal 2001) presented directions for folding an origami animal in a number of textual and visual combinations, as well as textual or visual alone. We found that user performance on the animal folding task was much improved when users had both styles of information presented together. It is also important when presenting textual and visual information to engage or make users aware of both styles of interaction. In Instone, Brown, et al. (1993), we presented some visual and spatial information related to the Sherlock Holmes stories. This information was accompanied by textual information. We found that when users were forced to interact with both the text and visual information, via a mouse click, their performances on a delayed question-and-answer task were greatly improved. The following is a guideline concerning the role of text in a graphical interface:

- Where appropriate, consider using a dual (textual and visual) presentation. For many tasks, presentation of information in both textual and visual form leads to better performance than textual or visual information alone.

### Direct Manipulation Open Questions

Direct manipulation interactions have emerged as a major interaction style. While other styles are in use, the marketplace is dominated by direct manipulation interactions, which are constructed around the idea of the user manipulating screen objects to initiate actions. Direct manipulation interface objects may themselves be of another interaction style. For example, the familiar WIMP (windows, icons, menus, pointing devices) interfaces from contemporary personal computers are themselves composed of windows, menus, forms, question-and-answer dialogs, virtual reality, and even video.

A number of issues must be considered in the design of direct manipulation interactions, for example, varying levels of directness. An interaction may incorporate direct manipulation features and still include features of other interaction styles. For example, one common misconception among users is that mousable user interfaces are direct manipulation interactions while keyboard driven user interfaces are not. This is false. In fact, so long as the interface includes some mechanism for the user to physically manipulate interface objects, whether by mouse, arrow keys, or another pointing mechanism, this requirement is being addressed.

The roles of space and motion of objects in direct manipulation environments are not well understood, particularly from a behavioral perspective. The user's perceptions and formation of mental models about a real space and objects in that space are complex cognitive operations. So it is not always possible to predict how well a space and objects in a particular direct manipulation interaction will support user perception and mental actions.

Finally, taking actions from the keyboard to a pointing device strategy may be distracting or interfere with task efficiency. For example, most of us would probably find it easier to type in calculator instructions rather than pointing to individual keys.

## 8.4 *Conversational Interactions: Verbal, Symbol Exchange*

A number of interaction styles involve the exchange of verbal information in the form of symbol exchange similar to a conversation. The user may be responsible for remembering the words to use in the exchange. In command-line interactions, the verbal information on the user's part is limited to a specific set of symbols and syntax for organizing the symbols. In a natural-language interaction, the user "converses" using a subset of a natural language.

### 8.4.1 *Command-Line Interactions*

In the old days of computer science, when a person wished to interact with a computer, he or she would use a *command-line* interaction style, in which the computer sat waiting passively for a user command. The user would enter a command string in some prespecified syntax; the command string would constitute the instructions to the machine. Command-line interactions rely on the user's recall of instructions and, as such, impose more memory requirements on the user than menus or forms. Command-line interactions essentially are a verbal or symbol exchange between the user and the computer; in other words, the user is not presented with a visual environment in which to operate.

Command-line interfaces still exist in contemporary computer systems such as UNIX and MS-DOS. Interestingly, even visual interfaces such as Macintosh OS X and Windows 2000 offer the opportunity to the user to open windows for command-line interactions, which have remained a viable interaction style for a number of reasons. Obviously since the interactions involve alphanumeric symbol exchange, they do not require sophisticated input and output hardware. For interactions that are intended to run on slow processors or across slow communications lines, command-line interactions require minimal screen refresh, compared to more visual interactions. For expert users, command-line interactions may be fast and efficient. Expert users may feel in control of systems with command-line interfaces and able to work at speeds that are appropriate. With a command-line interaction, experts may be able to customize their task to their exact needs. Even for novice users, a simple command structure and instruction sequence may tighten the task and aid in the formation of conceptual models.

Command-line interfaces also have disadvantages. Because their use involves recall, the burden for remembering commands and their syntax falls to users. Typically, command-line interfaces have a fairly stiff learning curve for novice users. Because many command-line languages strive to minimize user typing, the language itself involves numerous abbreviations and occasionally apparently random grammar rules. From Norman's (1988) perspective, we could probably conclude that command-line interactions have low visibility, since the consequences and constraints of one's actions are not available until after the work is done. Finally, because command-line interactions are not visual, it is usually more difficult to impose an analogy or metaphor onto the command language.

Command-line interfaces appear to be here to stay. They have a number of advantages, especially for expert users. They can be well designed. In user interface design, you should consider them to be a viable interaction style choice.

Command-line interfaces have gotten some bad press, especially with the preponderance of more visual interfaces in the commercial marketplace. When we ask our students about interfaces that they like, we find that most of them secretly like command-line interfaces but do not want to admit it to their usability engineering teachers. They are afraid that they will seem old-fashioned and out of touch with new technologies. Well, we love command-line interfaces in some settings, too! Sometimes command-line interfaces are a good choice.

Table 8.5 summarizes some of the situational variables and guidelines that suggest the use of command-line interactions.

**Table 8.5**   Summary of Situations that May Call for Command-Line Interfaces.

| User Characteristics | Task Characteristics | User Interface Variables Supported | Guideline Supported | Guideline Reference |
|---|---|---|---|---|
| User knowledge level—Expert | Task is not rigid. | Ease of use<br><br>Expert users can follow a large or infinite number of steps through the interface. | Facilitate the development and use of workable mental models.<br><br>The expert has a working mental model of the task. | Guideline 1, Chapter 7. Facilitate the development and use of workable mental models. |
| User knowledge level—Expert | Task is rigid. | Task match<br><br>The user can make the sequence through the interface match the model of the task exactly. | Facilitate the development and use of workable mental models.<br><br>The expert has a working mental model of the task. | Guideline 1, Chapter 7. Facilitate the development and use of workable mental models. |
| User knowledge level—Novice | Task is tightly structured and rigid. | If the command structure is closely matched to the task structure, the command structure may help the user build a working mental model of the task. | Facilitate the development and use of workable mental models. | Guideline 1, Chapter 7. Facilitate the development and use of workable mental models. |
| Any user | Task is situationally constrained by low bandwidth or limited display capabilities. | User satisfaction<br><br>While users may be required to remember the command set, they may be satisfied with the faster response in a limited situation that a simple command interaction can offer. | User satisfaction can contribute to high usability. | Our model of usability. User satisfaction can contribute to high usability. |

### Command-Line Language Design Decisions

A number of potential design decisions have to be made for command-line languages. Not surprisingly many decisions are centered around the choice of actual words for the command set and the order in which the commands can be given. Recall that a command-line interaction often relies on the user's ability to recall the commands. Selecting command words that are meaningful to the task will facilitate user recall because users should be able to apply their knowledge and understanding of the task to the interaction. For example, suppose that we were implementing a command-line interaction for the audio catalog problem from Chapter 6. Our rationale for going with a command-line interaction might be that our user is very expert and does not need or want to wait for the prompting inherent in a menued interaction. A command set for the audio catalog might include the following two commands:

> FindSongInformation *Name of Song*
>
> FindArtistInformation *Name of Artist*

What design decisions were involved in these choices of commands? First, we have decided to have two separate Find commands, one for *Artist* and one for *Song,* and each command has a unique name. Second, we have decided to have long but descriptive command names, rather than shorter and more abbreviated names. Were these good decisions? Landauer, Galotti, and Hartwell (1983) suggest that names of the commands should be meaningful and distinguishable. Do you think that these names have enough detail to be distinctive and informative?

These command names are long and require a lot of typing. Is that a good choice for expert users? If not, should we keep the command names as set but allow them to be abbreviated for our expert users? Hirsh-Pasek, Nudelman, and Schneider (1982) suggest that abbreviations can be used but recommend that the design follow a consistent abbreviation strategy. Perhaps we could include these abbreviations:

> FSI *Name of Song*
>
> FAI *Name of Artist*

Do you think that these abbreviations would facilitate expert use and still be distinctive and memorable?

What about the commands themselves? Is it really essential to have two different Find commands? Clearly, it is critical to include enough commands to cover the needs of the task, but according to Mynatt (1990):

> One of the major design flaws in many command languages is simply that they contain too many commands and allow the user too many alternate ways of accomplishing a task (Rosson 1983). This makes the command language difficult to remember.

Following Mynatt, we might want to substitute just one command:

> Find *Name of Information*

Would the user be more likely to remember the one command with a shorter name rather than the two longer commands? Do you think that the user would find it confusing to use the same command to find information about different kinds of information in the catalog?

What about the use of the term "FindSongInformation" over something more specific to the internals of the software, such as "Table Lookup 732.5"? Mayhew (1992) suggests that it is essential to couch the command names in the task and to make the terms meaningful to the user. Do you think that these commands have good task match and would be meaningful to the user?

What about the syntax of the command strings? Clearly both commands have the same structure of command followed by name information. Green and Payne (1984) indicate that structure of the command syntax should be consistent. Is this the best structure or should we select one of the following?

*Name of Song* FindSongInformation

*Name of Artist* FindArtistInformation

Mayhew (1992) recommends the use of an active or action-oriented syntax, suggesting that our original choices were probably better.

Finally, in Chapter 7, we suggest in Guideline 6 to *Provide appropriate feedback to the user.* How can we enhance feedback in a command-line interaction? Suppose that we have the following command:

FindArtistInformation *Name of Artist*

It is possible that this command will generate a lot of information on the screen. How will users know for sure which command they issued to get this information? If possible, we could leave the command in a visible and consistent place on the screen as the generated information is being presented.

In summary, we suggest the following guidelines in the design of a command-line interaction:

* Choose command names that are meaningful in the context of the task and are appropriate for the user.
* Choose a command structure that is consistent.
* When a user enters a command, include the command in a consistent and visible place in the response to provide feedback.

What if the user is interacting in an audio command-line interaction? For example, suppose that the user is interacting via a telephone with a variation of the audio catalog and receives the following instruction:

*Please enter your command-instruction*

Would the rules be different for an audio command-line interaction than they were for an interaction that involved a keyboard? We would say in general that the rules would be very similar. The user in this circumstance might respond with this phrase:

Find Artist Information *Name of Artist*

One challenge to the designer of the audio-based command-line interaction may be to provide feedback regarding the command. In the case of the audio catalog, the interaction might respond with this:

*Your request for Artist information for Name of Artist is . . . .*

### 8.4.2 Natural Language and Speech-Based Processing Interfaces
In the future, we expect that we will have opportunities to communicate with computers directly via a natural language, such as English or French, rather than in a constrained command set. Natural

language interactions have a number of apparent advantages. First, Yankelovich, Levow, and Marx (1995) note that the set of available commands in a natural language are much more numerous than the set of commands in more traditional command-line interactions. In addition, Rosenfeld, Olsen, and Rudnicky (2001) point out that with natural language a user can describe objects rather than the name of a target object. Both these advantages suggest that users of this kind of interaction could focus on the task rather than the operational details of the interaction because they could specify their command in a way that is more natural to them.

Unfortunately the very advantages of natural language interactions have made them difficult to build. Natural languages, as a system, are complex and contain ambiguity. Consider the statement "I saw the show with the television." What is the right interpretation? Did I see the show on the television or did I see a show that included a television? Natural languages contain huge vocabularies that are complete with idioms and cultural influences. Interpreting natural language statements involves interpreting context dependencies. Consider the following: "I read about Caesar and Octavian. He was murdered." Who was murdered? You probably knew that Caesar was murdered, but nothing in the two statements says whether it was Caesar or Octavian. Finally, when we use natural language to communicate via speech, we not only speak and interpret speech, but we use nonverbal cues, such as gesturing and facial expressions, to communicate.

What would be needed to build a successful natural language interaction? Hayes and Reddy (1983) suggest that, to be successful, natural language interactions must include the infrastructure so that the language inputs from the user can be understood. This means that the underlying system has to be able to dissect user inputs, whether they follow grammatical rules or not, and they must generally get the gist of what the user is saying.

Processing speech and processing natural language obviously have a number of characteristics in common. However, they are not identical. Processing speech involves management of spoken and gestural inputs and generation of realistic speech outputs but could potentially use a limited language set. Natural language processing may include speech but may also include textual (written) inputs and outputs and might be expected to deal with the true richness of natural languages. Rosenfeld et al. (2001) describe several strategies for speech interfaces, ranging from interactions that use unlimited natural language to interactions that are simply spoken command-line interactions. Several lessons are to be learned here. First, the designer faces a trade-off when working with natural language interactions: let the user truly converse with the interaction in his or her natural language and the system will require sophisticated recognition and translation infrastructure. On the other hand, if the designer constrains the language enough, he or she essentially will have a command-line interaction with all the associated issues of recall for the user. Second, even the most constrained language, if it uses speech inputs, still requires recognition of the speech strings but may enable the user to work in a hands-free or multiple modality setting.

So how does the designer build an interaction for natural language and/or speech? In describing their experiences, Yankelovich, Levow, and Marx (1995) state that designing a speech-based user interface was different from designing a GUI. In particular, they note that some of the conventions of GUIs do not translate well into the speech interaction style. For example, the organization and sequencing in a graphical interaction may have an unnatural feel in a speech-based setting. Rosenfeld et al. (2001) also point out that speech does not leave the memory trail that we typically see with a

GUI. Because speech is transitory, the user has to remember what was spoken. Rosenfeld et al. have suggested that when designers follow a GUI analogy they may produce viable speech and natural language interfaces. Within that vision, natural language and speech interactions, as a group, could follow a similar metaphor. With this approach, users would be familiar with the speech interface metaphor.

Table 8.6 shows the situational variables that call for natural language interactions.

Table 8.6    Summary of Situations that May Call for Natural Language Interactions.

| User Characteristics | Task Characteristics | User Interface Variables Supported | Guideline Supported | Guideline Reference |
|---|---|---|---|---|
| Any user | Task is not rigid in a linguistic sense and often has multiple linguistic paths to the solution. | Task match between the nonrigid nature of the task and the nonrigidness of direct manipulation interaction. | Good task match | Our model of usability. Good task match can contribute to high usability. |
| Any user | Task is situationally constrained to be hands free and requires a speech-based interaction. | User satisfaction. Goals and setting of task supported by the interaction. | Good task match | Our model of usability. High user satisfaction can contribute to high usability. |

### 8.4.3 Question-and-Answer Interactions

One kind of user interaction that could be presented as either a menu, a visual, or a conversational interaction is a question-and-answer interaction, in which the application asks the user a series of questions. For each question, the user provides answers; the options for the answers may be presented in menu format or may be of a more conversational nature, with the user recalling the answer options. This style of interaction may be a good choice when the underlying task is tightly structured and has clear paths to accomplish it. One example of a question-and-answer interaction is the interaction of a user with an automatic teller machine.

A number of design decisions have to be made with the question-and-answer interaction. For example, the pattern of questions and user answers should closely follow the task. The wording of the questions and answers should also be a close fit with the task. Other issues concern the user's ability to go back through the question chain and the user's ability to make changes in their answers. These decisions should also be driven by the task itself. Finally, if the question-and-answer task is lengthy and tedious, the designer might wish to consider presenting more than one question at a time.

Question-and-answer interactions can be very useful when the task is highly structured and when it is critical that the user not get lost in the interaction sequence. For example, in an electronic voting interaction, where it is critical that close to 100 percent of users successfully complete the voting task, breaking down the task into a sequence of short questions and answers may help to broaden usability success to even very novice users.

Table 8.7 lists some situations that may be appropriate for question-and-answer interactions.

Table 8.7 Summary of Situations that May Call for Question-and-Answer Interactions.

| User Characteristics | Task Characteristics | User Interface Variables Supported | Guideline Supported | Guideline Reference |
|---|---|---|---|---|
| Any user | Task is rigid and is inherently structured as a question-and-answer sequence. | Task match between the question-and-answer dialogue in the task and question-and-answer interaction is high. Ease of use if the user knows or is cued to the set of legal responses. | Good task match. | Our model of usability. Good task match can contribute to high usability. |
| User knowledge – all levels, but particularly helpful for novice users. | Task is rigid and is inherently structured as a question and answer sequence. | Ease of use. User is not likely to get lost in response sequence if there is just one path through the interaction. | Facilitate the development and use of workable mental models. | Guideline 1, Chapter 7. Facilitate the development and use of workable mental models. Enhance wayfinding and help prevent users from getting lost. The rigid structure of question-and-answer applications makes it difficult for users to get lost. |

## 8.5 Manipulable and Combination Interactions

A number of emerging interaction styles are not easily categorized as necessarily verbal or visual. The common feature of these interaction styles is that they typically involve manipulations and are relatively new or emergent in the interaction scene.

### 8.5.1 Haptic Interactions

The word *haptic* refers to touching. A growing number of interfaces involve human touch as a critical part of the interaction. By using touch as part of the interaction, humans can detect features of texture, resistance, and vibration. Haptic interactions integrate touch feedback, as well as positional or location information, within the context of the interaction.

Haptic interactions seem particularly well suited to tasks in which tactile feedback is important. For example, surgical training simulations are an ideal venue for haptic interactions. Haptic interactions can be used in conjunction with virtual simulations of three-dimensional environments. Some of the key design decisions for haptic interactions involve these specifics:

• What kind of touch should be supported? Touch actually involves detection of changes in the presence, or absence of contact, degree of pressure, and/or level of temperature.
• What hardware should be chosen for the interaction?
• What will be the style of the interaction? Should the interactive device have one level or only one location of haptic feedback?
• How is the haptic interaction coordinated with other kinds of interactions?

In some regards, haptic interactions can be just a highly sophisticated form of direct manipulation. In both styles, the user is manipulating screen objects. In direct manipulation, the feedback is visual, and in haptic interactions the feedback is tactile and positional.

Table 8.8 lists some situations that may be appropriate for haptic interactions.

Table 8.8    Summary of Situations that May Call for Haptic Interactions.

| User Characteristics | Task Characteristics | User Interface Variables Supported | Guideline Supported | Guideline Reference |
|---|---|---|---|---|
| Any user | Task is constrained in some way so that the task inherently has or benefits from tactile elements. | Task match between task and the interaction. | Good task match. | Our model of usability. Good task match can contribute to high usability. |

### 8.5.2  Multimodal and Multimedia Interactions

Multimedia interactions, such as interactive stories and role-playing simulations, have become so commonplace that you are probably surprised that we have highlighted them as a separate interaction style. Multimedia interactions are typically characterized by the presentation of information in a number of representational forms, including text, pictures, audio, video, animation, and virtual reality.

Multimedia interactions may integrate the presentation of information in visual and verbal forms. As we will see in Chapter 14, presentations with information in both formats are often superior to presentations with one format or the other. Multimedia interactions are appropriate under at least two circumstances, which often overlap:

• *Situations in which the task is by nature multimedia.* In other words, these are tasks in which we naturally think of a number of parallel representations. For example, a story about a treasure hunt may include, concurrently, both a verbal description and maps. The verbal description may tell us about the history, biology, and so on of the space that we are exploring. The maps may show us the composition of the elements that make up the space.

• *Situations in which information could be presented in any of a number of forms.* For example, if I am providing directions for the assembly of a child's bicycle, I could describe the steps in words, I could show the steps in a series of pictures, I could animate the series of pictures, I could show a realistic movie of someone actually building the bicycle, or I could immerse myself in a virtual bicycle and learn about assembly by building the virtual bicycle.

A number of task types would seem to fit into these situations. Assembly or construction tasks are one example. Educational tasks, in which I am trying to teach a richness of concepts, potentially benefit from multimedia presentations. Complex problem-solving tasks, such as complex scientific problems, may benefit as well. In such problems, the scientist may benefit from observing their data in a variety of visual and verbal forms.

As more and more sophisticated and integrated multimedia interactions emerge, a number of critical open questions and problems remain. For example, some questions concern the effectiveness of different combinations of informational forms for different tasks and the realistic roles of response time for complex presentations versus the payoff of the presentations (cf. Pausch, Proffitt, and Williams 1997; Zimmerman, Barnes, and Leventhal 2001). From a computing perspective, effective multimedia requires efficient and appropriate compression standards for such informational forms as video, audio, and virtual reality. As compression standards for multimedia information (MPEG 1, MPEG 2, and MPEG 4) emerge, the potential for powerful and interactive multimedia increases (cf. International Standards Organization 1993, 1995, 2000; Chiariglione 1996, 2000; Koenen 2002).

Design choices for multimedia would include the following:

- Determine which informational representation to include and how to combine multiple representations.
- Determine which parts of the presentation appear to the user to be active at any given time. Facilitate the user's ability to interact with the active element.

Table 8.9 lists some situations that may be appropriate for multimedia interactions.

Table 8.9    Summary of Situations that May Call for Multimedia Interactions.

| User Characteristics | Task Characteristics | User Interface Variables Supported | Guideline Supported | Guideline Reference |
|---|---|---|---|---|
| Any user | Task is situationally constrained such that presentation in multiple formats is superior to a single format presentation. | Task match between goals of task and interaction. | Reduce the cognitive (mental) workload of the user.<br><br>Good task match. | Guideline 5, Chapter 7. Reduce the cognitive (mental) workload of the user. Multiple representations (formats) of information may optimize Working Memory operations (see Chapter 14).<br><br>Our model of usability. Good task match can contribute to high usability. |

In some regards, multimedia interactions can be an example of multimodal interactions. Multimodal interactions are those where users are offered a selection of interaction modalities; they potentially support interactions in the many modes in which people communicate, including speaking, moving eye gaze, and gesture. In multimodal interactions, the user may have a number of parallel options for inputs. For example, a user might be able to type inputs on a keyboard for a while until becoming fatigued. Then the user could switch to speech input. Because multimodal interfaces do not seem to require the narrow skill band that pointing and typing interfaces do, they seem to carry much promise for a broader user population, including those with physical limitations. Multimodal interfaces would also seem to be appropriate for mobile applications when the user's hands are occupied with driving. Some proposals for multimodal interfaces propose the possibility of multiple, parallel, and concurrent user inputs. A design challenge is to synthesize and interpret multiple sources of user inputs (Oviatt and Cohen 2000; Oviatt 2001).

### 8.5.3 Virtual Reality Interactions

Over the last ten years another interaction style, *virtual reality,* has emerged into the mainstream of interaction styles. One definition from searchSMB.com defines virtual reality as "the simulation of a real or imagined environment that can be experienced visually in the three dimensions of width, height, and depth and that may additionally provide an interactive experience visually in full real-time motion with sound and possibly with tactile and other forms of feedback" (*TechTarget,* Whatis.com 2004–2006). While there are many definitions, the unifying feature seems to be the ability of the user to move or to manipulate objects in a simulated virtual world. The *world,* while a two-dimensional presentation in reality, gives the impression of being three-dimensional.

Use of virtual worlds varies in terms of the degree to which the user is *immersed* in the world. By *level of immersion* we mean the degree to which users actually see themselves as part of the world. Interactive devices such as head-mounted displays and interactive gloves can greatly increase the user's sense of immersion, and some research has suggested that for certain tasks more immersive environments may be more effective than less immersive environments (cf. Pausch, Proffitt, and Williams 1997). However, highly immersive interaction devices do not seem to be essential for all virtual reality interactions (cf. Robertson, Czerwinski, and van Dantzich 1997).

A broad range of interactions can be considered *virtual reality.* By using tools such as the Virtual Reality Modeling Language (VRML), Java 3D, or X3D, it is possible to build low-cost, Web-deliverable worlds that can be manipulated with a mouse or other input device. In augmented reality interactions, users wear special glasses that allow them to see both the virtual world and reality. In a CAVE (Computerized Automatic Virtual Environment), users may move or manipulate "objects" in a room with graphics projected from behind walls.

An interesting question for researchers in this area is to identify exactly what situations are good for virtual reality interactions. That is, it would be useful to identify the kinds of tasks and user groups that would best fit with virtual reality interactions. This is an open question, but some hints point to the answer. Some researchers have focused on virtual worlds as a mechanism for navigation. In this approach, users learn by "traveling" through a virtual world. So, tasks that involve navigation through some kind of space would seem to have good task match. In this case, "traveling" would seem to be a fairly nonrigid task that would benefit from the richness of a virtual reality world.

In our research work, we have focused on the use of virtual worlds to provide instructions for procedural or construction tasks. We have found that instructions presented in even simple virtual reality presentations, coupled with text and still pictures, can be more effective than text and pictures alone in helping people to build real things (Zimmerman, Barnes, and Leventhal, 2001). We believe that this is partly because the virtual reality allows users to off-load some of the spatial transformations onto the virtual reality that they would normally make mentally. The need for the user to off-load seems to vary with individuals, but it seems clear that tasks with extensive spatial transformations are good candidates for virtual reality presentations.

Virtual reality, because it is a kind of simulation, offers opportunities for people to train and work in environments that might not otherwise be accessible. For example, users of virtual reality can experience simulated trips to historic sites or the moon. Virtual reality is also a platform for creativity and artistic expression. Finally, it seems that virtual worlds that involve manipulation of three-dimensional objects and navigation in three dimensions may have good task match with their real-world counterparts.

Table 8.10 shows some situations that may be appropriate for virtual reality interactions.

Table 8.10   Summary of Situations that May Call for Virtual Reality Interactions.

| User Characteristics | Task Characteristics | User Interface Variables Supported | Guideline Supported | Guideline Reference |
|---|---|---|---|---|
| Any user | Task requires the ability to explore or to use the richness of an interactive and three-dimensional presentation and therefore is not rigid. | Task match between the richness of the task and the richness of the virtual environment. | Good task match. | Our model of usability. Good task match can contribute to high usability. |
| Any user | Task requires support for creative and nonrigid activities that lead to a creative outcome. | Flexibility of interaction allows it to be used in ways not anticipated by a designer. | Good task match. | Our model of usability. Using the interaction for artistic and creative purposes suggests that it may require flexibility. |
| Any user | Task is situationally constrained such that presentation in multiple formats is superior to a single format presentation. | Task match between goals of task and interaction. | Reduce the cognitive (mental) workload of the user.<br><br>Good task match. | Guideline 5, Chapter 7. Reduce the cognitive (mental) workload of the user. Multiple representations (formats) of information may optimize Working Memory operations (see Chapter 14).<br><br>Our model of usability. Good task match can contribute to high usability. |

### Design Decisions for Virtual Reality Interactions

Once again, because of the relative newness of virtual reality as an interaction style, we do not have a complete understanding of the design decisions that are at work. Some possible decisions may include these:

- Identify the type of platform for the virtual world. For example, it is possible to display a primitive virtual world on a mobile device. The advantages of the mobile device would be that it would be usable anywhere and anytime, but a disadvantage would be its inability to truly immerse the user. On the other hand, the virtual reality interaction may be very sophisticated and require the advanced technology of a CAVE. In these examples, the sophistication of the platform will influence the detail and reality of the interaction.

- Select how complete the presentation is. Is it essential for the task and the situation that the presentation has naturalistic, high-fidelity quality? Is it essential that the whole presentation be of uniform quality? How good is good enough to get the job done?

- Verify that a virtual reality presentation is justified for the task at hand. The development of a virtual reality interaction, especially one that uses complex hardware, is challenging both as a usability engineering problem and as a software engineering problem. Developers may need extensive training on the various elements of the delivered product. If the task at hand *does not* justify the use of virtual reality, it may not be worth the cost of the resources to build one.

### 8.5.4 Video and Electronic Game Interactions

User interactions for video and electronic games are some of the most exciting interaction design projects of all. The interfaces for contemporary video games involve extraordinary use of graphics and animation, as well as sound, verbal, and haptic coordination with the games. It is possible to build game interactions that are primarily verbal, but most involve a visual presentation and may have enough interactivity of three-dimensional elements to include virtual reality. The nature of the visual presentation may vary, but most popular contemporary games include predominantly direct manipulation interactions. Input and output devices for the interaction may include pointing devices, speech input, tactile or haptic feedback devices, and visual displays.

Design of interactions for video games, particularly those for entertainment purposes, may differ in many ways from the design of interactions for other applications. While the game task itself may be characterized in terms of our Chapter 3 usability model task variables of frequency, rigidness, and the situational constraint of making the task fun, it is the user characteristic variables that stand out for video games. One notable characteristic of successful video games is that playing the game is *intrinsically motivating* (cf. Malone 1981). That is, the motivation for playing the game is from playing the game itself. This style of motivation may be different from more traditional applications in which the software is a tool used to accomplish a task. In a traditional application the motivation is usually to complete the task as quickly and efficiently as possible. In a game, the user usually wants to be challenged and for the game not to finish quickly.

Malone (1981) and Lepper and Malone (1987) have identified a number of characteristics that make electronic games successful, including challenge, fantasy, an optimal level of complexity, and control. According to these studies, challenge means that the game provides goals that the user is uncertain of achieving. Fantasy means that the game leads the players to think in mental images of situations that are not actually present in reality. Complexity means that the game should not be too simple or too difficulty, and control means that both the user and the game are able to instigate control during the game.

Users of video games typically do not want to read a lengthy set of directions, so video games often have to present an interaction that even a novice can enjoy; ease of learning for novices is typically essential to the success of the interaction. On the other hand, most games must present challenges to experienced users. Many video games use the concept of skill levels embedded into the interaction to accommodate the different types of users.

We believe that the interactions for video and electronic games often lead the way in interaction design in general. Video games often include imaginative input devices and clever use of integration of various informational forms. The Web site http://www.pong-story.com/atpong1.htm, presents a description of the development in the 1970s of the early video game Pong. In this description, Winter (1996–1999) shows the clever paddle inputs that were developed for the game. These input devices were much different from the keyboard inputs of more traditional applications of the day. Neal (1990) suggests that player-defined scoring may be applied to the design of more conventional applications.

The design of interactions for video games involves a number of issues, including these:

- How does the interaction help to tell the "story" and the context of the game? What interaction elements are used, and which parts of the game "story" do they support? How does the interaction vary with user expertise?
- How realistic is the interaction in the context of the game? Does the game simulate a full three-dimensional setting, or is it more limited?
- How does the interaction support relationships among players?
- How are the motivational factors of the game built into the interaction?

Table 8.11 shows some situations, which may be appropriate for game interactions.

**Table 8.11** Summary of Situations that May Call for Video and Electronic Game Interactions.

| User Characteristics | Task Characteristics | User Interface Variables Supported | Guideline Supported | Guideline Reference |
|---|---|---|---|---|
| User motivation is high to play the game | Task is situationally constrained to be fun. | Task match between the user's expectation for fun and the interaction's capability to deliver fun. User satisfaction. High user motivation combined with constraint for fun should lead to high levels of user satisfaction. | Good task match. | Our model of usability. Good task match and user satisfaction can contribute to high usability. |
| User knowledge— Novice. | Task is situationally constrained to be fun. | Ease of learning. In video game interactions, novices will most likely choose to learn to use the interaction by exploration. Fostering learning by exploration in a "safe" mode will enhance ease of learning. | Facilitate the development and use of workable mental models. Let the user be in charge. | Guideline 1, Chapter 7. Facilitate the development and use of workable mental models Guideline 6, Chapter 7. Let the user be in charge. Allow the user to accomplish tasks directly. While your interface should support exploration, where appropriate, it is also important to provide direct paths to user's goals. |

### 8.5.5 Mobile and Handheld Computer Interactions

In recent years, a number of mobile devices have entered the marketplace, including personal digital assistants, cellular telephones, and other handheld devices for global positioning systems for navigation, weather measurements, and games. From the perspective of the usability engineer, these devices would seem to present a number of interesting challenges. On the one hand, the devices themselves can support most, if not all, of the interaction styles that we have already seen. What makes them different is that the characteristics of the device, including its size and the way in which it is used, may change the nature of even the most familiar interaction.

Most mobile and handheld devices support some form of visual interaction, but the visual interaction may be very limited. Because of screen space and legibility concerns, the designer may opt to use more text and conversational interactions than in a workstation setting.

Another challenge is to determine exactly which kinds of tasks are best suited for these kinds of devices. We have a very powerful handheld computer in our lab that includes an Internet browser. Through the browser we can play the multimedia for our research. The snag is this: to fit our presentation on the screen, we either have to use very tiny images or lots of scrolling. Neither solution is perfect, and nothing else has suggested itself. One conclusion is that the kind of task we are doing is better matched to a larger screen.

A number of interesting open questions surround the subject of mobile and handheld devices. For example, mobile and handheld devices have a variety of input devices. What is entailed in transferring from a keyboard to gestural inputs? The answer is not clear. In addition, the nature of interacting with a handheld device is qualitatively different from sitting at a desk and interacting with a workstation. We are just starting to understand some of the ramifications of this difference.

Table 8.12 shows some situations which may be appropriate for mobile and handheld computer interactions.

**Table 8.12**  Summary of Situations that May Call for Mobile or Handheld Computer Interactions.

| User Characteristics | Task Characteristics | User Interface Variables Supported | Guideline Supported | Guideline Reference |
|---|---|---|---|---|
| Any user | Task is situationally constrained by the projected location of the activity. | User satisfaction. Goals and setting of task supported by the interaction. | User satisfaction can contribute to high usability. | Our model of usability. High user satisfaction can contribute to high usability. |

## 8.6 A Reminder About Hardware

New and amazing interaction styles are most likely to arise because of some kind of hardware change or change related to hardware. You may remember from Chapter 2 that we discussed how the whole idea of interacting with the computer in any other way than in the batch mode was facilitated by improvements in hardware, most especially improvements in memory capacity and processor speed. Consider an interaction that involves your television only (no Internet for the sake of example). This interaction would converge television, video games, and a DVD player/recorder. To make this appliance work, you would need what Forman and Saint John have referred to as a "killer d-TV" (i.e., a digital television appliance) (Forman and Saint John 2000, 53). Such an appliance would integrate the three interactions of TV, DVD, and video games and be able to compress and decompress information for each of the devices for a uniform-looking presentation. Forman and Saint John (55) alternatively suggest that a "fat PC" might eventually support and converge a number of what are now disparate technologies. The key in either of these strategies is new and more powerful hardware. Once again we see that the results of hardware changes drive us to constantly consider new interactions and their usability issues.

### 8.7 To Web or Not to Web?

To Web or Not to Web? Does it make a difference when designing an interaction? A number of authors (e.g., McCracken and Wolfe 2003) emphasize development of Web interfaces or interfaces for Web browsers when they teach usability courses. You may be wondering why we did not treat Web interfaces as a special form of interaction style. In our view, the issues that drive design decisions—user characteristics, task characteristics, and other realities of the development situation—are what should be considered when selecting an interaction style. Presenting your interface on the Web is just another reality of the development situation: clearly, if your customer wants a Web application, then that is what you will build. We would argue that any of the interaction styles we have presented in this chapter could be used in a Web presentation.

Whether building an interface for the Web or for another platform, the technology of the platform is an important consideration. When interfaces are delivered over the Web, the download and interaction times of the interface are of real concern. However, other issues, such as the appropriateness of the interface to the user and the task, are key to usability as well.

### Conclusions

There are a number of interaction styles to choose from. Many can be combined, and a particular interface may incorporate a number of interaction styles. Some interaction styles are more appropriate for some users and tasks than others. In some cases, the interaction style is strictly described by its look and feel, but in other cases the underlying technology, input device, or mode of output is an integral and defining part of the interaction style.

### Exercises

1. Define the following terms: *linear menu, tree-structured menu, menu network, keyboard-based menu, pull-down menu, layered context-dependent menu, pop-up menu, picture menu, pie menu, check box, form fill-in interaction, command-line interaction, natural language interaction, speech recognition, question-and-answer interaction, direct manipulation interaction, windowed interaction, multimodal interaction, multimedia interaction, haptic interaction, virtual reality interaction,* and *game interaction.*

2. Suppose that you were designing a *smart house* in the year 2010. If you are not familiar with this term, go to the Web and find an example or two. What types of interactions do you think will be appropriate for a smart house? Do you think that the interactions will be primarily based on visual interactions? What other modalities will be important, and why?

3. This exercise will give you a chance to apply some of the design principles for menus.

A class of CS students has just received the assignment titled *Paradise Travel*. As part of the Paradise Travel problem, users are able to create trips to Florida, Barbados, Cedar Point, or Casino Windsor. For each trip that they create, users specify the dates of the trip, the number of travelers, and the price range of the hotel in which they wish to stay. The students are to use menus to allow users to build, modify, and delete their trips, as well as a menu to manage their trip portfolios.

The students are to write their solutions so that the menus they build will respond only to keyboard input. Tong and Melvin have each designed a menu to manage the trip portfolios.

For this exercise, you are to compare the solutions of the two students. Neither menu is uniformly better than the other one. Identify what is different about each. Then, using the guidelines that we have discussed (both general and specific to menus), indicate five guidelines that differentiate the two solutions and/or that have been violated in the designs.

Construct a table like the following for your answer.

| Characteristic of Tong's Menu | Characteristic of Melvin's Menu | Relevant Guideline that Was Not Supported |
|---|---|---|
| AE   Edit a trip | E   Edit trip<br>D   Edit destination | Categories should not overlap from the user's perspective, even if they seem to be different categories to the developer. In Melvin's menu, the destination would seem to be a subset of trip. |
| | | |
| | | |
| | | |
| | | |

PARADISE TRAVEL

Trip Portfolio Options

AA    Build a trip
AB    Remove a trip
AC    Quit Paradise Travel
AD    View a trip
AE    Edit a trip

Type your choice of option by typing the letters of the option

Tong's Solution

PARADISE TRAVEL

Trip Portfolio Management

B     Build
E     Edit trip
D     Edit destination
V     View
R     Delete

Q     Quit Paradise Travel

Melvin's Solution

4. Command-line interface development exercise. Design a command language for a home heating control system. Assume that the user will be using only a keyboard and a display screen (no mouse, no graphics—just text).

Assumptions:

> Each day of the week should be separately programmable.
> Each day has a maximum of four times that you can change settings. For example, the user might want the temperature to go to 68°F at 7:00 A.M. (wake-up time), go down to 55°F at 9:00 A.M. (leave for work), go back to 68°F at 5:00 P.M. (return time), and down to 60°F at 11:00 P.M. (sleep).

The following functions also should be available:

> Ability to temporarily override the current program (e.g., adjust temperature up or down for any arbitrary period). May cancel override.
> Ability to indefinitely override the current program (e.g., a vacation setting). May also cancel this override.
> Ability to display current settings/program.
> Display current temperature.
> Set current day/time.
> Turn off/on system entirely.

Your answer should include the syntax rules for your language, the vocabulary for your language, sample commands, and sample displays (i.e., current settings, program, and temperature).

5. Interaction development exercise. Consider your solution to the task analysis problems that were presented in Chapter 5. Recall that you were to develop a task analysis for a children's game. Pull out that task analysis and design a general mode of interaction for the game. Justify your choices. What situational variables were inadequately defined? Would you make different design choices for different values of these variables? For example, would it matter to your design if your game were to be designed for an adult? Justify your answer.

6. Many people consider the concepts of natural language interactions and speech recognition to be the same. Explain the differences between the two concepts and how you can have a natural language interaction without speech recognition and how you can have a speech recognition system without a natural language interaction.

# 9

# More Guidelines, Some Standards, and More Ideas for Interaction Design

## Motivation

We have already seen that we can improve the design of interactions by following guidelines. Being familiar with general guidelines gives the designer a set of tools or a pocketful of miracles, depending on your perspective. Guidelines are not perfect, and following them is no guarantee of usability success, but they are a start.

In this chapter we examine some more specific guidelines for visual design. We will also learn about some other guidelines and standards that a designer may need to use.

At the end of this chapter you should understand

- Some additional examples of guidelines and standards.
- Some advantages and disadvantages that occur when you follow guidelines and standards.
- Some principles of visual design and some common mistakes that designers make.

It is our assumption that you will be doing some design activities when you finish this chapter. These activities will give you a chance to practice what you have learned. In our class, we emphasize interaction design and spend much less time on interface (software) design. Your instructor may opt for you to spend more time on interface design (see Chapter 13).

## 9.1 Introduction

In our initial discussion of interaction styles in Chapter 7, we described six general guidelines or rules of thumb that seem to apply to all interaction styles. Under our discussion of specific interaction styles, we listed some more general guidelines as they applied to each specific interaction style. We hope that these have been helpful to you. In this chapter, we explore a few more general guidelines that apply to the visual appearance of user interfaces. We also discuss different types of guidelines (Hix and Hartson 1993). Specifically, we discuss the advantages and disadvantages of these guidelines.

## 9.2 What Are Guidelines?

Guidelines are publicly available wisdom or suggestions, such as the guidelines presented in Chapter 7. They are usually based on a combination of research and practice; as such they are not just common sense. Following guidelines does not in itself guarantee a quality interface. For one thing, guidelines are usually specific but carry context as well. For example, guidelines concerning color assume that the UI has a visual element. To use them effectively, the developer typically needs to have some background skill and training. In other words, a novice developer picking up a guideline book will probably produce limited results.

Most human–computer interaction books describe some common guidelines. One of the more entertaining and interesting sets of guidelines comes from Jeff Johnson's (2001) *GUI Bloopers.*

The collection of guidelines by S. L. Smith and J. N. Mosier (1986) developed at MIT in the 1980s is probably the best known compendium of user interface guidelines. These guidelines are oriented toward non-windowed, alphanumeric terminals with nongraphical displays. The guidelines are divided into a number of related areas and can be used in both design and evaluation. Some forms of the Smith and Mosier guidelines present the guidelines as weighted checklists. The developer can then weigh the relative importance of the various guidelines. Many developers feel that the Smith and Mosier guidelines are becoming dated and may be difficult to apply to today's graphical interfaces. However, as a testament to the continuing influence of Smith and Mosier, the guidelines have been ported to hypertext and Web page formats.

Guidelines, like rules of thumb, in any setting may help you get started. If the guideline is specific, like some of the examples in *GUI Bloopers,* you may be able to apply it directly to your design. However, proper application of guidelines usually requires experience. As we have mentioned, guidelines often include terms, such as *consistency,* which can be interpreted in numerous ways. Guidelines may also be in conflict with each other. The following is an example of two reasonable guidelines that seem to conflict:

- Guideline 1: Make all options available to use.
- Guideline 2: Limit the number of categories in a menu.

In this example, the practitioner needs experience to determine which option is more important in a certain context or must know what type of interfaces apply.

Sometimes you will be asked to comply with external standards and guidelines. Your interface design will be required to conform to these guidelines, even if they conflict with the guidelines that we have given you. In particular, these guidelines and standards may come in three additional forms, including project guidelines, platform guidelines, and external standards.

## 9.3 Commercial Platform Guidelines

No doubt you have noticed that most applications on the Apple Macintosh seem to look and behave in similar ways. This is because Apple Computer, Inc., in the early days of the Macintosh, issued a set of platform standards (cf. Apple Computer 1992). These standards dealt with a variety of issues such as interface elements (windows, menus, and icons), use of color, designing for international audiences, and the design process.

Using *commercial platform guidelines,* a vendor defines the guidelines and makes them commercially available. Application developers can then advertise that their user interfaces adhere to the platform UI standard of a particular vendor. The Common User Access for IBM platforms (Berry and Reeves 1992), the Microsoft Windows User Experience (Microsoft Corporation 1999), and the Open Look (Sun Microsystems, Inc., 1989a, 1989b, 1994–2005) standard for UNIX GUIs are other examples of commercial platform guidelines.

Developing an interface under platform guidelines has several advantages. In particular, following platform guidelines promotes consistency and standardization across applications. Users may more easily transition across applications that adhere to the same platform guidelines. In addition, commercial platform guides often have a commercial toolkit or development environment. Using such a package, the developer may not have to rebuild code for windows, and so on.

Following commercial platform guidelines also has some potential disadvantages. Adherence to platform guidelines alone does not ensure usability. If the guidelines were developed without evaluation or input from a user interface expert, they may point design toward lessened usability. Another issue is that the platform guidelines may spell out the appearance and behavior of an interface object but neglect to say when to use it. For example, platform guidelines may describe the appearance and behavior of both radio buttons and check boxes but neglect to specify the conditions for their use. Additionally, platform guidelines often neglect to specify how to combine interface elements.

## Examples of Platform Guidelines

### Common User Access
Common User Access was a set of Guidelines proposed by IBM (1990, 1992). The guidelines supported a graphical user interface for applications running on OS/2 and System Application Architecture (SAA, part of a layered architecture in which the architectural interface was standardized and independent of software or hardware platform). The guidelines fall into three categories:

- The keyboard, screen, mouse.
- The content (appearance and sequencing) of interface elements.
- The nature of the interaction.

### Making It Macintosh
In 1992, Apple Computer published *Macintosh Human Interface Guidelines* and later (1993) Apple Computer released a CD called *Making It Macintosh: The Macintosh Human Interface Guidelines Companion. Making It Macintosh* used over a hundred computer animations to demonstrate the Macintosh user interface look and feel and to illustrate solutions to designers. Both were packaged together in electronic form as *Electronic Guide to Macintosh Human Interface Design* for pre-OS X Macs (Apple Computer, 1994). The guidelines indicate that user interfaces for Macintosh systems are to follow principles of human–computer interaction, such as consistency, direct manipulation, use of metaphors, user control, avoidance of modality, and

presentation of stability. For information on user interface guidelines for OS X, as well as links to previous Macintosh guidelines, see *Introduction to Apple Human Interface Guidelines* (Apple Computer 2006).

### Microsoft Windows User Experience

*Microsoft Windows User Experience* (Microsoft 1999) is the official style guidelines for applications that were created for Windows 2000. In addition to the style guidelines, the book includes some hints about user interface design. The book includes additional guidelines for user interfaces for Windows 98, as well as some low-level detailed information, concerning such topics as the System Registry (cf. Microsoft 1992, 1993, 1994, 1995, 1999).

## 9.4 Project Guidelines

We have already discussed the importance of consistency in the design of interactions. One way to guarantee at least a minimum level of consistency within or across projects is to establish *project guidelines.* These guidelines may specify the format, look, or behavior of elements across your development project or even across all projects from your group or corporation. The following are some issues that may be standardized across your project (cf. Hix and Hartson 1993):

- Button size and appearance.
- Background color.
- Startup window size.
- Formats for information, such as date and time.
- Standard formats for system messages.
- Use of a metaphor.

Many development environments permit you to set these types of guidelines as defaults. As a rule of practice, user interface development teams should always produce a set of project guidelines. These guidelines can be used in the design decision-making process and also as a way to record your development group's thinking process. Whenever possible, it is a good idea to evaluate the quality of project guidelines. Clearly these project guidelines should be established early enough in the development process so that they can be used.

Suppose your company is developing an application to run within the Microsoft Windows environment. You have available to you the Microsoft guidelines (e.g., Microsoft, 1992). Why would you spend the time to develop your own project guidelines? Gale (1996) suggests several reasons:

- Your company may have a number of interface development efforts in progress that are all to be delivered as part of a larger system. Project guidelines help ensure consistency across applications and help the applications hang together as an integrated whole.
- The many different development and delivery platforms available for GUIs increase the likelihood of inconsistent interfaces.
- Having a tangible document, such as project guidelines, may make the characteristics of the target interface less esoteric and more concrete.
- Having project guidelines may reinforce a company's image in the marketplace by showing a uniform look and feel across products.

Platform style guidelines can fail to produce usable interfaces. Gale (1996) offers some reasons:

- The document is too long and unwieldy to use.
- The document covers many application types, and it is difficult for the developer to localize the guidelines that apply to a particular development effort.
- The management of the company makes the assumption that an interface developed within the style guidelines is usable and does not require any user or product testing.
- The guidelines contain no mention of how to use them within the framework of the development cycle.

## 9.5 External Standards

External standards are official specifications or documents. They are often developed by government agencies with the goal of protecting the public or of ensuring a minimum level of quality. External standards documents are usually publicly available or available for purchase and may be enforceable by law or form the basis of contracts. We are all familiar with the idea of government standards concerning zoning or amperage levels in appliances. You may be surprised to learn that standards concerning usability also exist.

The most well-known standard is called *MIL-STD-1472C Military Specification for Human Engineering Requirements for Military Systems, Equipment and Facilities.* A number of the elements of MIL-STD-1472C are drawn from the Smith and Mosier (1986) guidelines.

Other usability standards include ISO 9241 and ISO 13407 from the International Standards Organization (ISO). ISO 9241 describes requirements for ergonomics of visual display workstations. It concentrates on ergonomics of the work area and consists of seventeen parts covering the physical design of computers and terminals and the design of UI for software. These standards refer to distance from monitor, angle, position, and characteristics of keyboard and mouse. For example, keyboard spacing is set to between 18 mm and 20 mm. Tom Stewart's System Concepts Web site (www.system-concepts.com) includes a number of links and documents concerning the details of ISO 9241.

Why would an organization specify this kind of information about the physical and environmental characteristics of interactions? Research has indicated that repetitive stress injuries, headaches, and carpal tunnel syndrome may be caused by the poor ergonomics of a person's workstation. In an installation operating under ISO 9241, a person whose station is not in compliance and who has one of these injuries may be entitled to injury treatment paid by worker's compensation insurance.

ISO 13407 is another set of standards that relates to human–computer interaction. This set of standards focuses on the human-centered design processes for interactive systems and is directed toward project managers. Specifically, this set of standards elaborates the steps in the UI engineering process. (See EMMUS, 1999, for more details of ISO 13407.)

When external standards are specific and therefore measurable, they can be very useful. However, when standards use simple or general wording and do not give specific definitions to words, such as *consistent,* the feature can be difficult to measure and therefore it may be difficult to decide whether the product is in compliance. Simple or general wording leaves open many interpretations and thereby opens the door for any interface to be in compliance. Notice that hardware features may be easier to be in compliance, especially when the standard is in terms of a measurement. Software standards usually are more vague, especially those that relate to interface quality or usability.

## 9.6 Conclusions About Guidelines and Standards

It would seem that the more guidelines and standards a designer receives, the easier the job will be, but it is not so. For example, tell a designer to build a consistent interface. Is it immediately obvious how to do this? No way! Many guidelines are at best rules of thumb. Determining when to apply them and how well they are working is difficult. Use of guidelines can be particularly frustrating for programmers who have little user interface development experience. Tetzlaff and Schwartz (1991) found that inexperienced user interface developers were more frustrated than expert designers by design guidelines that lacked rules for building interfaces to solve complex problems. The inexperienced developers also tended to look more at the pictures in the design guidelines than to read the companion text.

What good is it to talk about guidelines then? Many of the guidelines we have discussed may seem like rules of thumb or common sense. Realistically, if the guidelines were just common sense, we wouldn't need to talk about them. Guidelines and standards are tools for the designer. Sometimes they explicitly constrain the type of interaction, and other times they serve as a starting point in design. To be useful they must be acknowledged and applied!

## 9.7 Guidelines for Visual Design

We are now going to change direction. Rather than specifically discussing types of standards and guidelines, we are going to focus on some additional guidelines for visual design. Many of today's interfaces have a strong visual element. A good visual design can improve the usability of your interface, and a bad visual design can doom you to failure. The following is an example before we talk about some specifics.

Consider the following Web page for the fictional company Julie's Cat Crafts. Suppose that this fictitious company contains numerous typical and hard-to-find supplies for crafts that involve cats, so the Web site is a must visit for cat-loving hobbyists. However, the opening page, as seen in Figure 9.1 is nearly unreadable. The letters on the top of the page are extremely difficult to distinguish from the background. The star banner at the top is the same size as the information at the top. Users have to scroll to the bottom of the page to find out where the Cat Crafts store is located and why they might want to visit the store. Also, note the very intriguing picture of the Florida sunset; while beautiful, how does the background contribute to the readability and presentation of information at the Web site? Finally, how important is it to know that this site was developed by catsweb.com? In this section, we discuss some errors in visual design, many of which are illustrated by the Cat Crafts Web site.

Visual design is sometimes described as *layout* design and is concerned with the visual appearance of your interface. A number of elements influence the visual appearance, including use of color (foreground and background), placement and size of interface objects, and the distribution of information versus noninformation. Numerous texts and articles have appeared on this subject, and our discussion is in no way complete. Many of the Smith and Mosier (1986) guidelines relate to visual design. Hopefully, the few suggestions that we give will help you avoid common errors, especially the kind we see from student usability engineering projects or the Julie's Cat Crafts Web site. For more information, see Mullet and Sano (1995), Weinschenk, Jamar, and Yeo (1997), Horton (1995), and Johnson (2000). The following guidelines should help you improve your visual designs.

**Figure 9.1**   Web Page for Julie's Cat Crafts.
(Photo courtesy of LML)

### 9.7.1 Color

How do we find ripe fruit in a leafy apple tree in late summer? The red color of ripe apples helps to draw our attention to the ripe fruit. In a black background, as in Figure 9.2, the yellow shape is easy to see, but in Figure 9.3 the blue shape blends into the blue background. The lessons that we can learn from these two examples are that color can attract our attention and that the contrast between foreground and background is critical to our ability to distinguish colors.

Color is one of the most powerful tools that the designer has available. It is also potentially one of the most misused. Shneiderman (1998) notes that color can add interest to an otherwise uninteresting display. It can draw the attention of users to important interface elements and events, such as error messages. Shneiderman suggests that the use of color for maps, architectural drawings, and graphs encourages greater information density than do monochrome displays. With the widespread availability of color displays, users expect to see color, but Horton (1995) warns against "Crayola Effect and Photoshop Envy," which occurs when the designer uses too many colors. Horton, Powell (1990), and Shneiderman all recommend using about four colors for a single display, even though thousands of colors may be available.

Figure 9.2    Yellow Shape Visible Against Black Background.

Figure 9.3    Blue Shape Difficult to See Against Blue Background.

In the Cat Crafts example, one of the problems is that the pink textual information was nearly unreadable on the red background. Some combinations of colors work better than others. For example, yellow on a blue background is often easier to read. Purple or magenta on a brown background may be very hard to read. Pace (1984) found that black on blue and blue on white led to lower error rates than did other combinations of colors. Certain color combinations may be especially problematic for some users. In particular, approximately 7 percent of the male population and about 0.4% of the female population are color-blind and have difficulties distinguishing among colors, especially shades of red and green.

### 9.7.2 Organizing Interface Elements

You have your screen and all your interface objects. So how are you going to arrange the objects on the screen? First, if you are transforming a paper form into an electronic form, you must determine how closely you should preserve the format of the paper form. Thus, the first question to ask your users is, Do they want an electronic duplicate of their paper form? They may reason that the retraining costs for their employees do not justify variations in the paper form. If, however, your users are willing to go along with a potentially new look and feel for the form, you will want to avoid what Horton (1995) calls "Horseless Carriage Thinking," in which the designer simply moves the paper form to an electronic media, ignoring potential usability improvements. For example, your paper form may fit onto an 8.5-×-11-inch piece of paper, but your user's screen is not this size. Rather than simply building a long scrolling form, you may consider dividing the form across multiple screens. You can use your electronic form to cue your user about valid data for fields. For example, a field for Grandmother's Date of Birth with some blank underscores gives visual cues as to the format of the expected data. The user should infer from the following template that the response *November 13, 1895,* is not correct but that *11/13/1895* is.

Grandmother's Date of Birth _ _/_ _/_ _ _ _

Johnson (2000) has pointed to another common and misleading visual design error relating to layout of interface objects. His "blunder" involves the layout and arrangement of controls on dialogues. Given a context-specific dialogue, designers will simply integrate the context-specific controls and generic or general-purpose controls. This practice may hide the context-specific controls. For example, dialogue boxes often have general-purpose buttons such as *OK* and/or *Cancel.* Suppose a specialized dialog also has a *Sort* option. According to Johnson, it would be unwise to make the *Sort* button look and be positioned like the *OK* and *Cancel* buttons. Johnson suggests moving the context-specific controls close to the context-specific information.

### 9.7.3 Fonts

When we present information with text, we need to select the appearance of the specific characters. Unfortunately, many of the choices that we might make may actually reduce usability. For example, if we select tiny font sizes that can only be read by a person with normal vision, those with less than perfect vision may be left squinting or unable to see the information at all. Consider where possible selecting at least a 12-point font and allowing your user to adjust the font size. Serif fonts (like this one) are generally considered easier to read for those who are expert in the language presented. Nonnative readers may find sans serif fonts (like this one) easier to read because they can more easily distinguish individual letters.

Another font error to avoid is what Horton (1995) has labeled "Ransom Note Typography," for example, "RaNsom note eXample." In this example, textual information is presented in a number of fonts. When you try to read something that looks like a ransom note, chances are that you end up reading each word separately instead of reading a multiword string. Reading each word separately is slower than reading strings.

For another font error, consider the following e-mail exchange between Skipper and Cho.

From: Skipper

To: Cho

Dear Cho—I have to work late tonight at the club.

From: Cho

To: Skipper

DEAR SKIPPER—THIS IS THE THIRD NIGHT THIS WEEK. WHEN WILL YOU BE HOME TONIGHT?

Cho's response resulted in Skipper being offended. Skipper interpreted the all capitals to indicate shouting, so Cho's e-mail contained two messages: the question about when Skipper would be home and the shouting. Avoid using all capitals in your routine text presentations. Some users will perceive that the interface is shouting. Also, all capitals are typical of the output of older interface styles. Some users may interpret all capitals to be "computerese."

### 9.7.4 Labels

We are inundated with interface objects with labels. Unfortunately, many of those labels are confusing or misleading. For example, consider the dialogue box in Figure 9.4. What does "Cancel" mean? It could mean to cancel the input or to end the dialogue. Perhaps a better label would have been "End Name Entry." However, Johnson (2000) suggests that very long labels can also be problematic because they contain too much information or the user simply does not read them. In the Julie's Cat Crafts store, the label "Click Here" signifies a link but might have been improved by using "Satisfied Customers" to signify it.

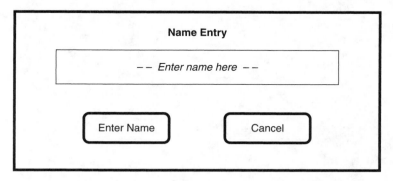

**Figure 9.4**    Poor Labels.

### 9.7.5 Drawing Attention to the Wrong Information

Unfortunately, it is very easy to draw a user's attention to the wrong element of your interface. As we have already seen, misused colors and color combinations can achieve this nefarious goal. Numerous other ways can draw attention as well. For example, consider the Web page for the fictitious company Over the Mountain, shown in Figure 9.5. The background, which is really just

Figure 9.5    Example of an Overpowering Background.

for decoration, overwhelms the foreground information that contains information for the user. Horton (1995) has called this type of design flaw a "Bullying Background."

Be careful with designs with graphics! That old bit of wisdom that a picture is worth a thousand words is not an ancient Chinese proverb, nor is it always true. (Blackwell [1997] reports the origin of this proverb to be Western and related to a scheme to sell advertising on public transportation in the 1920s; see also Mieder 1990.) To the point, humans like to look at graphics and will look at graphical information when it is presented. Often graphics draw our attention even when the graphic itself has little informational content. However, recall that graphics and text that work together can actually present information more effectively than either text or graphics alone (Teasley, Instone, Leventhal, and Brown 1997).

Have you noticed how many infomercials are on TV these days? The products they market look great, but are they as good as they appear? How is it that things look great on TV, but get them home and you may have wasted your money? My brother (LML) and I once bought a TV product as a gift for our parents. It was a piece of junk. The advertising on TV, through the clever use of lighting, angles, and other visual effects made the product appear to be something more than it was. In interface design, it is possible to do the same thing with graphics, especially with graphs. Suppose you are trying to sell product B and your competitor is selling product A. Usability of these products has been evaluated on a 100-point scale with 0 the lowest and 100 the highest. Figure 9.6 shows a graph of the usability for product A and product B. If you look closely at the values (1.10 and 1.20), product A and product B both have terrible usability, but the graph makes product B look a lot better than product A with the creative use of scaling and manipulation of context. The scary thing is that you actually might be able to sell product B as more usable than product A. The lesson here is to be cautious with your presentations of graphical or chart information.

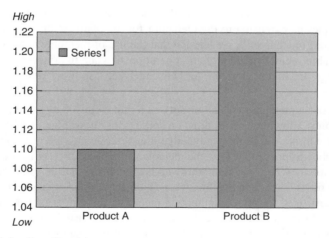

Figure 9.6   Misleading Graphics.

You can use a number of other techniques to draw attention to the wrong information. For example, humans are drawn to blinking or movement, so unless you really wish to get attention, use blinking and movement sparingly. Smith and Mosier (1986) recommend a blink rate of 2 Hz to 5 Hz.

### 9.7.6 Using Symbols and Visual Metaphors

Many symbols and colors carry information additional to the color or symbol itself. For example, in many Western cultures white is a color symbolizing purity, while in some Eastern cultures white is a color symbolizing death.

Consider the symbol in Figure 9.7. How would you interpret it? Perhaps you thought it had something to do with seeing or with opening something. According to Deurer (1996) this symbol in ancient Egyptian mythology was called an *Udjat*. It was the eye of the god Horus and symbolized healing. The lesson here is that you can easily mislead your user by using symbols with one meaning to the user and another to the interface.

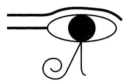

**Figure 9.7**    Udjat.

The Julie's Cat Crafts Web site drew our attention away from the important information on the screen in a number of ways. The big graphic about being developed by catsweb.com and the "Click Here" link, as well as the sunset background, stole our attention away from the text.

Platform guidelines may dictate your use of visual metaphors in your user interface. What if your project includes an extension to the metaphor for the platform or you are going to choose your own metaphor? In Chapter 7, we learned that the use of metaphors and analogies can help users build workable mental models of the operation of your interface and can help them to transfer knowledge from one domain to your interface. So how do you choose a visual metaphor?

When you choose a metaphor (visual or not), two things must be kept in mind. First, the use of the metaphor must allow the user to draw on some prior knowledge. A metaphor that is unfamiliar to the user will not aid in this knowledge transfer. Second, the user must understand the limit of the metaphor. Suppose that I use the metaphor of a flamethrower for the operation *Delete File*. In my metaphor, when my flamethrower is pointed at a file name and I activate the flamethrower, the file is deleted. In real life, when an object is struck by an activated flamethrower, it will likely be destroyed. In my computerized metaphor this might be true or it might not be. Perhaps, like in real life, my file will be destroyed or perhaps it will be recoverable. This question is only answerable if I understand the limitations of the metaphor. For the metaphor to be useful, the user must understand the reference and the extent of the match between the current situation and the metaphor.

Metaphors are oftentimes conveyed with visual symbols. In your choice of symbols, be sure to reflect the metaphor that you are trying to convey and that your users understand that a goal of the symbol is to indicate the metaphor.

### 9.7.7 Use of Spacing, Groupings, and Balance Within a Window, Field, or Dialogue

Your eye perceives groupings of text even before you read the content of the text. Clever use of space to show groupings can greatly enhance the information that is presented. The spacing of information within a window, field, or dialogue box can give your user visual clues about what information belongs together.

One of the key elements of spacing is the use of blank or dead space. This blank space is often called *white space.* White space can be used to separate groups of information and, in general, to aid readability. How much white space is enough? Surprisingly, Tullis (1983) found that performance was significantly degraded if less than one-fourth of the available space was used as white space. Powell (1990) has suggested the use of at least 50 percent of available character space be filled with white space.

You should consider using separate screens when you have clear groupings of information. When users scroll through long windows, they may forget the elements that they have seen together.

Powell (1990) suggests that screen balance is helpful to readability. He suggests the use of approximately the same number of screen elements at top and bottom, left and right. Use of columns for text is helpful to achieve this balance. To aid in the legibility of information in columns, he recommends at least $\frac{1}{8}$ inch between columns and alignment and justification of the columns.

Mullet and Sano (1995) have suggested a simple test to check the groupings of your interface elements. This *squint test* works as follows:

- Close one eye and squint with the other one. If the organization of your screen is obvious while squinting, it is probably okay.

## Conclusions

Following established standards and guidelines can help you build user interfaces that are internally consistent and consistent with other applications. A number of types of standards and guidelines exist, including general guidelines, platform guidelines, project guidelines, and external standards.

Visual designs are a powerful way to present information. Unfortunately, visual designs can go wrong in many ways.

## Exercises

1. Define the following terms: *external standards, guidelines, commercial platform guidelines,* and *project guidelines.*
2. What are the advantages and disadvantages of developing a project in compliance with platform guidelines?
3. What are some of the elements in an interaction that could or should be standardized in a project?
4. Find some examples on the World Wide Web that have really poor visual design. Describe, in terms of our guidelines, why you consider them bad.

5. Find a copy of the Smith and Mosier (1986) guidelines. Smith and Mosier provide guidelines for six areas of user interface design. List each of the six areas and give a two- or three-sentence description of the types of problems that are discussed in each area.

6. Pick three of the following four user interaction design problems. For each problem you select, find three Smith and Mosier (1986) guidelines that are applicable to the design of this interaction. Completely specify the location of the guideline. List the content of the guideline. How did you find the guideline? How do you think the guideline is related to the problem?

*Note:* The point of this exercise is *not to design* the interaction, but *to understand how* one uses guidelines in design. You are not to actually design the interactions. You are to identify which guidelines are appropriate.

### Interaction Design Problems

*Flyfast Airlines:* You are designing an interaction for the ticket agents for Flyfast Airlines. At one point, the ticket agents choose the type of seating from a menu. Design a feedback window that alerts users when they have made an erroneous entry or choice. In the box, they will need to choose from a list of correct options.

*HappyTemps:* You are designing an online form that potential employees will use to enter personal information about their background and skills. As you organize the data to be collected, determine how many pages (screens) will be necessary and how the user will navigate among the pages.

*FoodWorld Grocery Store:* You are designing a system with which a user can conduct a complex set of transactions for inventory control, such as demand analyses, sales projections, theft-loss reports, and purchase orders. The user will navigate through a series of screens to find information and/or to enter data. Some transactions will require multiple screens, and some will require one screen. Users may need to interrupt one transaction and go to another.

*SPIES Database:* You are designing a user interface that protects the SPIES master database from unauthorized users. Different users will have different levels of privileges.

# Part 5

# Revisiting the Process

# Prototyping Your Interaction

## Motivation

In this chapter, we revisit the development process. You may recall that in Chapter 4 we learned that the stages of the Waterfall Model form the basis for many software development methodologies. In that chapter, we mentioned that one of the basic problems with the Waterfall Model, especially for user interface development, is that the model does not support iteration—that is, the model does not support the notion of being able to go backward in the process, even if some aspect is incomplete or not exactly what the user had in mind. In this chapter, we revisit the idea of iteration and prototyping. We also discuss some types of development tools that can be especially useful in a development project that includes prototyping. At the end of this section, you should be able to answer the following questions:

- What are the different types of prototypes?
- When in the development cycle are the different types of prototypes most likely to be used?
- What do we mean by *fidelity* in the context of prototyping?
- What are some of the hazards of prototyping?
- What are some of the benefits of prototyping?
- What types of tools should you consider?

## 10.1 Why Discuss Prototyping Here?

In Chapter 4, we discussed different variations on the process of software development. The Waterfall Model is the oldest and best known model for the software development process. As we saw in Chapter 4, following a Waterfall-based methodology imposes discipline upon the process and facilitates scheduling and resource allocation. However, a number of difficulties arise when following a strictly Waterfall-based methodology, particularly for a project that has a significant user interface component. In a project with a significant user interface, it is likely that the developer will not be able to answer all the questions in one development phase before going on to the next phase. Iteration or repetition of phases is an integral part of the user interface life cycle. Prototyping is one mechanism for iterative design; building and evaluating prototypes helps us to decide whether to move forward in the development process or to iterate back to a previous state. Other strategies incorporate analysis of risk or expected value to the evaluation of prototypes in determining whether to go forward or backward (cf. Boehm 1986, Boehm 1988, Boehm and Huang 2003). While some studies indicate that prototyping can actually reduce development time, developers must schedule and integrate iteration into the development process. Finally, the very tools we can use to build interfaces can be used as prototyping tools.

## 10.2 Introduction to Prototyping and Iterative Design

Building a software system that a user actually wants is challenging. Often users are not sure of exactly what functions they would like the system to perform. Many times users have difficulty communicating their needs to the system developers. In addition, users may have faulty expectations regarding computing and may be unaware of some of the power, flexibility, and features that computer applications can offer. Alternatively, they may overestimate the functionality they can obtain for their projected investment. Finally, developers may be unsure how to distribute operations, especially those that can be automated.

Being able to see *something* in order to provide feedback for the designers often empowers users. They find that they can better articulate their project requirements. Prototypes are the *something* that users can see and are the artifacts that support iteration in software development. A prototype is a model and is not a refined and finished product. Specifically, according to Sommerville (2000, p. 172), a prototype is

> an initial version of a software system which is used to demonstrate concepts, try out design options and, generally, to find out more about the problem and its possible solutions.

Luqi (1989) adds that

> a prototype is a concrete . . . model of selected aspects of a proposed system. Rapid prototyping is the process of quickly building and evaluating a series of prototypes.

To support iterative development, usability engineers must be able to generate prototypes more quickly than a finished product. *Prototyping* is the strategy by which we generate prototypes quickly.

## 10.3 Steps for Prototyping: The Prototyping Life Cycle

In general, prototyping can be described as having a series of steps (Scharer 1983; Leventhal and Mynatt, 1991). You will probably notice that these steps look like a mini software engineering lifecycle. That is really not surprising if you remember back in Chapter 4 that we discussed the role of iteration in software engineering. The steps, based on Scharer (1983) and Leventhal and Mynatt (1991), include these:

- *Context setting and information gathering.* In this first step, the existing system is reviewed, the proposed system's feasibility and costs are evaluated, and some user requirements are gathered. In other words, we are defining the problem that we are targeting with the current prototype. Luqi (1989) calls this stage *determine requirements.*
- *Prototype design.* In the second step, the user evaluates a preliminary description (written) of the solution system. Luqi (1989) calls this stage *design prototype system.*
- *Prototype construction.* In the next step a baseline prototype is generated, along with a plan for its incremental growth. Luqi (1989) calls this stage *demonstrate prototype.*
- *Prototype finalization.* The final step has users evaluate the prototype, and the developers revise the prototype accordingly. Luqi (1989) calls this stage *user validation.*

Building prototypes should be a planned activity. A chaotic approach to prototype development potentially can create many of the same problems that we discussed for a chaotic approach to software development.

## 10.4 Advantages to Prototyping

Prototyping seems to have numerous advantages. First, users only truly understand the system requirements when they can see some form of implementation in action. Prototyping can lead to improved functional requirements, improved interaction requirements, and easier evolution of requirements. In addition, experiments show improvements in products and communication. Boehm, Gray, and Seewaldt (1984) performed an experiment comparing the prototyping approach to the conventional approach. They found that prototyping led to products with approximately equivalent performance, but 40 percent less code and 45 percent less effort. They also found that the prototyped systems were easier to learn and to use but somewhat less robust. In another experiment that compared a prototyping approach to a conventional approach, Alavi (1984) reported that prototyping led to enhanced communication between users and designers. However, she also reported that the use of prototyping led to difficulties in controlling the design process. From a study of thirty nine projects involving prototyping, Gordon and Bieman (1995) reported that prototyping improved the match between the final system and user needs, improved usability, and reduced development resources. Nielsen (1993b) describes a study of iterative design that was conducted by Clare-Marie Karat, in which Karat estimates at least a two-to-one savings in improved design as compared to increased development costs.

From the perspective of the usability engineer, prototyping offers a number of additional advantages. For example, the user interface is more carefully designed and tailored to the user's needs. The user becomes involved more completely in the evolution of the product. The low cost and availability of at least some prototyping tools make their acquisition feasible even with a small budget and less productivity. Luqi (1989) has added that prototyping moves some changes to the development phase that would otherwise be delayed to the maintenance phase; most notable of these changes are those that are related to mismatches between requirements and design or product.

## 10.5 How Extensive or Complete Should the Prototype Be?

During the prototyping process, the developer must decide whether to build a full prototype of the target system or only a portion of the system. A developer might choose to build a *local* prototype if he or she only has to deal with an isolated, tricky part of a system. On the other hand, if the developer is unsure of many aspects of the interface, he or she may choose to build a *global* prototype. Another issue that developers must decide is whether the prototype will be incorporated into the final system or if it is to be a throwaway effort. According to Luqi (1989) prototypes may not include all aspects of the target system and may be implemented in environments other than the final operational environment.

## 10.6 Styles of Prototypes

Prototypes may be distinguished by the amount of detail that they include and the goal of the prototype (Mynatt 1990; Leventhal and Mynatt 1991).

Some authors divide prototypes into two types (cf. Rudd, Stern, and Isensee 1996):

- Low-fidelity prototypes.
- High-fidelity prototypes.

Carey and Mason (1983) and Leventhal and Mynatt (1991) divide prototypes into three categories:

- Scenario/storyboard prototypes.
- Demonstration prototypes.
- Version 0 prototypes.

In the following sections, we discuss both categorization schemes and how they fit together.

### 10.6.1 Low-Fidelity Prototypes

Rudd, Stern, and Isensee (1996) define *low-fidelity prototypes* as prototypes with limited functionality and limited user interactions. Such prototypes are generated quickly, sometimes on the fly with users, and are used as a presentation of concept to the user. Rudd et al. point out that because the user is not interacting with the prototype in any realistic way, it is likely that a facilitator will be necessary to lead the user through the prototype.

Low-fidelity prototypes are especially useful in the early stages of the development life cycle. Sometimes looking at a quick and rough prototype can help users better express what they really want and what problem they really need to have solved. Low-fidelity prototypes are usually inexpensive to generate and do not require a lengthy development time.

Using low-fidelity prototypes has potential disadvantages as well. For example, users may simply watch low-fidelity prototypes since they have only limited interactivity. If users do so, their feedback may not be particularly detailed or even accurate because they may not see subtlety or detail. Also, because the low-fidelity prototype is usually short on details, the persons implementing the prototype may fill in the details themselves (cf. Rudd, Stern, and Isensee 1996). Under the Carey and Mason (1983) categorization, there are two types of low-fidelity prototypes: storyboard and demonstration prototypes.

### Scenario and Storyboard Prototypes

The terms *storyboard* and *scenario* are intended to give the impression of "paper and pencil." In a *storyboard prototype,* the user is presented with an example of the interface on paper or as a screen display. The prototyped presentation may illustrate the look of the interface for a scenario or scenarios. In general, each frame of the storyboard represents one page or screen that the user might actually see from the interface.

Storyboard prototypes can be produced relatively inexpensively with a minimum amount of programmer time or computing resources. However because such prototypes are tangible, real users can give feedback and designers can brainstorm while looking at them. Many usability engineers find that scenario prototypes are especially useful in the early stages of development or to hammer out a piece of the interface in which the requirements are not well understood. Storyboards, by their nature, tend to focus attention on high-level details. In addition, it may be difficult for both designers and users to grasp the dynamic behavior of an interface on the basis of storyboards.

The tools to build storyboard prototypes may be very simplistic and include colored pens to actually draw screens, sticky notes to represent buttons or menus, and so on. Drawing software can be used in place of paper and pencils to produce screens or report mock-ups. The advantages of using these tools are the ease of modification, the ability to reproduce portions of each page, and the neatness of the product. The major disadvantages of these tools are that the screen size, page size, and other characteristics of the target system must be known and taken into account in creating each storyboard frame.

In the audio catalog project, team members might elect to start the design of their overall interaction, as well as the design of individual screens, by drawing storyboard prototypes. Team members will collect paper and some pens. Perhaps the first designer has a great idea and draws a sketch of the idea. Then a second team member looks at the sketch, makes some changes, and shows it to the group. The team has not invested a lot of money or time in the construction of the prototype, but the team has been able to convey many of the static visual characteristics of its design in a way that all team members can understand.

### Demonstration Prototypes

In the demonstration prototyping approach, users are allowed to enter their own restricted sets of data or to perform some limited sets of functions with the prototype. The prototype then processes some limited range of user queries or data, using limited files, and generates one of a limited set of outputs. *Demonstration prototypes* are intended to show the look of the interface and a notion of the expected behavior of the interface and may draw upon the user's scenarios that were described during task analysis.

Once the usability engineer has a clear idea of the requirements, the usefulness of this type of prototype may be greater than the scenario/storyboard approach. A demonstration prototype can show some true system functionality, giving the user and the designer a better picture of the look and feel of the proposed system. The user and designer can evaluate the proposed behavior of the interface in some detail. Because the demonstration prototype has some interactive characteristics, the user may find it more realistic and may take the evaluation more seriously than with storyboard prototypes. However, you should be cautious with demonstration prototypes. Your users may not understand that this is not a working system because the demonstration may be pretty convincing from their perspective. Your users may also be confused by the "canned" reactions that are the nature of demonstration prototypes.

Several types of software can be used to support the creation of demonstration prototypes. One approach is to use a programming environment that can handle user input and connect the input with a preplanned output. If the usability engineer selects this approach, it is important to select a programming environment that supports the expected user input. For example, if the user will be expected to push an interface button via a mouse click, Visual Basic might be a good choice as it includes buttons and a template for a mouse-click event (cf. Microsoft 2003). The C programming language would likely be a poorer choice as it has none of these features built into it.

Another approach to creating demonstration prototypes is to use a hypermedia environment. Used in a simple way, hypermedia systems can be used to create prototypes that are essentially storyboards. These prototypes can be shown as a sort of slide show. With more complex programming, the hypermedia prototype can present menus and respond differently, depending on which choice was selected.

In the audio catalog project, the team may wish to build a demonstration prototype to show both the visual appearance and some of the dynamics of their design. The team might choose to build the visual elements of the design using a prototyping or visual design tool. Now, rather than fully implementing the features of the design, they may wish to hard code some data into the prototype. Perhaps they hard code information about two CDs: (1) *Highland Howliday* and (2) *Simon Carlson: Greatest Hits.* When the test users scan through the CD records in the catalog, they will see only the two CDs that were hard-coded into the original demonstration. Suppose the team also hides a hard-coded record for the CD *Chasing Mice* by Fast Cat. When the user goes to add a record, regardless of what is typed, the information about the Fast Cat CD will be entered. While the prototype is not truly "functional," it still can show users and other designers how the interaction would go.

### 10.6.2  High-Fidelity Prototypes

According to Rudd, Stern, and Isensee (1996), *high-fidelity prototypes* have complete or nearly complete functionality and are interactive. Users are able to navigate a high-fidelity prototype. The timing behavior of the prototype is similar to the final product.

Using high-fidelity prototypes has a number of advantages. For example, developers can utilize high-fidelity prototypes to gather realistic user feedback. Because the high-fidelity prototype appears to be fairly complete, the developer also can use the prototype as a marketing tool. On the other hand, high-fidelity prototypes require much more development time and resources, as compared to low-fidelity prototypes. Because of the amount of work involved in building high-fidelity prototypes, they are not particularly useful in the early parts of the development cycle and should not be used to help users clarify their requirements (cf. Rudd, Stern, and Isensee 1996). Version 0 prototypes (cf. Carey and Mason 1983) are an example of high-fidelity prototypes.

### Version 0 Prototypes

The term *Version 0* is based on the idea that systems under development go through a series of different versions. Usually the first working version would be Version 1, so a pre-working version would be Version 0. In a *Version 0 prototype,* the prototype is a working release of the system. The prototype is intended to be used under conditions similar to the final, targeted environment. A Version 0 prototype lacks the full functionality of the final interface but is typically developed with the tools for the final product. The Version 0 prototype resides in the environment of the final product. It is a goal of the Version 0 approach to create code that will eventually evolve into the released version of the system.

What kind of functionality is left out of a Version 0 prototype? Typically the developer may choose to leave out help and error messaging or parts of the system that are incompletely understood. The Version 0 prototype may purposefully leave out those elements of the interface that the developer expects to be altered through suggestions from the user.

Version 0 prototypes have a number of advantages. For example, the prototype evolves into the final product. There is less need for eliminating throwaway code than in the other approaches. The user sees progress being made on the real product and can feel that the project is moving forward.

The main disadvantage of Version 0 prototyping is that the developers, after spending time and resources on the prototype, may be reluctant to throw away a bad design. They may be hesitant to abandon a particular approach even if it does not meet the user's needs. Think of your own experience in your programming classes. Perhaps you have an assignment that is due on Thursday that by Monday is about 95 percent finished. You realize on Monday that if you would have taken a different approach from the beginning, your final product would have been better and your overall development effort easier. You also realize that that last 5 percent of your project is going to be tough to complete because it is going to take some convoluted coding to get it to work. What do you do? Do you start over again, or do you try to hack what you have into shape? Most of us would continue to work with what we have already finished, even if we rationally know that we might actually save time by starting over. This happens with Version 0 prototypes as well. Developers are hesitant to abandon a bad design, often choosing to try to retrofit it into the user's needs even if the fit is poor. Even when a developer has a good design, he or she may be reluctant to incorporate refinements that significantly alter the prototype because the refinements change the original work.

Suppose that we have a team of designers for the audio catalog project who build a Version 0 prototype. What exactly would be implemented? Looking back at the original task description in Chapter 6, we can see that some of the most important functions involve adding, changing, and removing CDs and songs, so we would expect to see at least some of these functions implemented. Searching seems to reappear in a number of the usage scenarios, so some form of searching probably would be implemented as well. However, error handling and sorting seem to be less critical and might not be included in the Version 0 prototype.

### 10.6.3 Horizontal and Vertical Prototypes

Rudd, Stern, and Isensee (1996) describe two types of compromise prototypes: horizontal and vertical. These types compromise on the placement of detail and interactivity in the prototype. Vertical prototypes have high-fidelity on only a portion of the final product, leaving the rest of the product as a low-fidelity prototype. Horizontal prototypes are highly detailed and interactive at a high level but have minimal details at lower levels. Rudd et al. suggest that these prototypes may be used when the developer needs the advantages of a high-fidelity prototype but only has the time or resources to develop a low-fidelity prototype.

### 10.6.4 Wizard of Oz Prototypes

Maulsby, Greenberg, and Mander (1993) have proposed a prototyping strategy that involves the use of what they have called *Wizard of Oz prototypes*. Like the Great Oz in *The Wizard of Oz* (LeRoy and Fleming 1939), the Wizard of Oz prototype also has a hidden operator. Unknown to the person experiencing the prototype, the operator actually runs the prototype; he or she receives input from the user and simulates output. An advantage of this style of prototyping is that the developer can observe the user in their interactions with the prototype, even though the real system has not been finished. The primary difficulty of this approach is that the "wizard" must provide a compelling simulation in order for the user to interact with the system in a meaningful way.

## 10.7  Conclusions About Prototypes and Prototyping

Integrating prototyping into the development life cycle can help users clarify their requirements and give feedback on design alternatives. Prototypes can differ based on the amount of detail in the prototype and how close the prototype is to being the actual product. Developers should not be concerned as to which type of prototype to choose for exclusive use: low- or high-fidelity. Rather they should recognize that all the types of prototypes can be used effectively at different points during the usability engineering life cycle. Selecting a style of prototype also means that developers may be weighing the trade-offs. Users may not find as many errors in low-fidelity prototypes as high-fidelity prototypes, but the cost to develop low-fidelity prototypes is generally much less than the development costs of high-fidelity prototypes (cf. Nielsen 1990).

## 10.8  Tools for Interface Construction and Version 0 Prototypes

Choosing tools for Version 0 prototypes really is a choice for interface developers, since the Version 0 prototype eventually will evolve into a functional system. Using development tools can make prototype generation easier and can facilitate several rounds of iteration. A number of choices are available. *Event-driven programming languages* are general-purpose tools that can be used to build interfaces, while *User Interface Management Systems* (UIMS) and *Dialog Management Systems, toolkits,* and specific prototyping tools are generally directed to the construction of user interfaces. Myers, Hudson, and Pausch (2000) review tools for user interface development.

### 10.8.1  Event-Driven Programming Languages

A key concept in the construction of software to drive user interfaces is the notion of an *event loop,* which is a programming notion in which the loop waits continuously for a user event. When that happens, the program responds. In this way, an event loop is similar to a loop that waits for a real-time event. Event-driven programming languages allow usability engineers to build programs with an event loop structure.

Visual Basic is an example of a programming language that contains support for event-driven programming. In Visual Basic the programming environment may be set up to wait for a user event, such as a mouse click, and then to respond to that specific event. Events are defined as user actions; these actions are managed by event handlers that are procedures or subroutines that are defined to process user inputs (cf. Microsoft 2003).

Hypertalk, released for the Macintosh as part of Hypercard, was a well-known example of an event-driven programming language. Hypercard was a development environment, invented by Bill Atkinson. The idea was that the user would see a series of "cards." These cards typically did not have a linear order, although a specific order could be programmed into the card stack. The objects in the Hypercard presentation included stacks, backgrounds, cards, fields, and buttons. The programmer could write scripts for any of these objects using Hypertalk. Hypertalk was a full, structured programming language that also included event handlers as primitives. It included inheritance of characteristics with stacks at the highest levels. Unless a specific script was set for a low-level object, the low-level object inherited the script of the higher level object. Hypertalk included event handlers for events such as "on-mouse-up" for buttons (cf. CocoaDev 2006).

Event-driven programming languages seem to have a number of advantages as interface development tools. Response to user events is what user interface programming is usually all about, so event-driven programming languages may be a natural choice for building interfaces. They often include built-in interface objects, such as buttons and windows. They typically include a true programming language that uses structures familiar to programmers (e.g., *do-while* and *repeat-until* loops). The base programming language may itself be familiar, so that programmers may be able to use prior knowledge during development. For example, Visual Basic is an extension of qBasic, and Hypertalk was similar to Pascal.

Event-driven programming languages also seem to have some disadvantages. Perhaps you have encountered some of these problems yourself. For one thing, the very familiarity of the language may cause difficulties as the programmer is trying to use a familiar tool to write code under a different paradigm. Interface code and application code are often mixed together. Tracing of program events may be difficult to follow since there is not necessarily a linear flow to these events. In addition to variables, the programmer also needs to keep track of the program state.

Testing event-driven programs seems to be somewhat different from the testing of conventional programs, at least at the logic level. In conventional software development, software testing typically consists minimally of testing the code against the specifications (functional testing) and testing the flow of control through the code (logic level). For example, in an *if-then-else* structure, two paths of control run through the structure. The programmer typically would run at least two test cases, one to test the *if-then* component and one to test the *else* component. In an event-driven program, potentially many paths lead through the code, depending on the states of the events, necessitating many more test cases. Finally, programmers may set up important state variables as global variables in an event-driven program. If the state variables were not global, they would have to be parameters to almost every subprogram. Global variables tightly couple the modules in a program and should be avoided. When a program goes through maintenance, global variables make it virtually impossible to localize changes.

### 10.8.2 Specific User Interface Development Tools

Myers (1989) pointed out that using tools that are targeted specifically to user interface development can lead to both better interfaces and code that are easier to engineer and maintain. He points to a number of advantages:

- User interface designs can be prototyped without developing the application. Comparing alternative designs is easier when the designs can be prototyped efficiently.
- Across applications developed with the tool, the user interface should have consistency.
- The code will be more localized and hence easier to maintain because the interface code is separate from the application code.

One choice is to select a specific prototyping software package. With this kind of development tool, the usability engineer will describe the look and behavior of the interface using components of the tool. The tool will then generate the code to drive the interface. These tools support screen, window, and report generation. The tools often force the developer to build a "standardized" interface for an established commercial platform. The source code that is generated is in a familiar programming language, such as C++. The code is modular and documented. This generated code usually is suitable for expansion by adding additional functions or by combining the modules with others. A common criticism of specific prototyping software is that the code produced is somewhat inefficient and has poor style. The poor coding style may make integrating functional, noninterface components with interface components more difficult.

### 10.8.3 Toolkits

A second type of user interface construction tool is a *toolkit,* which includes definitions of interface widgets or interaction techniques, where widgets are typically defined as low-level interface elements. A widget might be a button or a menu. The idea is that a programming or scripting language describes the specific structure of the interface and the toolkit provides the definitions for widgets that are included in the interface. One criticism of toolkits is that the widgets and their codes are so low level that the toolkits provide only limited assistance in building interfaces. On the other hand, use of toolkits does encourage reuse and, depending on the level of the widgets, may encourage some consistency across applications.

### 10.8.4 User Interface Management System and Dialogue Management

Another approach to the development of Version 0 prototypes is to use a *User Interface Management System* (UIMS) (see Hix 1990 for an overview). UIMSs were originally envisioned as systems that separated the user interface and its operation from the functional components of a system. According to Myers (1988), the first UIMS was created in 1968 by Newman. The notion was that the code for the interface and the code for the function would communicate only as necessary through a mechanism called a *dialog controller* (Bennett 1986). However, function and interface would be separate and could support separate development and maintenance cycles. UIMSs would include tools for user interface development and, in particular, would facilitate the structuring of the screen, the handling of the dialogue between the human and the computer, and the sequencing of events. Bennett points out that a UIMS is both a tool for user interface construction and a run-time system that supports the interaction between the user and applications. Myers adds that a UIMS will typically have a programming environment that is targeted to user interface development rather than general-purpose programming.

A number of techniques for describing interfaces in UIMSs have been offered, including menu networks, state transition diagrams, context-free grammars, event languages, and declarative languages. Some UIMSs are now evolving more toward graphical programming languages by allowing the graphical objects created within the interface to connect with functional objects (cf. Myers 1988).

Two of the goals of UIMSs are to encourage code reuse and to encourage style consistency across interfaces that were created with the particular UIMS. The biggest disadvantages of UIMSs to date seem to be their limited availability and the difficulties of specifying interfaces in these systems. Because UIMSs are not widely marketed, when they are used, they may have high cost, limited availability, and sometimes require special hardware.

### Conclusions

In Chapters 5 through 9, we presented methods for specifying and designing an interaction. The presentation was in a quasi-linear order, much like the Waterfall Model of software engineering described in Chapter 4. While the Waterfall Model can be used in usability engineering, it is a more common practice to follow an iterative model. Prototyping is a widely used mechanism to support iteration in the usability life cycle. Consistent with iterative development models, development and evaluation of prototypes actually occurs through a mini life cycle. The use of prototypes potentially improves usability and user satisfaction and may actually reduce the resources needed for a development effort.

Designers must choose the amount of detail to include in a prototype. The goals of the prototyping effort determine which style of prototype to choose:

- Choose a storyboard prototype to evaluate high-level design details and to facilitate brainstorming.
- Choose a demonstration prototype to evaluate low-level details of interface behavior.
- Choose a Version 0 prototype for user testing and to lead to the development of a full system.

Numerous tools are available for prototype development.

## Exercises

1. Define the following terms: *local prototype, global prototype, low-fidelity prototype, high-fidelity prototype, storyboard prototype, demonstration prototype, Version 0 prototype, horizontal prototype, vertical prototype, Wizard of Oz prototype, event-driven programming language, event loop, User Interface Management System,* and *toolkit.*
2. Name and describe the different steps in the prototyping lifecycle.
3. Describe the advantages and disadvantages of building prototypes.
4. In this exercise, you will develop a prototype for the children's game we have been working on. You are to pick one of the three categories of prototypes and develop a prototype for your game within that category. Answer the following questions as you work on your prototype:
   a. Describe the three categories of prototypes (storyboard, demonstration, Version 0).
   b. Which of the three types of prototypes is the one that you are building?
   c. Where in the software engineering/usability engineering life cycle would you see your prototype fitting in? Justify your answer.
   d. What are the advantages and disadvantages of the type of prototype that you are building as opposed to the other two types?
   e. What tools did you use for your prototype? Were they appropriate to the type of prototype that you are building?
5. We have now seen life cycles for *software engineering, usability engineering,* and the *development of prototypes.* What do you infer about the presence of a development cycle for each of these processes? Relate the necessity of a life cycle for the development of complex artifacts back to our discussion of wicked problems.

# 11

# Usability Assessment

## Motivation

So far we have been focused on what to aim for—usability—and how to achieve it via good usability engineering. But how do we know that we have achieved usability, even if we have followed good practice? The answer is *usability assessment.* In traditional software engineering, we test designs and implementation in order to match the requirements and to check the correctness of logical flow. Add a significant user interface and you add a third kind of assessment: usability assessment. In this chapter, we focus on usability assessment.

When you are finished with this chapter, you should be able to answer the following questions:

- What is the process of usability assessment?
- What are some techniques of usability assessment?
- When should usability testing be performed in the development cycle?
- Where should testing take place: a laboratory or on-site?
- What is the difference between qualitative and quantitative data?
- What is the difference between subjective and objective measures?
- How are data collected?
- What is informed consent?

## 11.1 Introduction

Why do we worry about the evaluation of usability? After all, if a developer has gone through a good development cycle and followed reasonable guidelines all the way through the process, shouldn't the product turn out pretty well? Of course, you know the answer already: without evaluation, you cannot be sure that your final product meets your requirements and is usable. You won't even know if you are on the right track.

Usability assessment is a critical step within the usability engineering life cycle. It may take a number of forms, from analysis to user testing of a product to an evaluation by experts. Good usability assessment takes place a number of times in the development cycle and may take different forms, depending on where the project is in the development cycle. The goals of assessment may vary somewhat as the cycle proceeds.

Humphrey (1994) has made the following points about usability and software quality:

> You must recognize the hierarchical nature of software quality. First, a software product must provide functions of a type and at a time when the user needs them. If it does not, nothing else matters. Second, the product must work. If it has so many defects that it does not perform with reasonable consistency, the users will not use it regardless of its other attributes. This does not mean defects are always the highest priority, but they can be very important. If a minimum defect level has not been achieved, nothing else matters.

Clearly these points also apply to usability assessment.

## 11.2 Evaluation Is a Process

Evaluation is a process, and useful evaluations follow a process. In planning an evaluation, the usability engineer must answer a number of questions, including these:

- What steps are part of the evaluation process?
- When should usability assessment be performed in the development cycle?
- What kind of evaluation (or evaluations) can be used?

We first present overviews of these issues. Then we present more detailed descriptions of each issue.

### 11.2.1 What Steps Are Part of the Evaluation Process?

In general, we think of the process of developing and executing an evaluation to be similar to the process of usability engineering. In other words, we need to understand what it is that we are trying to evaluate—design an evaluation, try the evaluation out, remove its defects, and so on—until the evaluation addresses the issues at hand. You may develop and test a prototype evaluation before the full assessment, especially if chances for real testing are limited or expensive. You want to make sure that your assessment addresses the issues that you are interested in assessing.

### 11.2.2 When Should Usability Assessment Be Performed During Development?

When we think of assessing usability, we often think of assessing a finished product. It may surprise you that usability can be assessed just about anywhere during the development cycle. In a discussion of software testing and defect detection, Humphrey (1994) states this:

> An unpublished IBM rule of thumb for the relative costs to identify software defects: during design, 1.5; prior to coding, 1; during coding, 1.5; prior to test, 10; during test, 60; in field use, 100.

In other words, the cost of detecting software defects increases dramatically as the detection activity progresses. Does this mean that all testing should be at the beginning of the development cycle? It should be obvious that the answer is no—clearly some assessment is necessary on the finished product. Assessment should take place throughout the development cycle. In fact, repeated assessment is the basis of iterative development. Early testing may identify mismatches between the specification and user needs or gross misdirection in concept. Later testing may identify these types of errors, as well as fine-grained design flaws and software errors.

Scriven (1967) first distinguished between evaluation during design *(formative evaluation)* and evaluation of a final product *(summative evaluation)* in the context of curriculum development and evaluation. Hix and Hartson (1993) further distinguish between these two types of evaluation, indicating that the goal of formative evaluation is to help *form* the design, while the goal of summative evaluation is to *summarize* the usability of the final product. In Robert Stakes's words, as quoted in Scriven (1991):

> When the cook tastes the soup, that's formative evaluation; when the guest tastes it, that's summative evaluation.

### 11.2.3 Analytic, by Experts, or by Users?

A number of strategies have been offered for evaluation. Broadly speaking, evaluation strategies fall into three categories: analytic evaluation, evaluation by experts, and evaluation by users. Briefly, *analytic evaluation* uses a description of the proposed interaction or interface to project performance information about the interaction. *Evaluation by experts* typically involves experts applying principles of good design to determine the effectiveness of the interaction. *Evaluation by users* or *user testing* utilizes qualitative and quantitative methods to collect feedback data about the interaction.

Do we need all these techniques? We feel that the answer is yes. Analytic assessments give good information. They allow a designer to make comparisons between designs or to identify potentially poor elements of design. Evaluations by users and by experts can enhance or explain the predictions made by analytic evaluations.

If your evaluation is not an analytic evaluation, who performs your assessment turns out to be a very interesting question. Should your evaluation be done by usability experts or by users? Not surprisingly, this question has several good answers. Feedback by experts can identify poor design choices and failure to adhere to guidelines, but the evaluation of users may ultimately explain or predict the reception of the final product in the target setting.

## 11.3 Getting Started: The Process

Good evaluations do not just happen. Rather, they are the result of an engineering process. It would be a complete and total surprise if the developer of an evaluation sat down and generated a top-quality evaluation the first time, just as it is a surprise if a software developer can go right to the code and generate a successful piece of software. The reality is that you probably will not get it right the first time in usability assessment. The person or persons developing the assessments must still understand the evaluation problem or goal, design an evaluation, and test and implement this evaluation. In this section, we highlight the steps of the process.

### 11.3.1 What Are the Steps in the Process?

As we saw in the previous section, evaluation is a multistep process that you need to plan. This is one possible approach to the process:

- Understand the evaluation: What is to be evaluated? What is the meaning of the outcome of the evaluation?
- Design the evaluation at a high level: What is to be evaluated? What is the setting of the evaluation? What precise interaction/interface features will you evaluate?
- Design the evaluation at a low level: What measure or data are to be collected? How will you operationalize abstract constructs? What task scenarios and benchmark tasks will you use? Where will you administer your evaluation? What will your procedure be?
- Pilot test your evaluation and revise it.
- Do it! Perform the evaluation.
- Analyze the results and compare them to the expected outcomes.
- Make recommendations based on the results of the evaluation.

Note that this set of steps sounds like a linear sequence of activities or a kind of Waterfall Model for evaluation. Similar to software and usability engineering, while these steps could take place in sequence, they could also follow an iterative pattern.

### Understand the Evaluation

What does it mean to "understand the problem" in the context of evaluation? It means that we need to understand what we are evaluating and what the outcome of the evaluation means. The answers to these questions may vary, depending on when and what you are evaluating. For example, during summative evaluation, you may define your evaluation in terms of the usability requirements that were set during the specification of your project; in this case, the "problem" that you are solving in the evaluation is a verification that your product matches the product that was described in the specification. On the other hand, earlier in the development cycle, the "problem" that you are solving in your evaluation may be to make a comparative evaluation between two interaction alternatives.

### Design the Evaluation at a High Level

Once you have identified the goal of your evaluation, you are ready to design your evaluation at a high level. For example, suppose your specification indicates that your product will support a number of usability attributes, including *ease of learning*. During the high-level design of your evaluation, you decide to evaluate *ease of learning*. You further decide to perform an evaluation by users because you reason that their responses to your interaction will really reveal something about ease of learning.

Other commonly used usability attributes that are used as the basis of an evaluation and that might have been specified for your project include first-time performance, long-term performance, ease of remembering (memorability), advanced feature usage, first impressions, and long-term user satisfaction.

Some other questions you may address during your high-level design of evaluation may include these:

- What part of the user interaction/interface will you actually access? If you are using human evaluators, what will your evaluators do with your interface during the evaluation?

- Suppose we have decided that this will be an evaluation by users. Will you collect user opinions and/or information about performance? Why will this measure be useful in your evaluation?

- Suppose we have decided that this will be an evaluation by users. Will your measure of *ease of learning* be based on observation of users in a naturalistic setting or will it be based on data from a controlled or laboratory setting? What are the advantages of the choice of setting?

### Design the Evaluation at a Low Level: Operationalize Variables and Benchmark Tasks

Low-level design activities are focused on filling in the details to the high-level design. As we continue with the design process and our example, we now need to designate what *ease of learning* is really going to mean in our assessment. Specifically, these are some questions you will need to answer about *ease of learning* as you design your evaluation:

- What does *ease of learning* mean in the context of your users and tasks? How will you define and measure ease of learning in your evaluation? Did your original specification define ease of learning? What is the acceptable level of ease of learning in the context of your system, tasks, and users, especially if this was not precisely specified in the original specification of your user interaction?

*Ease of learning* is an abstraction. What it means in reality could be any one of a number of things. Turning an abstraction into a measurable or observable value is called *operationalizing* the concept; the concept may have been operationalized in the specification, or the usability engineer may need to do this. Some possible operationalizations for ease of learning could include these:

- The length of time for the user to successfully perform a task scenario the first time that the user encounters the interface.

- The number of training sessions required for a user to perform a task scenario at an acceptable performance level.

During evaluation, the usability engineer frequently will develop a set of *benchmark tasks.* A benchmark task is a standardized task that is representative of the normal use of the interface and will likely follow from the task scenarios in your task analysis. Recall that the scenarios are descriptions of real-world tasks that the user might do with your product; a scenario describes a task to complete rather than the sequence of interface actions to complete the task. Consider this scenario from Chapter 6:

> I go shopping and buy some CDs, including *Simon Carlson: Greatest Hits.* I add the songs and the CD to my catalog. I make a note in the catalog entry for this CD that I want to skip "Your UI Is So Plain" when I listen.

Note that this scenario specifies several outcomes from the task (adding songs and CD, making a note) but does not specify the sequence of interface actions to achieve the goals. A benchmark task based on this scenario might be "Add the song 'Meowing in the Rain' from *Simon Carlson: Greatest Hits* to the audio catalog." Benchmark tasks may also be at a lower level, like "Capitalize the names of all artists whose names begin with S." Part of the outcome of any assessment will be to see if the outcomes in the benchmark task can be accomplished with the design; identifying benchmark tasks is part of the design of the assessment.

## Design the Evaluation at a Low Level: To Measure or Not to Measure—Opinions or Performance

As the person making the assessment, one question you must answer is, What form of data will be most useful to you? Data are generally divided along two dimensions: (1) qualitative versus quantitative and (2) objective versus subjective responses.

Qualitative data is nonnumeric data. In other words, when you collect qualitative data, you are collecting data that is not numerical. What can you do with qualitative data? For an example, suppose you are interested in ease of learning for a children's game but that the prototype to assess is a very minimal Version 0 prototype. In terms of time to master a skill, measuring performance using this prototype may be misleading. The design may actually enhance ease of learning, but the implementation as it stands, because it is minimal, may interfere with ease of learning. So, the usability engineer may choose to collect qualitative data, in the form of user conversation and interviews, while learning to use the prototype. As users are learning about the prototype, they may say out loud what they are doing and where they are having problems. From this information, the person making the assessment can separate feedback that is related to the design and feedback that are artifacts of the prototype.

On the other hand, quantitative data is numeric data. Some examples of quantitative data might be time to complete a benchmark task or number of errors experienced in a half-hour exploratory learning session. Performance measures of time and accuracy are common quantitative operationalizations for ease of use and ease of learning.

Useful feedback from users can be based either on opinions or on measures outside of opinions. User data in which the user's opinions are not considered are called *objective* data. For example, measuring the number of user errors on a benchmark task is a good example of objective data. On the other hand, asking users their opinions produces *subjective* data. For example, the answer that a user of a video game gives to the question, "Was the 'C' button useful?" is an example of subjective data.

Table 11.1 illustrates the two dimensions of qualitative versus quantitative and objective versus subjective. As you can see from the table, it is possible to have any of the four possible combinations of types of data.

Back to our example, suppose we have operationalized ease of learning as the length of time to successfully perform a benchmark task the first time that the user encounters the interface; this would be a quantitative, objective measurement. On the other hand, if a user discussed his or her opinions about ease of learning for the interface in question, this would be a qualitative, subjective measurement.

**Table 11.1**   Dimensions of Data.

|            | Quantitative | Qualitative |
|------------|--------------|-------------|
| **Objective** | *Examples:* Time to complete benchmark task; number of errors on a benchmark task | *Example:* Observation of performance to complete a benchmark task |
| **Subjective** | *Example:* Responses to a questionnaire about an interaction in general or after completing a benchmark task | *Example:* Observation and collection of responses to open-ended questions after completing a benchmark task |

## Design the Evaluation at a Low Level: Where to Evaluate—Laboratory, Controlled Setting, or Real Site?

For a usability engineer, another design decision is to identify the setting for the evaluation. For instance, in user testing, it is often easier to focus your assessment on specific target interface features if your user is in a controlled setting, such as a laboratory or a simulation of the target setting. In a *controlled setting,* the usability engineer can control the choices and distractions that the user might otherwise deal with in a real setting. For example, in a controlled setting the user's access to distractions, such as answering the phone, can be limited. User testing in a laboratory can be artificial and can artificially filter out some of the situational factors (see Chapter 3) that may come into play when your interface is put to actual use. Alternatively, the usability engineer may either observe the users by using cameras or one-way windows or become an active participant in the real environment in order to observe usage patterns.

Clearly the choice of settings involves trade-offs. In user testing, a key concern about laboratory studies is how closely they match reality. Are the users who come to the laboratory representative of real users? Are the tasks and settings similar to reality? On the other hand, in an evaluation at a real site, interference from other factors may confound your results. In evaluation by experts, practical concerns, such as the cost of the experts' time, may dictate the choice of setting.

## Design the Evaluation at a Low Level: Developing a Procedure

A part of the low-level design of your evaluation is the procedure that you will follow during the evaluation. The procedure should be fixed and should be focused on answering the questions that you identified in the "understanding the evaluation" stage.

## Design the Evaluation at a Low Level: Developing the Structure of Experiments

Some usability assessments involving user testing will include a determination of causality in an experimental setting. For instance, in Chapter 3, we introduced the notion of controlled experiments, when discussing Eason's usability model (1984) and our own usability model based on Eason. You may recall that Eason's model of usability is a causal model, meaning that the inputs to the model impact the outcome of the model in such a way that there is a causal relationship between inputs and outputs. In Eason's model the inputs and outputs are abstract notions, like *ease of learning* and *usability.*

Suppose that the interaction specification for the product MmM Bags of Marbles, indicates that the usability attribute of ease of learning would be provided as a result of features of the interaction. In our design of the interaction, we have thought of two ways to promote ease of learning. In one approach, we have designed a button that the user can push to bring up an online tutorial. In the other approach, the online tutorial is on the screen at all times. How would we build an experiment to test that our feature (button or continuous display of the tutorial) influenced ease of learning?

In an experiment, one starts with a hypothesized causal relationship between abstract notions; in this case, the hypothesis is that the UI features influence ease of learning. Next, these abstract notions of features and ease of learning are operationalized into specific independent and dependent variables, respectively. The values of the independent variables are hypothesized to influence the values of the dependent variables. That is, the experimental hypothesis predicts the impact on the dependent variables, given the experimental manipulation of the independent variables. In an experiment, the experimenter controls (keeps the same) all factors besides the independent variables that might affect the outcome. Only in this way can the experiment demonstrate a causal relationship between the independent variables and dependent variables.

How do we know that a causal relationship exists between the independent variables and dependent variables? Assuming that the data are quantitative, a number of statistical tests can be applied. The statistical tests will tell the experimenter whether a true causal relationship exists and can be generalized or whether the outcome is simply due to chance.

So for the MmM Bags of Marbles product assessment example, our independent variable representing UI features might be "access mechanism for online tutorial." The levels of the independent variable could be button or onscreen display. The operationalization of ease of learning for the dependent variable might be the score on a quiz about the interface after using it for ten minutes. If we can demonstrate statistically that there is a causal relationship between the independent and dependent variables, we can conclude with some confidence that the notion of features for this product did influence ease of learning.

For another example, in some of our research we have been interested in how one might best display instructions for procedural tasks in a Web browser. Our idea was that when instructions are displayed in both a graphical and textual form, people would be more likely to carry out the procedure than when the instructions are displayed either textually or graphically alone. The abstract concepts are "Best" and "Display instructions for procedural tasks." We operationalized "procedural task" to be folding an origami whale. We operationalized "Display instructions textually and graphically" by building a set of step-by-step instructions that had three forms: text only, text and pictures, and pictures only. We operationalized "Best" as the number of errors subjects made in folding a whale. Clearly in this experiment, some other factors, such as the quality of the output display, might also influence the outcome of our experiment. In our research, we held constant the other factors that could potentially influence the outcome so that we could determine the impact of the variables of interest only (cf. Leventhal 2001).

Designing and executing an experiment involves careful attention to the control of extraneous variables to demonstrate causality, but it may be that to maintain experimental control you lose the question that you wanted to ask. On the other hand, should you design and run an experiment with a significant result, you can feel confident about the causality between your experimental variables and can create support for your theory about the relationships among the variables.

### Evaluate: Pilot Test or the Real Thing

Once the evaluation has been designed, it is time to try it out, to make corrections to your design iteratively, or to implement the evaluation. Once the evaluation is made, the usability engineer will evaluate the results and make recommendations based on the results.

## 11.4 When to Evaluate?

Evaluation can take place when the interface is being formulated or at the end of the development. In this section, we discuss formative and summative evaluation in more detail.

### 11.4.1 Formative Evaluation

Formative evaluation is assessment that occurs during the formation of a design. As an assessment of a design under development, formative design typically is used to identify missing elements of the problem specification or potential problems in the design while there is still time to fix them. Formative evaluation surprisingly should take place as early as possible in the development cycle. Hix and Hartson (1993) describe a good rule of thumb called the *10% rule,* which goes something like this:

> By the time that 10 percent of the money has been spent, you have something to evaluate.

In other words, by the time you have used 10 percent of your resources, you should already be thinking about evaluation. In general, you should conduct at least three major cycles of evaluation and redesign (Hix and Hartson, 1993, p. 285). Expect the most improvement and feedback on the first iteration of your formative evaluation. Although you may be only evaluating the most bare-bones pencil-and-paper interaction design, at least you will be comparing it to your specification. If you misunderstood the specification in your design, this is the earliest time to find your error.

Formative evaluation has a number of benefits. Most particularly, a formative evaluation can identify inconsistencies, incompleteness, or infeasibilities in the specification of the interface or the design. Furthermore, formative evaluation can point to mismatches in the design and the specification, failures to conform to standards and guidelines, or poor design choices that will impact user performance and/or satisfaction. Finally, in some regard, formative evaluation can be used as a kind of prototyping tool and vice versa; in this sense, formative evaluation can be used to provide iterative feedback on both the specification and the design.

### 11.4.2  Summative Evaluation

Summative evaluation is an evaluation of the final user interface. It is helpful in summative evaluation to have quantifiable or measurable goals that can be used to determine if the product is "good enough." For example, a product may be viewed as "usable enough" if novice users can use the product with fewer than ten errors on a standard task after thirty minutes of exploratory use. In general, in summative evaluation the usability engineer will need to determine how to measure usability and to interpret the results of that measurement.

### 11.4.3  Connection Between the Type and the Time of the Evaluation

Evaluation by experts or users can happen any time in the development cycle. Early in the development cycle, experts may be able to foresee problems that will crop up later in the development process. On the other hand, real users may have a better idea of the real task requirements, especially when evaluating a finished product. What about analytic evaluation? Analytic evaluation requires some kind of formalized description of the interaction and the interface. Depending on the particular analysis technique, this information might be available almost as soon as design begins.

## 11.5  What Kind of Evaluation?

There are three major types of usability assessments: analytic evaluation, evaluation by experts, and evaluation by users. In the next three sections, we investigate these three strategies.

### 11.5.1  Analytic Evaluation

Analytic evaluation techniques allow us to predict how a design will perform or to explain the performance of an existing interface. They can be used to predict, for example, how long it will take users to operate a screen; this information can help us to compare alternative designs, as well as to anticipate the success of a design.

The most well-known family of these techniques is called *GOMS* (Goals, Operators, Methods, and Selections) analyses and follow from the Model Human Processor suggested in the book *The Psychology of Human–Computer Interaction* by Card, Moran, and Newell (1983). The idea behind a GOMS analysis is that a user's knowledge and skill in an interface task can be broken into small mental and physical actions. Each of these actions has a characteristic time associated with it. Based on these characteristic times, one can make a prediction as to how long the interface task will take with a specific interface. Given interface designs, one can then compute the time for some standardized tasks or can compare the predicted times between two interfaces and make a comparison.

In GOMS analysis, a *goal* is the user's objective relative to a task. The goal may be subdivided into subgoals. An *operator* is a low-level action that is either a mental or a physical action; however, mental operations typically correspond to rote actions. An action is an operator if it changes the task environment or the user's mental state. Goals and operators differ in the level of detail; an operator is a low-level action, and a goal is usually more abstract. A *method* is a sequential set of operations. A *selection* rule is a rule or test that allows a user to select a particular method. These four elements can be combined in a number of ways to build analytic models of use of an interface (Bennett 1986; John and Kieras 1996a, 1996b).

Four variations on GOMS have been suggested. The *Keystroke-Level Model* (KLM) is probably the simplest. The focus of the KLM method is on keystroke- and mouse-level operators and their characteristic time to perform. KLM does not focus on goals, methods, or selection. It also includes a number of heuristics to describe the use of the mental operator (cf. John and Kieras 1996a, 1996b).

A second variation of GOMS is called *CMN GOMS* for Card-Moran-Newell GOMS. This variation of GOMS was suggested in Card, Moran, and Newell (1983). In CMN GOMS, the analyst develops a detailed goal hierarchy. The analyst then generates methods to accomplish the subgoals, using a method description similar to pseudocode. Methods are described by other methods, operators, and conditionals. According to John and Kieras (1996b), the main differences between CMN and KLM are the emphases in CMN on the explicit goal hierarchy and the applications of methods to subgoals. CMN supports the idea of conflicting goals and multiple methods for a given goal or subgoals.

Two other more sophisticated forms of GOMS have been suggested. *NGOMSL* (Natural GOMS Language) was developed by Kieras (1988) and is described in John and Kieras (1996a, 1996b). NGOMSL shows a GOMS model with a structured language and is tied to a more detailed theoretical model of the mental activities of the user than either CMN or KLM. *CPM-GOMS* (Cognitive-Perceptual-Motor GOMS) is described in John (1990) and in John and Kieras (1996a, 1996b) and supports parallel sequences of operators, if this is appropriate to the task.

GOMS analyses have been used successfully as a predictive tool in a number of instances. For example, Gray, John, and Atwood (1993) did a CPM-GOMS analysis on a proposed workstation replacement for telephone operators at NYNEX. They found that operators were actually more effective with the existing workstations than with the proposed one. The project was scrapped and saved NYNEX about $2 million per year!

However, GOMS analyses have some limitations. For example, they typically assume idealized or expert performance on the part of the user. The GOMS hierarchy of operations is somewhat subjective. Two different designers may develop two different GOMS models for the same interface task and come up with different predictions. Rosson and Carroll (2002) note that models such as the GOMS models do not include parameters to model learning or social and organizational relationships that potentially impact usability.

Where is the relation between the specification of the problem (the task specification) and the GOMS analysis of the design? The task analysis of the problem and the GOMS analysis of the design seem to be potentially related. It is possible to define a goal hierarchy from the design that corresponds to the problem decomposition of the task analysis. In fact, the GOMS analyst may start with the task analysis as a basis of the goal hierarchy. However, particularly with the KLM variety of GOMS, the sequence of actions probably describes the solution to a low-level task in the task analysis.

### 11.5.2 Evaluation by Experts

Experts have a number of skills that they can bring to the evaluation process. They often are knowledgeable about standards and guidelines and can evaluate the conformance of a design to those guidelines. Also, experts often have a wide set of experiences with users and designs. While they cannot necessarily experience a design, in the same way that a user does, they still may be able to project or predict how a user will respond to a design. In addition, when experts perform the evaluation, they may also be able to help designers to fix their product.

Assessment by experts often takes the form of reviews, similar to the notion of code or design reviews in software engineering. These reviews may focus on adherence to design guidelines. Not surprisingly, reviews by experts usually are used in formative evaluations, although they also may be used in summative evaluations. Only a few studies have looked at the effectiveness of expert reviews (cf. Jeffries, Miller, Wharton, and Uyeda, 1991; Karat, Campbell, and Fiegel 1992). Both these studies indicate that expert reviews can be an effective assessment technique. In the next section, we discuss two evaluation techniques used by experts: *heuristic evaluation* and *cognitive walk-through.*

### Evaluation by Experts: Heuristic Evaluation

Nielsen (Nielsen and Molich 1990; Nielsen 1994) has proposed a kind of usability assessment technique called *heuristic evaluation.* Under this strategy, a group of experts, working independently, evaluate an interface or prototype against a set of heuristics or guidelines. The idea is that while no one individual assessor will find all violations to the heuristics, several expert evaluators, working independently may be very effective. The end result of the evaluation should be a list of problems or conflicts with the list of heuristics.

According to Nielsen (2006a), in addition to the benefit of finding problems, the heuristic evaluation may be interactive between the expert assessor and the developer, so that the developer can also see problems as the expert is evaluating the system. Nielsen (2006b) lists ten heuristics as a focus for heuristic evaluation; Nielsen's heuristics and the guidelines given in earlier chapters are very similar. For example, Nielsen points to the importance of matching the information in the interaction to the user's model. In addition to heuristics for the interaction itself, Nielsen also includes guidelines for documentation and help materials.

### Evaluation by Experts: Cognitive Walk-through

A commonly used assessment technique in software engineering is the *walk-through,* whether it is a walk-through of code, design, or a test plan. In software engineering, the idea is that a group of software developers carefully "walk through" or step through the artifact under review, looking for such things as inconsistencies, irregularities, or inefficient design. These walk-throughs may be formalized with a secretary and a formal report or less formal with just note taking. The developers may be participants or may simply receive the reports. The expert evaluators may identify potential problems and/or make suggestions on how to improve the system.

The notion of *cognitive walk-through* is similar in many ways. This approach was suggested by Polson, Lewis, Rieman, and Wharton (1992) and in a revised form by Wharton, Rieman, Lewis, and Polson (1994). In the cognitive walk-through, the expert evaluator or evaluators ask several questions about a representative task within a prototype or finished user interface. The questions are intended to determine how closely the actions within the task match the user's goal for the task.

### 11.5.3 Evaluation by Users: User Testing

Ask most computer scientists what they think usability assessment is all about and they are likely to tell you something about having a group of users do something. In other words, when most of us think of usability assessment, some form of evaluation or feedback from users, most often called *user testing,* comes to mind. As we will see, there are many approaches to user testing, and user testing may be formative or summative. Testing your interface with real users potentially has the advantage of providing data that are predictive of how your interface will fare in its actual setting.

Successful user testing can take a number of forms. For example, the users may provide qualitative, quantitative, subjective, or objective data. In the next section, we overview some of the most common types of measurements utilized in user testing.

### 11.5.4 Performance Measurements

Performance measurements are often collected from users during evaluation and often reflect an operationalization of some kind of success construct. One common type of performance measurement is accuracy measurements. As a measurement, accuracy can be positive (e.g., "The user selected 75 percent of the correct interactions.") or negative (e.g., "The user made 4 out of 10 possible errors."). In our study (Leventhal 2001) on the presentation of instructions for folding origami animals, we counted the number of correct folds of the animals that the participants made; from this quantitative measurement, we were able to compare several different styles of presentations.

One potential challenge with accuracy data is to decide when a user actually makes a correct or incorrect response, as opposed to an incidental response, in the context of the software. So if I am user testing a piece of software and the user accidentally makes a typing error, I may or may not wish to count it as an "error" in the context of the test.

Reason (1990) has distinguished errors by the intent of the person performing the action and making the error. He describes *violations* as actions in which the individual intends to perform an action that is contrary to procedure. He defines *errors* as actions that the individual unwittingly performs contrary to procedure. This is an important distinction as it provides the usability engineer with a starting point for discovering why an error occurred. For our origami studies, we observed that our participants sometimes would fold the paper correctly and then refold correctly again. In our evaluation of instructions for origami animals, we found it useful to distinguish between an initial accurate fold and repeated accurate folds; folding the same fold accurately several times did not increase the overall accuracy of the finished origami animal and did not necessarily mean that the presented information was better than some other form.

Accuracy can be either a quantitative or qualitative measurement. In the preceding examples, we illustrated some quantitative measures of accuracy. Other quantitative examples might include scores on a quiz or the number of screens visited. Qualitative measures of accuracy might include patterns of user strategies, patterns of errors, and so on. Additional performance measures include time to do something, number of keystrokes, and usage frequency counts of particular interface features.

### 11.5.5  Subjective Measurements

Oftentimes, it is useful to get users' feedback about their subjective responses to an interface as a whole or to specific interface features. A number of techniques to gather this feedback have been suggested, ranging from interviews and discussion to the use of surveys and questionnaires. For instance, the usability engineer might construct a survey in which users respond about their preferences or satisfaction levels. The following is an example of a survey question to elicit a subjective response.

In Chapter 3, we described the following product:

> Alice and Darius are developing a product for Woodrow Wilson High School. The product is called "Señores y Señoritas" and is intended to help high school Spanish students with vocabulary drills. The contractors for the product are the teachers at Woodrow Wilson High School.

This might be a quantitative, subjective evaluation of this product:

> Rate your overall satisfaction with this product (circle your response).
> 1 = not at all satisfied    2 = not satisfied    3 = no opinion
> 4 = somewhat satisfied    5 = very satisfied

Numerical responses to survey questions produce quantitative data and are often presented as closed-ended questions where the user selects from a set of responses. Alternatively, observed responses to interview questions and open-ended questions are most likely qualitative and allow users to respond in their own words.

The *QUIS* (Questionnaire of User Interface Satisfaction) is an example of an interface assessment questionnaire. Chin, Diehl, and Norman (1988) developed the QUIS and conducted usability studies based on its use. In the QUIS, users are asked to provide subjective responses by rating various interface features and characteristics.

In general, tools such as questionnaires and surveys are not easy to construct. The usability engineer must be aware of his or her own biases so as not to influence the results by how questions are constructed. For example, the following satisfaction question for "Señores y Señoritas" is biased and would present potentially unreliable data:

> Rate your overall satisfaction with this product (circle your response).
> 1 = very satisfied    2 = very very satisfied    3 = most satisfied with any product

Often questionnaires ask the same question in slightly different ways multiple times; the idea is that the outcome of the measurement may be more valid if the user has had a chance to respond to variations of the same question.

### 11.5.6 Observational Measurements

With contemporary technologies, it is often easy, with the permission of the users, to record users' movements, interactions, spoken comments, and responses to interview and follow-up questions. Or the usability engineer may simply observe and take notes. Recorded observations are a potentially rich data source that can provide evaluative insights beyond simple performance measurements of time and accuracy. However, the very richness of observational data often makes data difficult to analyze.

Observations can be directed. For example, Ericcson and Simon (1984) describe a strategy called *verbal protocols* in which subjects are directed to speak aloud the information that they are thinking. These protocols can then be analyzed systematically and at a very detailed level.

Additional code can be added to an application so that all user inputs/actions are recorded. The files in which this information is saved are called *clickstream data.* Not surprisingly, clickstream data may generate huge quantities of data requiring considerable effort to analyze. On the other hand, clickstream data may reveal information about users' strategies that are not apparent from time or accuracy data. For example, we recently were interested in the ways that people used interactive three-dimensional models to solve a particular task. When we analyzed the accuracy of our users on the task, we found that everyone was actually pretty good at solving the problem. However, when we analyzed the clickstream data, which in this case revealed how the users had interacted with the models, we noticed two clear patterns of clickstreams. Over a number of repetitions of the task, users tended to stick with one of the two patterns of clicks suggesting that users were following two different strategies to accomplish the task.

### 11.5.7 Users as Informed Participants

Sadly, in the history of science, people have been forced or manipulated to participate in experiments without their informed consent. Regardless of the setting for your user evaluation, it is unethical to force or manipulate users to participate in any evaluation without their consent.

## Conclusions

Successful usability engineering projects include evaluation. Evaluation done as an afterthought, rather than a planned and process-based activity, will likely yield little useful feedback or assessment. Evaluation is a process that occurs in multiple steps. A number of strategies are used for evaluation; each strategy has the potential for providing meaningful information to the usability engineer.

## Exercises

1. Define the following terms: *usability assessment, analytic evaluation, evaluation by experts, evaluation by users, user testing, benchmark task, objective data, subjective data, qualitative data, quantitative data, controlled setting, formative evaluation, summative evaluation, GOMS analysis, heuristic evaluation, cognitive walk-through, QUIS, clickstream data,* and *verbal protocols.*

2. Suppose that the ABC Company is going to implement a companywide instant messaging system as part of its technology plan for this year. ABC has never had companywide instant messaging before and is considering several instant messaging systems.

   a. Develop a usability assessment strategy to analyze and design an evaluation for the candidate instant messaging systems. What usability attributes will you focus on? Will your tests be summative or formative? What type of assessment will you perform?

   b. Continuing, address low-level design questions for your evaluation. What types of measurements and usability assessments will you use? For each, be sure to identify *what* and *how* you are measuring. What procedure will you follow?

# Part 6

# A Little More About Design

# 12

---

# Interaction Design and Evaluation Example

## Motivation

In the previous chapters, we showed you how you might choose an interaction style or styles for a project, how to prototype a user interface and how to do evaluations. This chapter continues with the audio catalog and shows how we might use the information in Chapters 7 through 9 to build an interaction for the audio catalog. We evaluate prototypes as we go, from the perspective of an expert (you). Finally we also introduce how you might use an analytic evaluation to compare designs.

When you are finished with this chapter, you should be able to do the following:

- Design a prototype using the design process outlined.
- Conduct an analytic evaluation of a prototype and use the information collected to make design decisions.

## 12.1 Introduction

We are now going to design an interaction for the audio catalog problem, which was introduced in Chapter 6. We will make design choices based on the ideas that were presented in Chapters 7 through 9. We will evaluate a prototype following the concepts presented in Chapters 10 and 11.

Recall that by the end of Chapter 6, we had a set of user scenarios about how someone would use a computerized audio catalog. We also had a high-level use case diagram that divided our user tasks into eight categories. Our task analysis and task descriptions then broke down those eight user tasks into detailed subtasks. Now we are ready to actually start designing an interaction that (a) covers the task set for the audio catalog and (b) complies with the design guidelines and directives from the previous chapters.

Let's assume that our customer has already read through our task specification and has agreed that our problem description is acceptable. What now? The following is a list of steps that you will need to go through in designing your interaction.

### Design of Interaction: High-Level Design

**STEP 1.** Review your situational variables vis-à-vis our hybrid model of usability from Chapter 3. In other words, fill in the "values" for these variables or any other variables, which may give you insights about the constraints of your situation.

**STEP 2.** Choose an interaction style or styles. One part of this activity may be to eliminate all unsuitable interaction styles. The "values" of your situational variables and the general guidelines from Chapter 7 may help you limit the set of reasonable interaction styles.

**STEP 3.** Review the general guidelines from Chapter 7. Can you use the general guidelines to eliminate inappropriate components within your interaction style? For example, if you have a metaphor in mind, does it match the problem closely enough to be workable?

**STEP 4.** Identify and make specific decisions for your interaction style. If your interaction involves multiple styles (i.e., menus and forms), use the design decisions for each of these styles as a possible check-off list.

**STEP 5.** Identify a standard look and feel for your screens. Some suggested ways to do this are (a) to select standard locations and sizes for buttons and other interface objects, (b) to select standard language styles for text, and (c) to select standard colors and other visual characteristics.

**STEP 6.** Think about the dynamic behavior of your interaction. Design the "feel" of the interactions.

**STEP 7.** Review general and visual guidelines. Redesign and reevaluate your standard look and feel. Build templates of your standard that everyone in your design group can use.

### Design of Interaction: Low-Level Design

**STEP 1.** Map the task structure onto your design. Do not wait until your interaction is fully designed and then go back to your task analysis to confirm that you have covered everything. Rather, once you have made some global decisions about interaction styles and choice of metaphor, start your particular interaction by following your task structure, at the very least.

**STEP 2.** Using your task analysis and specification as a guide, design your individual interactions to support the tasks that you identified in your task analysis. To ensure coverage, document that each task is included somewhere in your interface.

**STEP 3.** Check the design of your individual screens or interactions against both the general guidelines and the visual design guidelines from Chapter 9 and any other project or commercial platforms that you have.

Note that you may iterate through these steps several times. In both Chapter 11 and Chapter 12 we discuss some ways that you may assess your design. For now, we show the steps as if they were linear.

## 12.2 Design of Interaction

Recall that our first design task is to design the overall look and feel. Some critical design activities during this phase are to review the values of the situational variables that describe the environment in which the interface eventually will be used. With a good understanding of those variables, you will select an interaction or interaction styles. Finally, for your selected interaction style(s), you will focus on the design decisions that were presented in Chapter 8.

### 12.2.1 Step 1: Review the Values of the Situational Variables for the Project

You may recall that in the Eason (1984) model of usability, Eason makes the point that usability is an outcome of system (user interface) characteristics, task characteristics, and user characteristics; we offer a similar perspective in our hybrid model. As the designer, you control the characteristics of the interaction and ultimately the user interface, but the characteristics of the task and the user are generally set. Before you begin the design of your interaction, it is a good idea to review the task and user characteristics for your project. During your analysis and specification phase of your project, you should have identified a number of user characteristics in your user profile and task characteristics in your needs and task analysis. Now, you should be prepared to answer the following questions:

**What are the user characteristics for your project?**

1. How expert or knowledgeable are your users about the task or tasks that they will perform with the interaction that you design? Other related questions might be, How experienced is the user for this task, and how much does the user know and understand about the possible action sequences through the task?

2. How motivated are your users to complete their task or tasks?

3. How knowledgeable are the users about computer systems? (Mynatt 1990)

4. What do we know about the users' work environments? What types of hardware will they be using? What type of software platform will your product run on?

5. Are any other user characteristics important to consider?

To answer these questions, you should refer to the user profile that you developed. (See Chapter 5 to review.)

**What are the characteristics of the tasks in your project?**

1. How rigid is the task or tasks?

2. How frequently is the task, or tasks, performed?

3. Is there anything about the task situation that is constraining?

4. Are any other task characteristics important to consider?

5. Did the user specify any explicit usability goals for any tasks that we need to consider?

To answer these questions, you should refer back to your specification of the task analysis and, in particular, to the textual information that accompanies each task. For example, for the rigidness question, tasks can be open in terms of in how many different orders the subtasks can be completed or in the range of input values. If a task has a critical ordering or sequencing of subtasks, it probably is not particularly open.

Specifically, we ask you to answer these questions, at least for the high-level tasks. For the audio catalog, we have assumed the following answers to these questions:

### What are the user characteristics for the audio catalog?

1. How expert is the user? Based on the user profile from Chapter 6, we assume that the users are knowledgeable about the task of using a paper audio catalog. For example, we assume that users are able to distinguish between the uses of the different types of entities, such as songs, CDs, and shopping lists. We note, however, that as the size of the audio catalog grows, it will be increasingly difficult for the user to remember and to distinguish between each data item that resides in the catalog.

2. How motivated are your users to complete their tasks or tasks? We assume that the users are very motivated. The user expects to use this system often and would like to have fast response and the capability to build a large catalog.

3. What do we know about the user's computer system expertise? The typical user is computer literate and familiar with a windowed operating system environment.

4. What do we know about the user's work environment? What type of hardware will be used? What type of software platform will our product run on? We note that the user will be using a workstation type of machine with a fast processor, so we can expect to deliver generally fast response, regardless of the type of interaction that we choose. We also note that the user will be running in a windowed system environment.

5. Are any other user characteristics important to consider? We are not aware of any at this time.

### What are the characteristics of the tasks in the audio catalog?

1. How rigid is the task or tasks? The overall task (*Use audio catalog*) is somewhat rigid because we do not believe that new variations will be added. The high-level tasks, such as *Manage songs* and *Manage CDs* also seem rigid, as it is unlikely that the user will modify the tasks, outside of what we have already specified. However, the actual content of the data that will be entered during these tasks is very nonrigid; the precise content is impossible to predict in advance. Also, the user has some discretion as to which fields are actually filled in for a given item, lessening the rigidness of these tasks.

2. How frequently is the task or tasks performed? The task (*Use audio catalog*) will be performed frequently. Depending on the size and dynamics of the user's physical audio collection, the subtasks could be performed very frequently.

3. Are there situational constraints? No. We saw no specification relating to fun, security, or collaborative work.

4. Are any other task characteristics important to consider? Once again we notice that the overall task (*Use audio catalog*) includes some data entry of song, CD, artist, and other information. However, once data are entered, some tasks involve retrieval of data from a potentially large set of data items.

5. Did the user specify any explicit usability goals for any tasks that we need to consider? From Chapter 6, we have the following:

> Overall we expect that the use of the interface for *Manage CDs* will be satisfying. Specifically, we define satisfaction for this task as follows. After a group of users has been using this system for ten hours, so that all are proficient, we will ask them to rate their satisfaction on the following scale to each of the tasks that corresponds to the subtasks of *Manage CDs*. We expect that the average rating should be 4 or above. A sample question is:

> On a scale of 1 to 5, indicate how satisfying this user interface will support the subtask of *Fill in Subtask*.

**1 = Not at all   2 = Marginally   3 = OK   4 = Pretty good   5 = Excellent**

For the task *Add a new CD to catalog,* we have two expected characteristics of the eventual user interface, ease of use and ease of learning, defined as follows. If the user adds CDs often, he or she may wish to be able to add a CD in less than some number of minutes, once trained on the system. This would be an operationalization of ease of use.

In Chapter 3, we suggest that we might define ease of learning for this task as how long it takes a beginner to the system to do this task in the computerized system. We might give the user ten practice exercises during which they have to add new items. Then we might ask the user to add another item and measure performance time.

For the task of *Paste, existing CD,* we have the following information: ease of use might be of importance here. Users may expect this task to lend itself to minimal errors and minimal keystrokes, especially in the selection of the spot of the paste. Minimal errors might be 10 errors in 100 tries. Minimizing keystrokes might be less than 5 keystrokes per paste. Note that minimizing keystrokes may improve usability if the task is performed frequently.

### 12.2.2 Step 2: Choose an Interaction Style or Styles

Once you have reviewed your situational variables, you need to choose a specific interaction style or styles. Many successful interactions use a combination of interaction styles. The styles presented in Chapter 8 included these:

**Manipulation of visual elements interactions**

- Menu interactions
- Windowed interactions
- Form fill-in interactions
- Direct manipulation interactions

**Conversational interactions**

- Command-line interactions
- Natural language interactions
- Question-and-answer interactions

**Manipulable and combination interaction styles**

- Haptic interactions
- Multimedia and multimodal interactions

- Virtual reality interactions
- Video and electronic game interactions
- Mobile and handheld computer interactions

Which of these styles can we eliminate for the audio catalog? We would argue that the typical "fun" goals that characterize video games do not match the goal of the interaction for the audio catalog, so video game is out. The goals of the audio catalog potentially could be matched by a virtual reality presentation. However, since the user is at a workstation type of computer, he or she would not have equipment to support a highly immersive virtual reality interaction. While the user's equipment could support a low-cost virtual reality presentation, there is nothing that we know about the user or the task that suggests that this would be a superior presentation as compared to more familiar presentations. In fact, considering that the user may be only moderately knowledgeable, the unfamiliarity of virtual reality probably rules it out.

We can now go back and review the software characteristics of the platform that the audio catalog software will run on. Recall that in Chapter 6 the feature list characteristics indicated that the software will run on a windowed operating system setup. This eliminates a mobile interaction. The only pointing device available to us will be a mouse, and the user will also have a keyboard available. No hardware is available to collect speech, pen, or gesture inputs. We can probably eliminate a haptic or speech-based interaction. Multimodal inputs are not possible. We still could present the outputs in a multimedia presentation; however, there is a strong reason why the "multimedia" aspect of this interaction will likely be minimal. We note that the only role of pictures in this task is as data for pictures of CD album covers. There is no sense in the problem definition that the user will need to be interacting with parallel representations (text and graphics, for example) of the same information. So, if our eventual interaction supports multimedia, it will likely be in a limited way.

Thinking back to the task analysis and specification, we recall that overall the set of tasks is very well defined and rigid, so that extending the functionality of the interface by the user is probably not necessary. This would eliminate a programming language interaction. Because the user is computer literate and the associated implementation issues of a natural language interface can be difficult, we also eliminate natural language.

This leaves us with windows, menus, direct manipulation of interface objects, command-line, form fill-in, and multimedia. Our users are experts in the task, and so a command-line interaction might actually be the best choice. However, suppose that our user is really uncomfortable with the idea of a nonvisual interface. For now, we will go in the direction of a visual interface that includes visual elements, such as windows, menus, and forms. The cues that we can give from these interactions should be able to promote recognition over recall, which should be helpful if there are any intermittent users. We note again that the user will likely be performing some data entry, so forms may be useful.

### 12.2.3 Step 3: Use General Guidelines to Eliminate Unworkable Ideas and Expand Workable Ideas

Reviewing the general guidelines that were given in Chapter 7, we find that the first two guidelines were these:

- *Guideline 1:*   Facilitate the development and use of workable conceptual models.
- *Guideline 2:*   Use meaningful analogies and metaphors.

You may recall that the point of these two guidelines was to allow the user to make use of prior knowledge to accomplish goals with the interface. A mechanism to achieve this was to use meaningful analogies. Looking back at the scenario descriptions for the audio catalog, we see that the user already had some experience with a paper-based audio catalog. To get started, let's build on what we have in the scenarios and use a metaphor of a paper catalog.

What could go wrong with this metaphor? First, we may find that the computerized catalog behaves differently than the paper catalog. If this is the case, the metaphor could be potentially misleading. If compliance with the metaphor forces the interface to be cognitively indirect or inhibits wayfinding, the mental price for the user will not be worth the metaphor and we will need to rethink our starting point.

Let's sketch a quick picture of a paper audio catalog, shown in Figure 12.1. Lots of paper catalogs are stored in index boxes, with the entries on index cards. The dividers are made of thumb tab cards.

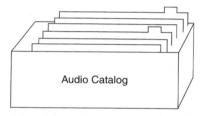

Figure 12.1    Sketch of the Paper Audio Catalog.

Now we need to do a reality check on our metaphor. What kind of data entities would be on the paper cards in a physical audio catalog? From our task specification, we know that at a high level we envision a set of management functions for each of the primary classes: CDs, songs, shopping lists, reports, queries, labels, and the catalog itself.

In our metaphor, perhaps we can start with the idea of the thumb tabs that include references to each of these primary classes, as shown in Figure 12.2. This setup seems applicable because it follows the structure of our task breakdown.

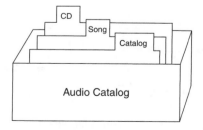

Figure 12.2    Audio Catalog: Primary Classes Represented as Thumb Tabs.

So far, we are trying to see if the paper catalog metaphor translates into the computerized version without imposing extra work on the user. We have divided the catalog in our metaphor by primary classes.

For now, let's assume that the metaphor is working. Can we extend it to a computerized design? Looking at our sketch, we are presenting the user with a choice of primary class types. This choice is closed (that is, we know what all the choices are). Remember from Chapter 8 that menus are a good way to explicitly present a set of options. We can build a menu of our entity types, as shown in Figure 12.3. Does this mean that we should rush to build a menu that looks like a pull-down menu that matches many common commercial applications? There is no reason to do so at this point. We have not run into any major screen

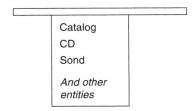

**Figure 12.3**    Audio Catalog: Sample Menu Interaction.

space restrictions yet! We might as well stick with the metaphor that we have chosen, since it has not collapsed. What we can imagine is something more like what we have been working with. We can use the thumb tabs as a set of visual menu options. For now, we will just highlight the selected menu option by highlighting the corresponding thumb tab, as shown in Figure 12.4.

**Figure 12.4**    Audio Catalog: Highlighting A Thumb Tab to Indicate Selection.

### 12.2.4 Step 4: Identify and Make Specific Decisions for Your Interaction Style

In this section, we review some design decisions that we might consider for an interaction in the audio catalog.

### Design Decisions for Menus

- *Menu architecture:* Do we have breadth versus depth trade-offs? This is not clear. We will delay any decisions on this issue for now.

- *Specific content and layout of menu choices:* For now, we will use the primary classes and the task analysis to determine the choices. One menu for each of the types of primary classes (represented as thumb tabs) and the choices for each class based on the task analysis, with one choice per subtask.

- *Organization of the menu options:* Content and structure of categories (what to group together). We are grouping the primary classes into one menu and the choices of operations for each class, into another menu.

- *Navigational structure of menus:* Choices are single menus, linear navigation, tree navigation, or network (cyclic) (Shneiderman 1992). Let's look at our task analysis and in particular our task write-ups. What we see is that there is little sequencing between the high-level subtasks (e.g., *Manage CDs, Manage Songs*). Even at the lower levels of the task breakdown, we see little inherent sequencing. For now, we should not need a linear menu structure. However, as the task breakdown shows, the choices of operations are context dependent. It does not make sense to jump from *Add a new CD to catalog* to *Add new song to catalog* without selecting Song. Our menu architecture should be hierarchical.

- *Type of menu (pull-down, pop-up, pie):* Our task structure seems best matched with the horizontal context dependent (Lotus-style) menus, allowing ourselves some variations in appearance. If we consider our choice of primary class to be our first-level menu selection and we turn on the menu choices that correspond, in some respects this is a layered menu.

- *Physical access to menus:* How does the user access the menu from the screen? The style of selection could be enter a number, use a pointing device, or use function keys. Our design includes thumb tabs to be selected with a mouse as our way to specify the menu choices of the primary classes.

- The next iteration of the interaction is shown in Figure 12.5. In this picture, the CD menu is activated.

Is there support for experts? What about the variables of satisfaction, ease of use, and ease of learning that we have already defined? We have no idea how to answer these questions yet.

### 12.2.5 Step 5: Identify a Standard Look for Your Screens

Some suggested ways to do this is to select standard locations and sizes for buttons and other interface objects, to select standard language styles for text, and to select standard colors and other visual characteristics. At this point, you may wish to consider developing a template for your screens that you can use across the interaction. Some issues to be aware of include these:

- In Chapter 9, we described a number of strategies to improve the visual layouts of your presentation. Check your template against these strategies.

- We learned in Chapter 7 that the use of the user's mental model can be enhanced if the presentation is consistent in appearance. Now is a good time to check the appearance of your interaction objects for consistency. Developing and following a template for your screens can help to promote consistency.

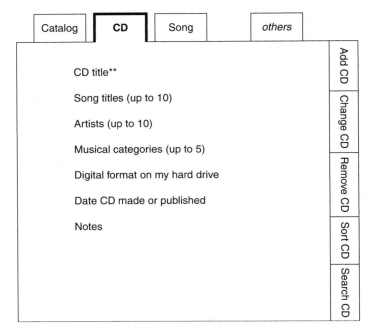

Figure 12.5    Audio Catalog: CD Tab Selected and Secondary Menu Visible.

- We learned in Chapter 7 that it is important to reduce the user's cognitive workload. When designing the appearance of your interactions, do not introduce superfluous colors, motion, and so on that might distract the user or "steal" the user's attention. Check your template. Have you introduced any superfluous elements to the look of your screens?

### 12.2.6 Step 6: Design the Feel of the Interactions

So far, much of what we have designed involves the static appearance of our screens. Some of our general guidelines also give us some hints about the behavior or feel of the interaction. Take some of the screens that you have designed and interact with them as your users might. As you execute some interactions, the following are some issues to consider:

- In Chapter 7, we learned that it is important to reduce the strain on the user's working memory by utilizing clear, closed, and, when possible, short sequences of user actions to accomplish a task. Evaluate your interaction sequences in this context.

- In Chapter 7, we saw that it was important to let the user be in control. One suggestion was to allow the reversal of user actions. Try some user actions and ask yourself if they are reversible.

- In Chapter 7, we learned to provide appropriate feedback to the user. We have already given some ideas for feedback. In our audio catalog design, selected buttons were highlighted. What other forms of feedback do you plan to provide?

### 12.2.7 Step 7: Review General and Visual Guidelines, Redesign, and Reevaluate

At this step you should review all your design choices in light of the guidelines that have been presented. For example, suppose that I was reviewing the guidelines regarding my proposal for the audio catalog. Chapter 7, Guideline 4, says to minimize modal interactions. Right now, for our second-level menu choices, we are still including the type of primary class in the title. For now, by avoiding a menu title of "ADD" we are not modal. Other guidelines you may wish to consider include these:

- Guideline 6: Let the user be in control. Reduce opportunities for user errors.
- Guideline 5: Reduce the user's cognitive workload.
- Guideline 1: Facilitate the development of mental model.

Let's check the audio catalog design one more time against our visual design guidelines. Well, yes, it looks ugly. The thumb tabs down the side look funny and are out of balance. Let's just make them buttons and see if we can balance our appearance. The next version is shown in Figure 12.6.

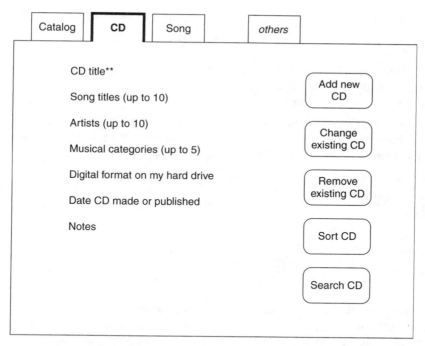

**Figure 12.6** Audio Catalog: Thumb Tabs as Buttons.

Now, recall what we learned about forms. First, users do better if they have an idea of what kind of data they are supposed to input. Some kind of input box is a good idea for any of the fields, as shown in Figure 12.7.

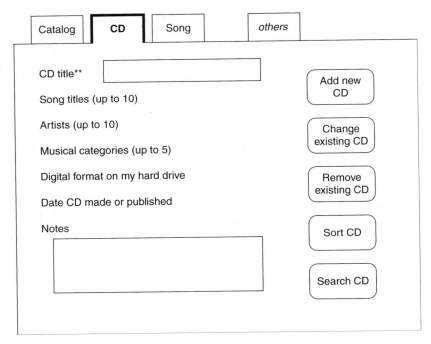

Figure 12.7    Audio Catalog: Input Boxes for Data Entry.

Now, let's take on a more difficult problem. What happens when the user has selected one of the buttons that is on the form? Let's start with what happens when you select *Add new CD*. According to the task analysis, this task involves the following subtasks:

- Add CD title (required)
- Add song titles
- Add artist
- Add category
- Add format
- Add date
- Add notes

From our task specification, we know that the particular order of adding this information is unimportant and only the CD title is required. As long as the user can see that all the fields can be put in, no particular order is required. However, following our form fill-in guidelines, we would like to lead the user to input the actual data. We also need to tell the user what to do next: either to add the new CD or to stop this entry.

## 12.3 Low-Level Design of Interaction

In this section, we discuss some issues to consider as you design your individual interactions. You will note that we will revisit a number of the guidelines that we presented in Chapters 7 through 9.

### 12.3.1 Step 1: Map Your Task Structure onto Your Design of Interaction

Regardless of the interaction you have in mind, you are more likely to be successful if the structure of the interaction matches the structure of the task. Don't wait until your interaction is fully designed and then go back to your task analysis to confirm that you have covered everything. Rather, once you have made some global decisions about interaction styles and a choice of metaphor, your particular interaction should at least start by following your task structure.

Let's reconsider our thumb tab and cards idea for the audio catalog. Now let's ask ourselves what should go onto the cards. In keeping with the metaphor, we could put on the card the attributes of whichever thumb tab and entity had been selected. For example, for a CD we might have something like Figure 12.8. Well, that is the idea even if it looks kind of funny. This card is starting

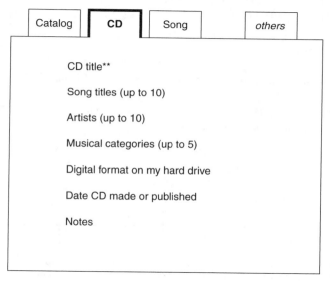

**Figure 12.8**    Audio Catalog: Sample Organization for CD.

to look like a form, and given that we cannot predict the actual value of the fields in advance, form fill-in might be a good choice. What kinds of lessons did we learn about forms? First of all, layouts are critical. We want to make good use of white space, balance the presented fields, and group the fields in a reasonable way.

Also, recall that you can prevent some user errors by providing clues as to what would constitute good data or by providing visually clear delimiters of the fields. Figure 12.9 contains clues as to appropriate inputs for digital format and date. This form is incomplete, however. It does not really tell us what we can do with the form, even if we have the data in front of us. Are we browsing, and if so, how? Are we adding a new CD, adding a nonessential attribute to an existing CD, or what?

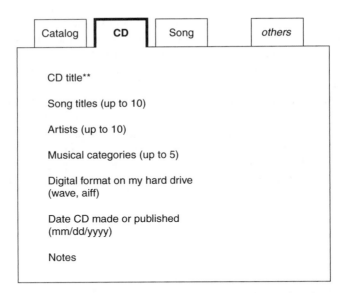

Figure 12.9    Audio Catalog: Information to Indicate Type of Data in a Form.

Looking at the task analysis, you can see that you can do a set number of things with a CD. Figure 12.10 shows the subtasks of *Manage CDs*.

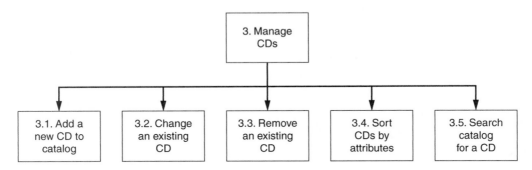

Figure 12.10    Subtasks of *Manage CDs*.

This is a limited set of alternatives. If we follow the task structure, are we thinking of some kind of menu? What kind of menu would be most appropriate for our idea? Remember that we are working in the direction of the prototype in Figure 12.11. In other words, we have the thumb tabs as menu entries to select the appropriate forms. Now we have to make some other design decisions about our second-level menus.

### 12.3.2 Step 2: Design Individual Interactions to Support the Tasks Identified in the Task Analysis

Your task analysis should drive your design of individual interactions because, after all, your task analysis defines the interface that you are ultimately to build. The following are several specific ways that you can use your task analysis to drive your design.

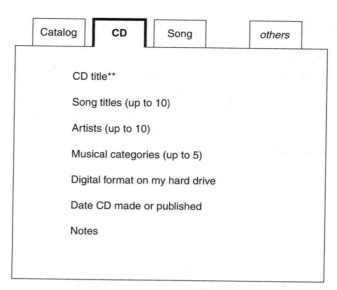

**Figure 12.11** Audio Catalog: Prototype.

1. Using the tasks from your task analysis, check off all tasks that have an interaction or interactions. If you used a numbering scheme for the tasks in your task analysis, carry that scheme forward and use the numbering scheme to identify corresponding interactions.

2. Identify which of your task subtrees have sequencing concerns. How are you going to make sure your user follows the correct sequence? Will the user be able to quit the task before the sequence is finished? How will the user know where he or she is in the sequence?

3. Identify those tasks, which could fail because of inappropriate or incorrect user inputs. In the interactions for those tasks, consider ways to guide users to appropriate or correct inputs.

4. Identify those tasks, which are to generate an automatic action, such as an alarm. Document in your design of these interactions that an automatic action is expected.

5. Identify those tasks, which rely on a noninterface function, such as a sorting routine. Document in your design of these interactions that a noninterface function is expected.

### 12.3.3 Step 3: Check the Design of Individual Screens
At this point, you should refer to your project and other guidelines for conformance.

## 12.4 Reevaluate Your Design Decisions
Here we present some additional examples of how we might reevaluate and change our design for the audio catalog.

Adding the CD title seems to be a straightforward text entry, especially if we assume for now that the title is not already in the catalog. Adding the artist and notes is just a matter of text entry as well. For now, we can just use the simple text-entry box that we have shown in Figure 12.7 above.

What about adding a song? Song is a primary entity in the catalog, so the user might want the new song to be one already in the catalog. Or, the user might want to type in a new song title, in which case adding the song to the CD also adds the song to the catalog. The primary class of Category behaves in the same way as Song. Think about this data—sometimes we know the value and sometimes the user will need to tell us what it is. If the user has to tell us the value, we will need to use a text-entry box. However, if the song or category already exists in the catalog, we might as well let the user select from a list of the existing information.

One strategy would be to use a combination text and menu selection tool: Using this strategy, the user could rely on recognition if the song is already in the catalog, as shown in Figure 12.12.

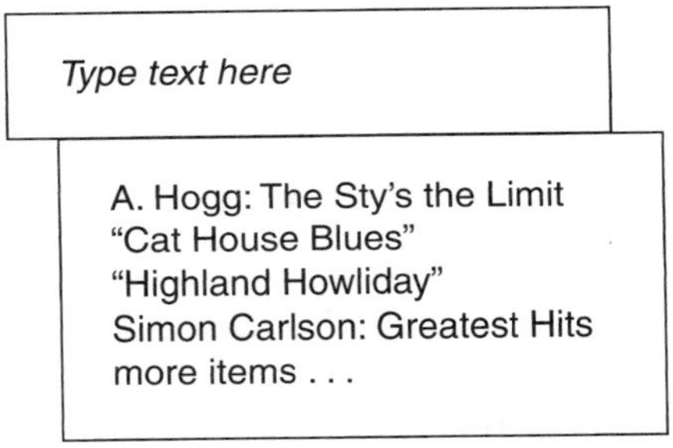

*Type text here*

A. Hogg: The Sty's the Limit
"Cat House Blues"
"Highland Howliday"
Simon Carlson: Greatest Hits
more items . . .

Figure 12.12   Audio Catalog: Sample Combination Text Entry and Menu Selection

This approach will probably work out as long as we do not have too many menu entries. Remember, we learned that long menus can be problematic and that it is probably better to favor breadth over depth. Suppose that our audio catalog manager is really useful and that the typical user includes 5,000 songs on average. Clearly, a menu of 5,000 elements is too large.

## 12.5 Analyzing the Design

In Chapter 11 we learned that analytic evaluation methods can be used to compare alternative designs. In this section, we show a simple example of a GOMS analysis. There are a number of flavors of GOMS; for this example, we will use the simplest GOMS technique: the Keystroke-Level Model, or KLM.

Recall the partial design of the interaction for the audio catalog from previously in this chapter. We had included a dialogue with thumb tabs for the objects and the name of the active object in bold. For the sake of this example, we suppose that we have modified our design for the audio catalog to include the screen shown in Figure 12.13. Remember that this is not the best design; we are using it to illustrate the method.

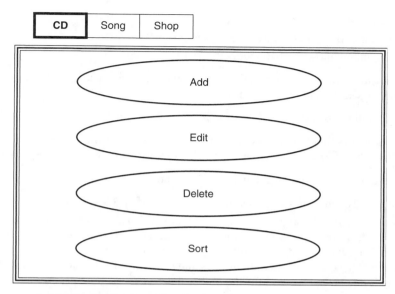

Figure 12.13    Audio Catalog: Alternative Design 1.

We will now do a KLM analysis for the interaction of pushing one of the category buttons. To push a button, the user will apply the following sequence of physical actions:

1. Move hand to the mouse.
2. Mentally select the target thumb tab.
3. Move the mouse to the thumb tab.
4. Click on the thumb tab.

We call this sequence of actions a *method*. Each physical action involves an operator. The KLM method includes at least eight operators from to which choose. Each of these actions has empirically derived time value (cf. Kieras n.d.). These are the eight operators:

| | |
|---|---|
| K | Press keyboard |
| B | Press or release mouse button |
| BB | Click mouse button |
| P | Point with mouse |
| H | Move hands to and from the keyboard |
| D | Drawing |
| M | Mental activity (thinking or perceiving) |
| W | Waiting time for system to respond |

Reconsidering our action sequence, we can now categorize actions into one of the KLM operators:

1. Move hand to the mouse—the H operator.

2. Mentally select the target thumb tab—the M operator.

3. Move the mouse to the thumb tab—the P operator.

4. Click on the thumb tab—the BB operator.

In our sequence of physical actions, we assumed that no mental activity was occurring. So our time for pushing a single button would be:

Time for thumb tab = Time for H + Time for M + Time for P + Time for BB

Kieras (n.d.) suggests times of 0.4 second for H, 1.2 seconds for M, 1.1 seconds for P, and 0.2 second for BB. Thus, our analysis suggests that the total time for this action sequence should be:

Time for thumb tab = 0.4 + 1.2 + 1.1 + 0.2 seconds

Our time for this sequence of actions should be approximately 2.9 seconds.

Think about this simple analysis. First, we assumed that the user already knew the action sequence to click on the thumb tab and did not make any errors when clicking on a choice. Second, we did not include any waiting or down time for the system to respond or redraw the mouse position. Third, we assumed that the "standard" times for the actions made sense. This latter assumption is probably valid for the physical actions, based on prior empirical data. According to Kieras (n.d.), M represents routine thinking, so as long as our user's choice of thumb tabs is routine, the time value of M is probably a good choice. If the user needs to study the choice, however, our value of M is probably low. Finally, if our action sequence included several parallel paths, we would not have captured the timing of the user selecting which path to take.

Assuming that our assumptions were relatively valid, however, we could have used the keystroke analysis to compare selection of the thumb tabs to the alternative design shown in Figure 12.14. In our alternative design, we will use horizontal context-dependent menus. The idea is that the user moves the mouse across the choices in the first row. Suppose that in this interface the user activates a particular entity by clicking on it. So, if I click on Song, the options for Song show up on the second-level menu.

| **CD** | | | **Song** | **Shop** |
|---|---|---|---|---|
| Add | Edit | Delete | Sort | |

Figure 12.14    Audio Catalog: Alternative Design 2

The sequence of user actions for this design is:

1. Move hand to the mouse—the H operator.

2. Mentally select the menu entry—the M operator.

3. Move the mouse to the menu entry—the P operator.

4. Click on the menu entry—the BB operator.

Once again, building a time model, we have:

Time for HCD menu = Time for H + Time for M + Time for P + Time for BB

Using the values suggested in Kieras (n.d.), the total time is:

Time for HCD menu = 0.4 + 1.2 + 1.1 + 0.2 seconds

Our time should be around 2.9 seconds, which is the same as for the other presentation. The fact that the times for the two presentations are the same should not be a surprise because they are actually very similar. The thumb tab presentation is something like a horizontal layered menu with two types of information showing. The main difference is whether the user actually clicks the mouse to see the choices that go with each entity type or simply moves the mouse over the entity.

## 12.6 Another Evaluation of Our Design

Recall from Chapter 11 that we need to go through a design process to develop an evaluation. In this section, we illustrate an example evaluation for our prototype for the audio catalog interaction.

STEP 1. Understand the evaluation: What should we evaluate? What is the meaning of the outcome of the evaluation?

Let's assume that the goal of this evaluation is to perform an evaluation of the prototype interaction shown in Figure 12.11 and again in Figure 12.15. Because we are evaluating a prototype, our evaluation is formative.

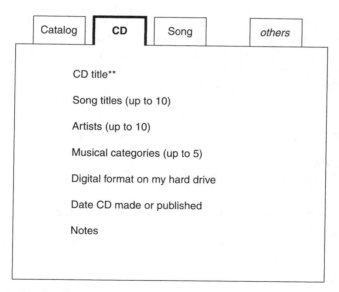

Figure 12.15   Audio Catalog: Prototype to Evaluate.

STEP 2. Design the evaluation at a high level: What should you evaluate? What is the setting of the evaluation? What precise interaction/interface features will you evaluate?

Recall from our specification in Chapter 6 that we had some specific usability goals that included a goal of *satisfaction:*

Overall we expect that the use of the interface for *Manage CDs* will be satisfying.

**STEP 3.** Design the evaluation at a low level: What do you measure? What data do you collect? How will you operationalize abstract constructs? What task scenarios and benchmark tasks will you use? Where will you administer your evaluation? What will your procedure be?

Our specification included an operationalization for *satisfaction:*

Overall we expect that the use of the interface for *Manage CDs* will be satisfying. Specifically we define satisfaction for this task as follows. After a group of users has been using this system for ten hours, so that they are proficient, we will ask them to rate their satisfaction on the following scale for each of the tasks that corresponds to the subtasks of *Manage CDs*. We expect that the average rating should be 4 or above.

On a scale of one to 5, indicate how satisfactorily this user interface will support the subtask of *fill in subtask.*

**1 = Not at all    2 = Marginally    3 = OK    4 = Pretty Good    5 = Excellent**

We can use this operationalization of satisfaction as the basis of our evaluation. Note that these data are subjective because they reflect an opinion, but they are also quantitative because they are numeric. However, as we are in the midst of designing the interaction, our prototype exists only on paper and is rather primitive. How useful will the quantitative data be to our future development? We would argue that at this early stage of evaluation we might be better off to describe a benchmark task and ask our evaluators to discuss how satisfied they think they might be with the prototype. Let's make the question open-ended so that we can hear any suggestions to our design that the evaluator makes.

Notice that hidden in the specification is the indication that this evaluation is to be done by users. Let's decide to bring some potential users of the audio catalog to our laboratory facility so we can listen to their feedback.

Now we have to identify a benchmark task. In Chapter 6, we have this scenario:

I go shopping and buy some CDs, including *Simon Carlson: Greatest Hits.* I add the songs and the CD to my catalog. I make a note in the catalog entry for this CD that I want to skip "Your UI Is So Plain" when I listen.

This scenario specifies several outcomes from the task (adding songs and a CD, making a note), but it does not specify the sequence of interface actions to achieve the goals. A benchmark task, based on this scenario might be "Add the song "Meowing in the Rain" from *Simon Carlson: Greatest Hits* to the audio catalog."

Our evaluation procedure will be as follows:

- Bring some potential users (say ten, so that we will have some diversity of perspectives) to our development facility.
- Show each user the prototype and the benchmark task. Ask to answer the open-ended question *Indicate how satisfying this user interface will support the benchmark task.*

- Evaluate our results. Did our evaluation give enough information to help us evaluate the prototype, or do we need to refine our evaluation? How can we use the evaluation results to refine our prototype?

Later in the interaction development, we will want to evaluate again. In these later evaluations we may wish to consider using the operationalizations from the specification.

## Conclusions

Students often ask, "Exactly how am I supposed to design an interaction?" In this chapter we have tried to identify a series of steps to help you get started on this process. The strategy that we have presented, while not algorithmic, is at least organized. If you keep careful records of the steps of your design and of your justification for design decisions, you will have a rationale to support the decisions behind your design. Should you need to change design elements later, you can always go back to this record of your design process to review why you made the design decision that you did.

In this chapter, the design process that we presented may have seemed to proceed stepwise. In reality, as we learned in Chapter 4, iteration is key to a good design. While we presented a series of steps that appeared to move in linear order, in fact you should be willing to go backward and forward. The results of an analysis and evaluation of your design, using KLM and/or user testing, should give you some idea of whether you are ready to proceed or whether you need to move backward.

You worked very hard to define your problem during your requirements and analysis stage of usability engineering. You do not want to lose the work that you have already done. You want to completely solve the problem that you have defined. In our discussion of low-level design, we suggested that you use your task analysis as a check-off list for the tasks that you were to cover in your design. This was just one example of how your requirements documents should be actively used in design and not simply shelved in a project notebook.

In Chapter 10, we learned about types of prototypes and how they can be used in design. For the early design stage that we showed in this chapter, you should consider using *paper prototypes*. Paper prototypes are made with the simplest of materials: paper, colored pencils, and crayons. Actual interactions and state changes in your design can be shown with sticky notes and tape (cf. Snyder 2003).

## Exercises

1. You or your instructor may wish to develop some documentation reports for your design that allow you to keep a record of your design decisions. Obtain or develop such a reporting form.
2. Using your reporting form, your task analysis, and your user profiles, go through a design exercise. What steps were difficult? What decisions were bothersome?

# Specifying and Analyzing Your (Quality) Software Design

### Motivation

At this point, we have been through the usability engineering process and also seen the audio catalog example evolve throughout specification, design and evaluation. Our focus has been on the development of the user interaction. However, there is a significant amount of *software* engineering in a user interface development project. This chapter focuses specifically on some of those software engineering activities.

When you are finished with this chapter, you should be able to do the following:

- Explain the difference between interaction design and interface design.
- Apply notations and documentation techniques for interface specification and design.
- Explain why interface specification, design, and notation are difficult problems.
- Explain the characteristics of a quality software design.
- Explain how an object-oriented specification and design strategy may help you to develop a quality design for your interface software.
- Describe the process of software testing.

It is our assumption that you have already done some interaction specification and design activities and that you are now starting to specify and design some software to support your interaction. The concepts and examples in this chapter, as well as activities related to your class project, will give you a chance to practice what you have learned.

The discipline of software engineering is huge and often receives the attention of two or more courses in a computer science curriculum. Our goal in this one chapter is *not* to teach you all of software engineering. Rather, we hope to show you something of the development process for quality interface software, once the interaction design is known.

## 13.1 Introduction

Once you have decided on an interaction design, you will want to develop documentation for both the *look* (anticipated appearance) and the *feel* (anticipated behavior) of the user interface. This complete description of the look and feel of your specific interaction will be the specification or problem definition for the software that will drive your interaction. Based on this specification, you will design the software to support the actual interface.

The documentation techniques that we explain in this chapter tend to be system centric in the sense that the techniques show the interface in terms that are more characteristically thought of as "computer science." This is not surprising, considering that you will need to express the desired interaction in a form that will lead to the construction of software to support that interaction. After all, we eventually have to write instructions for the computer to execute. In this phase, you will describe the elements and the behavior of the proposed interface from the perspective of the system and not the human user of the interface.

We are going to briefly discuss the translation of your interaction into software specification documents. This translation process is not trivial, and identifying just the right technique is still under consideration by usability engineering researchers. This discussion shows a simple example of how you might perform this translation using the tools of the Unified Software Development Process. Hopefully, this example will give you some ideas of how one might specify an interface and why this is a difficult problem. We also discuss the transition of your specification into design and some characteristics possessed by quality software.

## 13.2 From Interaction Design to Software Development

Once you have designed the look and feel of your interaction, are you finished with the design process? No way! You have completed your interaction design, but you still have to specify, design, build, and test the *software* to drive your interaction. In other words, you are not ready to code yet and, at this point, you may not even be sure of the specific requirements for the software that you have to build. You still have to reach decisions about the architectural design of the software that runs your interface. For example, you will need to design the classes, algorithms, and data structures for the software, as well as the communication requirements to link other software, such as external databases or drivers. Some of these design decisions may be made for you as an artifact of your development environment. Many of these decisions will likely be left to you.

## 13.3 Software Requirements Specification to Support Interaction

How do you get started with the development of the software for your interface? In Chapter 4, we learned that an early step in software development is defining the problem. Here is an example that shows how I might start to transform my interaction design into a problem definition. Suppose that during the design of interaction, you have designed a button for an interaction that looks like the button shown in Figure 13.1.

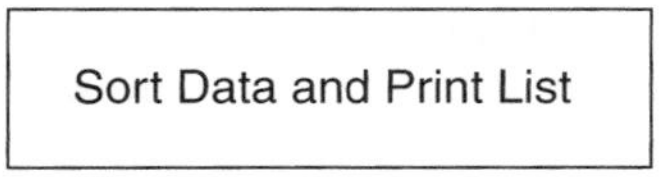

Sort Data and Print List

Figure 13.1   Sample Button.

For this example, we assume that "List" is defined in some other part of the interaction. We further assume that we have good reasons for this shape of button and the choice of text on the button.

What sort of software is required to support this button once it is selected? In other words, what are the requirements of the software to support the appearance and behavior of this button? To answer this question, I would need to know exactly what is supposed to happen when the button is pushed. For example, I would like to know if the button becomes highlighted when it is pushed. I would also need to know what noninterface functions occur when the button is pushed. In this example, it appears as if the software will need to find the list to be printed and sorted; printing and sorting are instances of noninterface functions.

As this example suggests, one aspect of specifying this button's requirements is to specify the expected behavior of the button, both in terms of events in the user interaction and in terms of functionality to be supported. The workflow that my software will have to support for the button push is probably similar to that indicated in Figure 13.2. This workflow shows both the sequencing and inherent parallelism in the activities that occur when the button is pushed. In addition, the activities related to noninterface functions suggest the use of noninterface or external programs. Many developers feel that it is good practice to separate the functions of the user interface (e.g., managing button states) from the functionality of the application software (e.g., sorting and retrieving data).

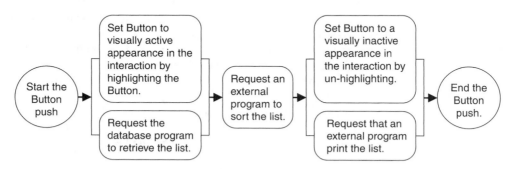

Figure 13.2   Workflow for the Sort-and-Print Button.

Now that I have specified requirements for the behavior of the button, I need to describe the requirements of the more static characteristics of the button. First, I will identify some of its attributes and their likely value. Some attributes are *color, shape, size,* and *position in the interaction.*

Hopefully, you can see that we have built a scaled-down software requirements specification for the button. We have described the behavior and the static characteristics of the button.

### 13.3.1 Specification of Interface: A Difficult Software Engineering Problem

As we have just seen, our first step in building the software for our interface is to define the problem that we are solving with the software; that is, we are defining the requirements of the software to support our interaction. We saw in Chapter 4 that software specification is generally a difficult and challenging problem in software engineering. It is a difficult problem in usability engineering as well. Thinking back to our button example from the previous section, suppose that in my specification of attributes for the button, I had forgotten to specify that the button had a size, even though the interaction team was quite specific about the button having a specific size. Eventually, in constructing the actual button, someone would define the size simply by building the button, but because I had not included the size characteristic as part of my specification, the actual size in the interface might not match what the interaction team had in mind.

A good software specification should have the following minimal characteristics (Fairley 1985):

- It should be complete. That is, there should be a full definition of the problem to solve. In usability engineering, this means that the behavior and appearance of every interaction and every object within the interaction should be completely documented. If not, the ultimate coders of the interface will use their own best guess as to what the interaction designer really wanted.

- It should be correct. That is, the specification for the interaction should faithfully describe the expected appearance and behavior of every interaction and every object in the interaction.

- It should be consistent. When describing the characteristics of an interaction or object in the interaction, I should not find one description on one page and a conflicting description on another page.

- It should be unambiguous. Specifications that are ambiguous leave designers no choice but to use their own best guesses as to what was meant.

### 13.3.2 Specifying the Requirements for Your Interface Software: What Information Should Be Included?

In the button example, shown in Figures 13.1 and 13.2, we identified some types of information that we might want to specify. Now we introduce another example and make the specification more explicit.

Let's assume that we are working on an interface development effort, as we have tracked in Chapters 6 and 12. Assume that in this example, thus far we have designed an interaction for our user that we feel matches the task specification as well as our situational variables. Just as in Chapter 12, we have drawn pictures of the screens or user interactions. These pictures are drawn with paper and pencil but have a fairly well-defined look and feel, at least in the mind of the interaction designer.

Suppose I am considering the data entry box shown in Figure 13.3. (We have made this a limited interaction design for the purpose of illustrating these concepts.)

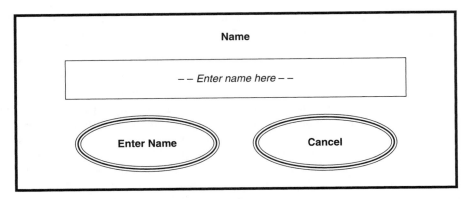

**Figure 13.3**    Data Entry Box.

Suppose I gave only this picture to a programmer. From the picture, the programmer would have a pretty clear idea of the size and layout of the box, the buttons, the label, and the text field. Some information is missing from the picture, though. Specifically, this picture gives no ideas as to how the elements of the interface, such as the buttons, are related or are similar. In other words, it is not clear from the picture if I was thinking that the buttons would be members of the same class or data structure. We need to include a lot more information. Hopefully, you can see that even in this simple presentation, the programmer could make several different interpretations of the behavior of the buttons. For example, the picture alone does not specify how the buttons are activated. Is it by a single mouse click or a double click? It is also not clear what happens when I push the *Enter Name* button. Is the name saved and then the text field emptied for another text entry? Or is the *Enter Name* button more like a submit button that will save the text string and then close the box? What is the behavior of the *Cancel* button? Does pushing this button erase the text field, or does it cancel the interaction and close the box?

Without specifying both the appearance and behavior of interface elements, we leave it to the programmer to guess our meaning. On the other hand, documenting the design of an interaction is difficult. Following is some of the information that must be captured:

- *The look of the interface and composition of the interface objects.* You must show the appearance and organization of the proposed interface elements. For example, if your proposed interface will have a window, a menu bar, and three menus, you must be able to explicitly show the appearance of these interface elements.

- *Services necessary from other parts of the system.* For example, an interface element may require a database access service to complete its goals.

- *The relationships and characteristics of interface objects.* For example, Figure 13.3, shows two buttons. Do they have the same pattern of behavior, so that they both react to mouse clicks in identical ways? Are they to be implemented as totally different data structures, or are they both examples of some more abstract object? What are the attributes of buttons? How do they interact with other objects?

- *Sequencing and behavior of interface objects.* What is the behavior of the interface elements? In particular, you must specify how interface elements become activated and how their behaviors interact.

In the next few sections, we present a highly simplified specification technique as we apply it to our interaction design of the audio catalog shown in Chapter 12. The presentation only samples some of the modeling techniques of the Unified Software Development Process and is purposefully incomplete. Our intention is simply to give you the flavor of the process and methodology.

### 13.3.3 Look of Interface and Composition Interface Objects
In your interaction design, it is likely that you have already captured the appearance and composition of many of your eventual interface elements and screens using paper-and-pencil drawings. You may have also written a narrative to justify your design decisions.

The look and composition of the interface objects form a starting point for specifying the objects and data structures that will ultimately support the interaction. For example, in Figure 13.3 we might have specified a button class that would have been instantiated for each button in the example interaction.

### 13.3.4 Using UML Models to Specify Look and Feel
What does it mean to be *object-oriented?* As you perhaps have learned in your other computer science classes, a growing emphasis within computer science has been placed on object-oriented software development methodologies. In the abstract, an object-oriented methodology means the analysis, design, and construction of a software system that is built around component parts. These components are called *objects;* objects contain both data and the operations associated with the data. Just as a factory builds products out of components, the hope is to construct software out of components as well. In theory these components would be reusable from product to product and would each be to some extent stand-alone. Initially, the hope was that this approach would greatly improve software productivity and quality. Sadly the object-oriented approach has not uniformly improved all aspects of the software industry, but it does provide a useful way of thinking about analysis, design, and implementation, and it is in widespread practice. Even better from the usability engineer's perspective, the object-oriented paradigm really does apply to user interfaces, especially graphical user interfaces. We can think of typical visual interface elements, such as windows and buttons, as objects. Many development environments even deliver their widgets as reusable components.

Object-oriented methodologies describe their specifications, designs, and programs in terms of communicating objects. Objects communicate via message passing; message passing among objects often represents requests for services from one object to another. Objects are made up of their characteristics or attributes and the methods or functions that they contain. Some of these attributes and methods are visible to other objects, and some are private. At any time, an object has a state that is made up of the current values of its attributes and its point in processing. Specific objects are typically generalized into classes.

Some background information about object-oriented software engineering is useful here. Several people, notably Booch (1991), Rumbaugh, Blaha, Lorensen, Eddy, and Premerlani (1991), and Jacobson, Christerson, Jonsson, and Övergaard (1992) have proposed object-based development methodologies. These three flavors of development methodologies have more recently been joined to form what is called the Unified Software Development Process. The Unified Software

Development Process is a true methodology, in the sense that it provides a way of thinking about software development that supports all phases of a project from the beginning of the project through its delivery.

*Unified Modeling Language* or UML is the modeling and notational strategy that is used to support the Unified Software Engineering Process. As such, UML consists of a number of models, in the form of diagrams that can be used throughout the software life cycle. These models permit the developer to describe system features, such as class structures and static characteristics, message passing patterns and requests for services among classes and objects, functionality, workflow, state change, and sequencing. UML can be used at both a high, abstract level and at a low, very detailed level, as we will show.

For user interfaces, several of the models from UML can be quite useful. However, the specific intent of UML is to model more traditional software development, so these techniques are not specific tools for user interface development. (See Hudson 2001 for a discussion of this issue.)

We will focus on just a few of the modeling techniques of UML, and our discussion of UML will follow the approach of Booch, Rumbaugh, and Jacobson (1999). We will use elements of UML to show:

- *Static characteristics of a user interface.* A model of these characteristics can be called a *structural model.* User interfaces are made up of various interface objects and relationships among these objects. In UML, interface objects can be viewed abstractly as *classes.* We will show how to use UML *class diagrams* to illustrate modeling of the structure and associations of (relationships among) classes.

- *Behavioral characteristics of a user interface.* Behavioral models show how the structural elements of the user interface react to user input and to each other. We illustrate these issues with behavioral models. From UML, we will use *state diagrams* and *activity diagrams* to illustrate the behavior of user interface components.

### 13.3.5 Static Structure of the Interface: Class Diagrams

UML class diagrams can be used to document the static structure of the interface and describe what the interface object classes are and how the classes are related. Because the class diagram presents a static view of the system, it is not intended to show system behavior. For example, the class diagram does not show the interactions among objects or the relationships in terms of communication patterns. Rather, they show the semantics of relationships among classes: who is the superclass of whom, and what classes exist only because of the existence of other classes. While not specifically showing message passing among classes, many class relationships imply message passing. Class diagrams provide information to the designer concerning the object structures in the eventual program.

The fundamental elements of class diagrams are *classes* and *relationships* among classes. Classes are abstractions of specific instances of objects (real world or in the mind of the designer) and may represent things, events, and so on. Classes potentially have characteristics, called *attributes,* and capabilities, called *methods* or *operations.* Operations are the actions that instances of the class can take; in other words, they are the methods that instances of other classes will ask for when requesting services. Classes can be represented either at a high level with just a name in a rectangle or at a lower level to include attributes and operations. Figure 13.4 illustrates a generic UML diagram of a class; the diagram includes space for the class name, attribute names, and operation (method) names, as well as parameters or data types.

```
┌─────────────────────────────┐
│                             │
│      Class Name             │
│                             │
├─────────────────────────────┤
│                             │
│      Attribute Names        │
│                             │
│   Characteristic properties for │
│   this class,               │
│                             │
├─────────────────────────────┤
│                             │
│      Operation Names        │
│                             │
│   Characteristic operations for │
│   this class,               │
│                             │
└─────────────────────────────┘
```

Figure 13.4    Generic Class Diagram.

### 13.3.6 Relationships Among Classes

While individual classes are critical in an object-oriented presentation, it is important to specify how they are related to other classes. Classes may be made up of combinations of other classes, generalizations of classes, or simply related by the problem.

In the class diagram, relationships show connections among classes. Classes can be related in at least three ways (cf. Rumbaugh, Jacobson, Booch 1999):

*Association.*    If two or more classes are related, then they have an association. Associations among classes are shown graphically as a simple line.

---

*Generalization.*    One class is a generalization or specialization of another class. In the entity-relation diagram approach (cf. Chen 1976) this is known as an *ISA relationship* (ISA stands for "is a"). In an object-oriented approach, generalization means that the subclass inherits the attributes and operations from the superclass. In a UML diagram, generalization is shown as an arrow.

⟶▷

*Aggregation and composition.*    One class is part of a group of classes that forms another class. In other words, one class is composed of, or aggregated with, other classes to form a new class. If one class is a part of another class (i.e., part of an aggregation that makes up another class), then we mark it with a filled diamond

### Associations

Associations typically have names. The name tells you something about the nature of the classes that are related via the association.

As associations represent relationships among classes, a relationship may be one to one, one to many, or many to many. This characteristic of the relationship is called *multiplicity*. Each association has a characteristic multiplicity for each of the classes in the association. Rumbaugh,

Jacobson, and Booch (1999) define *multiplicity of association* as the number of objects from a subclass that can be associated with an instance of a superclass.

Finally, sometimes in class diagrams it will be important to identify specific instances as compared to abstractions. A colon (:) is used to separate the attribute names from additional definitional information, such as data type.

Consider the dialogue box in Figure 13.3. A class diagram as a model for the buttons in this box can specify some aspects of the eventual interface design and implementation. In particular, a class diagram can answer the following questions:

- Are the two buttons totally different, or are they both examples of some more abstract object?
- What are the attributes of the buttons, and what are they supposed to do?

To answer these questions and make the specification for the buttons explicit, we will use a class diagram. In this diagram, we show that there is a class called *Button. Button* has one attribute, *Button Status. Button* has one operation, *Set Button Status.* Two button classes, *Enter Name Button* and *Cancel Button,* inherit the attributes and methods of *Button.* Each is a specialization of *Button* because each has its own set of methods; *Button* is a generalization of *Enter Name Button* and *Cancel Button.* Specifically, the *Enter Name Button* class has a method to send a name to wherever the name value is being stored. *Cancel Button* has a method to terminate the dialog. *Button* is called the superclass or parent, and *Enter Name Button* and *Cancel Button* are called the subclasses or children. In object-oriented terms, *Enter Name Button* and *Cancel Button* inherit the attributes and methods of *Button.* The class diagram for the buttons, including their generalization patterns, is shown in Figure 13.5.

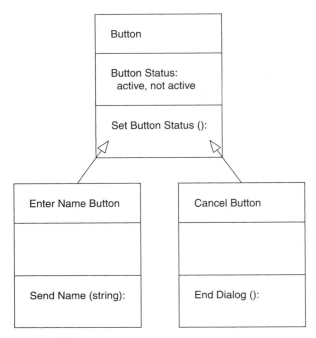

**Figure 13.5**   Class Diagrams for the Buttons in Figure 13.3.

Now the developers of our interface will have a much clearer idea of the specifics of the buttons in the dialogue than if they only had the picture of the interaction.

Let's think back to our task analysis and specification for the audio catalog. When we last saw the design of the interaction in Chapter 12, it looked like the image in Figure 13.6. Now let's consider developing a class diagram to show some of the classes and relationships to support the interaction that is shown in Figure 13.6. At a high level, we wish to show classes and their associations among the interface objects.

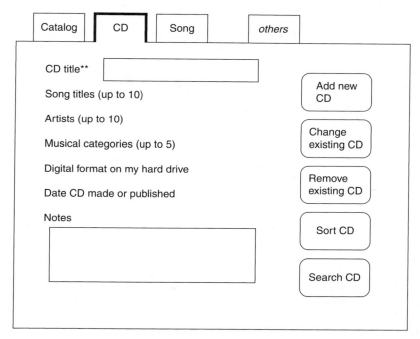

**Figure 13.6** Dialog for the Audio Catalog.

Recall that in the Figure 13.6 design, our menu type is similar to a context menu. When the CD thumb tab is active, the corresponding CD actions are displayed as buttons on the right side of the form. The interface objects that we can model include the form itself, the thumb tabs, the buttons on the form, the titles, and the text boxes.

Some of the corresponding class diagrams might look like the diagrams in Figures 13.7 and 13.8. First we notice that all of the interface objects are probably examples of a more general UI class, as shown in Figure 13.7.

Now we notice that several interface objects are on the display. In other words, the display is a composition of a number of interface objects. Also, for each instance of the display, there are six thumb tabs and one form, as shown in Figure 13.8.

Now let's see if we can fill in some of the attributes and methods for the Thumb Tab class and its subclasses. One attribute for all the thumb tabs would seem to be whether they are active. In

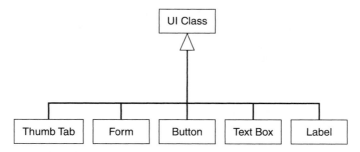

**Figure 13.7**    Generalization of Dialogue Objects.

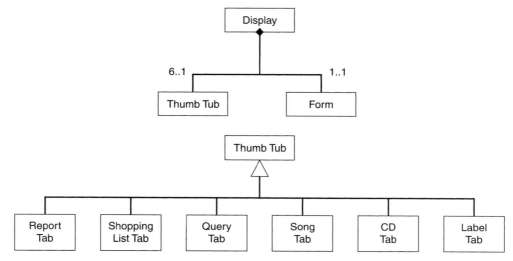

**Figure 13.8**    More Relationships Among Classes for the Dialogue.

terms of operations we would like to be able to SetActive as shown in Figure 13.9. In the example we have also included some prototypical data types associated with the attributes and methods.

What about the detailed and unique attributes for the tabs that correspond to the different entities? An example of the CD Tab class can be seen in Figure 13.10.

### 13.3.7 Showing Behavior

The preceding class diagrams illustrate the static structure of our proposed system and interface by showing some of the structure, attributes, methods, and relationships of the classes. Now we would like to show the behavior in some detail. What does "behavior" mean in an object-oriented design? At the beginning of this chapter, we showed an example of a model that described the workflow or sequence of activities that occurred when a button was pushed in our first example. One kind of behavioral information that we would like to show is the workflow or sequence of activities that occurs during an interface event. To accomplish this in UML, we use a model called an *activity diagram*.

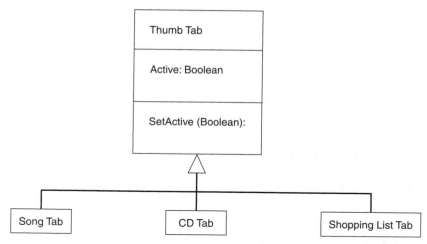

Figure 13.9  Details of Thumb Tab Class.

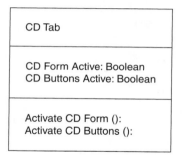

Figure 13.10  Details of CD Tab Class.

We have already learned that the *state* of an object refers to the values of its attributes and the status of the object's activities. To specify the behavior of interface objects, it is often useful to build a *state diagram,* which shows how an object moves from one state to another, particularly in response to external events. A state diagram shows explicitly all possible states of a single object or class; in this way, the state diagram is a very low-level description of a class or object behavior.

According to Rumbaugh, Jacobson, and Booch (1999), behavioral models play important roles in specifying and designing the dynamic behavior of a system. In this section, we visit several examples in which we use behavioral diagrams to specify interface behaviors.

### 13.3.8  Activity Diagram

Activity diagrams are used to show workflow through a system. In the Unified Software Development Process, activity diagrams are often used to describe the sequences of tasks that are necessary to support a use case similar to the use cases that we discussed in previous chapters.

Activity diagrams show the "states" not of only individual objects but also the "state" of part of our interface that may include several objects. In this way, it can also show some of the synchronization between objects and their behaviors. We will refer to the classes that we have already defined in our class diagrams. Remember that we are thinking of an interaction, such as the one shown in Figure 13.6, that uses thumb tabs for the interaction object with the active object highlighted.

This is the behavior: I know that when I click on the CD thumb tab, I want the CD form to activate and become visible. The buttons on the CD form will also activate. How can I describe this in a fairly rigorous way to a software designer or programmer? Each of the buttons and forms is an object, so a complete description of each button's state at this point is probably too complex. Rather, what I want to describe are the activities that will occur when the user event *Select CD Tab* occurs, relative to both the thumb tab object and the other objects in the interface.

### Activity Modeling and Diagrams
The UML symbols that are used in the activity diagrams are shown in Table 13.1.

Table 13.1    Symbols for Activity Diagrams.

| Name of Symbol | Symbol | Note |
|---|---|---|
| Activity State | | |
| Transition | → | Transitions indicate sequencing of activities or actions, so they are not always labeled. Transitions can branch and merge to represent alternative threads of activities, or they can fork and join to represent concurrent threads. |
| Decision Diamond | ◇ | |
| Start (Initial State) | ◉ | |
| Stop (Terminal State) | ● | |

When the user selects the CD tab, the user will see several options that represent tasks indicated by the buttons that are contained. We designate each of these tasks/buttons as activities that we want our interface design to support, as shown in Figure 13.11. Figure 13.12 indicates the activity flow for setting the buttons to active states when the CD tab is selected. Specifically, as the diagram indicates when the CD tab is selected, the CD form must become active first, and then the buttons for the CD-related tasks may become active concurrently.

### 13.3.9  State Diagram
State diagrams show the pattern of state changes for a class, and as such they present a much lower level of detail than the activity diagram. For example, we defined a class called *ThumbTab*. Suppose

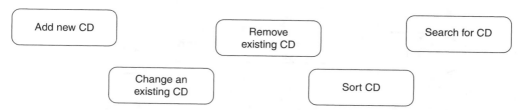

Figure 13.11  Buttons Representing Task Options when CD Tab Is Active.

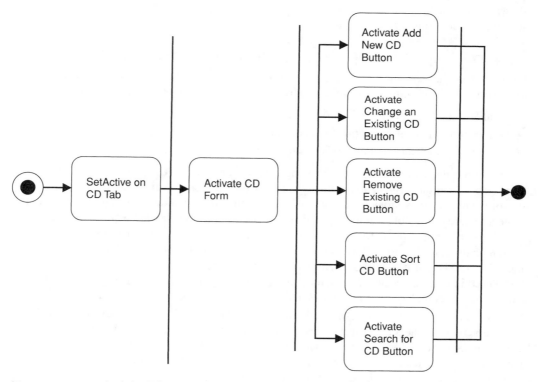

Figure 13.12  Activity Diagram for Manage CD: Display Task Buttons.

that ThumbTab has two states, Active and Not Active. A mouse click by the user would cause the ThumbTab to become active. A mouse click on another ThumbTab would cause the first to become inactive. The state diagram for the ThumbTab class is shown in Figure 13.13.

### 13.3.10 Conclusions: Unified Software Development Process, UML, and Specification of Interfaces

Specifying the software to support an interaction is a vital aspect of usability engineering. Without a clear specification of both the static structure of the interaction and its expected dynamic behavior, it would be nearly impossible to build the software that runs the interaction. We have

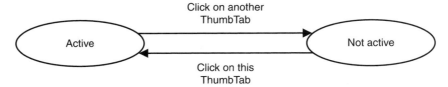

**Figure 13.13**    State Diagram for Thumb Tab Class.

shown some examples of how one might take a design of interaction and map that design into a specification for an interface.

## 13.4 Design of Interface: A Software Design Problem

Once the software specification is complete, it is time to design the software to support the requirements. Some specifics that I might address during the design process include these:

- Identify the information that is passed among classes.
- Design additional classes to provide necessary services.
- Develop the attributes and methods that define a class.

Based on our discussion of the software engineering life cycle in Chapter 4, it may seem as if once a specification is finished that the designer essentially starts over to build a design. In fact, one of the major motivations for using a software engineering methodology is that it should promote a seamless transformation of specification into design. As you were reading through some of our specification models for the audio catalog, did you feel that you could have almost gone right to code from the models? One of the interesting features of the Unified Software Development Process is that it provides a seamless transition from the models used in specification to those used in design, because for the most part, the models are the same. Design in theory is an expansion and completion of the models that were started during the specification process.

After I have completed my design activities, I should have a full software design that supports my interaction. If that is the case, the design is now ready to code. If my team is following an iterative approach to software development, we might have already developed some code from a partial design. My team members would have evaluated the code for, among other things, completeness and consistency with the interaction design.

You should consider these ideas carefully. The goals of software engineering do not always agree with the goals of usability engineering. The models that we built to specify our interface were drawn from the design of our interaction. If we did a good job of software engineering, our specification is a true representation of our interaction. That true representation of our interaction may not make the best design from a software engineering perspective. In traditional software design, the designer frequently will build a design that is different from the "design" suggested by the specification, because the structure of the problem definition may not produce the most efficient or robust design. The interface designer may be in a different position in this regard than the designer of a traditional software system and must always consider the usability goals of the project. The usability goals are key to a successful product and may conflict with a fast or efficient software design. When a software design can only be improved at the cost of some usability concerns, consider the dilemma carefully before you compromise. Always remember that the "best" designed software may be worthless if no one is willing to use it.

### 13.4.1  What Is Designed During Design of Interface?

You should recall that software design proceeds in two phases: high-level (architectural) software design and low-level software design. During architectural software design, the designer chooses the overall architecture. This means that the designer designs the component parts and identifies how they are related and how they will communicate. In an object-oriented design, the overall architecture describes these details:

- Major classes and their relationships.
- Messaging or communication architecture.

During low-level software design, the designer completes these details:

- Classes (structure and detailed behavior).
- Operations (member functions, class services, or subroutines).
- Attributes (data members).
- Issues of access (e.g., public, private), as well as storage strategies (e.g., static).

### 13.4.2  Software Design Quality

The software that we design to support our interaction can exhibit characteristics of high, low, or terrible quality. A software design is of high quality if the following are true:

- It is a solution to the problem that was defined in the requirements specification.
- It promotes functional independence.
- It promotes encapsulation and information hiding.
- It promotes software reuse.

We describe these ideas in greater detail in the next three sections. Note that what constitutes good quality for a user interaction differs from what constitutes good quality for a software component. User interactions and their resulting interfaces are judged by their usability. Software quality is judged according a very different set of criteria.

#### Functional independence

Stevens, Myers, and Constantine (1974) originally suggested that a high-quality design is one in which modules have limited connections among them and in which each module is focused on a single task. Designs with both of these characteristics are said to have high levels of *functional independence*. Functional independence provides design quality goals both within a module and in terms of the relationships among modules.

Two qualitative measures of functional independence have been suggested. *Coupling* is a measure of intermodule dependency, and *cohesion* is a measure of the internal functional strength of a module.

**Coupling**  *Coupling* is an indication of the interdependencies among software elements. Elements that are tightly coupled are highly dependent, and those that are loosely coupled are relatively independent. For example, consider two software procedures, X and Y. X and Y are loosely coupled if they share a simple data value or a data structure. They are more tightly coupled if they share control information or make direct reference into each other's code.

Consider a piece of software that has been in place for several months and now requires some maintenance. If the software has elements that are tightly coupled, changes to one component will likely necessitate changes to other components. If a component that is tightly coupled to another is changed without concern for the other component, the results may be unpredictable or catastrophic. In general, designers strive for low coupling among software components.

**Cohesion** *Cohesion* refers to the internal functional strength of a module. A module is highly cohesive if it accomplishes a single unified function. Modules that accomplish a number of functions, particularly unconnected functions, have low cohesion. Sometimes programmers will group similar functions into a single module. For example, a module that groups several input functions just because they involve the action of data input would have relatively low cohesion.

Modules with high cohesion are preferable to those with low cohesion. For example, a module has high cohesion if all the elements are focused on a single task. Once software is installed and requires maintenance, maintenance activities are much more complex for modules with low cohesion.

**Class Coupling and Cohesion** So far our discussion of functional independence has been in terms of modules, which could be subroutines under the procedural programming paradigm or member functions under the object-oriented programming paradigm. Page-Jones (1999) has made a similar observation and has noted that coupling and cohesion are defined at the code and subroutine level. He suggests that it also makes sense to consider class cohesion and class coupling. In his view, class cohesion level is an indication of how well the operations of the class are focused on one job. Class coupling is an indication of how tightly bound two classes are.

### Encapsulation

In the late 1970s, the idea was introduced that a data structure and its characteristic operations can be grouped together into an *abstract data type*. For the abstract data type to perform an operation, that operation has to be one of its characteristic operations, and abstract data types cannot use the characteristic operations of other abstract data types. Clearly, this idea has been further developed and refined in the object-oriented programming paradigm.

One outcome of the use of abstract data types and the object-oriented approach is *encapsulation*. Encapsulation is the grouping of related ideas into one unit that can thereafter be referred to by a single name. The idea is that the interface is a protective boundary between that which is encapsulated and that which is outside. A subroutine is an example of encapsulation. Classes can be considered a more extreme example of encapsulation.

In encapsulation, the abstract data type or object is protected from inadvertent changes from outside entities. If one object wishes to use the services or affect the data of another object, rather than doing this directly, the first object sends a message or request to the interface (boundary) of the second object. The first object does not care what the particular implementation of the request is, only that the job is accomplished. Meanwhile, the second object can evaluate the request and process it without disclosing information about its transitional states.

*Information hiding,* which is the use of encapsulation to restrict the external visibility of the implementation decisions that are internal to the encapsulated structure, is a by-product of encapsulation. Encapsulation and information hiding promote a form of low coupling and are generally very desirable.

## Software Reuse

One goal that has emerged from a number of software engineering paradigms is the idea of software component (modules, objects, and data structures) reuse. Software reuse can be viewed as essential for improving software productivity. From a practical perspective, if a component has been completed, why build it over and over again? Lack of reuse (continuous reinvention) is especially compelling when you consider that more than 50 percent of your development effort may be focused on testing. Each time a component is reinvented it must be reintegrated and retested. Imagine if vehicle manufacturers reengineered and retested each and every component in every car! We would all be walking.

How can one enhance reusability in software? The implication for software design is that functionality should be as broad as possible. Classes may need extra methods. Note that the goal of reuse may be in conflict with other software design goals, such as loose coupling.

Intuitively designing interface objects with an eye toward grouping similar objects may help you to identify conditions in which reuse is possible. Using an object-oriented programming language in your implementation may help you to take advantage of these reuse possibilities. Consider an alternative interaction in the audio catalog, as shown in Figure 13.14.

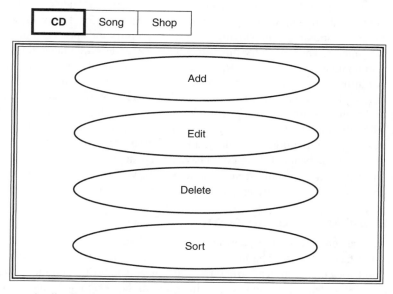

**Figure 13.14**   Audio Catalog: Alternative Interaction.

Suppose we decide that each combination of thumb tab and button click causes a different form to become active. We could write a separate function for each combination of tab and button click, or we could use an object-oriented approach to promote software reuse.

### 13.4.3 Object-Oriented Paradigm and Design Quality

Software that is developed under the object-oriented paradigm should promote the following:

- Functional independence, at least between classes. The designer is challenged to ensure high cohesion and low coupling within the member functions of classes.

- Encapsulation and information hiding.
- Software reuse.

When building the software to support your user interfaces, you should consider taking an object-oriented approach because it will result in higher-quality software.

### 13.4.4 Object-Oriented Design and User Interface Design

Hudson (2001) has pointed out that user-centered design and object-oriented design have continued to move in separate and, in many cases, unconnected directions. He points out several reasons (p. 216), including these:

- A number of open-ended questions address how use cases can be used as a specification technique for the richness of user tasks.
- No specific methodologies or models are focused on user interaction and interface design

In this book, we have shown how the UML notations and models could be used during the process of usability engineering. However, it is important to note that we did not follow a Unified Software Development Process. Our reasons have been aptly stated by Hudson (2001). For example, we showed an example in previous chapters about how the elements of use case diagrams could help a usability engineer abstract elements from scenarios. However, we *did not* use the use case diagrams and an accompanying analysis to identify the specific tasks that our user interface was to support. The reason for this is that use case models are intended to tell you what a system is to do relative to external agents. Use case models typically fail to capture the contextual and how-to information that we were able to specify in our task analyses and user profiles. Use case models typically do not describe the way that users experience their tasks; rather they show the tasks that the system will support. While we used other diagram techniques from UML for specifying and designing our interface, you may have noted that some aspects of the diagram usage were awkward. We required several dynamic diagrams to express interaction patterns. It would have been more convenient if we could have used a single model for behavior, analogous to the single class diagram for static structure. We look forward to the day when usability engineering and object-oriented software engineering are part of a seamless whole.

## 13.5 A Brief Note About Software Testing

During software design and certainly during implementation, it is essential to plan and execute tests of your interface software. The tests that you design should test the software against the specification and for correct logical structure. These tests should be conducted on individual modules, functional units, and whole systems. In addition, the design and execution of software testing should itself be treated as a type of engineering task in which the tester is responsible for developing a problem statement, designing the tests, and implementing the tests. Numerous software engineering books describe the testing process. We suggest that you consult one of these books as you are preparing to test your interface software.

## 13.6 Other Notations to Support the Specification and Construction of Interface Software

The specification and design of an interface constitute a difficult and somewhat unsolved problem in usability engineering. Several authors have suggested model-based user interface development environments (e.g., Puerta, Cheng, Ou, and Min 1999). Hix and Hartson (1993), recognizing the need for a notation to specify interface software, developed the UAN (User Action Notation) standard. Using UAN, an interface specification consists of descriptions for user tasks. The user tasks are derived from the task analysis and specification, and the UAN shows the precise interface correlate for the user task. The UAN specification is supplemented with state diagrams to show the way that the interface changes in response to user actions. The UAN may also include scenarios that describe in a step-by-step way how the user tasks would be accomplished in the proposed interface.

## 13.7 Challenges for Notations and Methodologies

Notations for specifying user interfaces continue to be an open challenge in usability engineering. The simple diagrams and models that we have shown are intended to give a flavor of using one technique: UML. No matter which technique you choose, you will be faced with a number of difficult challenges:

- Are you only able to model expert behavior? Are you able to show the behaviors of your interface in response to user errors?

- Many devices have characteristic behaviors. User actions can be primitive (e.g., mouse push down, push up). Does your modeling notion permit you to show interface characteristics at a low level, as well as at a high level, of description from your user?

- User actions may be contextual. Consider a drawing program. I can move an object by placing the mouse cursor on top of a graphics object, holding the mouse button down, and dragging, but I can also resize an object by placing the mouse cursor on one of the object's handles, holding down, and dragging. In other words, am I in one set of screens or another? Can your notational technique support concurrency at a number of levels?

- User tasks may have explicit usability goals, yet there may be no clear way to include those goals in the interface specification.

- Many actions within a user interface may be asynchronous and triggered by external events. Does your notation include a mechanism to respond to events?

- Will your design notation lead seamlessly to code? Is the design documentation thorough enough that the programmer does not have to guess what you really meant?

- How does your notational strategy fit into your development methodology? Use of UML complements a development effort in the Unified Software Development Process. However, the way we used UML may not be in compliance with the Unified Process.

In spite of these difficulties, it is important to choose a strategy to specify and design your interface software.

## Conclusions

The definition and development of software to support an interaction is itself a software engineering problem. Like any software engineering problem, the developer must be concerned with specification, design, and testing of the interface. However, the definition and development of interface software must always be considered in the broader context of usability.

## Exercises

1. Define the following terms: *noninterface function, message passing, abstract data type, class, object, static characteristics, behavioral characteristics, functional independence, cohesion,*

*coupling, encapsulation, information hiding, software reuse, association, generalization, composition,* and *aggregation.*

2. Describe what the following diagrams represent: class diagram, activity diagram, and state diagram.

3. Pick an interaction that you designed in your class project. Specify a class diagram and state diagram for one object in your interaction. If you do not have a class project, select another object from the audio catalog.

4. Discuss why the design of your interaction, if simply implemented as is, may not lead to the ideal software design. Consider how the design of interaction and the design of software often have different goals.

5. *Interface development exercise:* Consider your solution to the task analysis problems that were presented in Chapter 5 and your design of interaction from Chapter 8. Recall that you were to develop a task analysis, specification, and interaction for a children's game. Pull out that task analysis and design a general mode of interaction for the game. Justify your choices. Build the following UML models for the opening screen of your game: activity, class, and state diagrams.

6. *Interface design evaluation exercise:* Consider your solution to the task analysis problem that was presented in Chapters 5, 8, and 12. Recall that you were to develop a task analysis and specification, interaction design, and design definition using UML models for a children's game. Sketch out a likely architectural design for this game using a high-level class diagram. Where do you expect to see tight coupling or low cohesion?

7. Review your interface design for the class project. Find some elements that could be improved by limiting coupling, increasing cohesion, and encouraging reuse. Could you use object-oriented design concepts to improve encapsulation and information hiding?

8. Hudson (2001) states that user-centered design and object-oriented design have moved in separate and unconnected directions. What does this mean, and what is the implication in terms of designing user interfaces?

# Part 7

## Context, Constraints, and Responsibilities for User Interface Design

# 14

# The Human in Human–Computer Interaction

## Motivation

What is the "science" behind human–computer interaction (HCI) and usability engineering? As we saw in Chapter 2, a number of scientific disciplines are involved. Without any doubt, psychology is one of the most important. By the end of this chapter, you should be able to do the following:

- Describe examples of how knowledge of psychological phenomena can be applied to the design of user interfaces.
- Define and explain the concepts of input/output, storage, and processing as applied to human cognition.

## 14.1 Introduction

This chapter is a whirlwind tour of some of the important psychological characteristics of humans that impact HCI and usability. The goals of good user interface design are to improve efficiency and effectiveness of user performance and to build usable systems. One of the important challenges to HCI researchers is to understand how theories of psychology translate to the realm of HCI. This proves to be very difficult.

The problems and tasks of HCI are often radically different from the traditional laboratory and experimental domains of psychology. One of the first challenges in moving from laboratory studies to real-world problems is a scaling challenge. This upsizing of laboratory results to the real world can be really tough. Early in the history of HCI, a number of researchers performed traditional laboratory experiments and then tried to apply their results to larger-scaled problems.

The results simply did not always apply, especially in the larger venue. The experimental approach itself, with its heavy emphasis on controls, often controlled precisely those variables that were part of the overall phenomena. This was not a reflection on the researchers. Often there were simply too many variables to apply to an experiment. During the mid 1980s, a number of researchers switched to more qualitative and field study research methods in HCI. In our view, the main reason for this change in methodology was to address this scaling issue.

Another challenge in moving from laboratory studies to real-world problems has to do with theory. In most scientific disciplines, research and investigations are theory based and theory driven. While a number of good efforts have been put forth to generate a workable theory of human behavior in the context of HCI, based on theories of cognitive psychology and others, the translation problem is not trivial.

However, HCI has proven to be an excellent venue for psychologists who study complex behaviors. For example, many studies of programmers have provided valuable insights into the characteristics of novices and experts that can be generalized to other fields.

Of course, usability engineers can learn many things from psychology. The question is, What can we learn (quickly) from psychology? Here is one example:

**Psychological "Fact":**

- Humans are limited in their capacity to process information. Psychologists say that cognitive resources are limited.

**HCI Consequence:**

- When we build an interface, we want to utilize a person's limited cognitive resources wisely. For example, we want to limit the user's resources that are spent on operational tasks. Operational tasks are those tasks that are part of using the interface. So in a menu interaction, we want to minimize the resources that a user might use on actually making a menu selection, once the user knows what the selection should be. We want to build the menu interaction so that the user spends little of his or her limited resources on finding a menu selection. In general, we want to design interactions in such a way that a user's limited resources are focused on functional tasks.

## 14.2 The Person as an Information Processor

Okay, we all agree that the whole range of psychology is too much to present here. However, hopefully you are starting to get the idea that we can learn and remember things from psychology that will be helpful to us as usability engineers.

To start, we need a model that will help us predict how and why a user will react to an interface or situation. As designers, this may give us *realistic* expectations of what users will really be able to do with our user interface, or it may help us understand what went wrong when our interface fails. The model that we use must be straightforward and memorable.[1]

---

1. Ideally, we would like to have a model of user behavior complete and detailed enough that the model could be used as part of the engineering of a user interface. While models for elements of user interaction exist (cf. Card, Moran, and Newell 1983), no such model has emerged to cover the gamut of interactive user behaviors.

The model that we will use is called an *information processing* model of cognition. The idea is that we view human behavior in terms of its information processing and systems that support information processing. Does this sound familiar? What other entity, that we are familiar with, performs information processing? Of course! Information processing is what computers do, too. The idea of viewing human behavior in terms of information processing and information processing systems should be easy to remember because it should remind you of computing systems

Consider a computer. What are the primary systems that the computer uses for information processing? In our computer literacy course, we teach students that computers are systems that include components to provide input, output, storage, and processing. Human information processing activities can be loosely grouped into these categories as well. Computer input and output corresponds loosely to human sensation, perception, and effected behavior. Computer memory and storage bears some resemblance to cognitive structures, and computer processing has some similarities to cognitive processes. This analogy between human information processing and a computer works well for some aspects of human information processing; the limitations of the analogy are also helpful. For example, when a computer input device, such as a keyboard, receives information from the outside world, the information is digitized and translated to a form that can be used internally. Inside the computer, the information is then moved to a memory device, such as a register. In "a human input device," such as the vision system, the person receives light waves from the outside world and this information is translated into neural signals in the brain. However, visual inputs go through a number of filtering and interpretive stages that would not be the case for computer input. In traditional computing systems, an input device issues an interrupt to the central processing unit to perform input activities; in a person, "input" happens concurrently with processing at even the most primitive levels of activity.

Viewing humans as information processors is not a new idea. As computers grew in importance in the 1950s and 1960s, this model of human behavior gained increasing popularity among psychologists. Peter Lindsay and Don Norman, who we discussed in Chapter 1, even published a famous psychology textbook entitled *Human Information Processing* (Lindsay and Norman 1972).

In the next few sections, we visit each of these systems and touch on some characteristics that seem important to usability.

## 14.3 Human Input/Output

Human input/output (I/O) refers to a number of things, including the input activities of *sensation* and *perception* and the activities of the *motor system* driving body parts to accomplish output. Sensation refers to the activities in which external inputs from the environment are received and initially processed. Perception refers to the recognition and interpretation of that input information. As we saw in the previous section, human input systems do not simply collect input data. Rather, the information that enters the sensory system is filtered and interpreted so that it can be used. Imagine that you are walking on a path in a forest. What do you see? Most likely you "see" the path and the trees around you. Did you "see" the small hill beside the tree on your left? Your sensory system may have collected data about the hill, but you probably did not "see" it unless you were specifically attracted to it.

Typically, we combine the discussions of human input and output of information. We say that a person uses input and output channels to interact with the external world. By definition, the actual mechanisms for human input are called *sensors* or *senses* and include visual receptors in the eyes, auditory receptors in the ears, touch receptors, taste receptors, olfactory receptors for smell, balance, and a few other senses of self-awareness in space. The actual output devices include our limbs, fingers, eyes (direction of gaze), head, and vocal system. Clearly some components of human physiology can be used both to collect inputs and to produce outputs. Sometimes it is difficult to say that an element of human physiology is strictly input or output.

### 14.3.1 Attention

Sensory systems have limited capacity. We are constantly bombarded with stimuli, and we can only focus on and process a subset of these stimuli. For example, in a crowded room, there are often a lot of auditory stimuli (noise), but we notice (hear) when someone says our name. We use the processing strategy of *attention* to focus on things in the environment that are important. What is considered important might be based on experience (e.g., your name) or it might be "built in." For example, human visual perception is attuned to movement and built in because in our evolutionary environment, moving things usually meant predators or food; to survive, our evolutionary ancestors needed to detect and interpret movement without thinking about it.

The great American psychologist William James (1890) recognized that we attend to some stimuli involuntarily. He believed that some forms of attention happened without effort or directed activities. Examples of involuntary attention might include attention to certain colors, sounds, or objects in the environment.

### Designer Lessons: Attention

Why is this notion of attention important? We know that people involuntarily attend to certain stimuli. For example, certain colors (red) or sounds (alarm bells) draw our attention in spite of ourselves. From an HCI perspective, using sounds as alarms or alerts can draw a user's attention. Misusing alarm bells by attracting attention inappropriately can distract users. So floods of sounds or flocks of moving objects can draw a user's attention away from the intended target.

- *Lesson 1:* Draw a user's attention to important information with color, movement, or sound, but be careful not to use these techniques to distraction. Users can be involuntarily drawn to these stimuli. If you do not want their attention, don't include these in your design.
- *Lesson 2:* Use motion sparingly in interface design and only when you want to draw attention to an interface event. For example, adding dancing graphics to a Web site will draw a user's attention to the graphic. If the graphic does not add information to the presentation, you may wish to get rid of it.

### 14.3.2 Insights About Human Input/Output

Perception of inputs is often done in parallel, but generation of output tends to be more serial. Consider the following situation: Imagine that you are using a computer with a mouse, a keyboard, and an iconic user interface. What kinds of inputs are you receiving? The inputs are probably visual, auditory (from alerts), and tactile (touch). We are often able to take in multiple inputs and recognize and integrate them. We seem to push this capability to its limits. For example, many of us drive, talk on a cell phone, recognize instructions from street signs, and listen to the radio at the same time. On the other hand, many of us find it hard to walk, rub our stomach, and chew gum at the same time.

### Designer Lessons: Human Input/Output

- *Lesson 1:* The designer can present a number of pieces of information at the same time, especially if they are in different modalities. However, do not push the user too hard. If you have too many simultaneous inputs, your user's perception will become more serial.
- *Lesson 2:* While a lot of interesting ideas abound about nonvisual interactions, interfaces are dominated by visual elements. Auditory cues can be useful as supplements to visual cues. One of the intriguing aspects of auditory interactions, such as speech-based interactions, is that they have the potential to free our visual system for other activities.

### 14.3.3 Text and Human–Computer Interaction

Text is an integral part of most interfaces, even those that are primarily graphical. Reading from the interface can have a significant impact on the success or failure of the interface. The psychology of reading may give us some insights as to how to improve interfaces with text.

Once people learn how to read, they do not typically read character by character. Rather, we see a visual pattern that consists of whole words or phrases, syntax, and semantics. Dillon, McKnight, and Richardson (1988) reviewed a large body of research comparing reading from paper to reading from screens. They concluded from the review that reading from screens may be slower and less accurate than reading from paper—but not always. A number of variables seem to impact people's ability to read text from a screen image, including the quality of the presented image.

### Designer Lessons: Text and Human–Computer Interaction

- *Lesson:* The quality of a text image on a screen can be degraded in many ways. For example, overpowering backgrounds, as discussed in Chapter 9, can make foreground text difficult to see. When your interaction involves users reading text from screens, the better the quality of the image, the more likely it is that the user will be able to read the image at the same level of accuracy and speed as from paper.

### 14.3.4 Hearing and Audition

We are constantly bombarded with sound from the environment. We use attention to filter through the sounds, and some sounds get our attention. For example, the sound of a fire truck siren draws our attention.

### Designer Lessons: Hearing and Audition

- *Lesson 1:* Sound can be used to direct attention in an interaction, and the typical use of sound in interfaces is for alarms. However, one of the potential advantages of a sound-based interaction is that it frees the hands and eyes. Look for many more products with sound-based interactions in the future.

- *Lesson 2:* In Chapter 1, we emphasized the importance of perceptibility of informational cues to the user's ability to operate an interface. In some situations, sounds that are part of a user interface may provide useful and perceptible information. However, in the presence of too many sounds, the salient ones may not be perceptible.

## 14.3.5 Touch

Touch can be used in interfaces to provide feedback, and some psychophysics measures suggest that the bandwidth for touch is similar to that of vision or hearing (cf. Kokjer 1987). While we have the ability to sense temperature differences from the environment, most contemporary user interfaces that utilize touch use pressure to provide information. A number of studies suggest that information delivered via touch may be at least as effective as information delivered to other sensory systems. For example, Jeong and Gluck (2003) describe a study that compares the usefulness of auditory and haptic displays for showing information about different magnitudes of variables in maps; the haptic displays were vibro-tactile in nature. In this study, the fastest and most accurate performance came from the haptic condition.

### Designer Lessons: Touch

- Lesson: We learned in Chapter 7 that it was important to provide feedback. Keyboards and manipulative interface devices provide an excellent opportunity to provide tactile feedback. Many virtual reality (VR) environments use manipulative devices, such as head-mounted displays or even mice, to drive the user's interaction. When a user is engaged with the virtual world, it is potentially disconcerting if there is no "normal" feedback when encountering objects such as walls. While these experiences could be improved with tactile feedback, what if the VR is a simulation of a dangerous world, such as a military training situation? Should the feedback be painful?

## 14.3.6 What About Smell and Taste?

Interestingly, user interfaces involving smell and taste are becoming available. For example, Maynes-Aminzade (2005) describes an "edible" interface called *BeanCounter* for a memory monitoring application. These senses are still in a rudimentary state in terms of HCI.

## 14.3.7 What About Output? Fitts' Law

Consider moving your hand while you are moving a mouse; this is a kind of human output. Moving your hand actually consists of a series of small discrete movements and corrections. From prior research, we know that each small movement takes about 240 milliseconds. Fitts's law (cf. Fitts 1954) tells us that the time, $T$, to move your hand to a target of size, $S$, that is distance, $D$, away is

$$T = 100 \, \text{msec} * log_2(D/S + 0.5)$$

The time to move your hand depends on the relative precision needed ($D/S$). An interface event that requires a very precise corresponding hand movement will take longer than an event that requires less precision. Fitts's Law has been used to compare interfaces and interaction styles. For example, one can demonstrate that for a small number of choices (low precision) a pie menu is faster than a linear menu (Callahan, Hopkins, Weiser, and Shneiderman 1988).

## 14.4 *Memory and Storage*

Contemporary cognitive theories point to several types of memories, including these:

- Sensory memory.
- Short-term memory.
- Working memory.
- Long-term memory.

### 14.4.1 *Sensory Memory*

Information from the outside world enters the cognitive system through *sensory memory,* a kind of scratch pad to record information from the senses. Each input channel has a sensory memory. Information is held in sensory memory for a very short time, with fast access and fast decay. If the presentation of an interaction changes faster than the decay rate, the information from the interaction will be lost. Sensory memory also has extremely limited capacity. Interestingly, there is some processing of sensory data, even in the brief time that information resides there. The information in sensory memory is filtered by attention and passed into short-term memory.

### 14.4.2 *Short-Term Memory*

Information from the outside world enters the cognitive system into *short-term memory* (STM) via perception. Information from sensory memory is interpreted by the perceptual system and moved to STM. STM has limited capacity, fast access, and fast decay, although not as fast as sensory memory. Distractions make it even more difficult for STM to hold information.

Characteristics of STM have significant impact on nearly every aspect of human cognition because in order for us to do something with information, it has to be in STM. In terms of HCI, we focus on an interesting issue: STM limitations and how they impact usability engineering tasks. Even with this short overview, we can get some clues about why so many interfaces are failures for the majority of their users.

Consider the following question: What makes an expert? After all, we have mentioned experts quite a bit in this book. Well, cognitively, experts differ from novices in many ways. For instance, experts have more knowledge about their domain of interest. However they differ from novices in other ways, such as their ability to form and use longer and more complex *chunks* of information than novices.

What is a chunk? George Miller (1956) wrote a famous paper called "The Magical Number Seven, Plus or Minus Two," in which he theorized that short-term memory could hold about seven (plus or minus two) things; he called these things *chunks.* This notion was based on numerous studies of short-term memory. Miller noticed that across STM experiments, people organized information into approximately five to seven units of information. Miller theorized that the capacity of human STM is somewhere between five and nine things or chunks. Any human (expert or not) can extract, remember, or recognize only a limited number of chunks in a limited period of time. Thus, a chunk is a useful unit of information.

As a computer scientist, you may be wondering how many bits make up a chunk. That's a good question, but chunks are not like bytes with a set size. For an informal demonstration of chunks, glance at the two strings in Figure 14.1. (A glance is about one-tenth of a second.) Now write down both.

```
ELTON JOHN


JHTEO NNLO
```

Figure 14.1    Memorize the Strings.

How well did you do? Was there any difference in your recall of the two strings? Both of the strings have nine characters, plus a space. You probably did better with the string "Elton John." For most people, the nine characters of "Elton John" are encoded in STM as a single chunk. The nine scrambled letters of Elton's name are each encoded as a separate chunk.

One of the functions of chunks is to guide visual perception. When we see things in the visual field, we group them based on the way that we chunk visual inputs. A chunk is stored (remembered) and retrieved (recalled) as a single unit.

For another chunking example, imagine that the phone number for the Beverage Supply House is 800–555–2337. Which of the following two telephone numbers is easier to remember?

• 1-800-555-2337
• 1-800-555-BEER

Most people will say that the second version of the supply house number is easier to remember. For most people, BEER is a single chunk, but 2337 is not. Advertisers are anxious to have memorable URLs for their Web sites. Which of the following two URLs are you more likely to remember?

• http://www.SamsHouseSales.com
• http://121.3.177.89/content/~usergeek176/7654444.html

Two people may not group visual information in the same way. Consequently, two people may not see the same thing even though they are looking at the same visual field. Experience guides how a person will group visual stimuli. Therefore what we "see" is related to our experience. A person with experience in a domain (an expert) will group stimuli differently than will a nonexpert. But this "enhanced" ability only holds in the expert's area of expertise. For example, a computer science expert probably does not chunk medical information any differently than a physics expert would.

Experts perceive visual stimuli differently than novices do. The information in a chunk for an expert is different than that for a novice. Expert chunks are large and rich in semantic information. They may contain both semantic (meaning) and surface details. Novice chunks, by contrast, are small and focused on syntactic features

### Chunking and the Design of User Interfaces

Most user interfaces are designed by people with expertise in computer science. Based on what we have seen about chunking, we expect that what a computer scientist sees when presented with a computer-type stimulus may differ from what a nonexpert sees. Let's test that idea. For this demonstration, you will need an experimenter (maybe your teacher). We will refer to those of you participating in the experiment as *participants* and the person coordinating the experiment as the *experimenter.*

**Directions to the Participants:**

1. You will be shown two programs. The programs are written in C++.
2. You will see each program for three minutes.
3. You are to study and memorize as much of the program as possible.
4. When the program is removed, you are to write down as much of the program as you can remember.

**Directions for the Experimenter:**

1. You will need a stopwatch.
2. Show Program 1 (Figure 14.2) for three minutes. Participants are to write down as much of the program as they can remember.

```cpp
#include <iostream>
using namespace std;
int main ()
{
int < SID;
cout << "Enter your student ID: ";
cin >> SID;
while (SID !=0 )
        {
        if ((SID >= 1000) && (SID <= 9000))
                cout << endl << "Student ID " << SID <<
                        " is doing fine in CS"<< endl;
        cout << endl << "Enter your student ID: ";
        cin >> SID;
        }
cout << endl << " *END OF ENCOURAGEMENT" << endl;
return 0;
}
```

**Figure 14.2**   Program 1 for Chunking Experiment.

3. Show Program 2 (Figure 14.3) for three minutes. Participants are to write down as much of the program as they can remember.

If you were a participant, how did you do? Presumably you did better at recalling the "normal" first program than you did on the scrambled second program.

Why did you do better on the "normal" program? You, as an expert, perceived the normal program as chunks of program structure. For example, you may have seen the *while loop* in the first

```
int Counter = 0;
}
        if (Num/2 == 0)
        cout << "Enter a positive integer or -1 to stop: ";
{
int main ()
cout << "Enter a positive integer or -1 to stop: ";
cin >> Num;
using namespace std;
while (Num != -1)
return 0;
        {
        cin >> Num;
        }
#include <iostream>
int Num;
Counter++;
```

Figure 14.3    Program 2 for Chunking Experiment.

program as a single structure rather than as a collection of terms. To an expert, the scrambled program has no recognizable chunks. Experts experience the second program as disconnected code fragments. They see only randomly arranged lines. They must memorize "random lines" or "garbage." Amazingly, participants who are not programmers see both of the programs as scrambled! Their recall performance is the same on both tasks. To novices, the scrambled and meaningful programs both look random.

This demonstration is called a *deGroot-style task* (cf. deGroot 1965). Teasley, Leventhal, Instone, and Schertler-Rohlman (1991) used similar stimulus materials to demonstrate that perception and recall of programs is influenced by expertise. They showed two similar programs to computer science students of low and high expertise levels and asked the students to reconstruct the programs after viewing. The highly expert computer science students were much better at the reconstruction of the meaningful program, but the novice computer science students were equally challenged by both of the programs.

The deGroot-style task has been used in a number of fields, including chess and basketball, to demonstrate the relationship between expertise and recall as a function of short-term memory. Figure 14.4 shows the patterns of results presented in Teasley et al. (1991), which are similar to other studies of this type.

### Designer Lessons: Expertise
• *Lesson:* Expert designers cannot judge how users with different expertise levels are going to experience an interface because the expert and nonexpert see things differently. How does this impact the design of interfaces? Experts and novices see, process, and view exactly the same

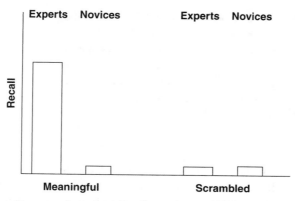

Figure 14.4    Pattern of results from deGroot-style studies.

stimuli (e.g., the screen) but in different ways. If you are an expert, it is impossible to interpret or use an interface in the same way as a novice does. Therefore, experts in usability engineering and computer science cannot rely on their intuitions about what makes a good interface when designing an interface for a nonexpert.

In Chapter 1, we learned that the perceptibility of cues in a user interface could impact a person's ability to operate that interface. In our model of usability, we mentioned the important user characteristic of expertise and noted that expert and novice users will experience a task differently. From this discussion, we see that expert users may "see" the values of the important parameters of the task differently than novices do.

### 14.4.3 Working Memory

More recent work has extended the traditional definition of STM to posit *working memory* (WM) (cf. Baddeley 1986, 1992, 1997). WM supports the short-term storage of information that was depicted previously with STM. Additionally, WM includes greater emphasis on information-processing capabilities than the traditional STM model. A key function of WM is to provide a place for the formation of mental models. Working memory is portrayed as a combination of several subsystems: a central executive that controls processing and two sketch pads. One sketch pad processes visual information, and the other one processes narration or auditory information.

### Designer Lessons: Working Memory

- Lesson: A number of researchers have found that multimedia presentations that are "dual," meaning that the information is conveyed both in auditory and in picture form, are more effective than single presentations for a variety of tasks, especially learning tasks (cf. Mayer, 2001). Because the sketchpads in WM have limited capacity, multimedia presentations that use both types of informational representations are more likely to be effective than those that are strictly visual or those that are delivered strictly by auditory methods.

### 14.4.4 Long-Term Memory

A fourth type of human memory is *long-term memory* (LTM). LTM may be permanent memory (as opposed to STM and WM). It is an open question whether people ever truly forget information that is stored in LTM. LTM has essentially infinite capacity, and it has slower access compared to STM.

Information gets into LTM from STM via rehearsal. Getting information out of LTM is called *retrieval*. Information can be retrieved in two ways: recall or recognition. In *recall,* information to be retrieved from LTM must first be found and then recalled. In *recognition,* an informational cue is provided and the information retrieved is matched against the presented cue.

### Designer Lessons: Recall

- *Lesson:* Generally, recall is a more difficult process than recognition. You will probably remember that in our discussion of interaction styles, we mentioned that menus might be easier for novices to use as compared to command-line interactions. With menus, all options are presented explicitly, so selecting a menu option involves recognition. When using command-line interactions, generating a command involves recall.

### Types of Knowledge in Long-Term Memory

Information in LTM is organized into two types of knowledge: *declarative knowledge* and *procedural knowledge.* Declarative knowledge or knowledge of facts indicates "knowing what." An example of declarative knowledge is knowing the answer to the following question: What is the capital of Ohio?[2] Declarative knowledge is easy to communicate. Procedural knowledge is know-how, for example, knowing how to change an automobile tire. In general, procedural knowledge may be more difficult to communicate than declarative knowledge.

### Representation of Knowledge

Knowledge is organized hierarchically (to represent categories), temporally (to represent sequences), and in networks (to represent complex connections). Both the information and its organization change over time.

Experts develop complex, multilevel bodies of knowledge in their domain of expertise. This knowledge is stored in LTM. Some knowledge is semantic, or about the meaning of things. *Semantic knowledge* is knowledge of general concepts and is independent of specific situations. For example, an expert programmer understands the concept of arrays regardless of the programming language. Some knowledge is about surface structure and is called *syntactic knowledge.* Syntactic knowledge is also stored in LTM, but it is more detailed than semantic knowledge and is less structured cognitively. Knowing the format of the C++ *while* statement is an example of syntactic knowledge. Syntactic knowledge is acquired by rote and is more easily forgotten than semantic knowledge. Semantic knowledge is acquired through demanding and meaningful problem-solving tasks. The acquisition of new syntactic information may interfere with previously learned syntactic knowledge, or vice versa. Hence, programmers often have difficulty learning a second programming language (cf. Shneiderman 1998).

There are vast individual differences among people in the quality and capabilities of building informational structures in LTM. Also, children and adults differ in the quality and capabilities of

---

2.   The capital of Ohio is Columbus.

these structures. Adults have an existing informational structure. Their challenge is to integrate new concepts into the existing structure. On the other hand, children are building their structures, so much of what they do is concept learning and formation.

### Designer Lessons: Knowledge

- *Lesson 1:* As stated, syntactic knowledge is acquired by rote and is more easily forgotten than semantic knowledge. In previous chapters, we have discussed "occasional" users who use systems only once in awhile. These users may more easily remember the semantic details of the task than the syntactic details of the interface's operations. Designers should provide cuing when possible for the operation and syntactic details of an interface's use.

  Learning, or the construction of knowledge, is a key focus of cognitive psychology and has been the subject of many studies and experiments. In summary, learning is the process of building knowledge; this may involve the formation of concepts. Learning is complex, and learners are not passive absorbers of information. Learning involves the integration of new information and experiences with our existing structures. What we learn may be wrong. We learn by rehearsal, by doing things, by vivid experiences, and through analogies. In addition, even within a narrow group of people, the ability to integrate new concepts will vary tremendously among individuals.

- *Lesson 2:* Research in HCI has suggested that people learn to use computer systems most effectively if learning is *active*. According to Mayer (2001), active learning that involves cognitive processing is more likely to lead to effective learning than active learning that is behaviorally active. For example, users may learn more effectively in environments in which they have to develop explanations for themselves of some novel phenomena than when they engage in a lot of hand motion. Active, cognitive learning may also be promoted if users are placed in problem-solving situations that allow them to connect prior knowledge to the current situation.

### Skill Acquisition

Some interactive activities involve *skill acquisition* or use of skill rather than complex knowledge. There are many "laws" of human factors that one can use in design. These generally apply to sensory-motor skills rather than knowledge. For example, the power law of skill acquisition suggests that our improvement is fast at first, then much slower. When you learn to do something, like use a mouse, you improve quickly at first. Subsequent improvements take longer. However, the more you practice, the better or faster your performance becomes. The power law (Newell and Rosenbloom 1981) states that task time, $T$, on the $n$th trial is

$$T_n = T_1 n^{-0.4}$$

where $n$ is a constant for the task.

## 14.5 Thinking Processes

Like a computer system, it is not enough to describe the input and output mechanisms and memory or storage. One also has to describe the information processes that utilize these facilities, and these processes are thinking processes.

### 14.5.1 What Is Thinking?

In his introductory psychology text, D. G. Myers (1998) states, "to think is to form concepts that organize our world, to solve problems, and to make efficient decisions and judgments." We focus on two aspects of thinking: problem solving and decision making, which are linked. One may make decisions in the context of solving a problem, and one may solve a problem during decision making. For clarity, we discuss them separately.

### 14.5.2 Problem Solving

*Problem solving* is typically defined as our ability, given a novel problem, to develop a solution to the problem. Typical examples of problems include arithmetic problems, finding a route to a restaurant in a new city, writing an HCI textbook, and writing a computer program.

Newell and Simon (1972) have suggested that problem solving can be viewed as a trip through a problem space. The problem space is made up of a number of problem states, starting with an initial state and ending with a goal state. The problem solver uses a number of heuristics to effect state transitions. For example, the problem solver may use a means–end heuristic with an operation or strategy that moves from the current state to a state closer to the user's goal (cf. Newell and Simon 1972).

Problems may be well defined (find the best route from X to Y) or sketchy (creating a poem). The problem solver may use heuristics (rules of thumb) or algorithms (a set of rules that guarantee a result if followed). In user interfaces, this distinction is usually the difference between following an event-driven sequence and a step-by-step process.

How is problem solving related to user interfaces, and how can user interfaces enhance problem solving? Using the Newell and Simon (1972) model of problem solving suggests that the problem solver is "taking a trip" through a problem space. If that problem space is small with few states, the problem solver can probably hold almost all the information about problem states in short-term memory. However, in the more usual case the problem space is likely to be enormous with many, many problem states. Because of the limited capacity of short-term memory, the problem solver can only work with information about a part of the problem at any one time. One way a problem solver can address this limitation is by using external aids during problem solving. These aids can come in a number of forms: tools to save intermediate results, tools that allow the problem solver to explore alternative transitions through the problem space in a safe way, and tools to lead the problem solver through the space and to suggest problem space transitions. Clearly, software systems have the possibility to serve as aids in any of these ways. The easier an interface is to use, the fewer memory demands using the tool demands, leaving the user more cognitive resources for the problem at hand.

### Designer Lessons: Problem Solving

- *Lesson:* Remember that your user interface may support problem solving. What can your interface do to aid in that process? Both problem solving and using the interface require cognitive resources such as memory. Reducing the cognitive resources required by your interface leaves more resources for problem solving. Recall that at the beginning of this chapter, we suggested that when we build an interface, we want to limit the resources that users spend on operational tasks and encourage them to spend resources on functional tasks. Interfaces with odd syntax, unpredictable behavior, and so on steal cognitive resources from problem solving and divert the resources to interface operations.

**Example: Problem Solving and User Interfaces**   Here is a story about problem solving and user interface operations. Before 1980, our local swim club used to calculate swim meet scoring by hand. Sometime in the late 1980s, our swim club switched to a computerized scoring system. The system had many good characteristics. For example, it transferred the results from the electronic timing system into the computerized system, it did scoring, and it was able to produce reports of results. The user interface was menu driven, so all the options were known in advance. The interface also had a number of problems. For one thing, the menu options were all expressed in terms of function keys, and the assignment of function keys to menu options was somewhat arbitrary. More critical was the fact that the individual menus and outcomes were very modal, and a variety of ways lead to the same result, or so it seemed from the labels.

I (LML) was using this package to build a report of the scores and results at a large meet sometime in the mid 1990s. The winners of this meet qualified for an additional championship, so getting the results correct was very important, and there was a team winner of the meet. The problem I was supposed to be solving was to build a report of the winners, results, and scores. Another issue I had to contend with was that people who are trying to qualify for a championship meet are not very patient, and neither are their parents, so it was critical to optimize my problem solving. Generating such a report is a kind of problem because it involves a number of choices and the outcome of one subproblem determines the next subproblem to solve. Using this package was not critical to solving the problem at hand because I could have used old-fashioned tools (pencil and paper), but it should have helped make the process go faster. I do not think I could have solved the problem without computer assistance as there were too many data points.

In the midst of trying to optimize my problem solving to generate the report of results, I followed what I thought was the fastest way to get to the results. Unfortunately, what I did not realize was that this route through the interface included all results except the results of the last race. A mere two minutes after the completion of the last race, I turned out the final team scores at the end of the meet and trophies were handed out. About a half hour later an irritated parent came by to tell me that the team scores were wrong because they did not include the last race. Turned out he was right, so I recalculated the scores by hand by adding what I remembered from the last race to the scores that we had used. Fortunately, the outcome was not changed, but now I had two problem-solving tasks. One was to correctly recalculate and verify the scores, using the software, as that was where the individual race results were stored, and two was to figure out what had gone wrong in my original heuristic. I did figure out that, for the operation I was doing, the two paths I thought were the same were actually different. The mistake was mine because I did not understand the operational differences of the word *Score* on two different screens. I never made this mistake again while we were using this application. However, in terms of solving the real problem at hand, the interface's demands on me to focus on operational tasks were certainly distracting, used lots of my memory and cognitive resources, and obscured the problem-solving process.

## More About Problem Solving and User Interfaces
A second way that problem solvers can manage the problem-solving process through large problem spaces is to decompose the problem into a number of subproblems and then to solve the subproblems. Of course, solving the subproblems may also require decomposition. It turns out this process of problem decomposition is related to HCI.

When it comes to problem solving in the expert's domain of expertise, expert behavior is different from a novice's behavior. It is no surprise that experts are better at problem solving within their domains. What is interesting, from an HCI perspective, is the way in which experts are different. In a study of programmers, Jeffries, Turner, Polson, and Atwood (1981) found that experts tend to use more of a top-down strategy than novices do. Novices were less able to use a problem decomposition strategy. In other words, experts tend to solve problems at a high level and then at successfully lower levels of abstraction and increasingly more detailed problem levels. On the other hand, novices attack problems by focusing on the details early. This means that novices may not grasp the big problem. Not only that, but without decomposition the problem reconstruction that would be helpful for insight probably would not happen.

### Designer Lessons: More Problem Solving

What does this mean for usability engineers? For one thing, these results suggest that novices may face considerable difficulties in complex problem solving because they don't solve or even understand the problem at a high level. In terms of knowledge representation from long-term memory, novices do not have the complex representations with many levels of abstraction that experts do. Experts are able to decompose the problem and work on it at many levels of abstraction because their knowledge of the domain supports many levels of abstraction.

As teachers of programming, we have seen this demonstrated many times. Beginning programmers invariably want to go right to the code when given a programming problem. Most beginners find it very difficult to step back and get the big picture, develop a design, (abstract problem solution), and then finally work on the code. Their knowledge of programming is mostly syntactic and not in terms of abstractions such as algorithms. When students acquire more abstract knowledge about syntax and we force them to go through more of a top-down problem-solving process, many of them have one of those "aha" experiences and realize that the abstract-to-details strategy is actually a lot easier. Perhaps this has happened to you. Do you ever notice beginning programmers and think, "Look at that chump, making the assignment a lot harder by going right to the code"?

- *Lesson 1:* How can your interface support problem decomposition? When designing interfaces to support problem-solving tasks to be used by novices, one idea is to use the interface to guide them through the process of problem decomposition. For example, if novices are interacting via menus during problem solving, hierarchical menus rather than network menus might be more appropriate.
- *Lesson 2:* Guindon, Krasner, and Curtis (1987) studied the strategies of expert software designers. Their results suggested that experts probably need more flexibility than novices to support their approach to problem solving. Interactions that permit experts to direct their problem solving, such as network menus or command-line interactions, may be better suited than those that force a particular path through a problem space.

### 14.5.3 Decision Making

*Decision making,* or choosing among alternatives, is another thinking process that has significant implications for user interface design. We like to believe that decision making is rational and logical, but lots of research indicates that it is not, in spite of any number of philosophical models to the contrary. If people are not rational in decision making, how do they make decisions? Research in this field indicates that they settle on a small number of hypotheses early on and tend to stay away from negative or nonconfirming hypotheses.

When is this important in HCI? When do we consider hypotheses? One time is when we are testing. As software developers we have to test hypotheses, such as "This software module functions as specified." In a series of experiments concerning software developers' ability to test hypotheses, Teasley, Leventhal, Mynatt, and Rohlman (1994) found that software developers tended to test their programs in very positive ways (i.e., in ways that supported the hypothesis that the software functioned in accordance with the specification). In other words, testers chose test cases that when applied to the software should have confirmed functionality. When testers found that software did not function correctly, the testers tended to dismiss the results as anomalies. This behavior was observed at all levels of tester expertise. For you this means that you will want to test your interfaces in ways that make the interface appear successful, even in the presence of counterevidence. As an assessor of usability, you must make a conscious effort to look for lack of confirmation.

### 14.5.4 Reasoning

*Reasoning* is defined as using prior knowledge to draw conclusions or infer something new about the domain of interest. Reasoning can be inductive or deductive. An important aspect of reasoning in interface design is *analogical reasoning* or reasoning by means of an analogy. In Chapter 7, we discussed the importance of good analogies and metaphors. Recall the difference between analogy and metaphor:

- Analogy means "acts like."
- Metaphor means "is a."

Now we can think of the use of analogy in its psychological context and see why good analogies are great and poor analogies lead users to misunderstand interfaces and to make errors. When people encounter an interface analogy, they reason or deduce the expected behavior of the interface based on what they know about the behavior in the analogy. If the analogy breaks down, their reasoning will be false. For example, a potentially misleading but commonly used analogy is found in the trash can or recycle bin of many contemporary windowing systems. New users may use analogical reasoning to infer the properties of the trash can. As such, beginners may think that dragging a disk to the trash can destroy or recycle (erase) the disk.

## Conclusions

This chapter provides an overview of some of the features of human psychology that are relevant to HCI. A human information-processing model is a useful way to think about human cognition. Understanding some aspects of human behavior can improve the design of user interfaces. Some elements of human behavior and performance are affected by expertise.

## Exercises

1. Define the following terms: *information processing model of cognition, sensation, perception, attention, Fitts's Law, sensory memory, short-term memory, working memory, long-term memory, chunks, deGroot-style task, recall, recognition, retrieval, declarative knowledge, procedural*

*knowledge, semantic knowledge, syntactic knowledge, skill acquisition, thinking, problem solving, heuristics, algorithm, decision making,* and *reasoning.*

2. After reading this chapter, go back to the guidelines that were presented in Chapter 7 and the design recommendations in Chapters 8 and 9. How many of those guidelines and recommendations are related to the material presented in this chapter?

3. Define and explain the concepts of input/output, storage, and processing as applied to human cognition.

4. Explain the difference between semantic knowledge and syntactic knowledge.

5. Describe the different ways that knowledge can be organized. What types of tasks are best supported by each type of knowledge organization?

# 15

# Usability for Everyone

## Motivation

In the previous chapters, we introduced many ideas concerning the process of usability engineering, as well as the characteristics and choices of usable interfaces. In this chapter, we discuss the issue of universal usability. At the end of this chapter, you should be able to do the following:

- Describe the concept of *universal usability*.
- Identify how a group of users might be left out.
- Understand some design strategies to better ensure universal usability.

## 15.1 Introduction

Isn't it a given that usability should be for everyone? Doesn't it make sense that when we build systems, they should be usable for all users, regardless of their ages or physical capabilities? Unfortunately, many systems are not universally usable. This is perhaps due in part to a failure to fully specify the prospective user's needs and in part to the incorrect belief on the part of some designers that all users are like them. It is also perhaps due to the perceived small size of special markets.

Universal usability appears under a number of related terms, including *universal usability, universal access,* and *access for specialized markets.* Shneiderman defines universal usability as "having more than 90% of all households as successful users of information and communications services at least once a week" (2000, 85).

The Association of Computing Machinery (1997) Code of Ethics and Professional Conduct suggests that universal access, via universal usability, is a goal all computing professionals should value.

> In a fair society, all individuals would have equal opportunity to participate in, or benefit from, the use of computer resources regardless of race, sex, religion, age, disability, national origin or other such similar factors.

In this chapter, we discuss some aspects of universal access and some populations who too often are excluded from access and usability.

## 15.2 Universal Access as a Matter of Law in the United States

The Communications Act of 1934, Title 1 Section 1 (1934, 1936), begins with the following description of the purpose of the act:

> For the purpose of regulating interstate and foreign commerce in communication by wire and radio so as to make available, so far as possible, to all the people of the United States, without discrimination on the basis of race, color, religion, national origin, or sex, a rapid, efficient, Nation-wide, and world-wide wire and radio communication service with adequate facilities at reasonable charges, for the purpose of the national defense, for the purpose of promoting safety of life and property through the use of wire and radio communication.

This legislation defined a governmental presence in the enforcement of universal access to communications technologies and established the Federal Communications Commission (FCC) as a regulatory agency. The act also established the idea of universal access to communications technology in the United States in its use of such as terms *without discrimination* and *reasonable charges.*

The Telecommunications Act of 1996, signed by President Bill Clinton, reaffirmed the notion of universal access to communication technologies at a reasonable price and extended the notion of universal access to schools, libraries, and health care providers (Kleiman 1998). It is interesting to note that the notion of universal access is not universally popular, especially when one considers that someone has to pay for it. Rohde (1998), for example, describes several monetary arguments against the concept, especially as set in the Telecommunications Act of 1996.

## 15.3 Diversity of Users

Both Eason's (1984) model and our model of usability tell us that user characteristics are critical variables in the usability of any system. From these models, we know that users with different characteristics may evaluate usability differently. Does this mean that universal usability is always a burden on the designer or a long-term source of cost to the developer? Emphatically *no*! In fact, some of our best usability inventions started as designs for specialized groups. Shneiderman (2000) explains how "curb cuts," originally intended for disabled users, have become widely used by everyone. Curb cuts became available initially to accommodate disabled users of sidewalks. However, the audience that benefited from curb cuts was much broader than only disabled users. The beneficiaries included bicyclists, people with baby carriages, and people with rolling suitcases. Now, most people using wheels look for the curb cut when leaving a sidewalk.

Previous experience suggests that products designed for a specialized audience may have much wider appeal. For another example, consider a blind Web user. Web graphics, especially those for decorative purposes, may be challenging for a blind user to understand and interpret while browsing the Web with a specialized screen reader. A Web site that is accessible to the blind might present graphics in an alternative text form, more amenable to an assistive screen-reading device. Someone who is accessing the Web using a cell phone that has a tiny screen may also appreciate a textual presentation.

Authors, such as Shneiderman (2000), have worried that designing for only a narrow band of user characteristics has the potential to create a society of usability "haves" and "have nots." This notion is a contribution to the *digital divide* (cf. National Telecommunications and Information Administration 1999; U.S. Department of Commerce 2000). As the functioning of society becomes increasingly dependent on technology and information, it is frightening to think that large groups of users may be closed out because their usability needs were not taken into account.

In the following sections, we discuss usability and access concerns for several populations who are potentially underserved.

### 15.3.1 Usability for Users with Disabilities

It is not a new idea to use technology to assist users with disabilities. The telephone was invented while searching for ways to assist the hard of hearing. Such technology may aid a person with a disability to perform tasks they could not do otherwise. However, it seems clear that persons with disabilities are an underserved population when it comes to computing access. According to *Falling Through the Net: Toward Digital Inclusion* (National Telecommunications and Information Administration of the U.S. Department of Commerce 2000, Introduction):

> People with a disability are only half as likely to have access to the Internet as those without a disability: 21.6% compared to 42.1%. And while just under 25% of people without a disability have never used a personal computer, close to 60% of people with a disability fall into that category. (Introduction).

The report continues:

> Technology offers enormous potential to increase the rates of computer and Internet use among people with disabilities. But technology can also be an additional barrier if products are not designed to be accessible. (Part III)

What does it mean for someone to have a disability? The Americans with Disabilities Act, civil rights legislation signed by President George H. W. Bush in 1990, defines a person with a disability thus (U.S. Department of Justice 2005):

> a person who has a physical or mental impairment that substantially limits one or more major life activities.

Disabilities may include vision problems, hearing problems, motor-skill problems, learning disorders, and such. In some cases, disabled users may not be able to extract meaningful perceptible cues from a user interface (see Chapter 1). Disabled users may employ additional assistive devices that improve their access to computing technology. Use of these devices alone does not ensure usability; rather, it promotes access. Technologies in which access is assisted with additional devices can be more or less usable in much the same ways that technologies are more or less usable.

### 15.3.2 Usability for the Elderly

Like fine wine and Etruscan artifacts, we are all getting older. Data from the year 2000 U.S. Census suggest that the population as a whole is aging as well. From a summary report on census data by Meyer (2001, 2), we see who are the fastest-growing age groups:

> Of the 5-year age groups, 50-to-54 year olds experienced the largest percentage growth in population over the past decade, 55 percent. . . . The second fastest-growing group was the age group 45 to 49, which experienced a 45-percent increase. . . . The third fastest-growing group in the past decade was 90-to-94 year olds, which increased by 45 percent."

In terms of technology, elderly users often get left behind. According to the report by the U.S. Department of Commerce (2000, Executive Summary), older individuals in the United States are "still less likely than younger Americans to use the Internet." But, as the executive summary also indicates, older Americans "experienced the highest rates of growth in Internet usage of all age groups."

So why do elderly users seem to lag behind the general population in terms of access? Let's explore several myths surrounding computing by the elderly.

* *Myth 1.* Older people came of age during a time when computers were not as widespread as they are now. Therefore, their use of computers is limited by their negative attitudes.

These statements are incomplete at best and judgmental at worst. Czaja and Sharit (1998) performed a study that considered age differences in people's attitudes toward computers. They found that, while older subjects felt less comfortable with and felt they had less control over computers than did other subjects, computing experience moderated these effects. Thus, more experience with computers can contribute to positive attitudes across all age ranges. In a study by Kubeck, Miller-Albrecht, and Murphy (1999) involving Web navigation for older and younger adults, the results indicated only small differences in attitudes. What is more, Kubeck et al. found that training and experience led to positive attitudes for both groups.

* *Myth 2.* Older people are just people with disabilities who happen to be old.

Older people may or may not have disabilities. Many older adults do not satisfy the definition of *disabled.*

* *Myth 3.* Older people are a homogeneous population.

In fact, the opposite seems to be true. Older people may be *more* diverse as a group than the population at large. What is more, an older person's characteristics may change dynamically over time (cf. Jorge, Heller, and Guedj 2001). Sight, hearing, and motor skills change with age and illness. An older user who has no problems with a computer application today may have different requirements in a year or two due to changes in sight, hearing, and health improvements due to medication, lifestyle, or arthritic changes.

### 15.3.3 Usability for Children

Mynatt and Doherty have published a wonderful introductory psychology textbook (2002). One of the themes of the book is that, psychologically, children are not just small adults. It seems that this view holds for usability as well. What makes an interface usable and appealing for an adult may not be at all appropriate for children.

For several years, the ACM'S Special Interest Group on Computer-Human Interaction (SIGCHI) conference held a kind of computer camp in conjunction with its annual meeting. The camp is called CHIkids and was the brainchild of Allison Druin. One aspect of the camp was that SIGCHI participants could bring their designs and products that they designed for children to CHIkids. The children (with proper consent) performed usability tests on these products. We have observed some of these usability tests. Designs that were not built with the specific characteristics of children in mind generally were not received well by the children. Those designs that were built with kid feedback during the design process seemed to fare much better (Farber n.d.).

Druin and her colleagues have designed a number of technology artifacts for children. What is especially interesting about her work is that she includes children as participatory designers as well as usability testers. She has found that children can help to specify and design products for their own use. These products are often much different from the original designs that the adult designers had in mind (Druin n.d.).

### 15.3.4 Usability and Gender

Are there usability differences between men and women? Can we predict these differences, and can we design for these differences? These are very difficult questions with no definitive answers. Some time ago, Aaron Marcus presented three interfaces for a word processing system. In his article, Marcus suggested that different genders and different cultural groups would differentially prefer one of the interfaces over the other two. Following Marcus's terminology, interfaces were proposed for the following user groups: (1) "an English-speaking European adult male intellectual," (2) "white American women," and (3) "English-speaking consumers who might prefer what is referred to . . . as international-style design." The interface for "women" was a round presentation; the other two were rectangular (Marcus 1993).

Leventhal, Teasley, Blumenthal, Instone, Stone, and Donskoy (1996) reported on an extensive study of people's reactions to the three Marcus interfaces. In this study, 105 subjects specified their preferences for the three interfaces. Of these subjects, 51 were males and 54 were females, 54 were U.S. citizens, 16 were native Russians, and the remaining subjects were international students at U.S. universities. Leventhal et al. found that subjects as a whole disliked the interface intended for women. In particular, women disliked the interface that was intended for women. From this study we can learn that designers should not dictate interface choices to a group or gender without input from that group.

## 15.4 Real Strategies for Universal Usability

The 2001 EC/NSF Workshop on Universal Accessibility of Ubiquitous Computing: Providing for the Elderly identified real strategies to improve access for older users (Jorge, Heller, and Guedj 2001). Four of these strategies appear to generalize to support universal usability. In this section, we consider those four strategies:

- To work within the context of established infrastructure to promote universal usability.
- To use good engineering practice to develop software systems with the flexibility to accommodate a wide variety of user needs and situations.
- To design for a diverse audience now rather than designing for a narrow audience and attempting to broaden the audience later.
- To use and accommodate a wide variety of technologies.

### 15.4.1 To Work Within the Context of Established Infrastructure to Promote Universal Usability

Jorge, Heller, and Guedj (2001) suggest that many of the elements of established infrastructure can be used to promote universal usability. For example, a number of laws and guidelines already exist. Consider that the Americans with Disabilities Act of 1990 (U.S. Department of Justice 2006) specifically disallows discrimination in situations involving employment, job training, commercial infrastructure, and services that impact persons with disabilities.

The Americans with Disabilities Act has been used successfully to promote universal access. For example, in 1999 the National Federation for the Blind filed a suit against America Online (AOL). In the case, the plaintiffs specifically argued that the screen readers used by persons with visual disabilities were often incompatible with the services of AOL. In 2000, AOL agreed to make its software more accessible to those with visual disabilities and the lawsuit was dropped (Cisneros 2000).

The World Wide Web Consortium has sponsored the Web Accessibility Initiative (W3C WAI) as a continuing effort to build guidelines to help developers build Web sites that are accessible to all users. The Web Content Accessibility Guidelines (WCAG) suggest that in a number of usage situations access may be limited; these situations range from those involving users with slow connection speeds, to users who need their hands free or sight-free access, to users with disabilities.

The Web Content Accessibility Guidelines, Version 1.0 (WCAG 1.0), were released in May 1999 and undergo continuing change and improvement. Key in the WCAG recommendations is the idea of separating content from presentation in the design of a Web site. In that way, a number of presentations are possible. The guidelines do not discourage complex multimedia presentations but instead suggest ways that the information conveyed can be communicated to a broad audience (Chisholm, Vanderheiden and Jacobs 1999).

Each guideline in the WCAG has associated checkpoints, and each checkpoint has an assigned priority number. Priority numbers range from 1 as the highest and 3 as the lowest. According to the recommendations, Priority 1 checkpoints *must be* satisfied for a Web site to be accessible; Priority 2 checkpoints *should be* satisfied; and Priority 3 checkpoints *may be* satisfied.

Depending on the checkpoints that are satisfied, the Web site may then be at one of three levels of conformance. In Level A conformance, all Priority 1 checkpoints have been met. In Level Double A conformance, all Priority 1 and 2 checkpoints have been met. In Level Triple A conformance, all Priority 1, 2, and 3 checkpoints have been met.

The WCAG are not the only guidelines or rules that exist. The Workforce Investment Act 1998, Rehabilitation Act Amendments of 1998, Section 508, is an amendment to the 1973 Rehabilitation Act. The act requires all United States federal agencies to provide access to information technology for people with disabilities. The act further specifies that information technology developed or procured by the federal government must be accessible to federal employees and/or members of the public seeking information, regardless of disability (see U.S. Access Board n.d.a).

Section 508 (U.S. Access Board 2000) states:

the Federal government will be in the forefront in ensuring access to electronic and information technology.

Section 508 includes a set of specific rules that require U.S. federal agencies to ensure that electronic and information technology be accessible to federal employees and to members of the public who are seeking information. The standards address accessibility issues relating to software, computers, and electronic office equipment. For example, Subpart 1194.22: Web-Based Intranet and Internet Information and Applications, contains guidelines for Web sites that promote accessibility.

Section 508 also establishes requirements for accessibility and maintains the Access Board to evaluate individual cases in question. The Access Board, "a federal agency committed to accessible design," maintains an extensive Web site with information about Section 508 and Web site accessibility.

Many of the provisions of Section 508 are identical or very similar to WCAG 1.0. For example, Guideline 1 of WCAG 1.0 states:

Provide equivalent alternatives to auditory and visual content.

This guideline recognizes that many individuals may not be able to use visual information but could use the same information if presented in a nonvisual form, such as text.

WCAG 1.0 states that in a conforming Web site:

A text equivalent for every non-text element shall be provided.

Suppose I have constructed a Web site for a recreation center. One activity at the recreation center is fishing. The site might have a graphic under its list of activities (Figure 15.1). This graphic represents "Fishing" as an activity. The Web site designer might consider using the following line of html at the site:

<img src="fishing.gif" alt = "Fishing is an activity.">

The "alt" description states the goal of this nontext object. This text description may facilitate usability for users with visual impairments. The text description should be to the point so that a user with a voice browser is not bombarded with long descriptions of nontext objects.

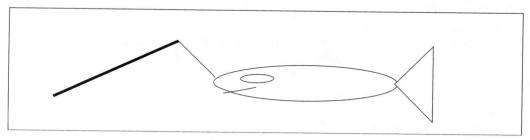

Figure 15.1   Sample Figure for Web Site.

In summary, a number of guidelines and laws promote universal usability. This information is itself accessible and available to designers.

### 15.4.2 To Use Good Engineering Practice

Much of what universal usability is concerned with pertains to supporting multiple redundant presentations (cf. Chisholm, Vanderheiden, and Jacobs 1999). Good engineering practice that builds products with flexibility in mind can support multiple presentations. These presentations may be of the type suggested by Oviatt (1999) or Oviatt and Cohen (2000) where the interface architecture and processing heuristics by their nature support multimodal interface, or they may use design tools to support separation of presentation from function. The notion of separating presentation from function is not a new idea in computer science and, in fact, is the whole idea behind usability engineering. However, a caveat is evident. As each new presentation technology hits the marketplace, developers are challenged to create alternatives. For display of information, text alternatives to graphics may be fairly obvious. Alternatives for navigation in virtual worlds may not be so obvious.

### 15.4.3 To Design for a Diverse Audience

We return to this theme from previous chapters: you are not your user. Your user's perspective is likely to be different from yours. Listen to your user. Practice user-centered design.

Throughout this book we have discussed a number of practices that should help you practice user-centered design. For example, defining your target interface in terms of your user's intended tasks is an example of a user-centered design strategy. Coleman, Heller, and Leventhal (2003) also suggest that putting emphasis on an interdisciplinary development team can help keep diversity in mind. Specifically, they suggest that you consider adding a person to your team who is an expert in the needs and realities of your users, especially if your user group is a specialized audience. For example, if you are designing an interface for elderly users, consider adding a physical or occupational therapist to your team.

### 15.4.4 To Use and Accommodate a Wide Variety of Technologies

Persons with disabilities may use a number of hardware and software technologies to aid their interactions with computers and to improve access. *Assistive technology* is defined as any item, piece of equipment, or system, whether acquired commercially, modified, or customized, that is commonly used to increase, maintain, or improve functional capabilities of individuals with disabilities. This definition is derived from the definition of assistive technology in the Assistive Technology Act of 1998 (U. S. Access Board n.d. b).

For example, a blind or visually impaired user may use a screen reader. Ability Hub, Assistive Technology Solutions (1997–2006), defines a screen reader:

> A Screen Reader software application reads aloud information displayed on a computer monitor screen. The screen reader reads aloud text within a document, and it also reads aloud information within dialog boxes and error messages. Screen Readers also read aloud and [sic] menu selections, graphical icons on the desktop. Recent upgrades are much better reading aloud information on the World Wide Web.

The Trace Research and Development Center of the University of Wisconsin–Madison has an extensive Web site that contains links and provides information about technologies for persons with disabilities. (See Trace R & D Center 2003.)

## 15.5 Universal Usability and the Marketplace

In a parody of an old-time beauty pageant, we once had a student equate a desire for universal usability to a beauty contestant's desire for world peace. Is universal usability one of those things like world peace that just sounds good? The answer probably lies in the marketplace. Shneiderman (2000) suggests by analogy that retrofitting existing sidewalks with curb cuts can be costly, but building them in a sidewalk initially is not. In other words, designing for universal usability can be cost-effective, but retrofitting is not.

## 15.6 Why Now?

Why are we thinking about universal usability now, when it was not a focus of attention twenty or even ten years ago in most quarters? We think that the answer harkens back to some of the ideas that we presented in Chapter 2. As computer science as a discipline has matured, we have become more concerned with usability in general. Three factors (diversification of software, more powerful hardware, and diversification of users) have pushed us toward usability as a discipline. In the same way, powerful Internet and networking technologies have opened up the possibilities of computer use to millions of users who had no opportunity twenty years ago. Unlike twenty years ago, those users potentially have different needs than a narrow set of programmers. Services that formerly were done in person, like banking or shopping, may be available in some cases only via the Internet. So once again, our three factors push us in the direction of usability— but now in the direction of usability for everyone.

Consider the audio catalog that we began to build in previous chapters. Who would have benefited in that project had we incorporated universal usability into our interface requirements? The answer is everyone. We might have included an audio feature so that a person with visual limitations could hear the answers to queries. A person driving a car and using the interface also would benefit from hearing the answers. Universal usability ultimately benefits everyone!

## Conclusions

Universal usability makes sense from a market perspective. Inclusion not only opens up markets but enhances opportunities for productivity across all segments of society. Changes to products to broaden a product's appeal to wider audiences often results in changes that are good for the population as a whole.

Across different potentially disenfranchised groups, we notice several themes that should come as no surprise:

- To accomplish usability, you must know your user because they are not you. By virtue of physical, cultural, or chronological differences, you cannot use yourself as the universal model of a user.
- User-centered design offers the best approach to really hearing what users have to say.
- Good usability and software engineering practice can improve usability.
- No group should be denied access simply because of an overbearing, negative attitude on the part of the developer.
- Universal accessibility is the law or policy in some quarters. Perhaps it will be so in all arenas at some point.

## A Final Thought

To all of you who have made it to the end of this text, thanks for sticking with us. We hope that you learned some things and enjoyed the book. Now that we are at the end, we have some parting thoughts. Technology can be a force for good or evil. It does not take much to identify some of the many ways that technology can be a force for good: improved health care services, safer transportation, and enhanced communication with those who are important to us. Sadly, as we know, technology can also be a great force for evil. Usability is a key element as to whether technology will be used at all. We believe that the usability professional has a responsibility to promote the use of technology, through usability as a force for good.

Interestingly, the first coda from the ACM Code of Ethics expresses much the same thought (Association of Computing Machinery 1997):

### 1. GENERAL MORAL IMPERATIVES.

*As an ACM member I will . . .*
1.1 Contribute to society and human well-being.

This principle concerning the quality of life of all people affirms an obligation to protect fundamental human rights and to respect the diversity of all cultures. An essential aim of computing professionals is to minimize negative consequences of computing systems, including threats to health and safety. When designing or implementing systems, computing professionals must attempt to ensure that the products of their efforts will be used in socially responsible ways, will meet social needs, and will avoid harmful effects to health and welfare.

## Exercises

1. Define the following terms: *assistive technology* and *universal usability.*
2. Visit http://www.w3.org/TR/WCAG10. Now go to a favorite Web site. Analyze the site in the context of the W3C Web Content Accessibility Guidelines.

# References

AbilityHub.com. (1997–2006). *Ability Hub Assistive Technology Solutions: Blind & Visually Impaired.* Retrieved July 5, 2006, from http://www.abilityhub.com/vision/index.htm

Alavi, M. (1984). An assessment of the prototyping approach to information systems development. *Communications of the ACM, 27*(6), 556–563.

Apple Computer, Inc. (1992). *Macintosh Human Interface Guidelines.* Reading, MA: Addison-Wesley. There is an interactive animated companion CD-ROM to these Mac guidelines called *Making It Macintosh,* 1993.

Apple Computer, Inc. (1993). *Making it Macintosh: The Macintosh Human Interface Guidelines Companion.* Instructional CD-ROM. Reading, MA: Addison-Wesley Publishing Company.

Apple Computer, Inc. (1994). *Electronic Guide to Macintosh Human Interface Design.* Reading, MA: Addison-Wesley Publishing Company.

Apple Computer, Inc. (2006). *Introduction to Apple Human Interface Guidelines.* Retrieved July 5, 2006, from http://developer.apple.com/documentation/UserExperience/Conceptual/OSXHIGuidelines/index.html

Artim, J. M. (2001). Entity, task, and presenter classification in user interface architecture: An approach to organizing HCI practice. In M. van Harmelen (Ed.), *Object Modeling and User Interface Design: Designing Interactive Systems,* Boston: Addison-Wesley, 115–158.

Association of Computing Machinery. (1997). *ACM Code of Ethics and Professional Conduct,* Section 1.4. Retrieved July 5, 2006, from http://www.acm.org/constitution/code.html

Baddeley, A. D. (1986). *Working Memory.* New York: Oxford University Press.

———. (1992). Working memory. *Science, 255,* 556–559.

———. (1997). *Human Memory: Theory and Practice* (rev. ed.). East Sussex, UK: Psychology Press Ltd.

Baecker, R. (1989). A vision of education in user-centered system and interface design. *ACM SIGCHI Bulletin, 20*(3), 10–13.

Baecker, R. M., & Buxton, W. A. S. (1987). *Readings in Human-Computer Interaction: A Multi-disciplinary Approach.* Los Altos, CA: Morgan Kaufman Publishers, Inc.

Barnes, J., & Leventhal, L. (2001). Turning the tables: Introducing software engineering concepts in a user interface course. *Proceedings of the 32nd SIGCSE Technical Symposium on Computer Science Education,* New York: ACM Press, 214–218.

Bellis, M. (2006). *Inventors of the Modern Computer: The History of the Graphical User Interface or GUI— The Apple Lisa.* Retrieved July 5, 2006, from http://inventors.about.com/library/weekly/aa043099.htm

Bennett, J. L. (1986). Tools for building advanced user interfaces. *IBM Systems Journal, 25*(3/4), 354–368.

Berry, R. E., & Reeves, C. J. (1992). The evolution of the Common User Access Workplace Model— Technical. *IBM Systems Journal, 31*(3), 414–428.

Billingsley, P. A. (1982). Navigation through hierarchical menu structures: Does it help to have a map? In *Proceedings of the Human Factors Society 26th Annual Meeting,* Santa Monica, CA: Human Factors Society, 103–107.

Blackwell, A. F. (1997). Correction: A picture is worth 84.1 words. In C. Kann (Ed.) *Proceedings of the First ESP Student Workshop* 15–22.

Blomberg, J. L., & Henderson, A. (1990). Reflections on participatory design: Lessons from the Trillium experience. In J. J. Chew, & J. Whiteside (Eds.), *Proceedings of the SIGCHI Conference on Human Factors in Computer Systems: Empowering People 1990,* New York: ACM Press, 353–360.

Bly, S. A., & Rosenberg, J. K. (1986). A comparison of tiled and overlapping window. In M. Mantei & P. Oberton (Eds.), *Proceedings of the SIGCHI Conference on Human Factors in Computing Systems 1986,* New York: ACM Press, 101–106.

Boehm, B. (1983). The hardware/software cost ratio: Is it a myth? *IEEE Computer, 16*(3), 78–80.

———. (1986). A spiral model of software development and enhancement. *ACM SIGSOFT Software Engineering Notes, 11*(4), 14–24.

———. (1988). A spiral model of software development and enhancement. *IEEE Computer, 21*(5), 61–72.

Boehm, B., Gray, T., & Seewaldt, T. (1984). Prototyping vs. specifying: A multi-project experiment. *IEEE Transactions on Software Engineering, May 1984,* 133–145.

Boehm, B., & Huang, L. G. (2003). Value-based software engineering: A case study. *IEEE Computer, 36*(3), 33–41.

Boehm, B. W., & Papaccio, P. N. (1988). Understanding and controlling software costs. *IEEE Transactions on Software Engineering, 14*(10), 1,462–1,477.

Booch, G. (1991). *Object Oriented Design with Applications.* Redwood City, CA: Benjamin/Cummings Publishing Company.

Booch, G., Rumbaugh, J., & Jacobson, I. (1999). *The Unified Modeling Language User Guide.* Reading, MA: Addison-Wesley.

Brooks, F. P. (1987). No silver bullet: Essence and accidents of software engineering. *IEEE Computer, 20*(4), 10–19.

Brown, J. R., & Cunningham, S. (1989). *Programming the User Interface: Principles and Examples.* New York: John Wiley & Sons.

Brown, J., Heller, R., Jorge, J., & Tremaine, M. (2001). Report on the EC/NSF workshop on universal accessibility of ubiquitous computing: Providing for the elderly. *SIGCHI Bulletin, 33*(5), 11, 14–15.

Budgen, D. (1994). *Software Design.* Reading, MA: Addison-Wesley.

Callahan, J., Hopkins, D., Weiser, M., & Shneiderman, B. (1988). An empirical comparison of pie vs. linear menus. In J. J. O'Hare (Ed.), *Proceedings of the SIGCHI Conference on Human Factors in Computing Systems 1988,* New York: ACM Press, 95–100.

Card, S. K., Moran, T. P., & Newell, A. (1983). *The Psychology of Human-Computer Interaction.* Hillsdale, NJ: Lawrence Erlbaum Associates.

Carelman, J. (1994). *Catalogue d'objets introuvables.* Paris, France: Librairie Générale Française.

Carey, T. T., & Mason, R. E. A. (1983). Information system prototyping: Techniques, tools, and methodologies. *INFOR—The Canadian Journal of Informational Research and Information Processing, 21,* 177–191.

Carroll, J. M. (2000). *Making Use: Scenario-Based Design of Human-Computer Interactions.* Cambridge, MA: MIT Press.

Chen, P. P-S. (1976). The entity-relationship model—Toward a unified view of data. *ACM Transactions on Database Systems, 1*(1), 9–36.

Chiariglione, L. (2000). *Short MPEG-2 description.* Retrieved July 5, 2006, from http://www.chiariglione.org/mpeg/standards.html

Chin, J. P., Diehl, V. A., & Norman, K. L. (1988). Development of an instrument measuring user satisfaction of the human-computer interface. In J. J. O'Hare (Ed.), *Proceedings of the SIGCHI Conference on Human Factors in Computing Systems 1988,* New York: ACM Press, 213–218.

Chisholm, W., Vanderheiden, G., & Jacobs, I. (Eds.). (1999). *W3C: Web Content Accessibility Guidelines 1.0—W3C Recommendation 5-May-1999*. Retrieved July 5, 2006, from http://www.w3.org/TR/WCAG10

Chrusch, M. (2000). The whiteboard: Seven great myths of usability. *interactions, 7*(5), 13–16.

Cisneros, O. S. (2000, July 28). AOL settles accessibility suit. *Wired News*. Retrieved July 5, 2006, from http://www.wired.com/news/business/0,1367,37845,00.html

CocoaDev. (2006). *Hypertalk*. Retrieved July 5, 2006, from http://www.cocoadev.com/index.pl?HyperTalk

Coleman, K., Heller, R., & Leventhal, L. (2003). Something old, something new: Designing for the aging population (tutorial). In *CHI '03 Extended Abstracts on Human Factors in Computing Systems*. New York: ACM Press.

Constantine, L. L., & Lockwood, L. A. D. (2001). Structure and style in use cases for user interface design. In M. van Harmelen (Ed.), *Object Modeling and User Interface Design: Designing Interactive Systems*, Boston: Addison-Wesley, 245–280.

Cunniff, N., & Taylor, R. P. (1987). Graphical vs. textual representation: An empirical study of novices' program comprehension. In G. M. Olsen, S. Sheppard, & E. Soloway (Eds.), *Empirical Studies of Programmers: Second Workshop 1987*, Norwood, NJ: Ablex Publishing, 114–131.

Czaja, S. J., & Sharit, J. (1998). Age differences in attitudes toward computers. *Journal of Gerontology, 53B*(5), 329–340.

DeGroot, A. (1965). *Thought and Choice in Chess*. The Hague: Mouton Publishers.

DeMarco, T. (1979). *Structured Analysis and System Specification*. Englewood Cliffs, NJ: Prentice-Hall.

Deurer, R. (1996). *Egypt Art: Symbols and Definitions*. Retrieved July 5, 2006, from http://members.aol.com/egyptart/symlst.html

Dillon, A., McKnight, C., & Richardson, J. (1988). Reading from paper versus reading from screen. *The Computer Journal, 31*(5), 457–464.

Dillon, A., McKnight, C., & Richardson, J. (1990). Navigation in hypertext: A critical review of the concept. In D. Diaper, D. Gilmore, G. Cockton, & B. Shackel (Eds.), *Proceedings of IFIP INTERACT'90: Human-Computer Interaction 1990*, Amsterdam: Elsevier Science Publishers, 587–592.

Dix, A., Finlay, J., Abowd, G., & Beale, R. (1998). *Human-Computer Interaction*, 2nd ed. London: Prentice Hall Europe.

Douglas, D. C. (1997–2005). *Useless Movie Quotes: Star Trek VI: The Undiscovered Country*. Retrieved July 5, 2006, http://www.uselessmoviequotes.com/umq_s010.htm

Druin, A. (n.d.). *Allison Druin—CHIkids activities*. Retrieved July 5, 2006, from http://www.umiacs.umd.edu/~allisond/chikids.html

Eason, K. D. (1984). Towards the experimental study of usability. *Behaviour and Information Technology, 3*(2), 133–143.

EMMUS. (1999). *Introduction to ISO 13407*. Retrieved July 5, 2006, from http://www.ucc.ie/hfrg/emmus/methods/iso.html

Ericsson, K. A., & Simon, H. A. (1984). *Protocol Analysis: Verbal Reports as Data*. Cambridge, MA: The MIT Press.

Fairley, R. E. (1985). *Software Engineering Concepts*. New York: McGraw Hill.

Farber, A. (n.d.). *Children as Design Partners: An Introduction*. Retrieved July 5, 2006, from http://www.cs.umd.edu/hcil/kiddesign

Federal Communications Commission. (1934, 1996). *Communications Act of 1934 as Amended by Telecom Act of 1996*. Retrieved July 5, 2006, from http://www.fcc.gov/Reports/1934new.pdf

Fitts, P. M. (1954). The information capacity of the human motor system in controlling amplitude of movement. *Journal of Experimental Psychology, 47,* 381–391.

Forman, P., & Saint John, R. W. (2000). Creating convergence. *Scientific American,* November 2000, 50–56.

Gaines, B. R. (1984). From ergonomics to the fifth generation: 30 years of human-computer interaction studies. In B. Shackel (Ed.) *Proceedings of IFIP INTERACT'84: Human-Computer Interaction 1984,* Amsterdam: Elsevier Science Publishers, 3–7.

Gale, S. (1996). A collaborative approach to developing style guides. In R. Bilger, S. Guest, & M. J. Tauber (Eds.), *Proceedings of SIGCHI Conference on Human Factors in Computing Systems: Common Ground 1996, vol. 1,* New York: ACM Press, 362–367.

Gane, C., & Sarson, T. (1979). *Structured Systems Analysis: Tools and Techniques.* Englewood Cliffs, NJ: Prentice Hall.

Gentner, D., & Gentner, D. R. (1983). Flowing waters or teeming crowds: Mental models of electricity. In D. Gentner, & A. L. Stevens (Eds.), *Mental Models,* Hillsdale, NJ: Lawrence Erlbaum Associates, 99–129.

Gibson, J. J. (1979). *The Ecological Approach to Visual Perception.* Boston: Houghton Mifflin.

Gilbert, P. (1983). *Software Design and Development.* Chicago: Science Research Associates, Inc.

Gordon, V. S., & Bieman, J. M. (1995). Rapid prototyping: Lessons learned. *IEEE Software, 12*(1), 85–95.

Grant, E. E., & Sackman, H. (1967). An exploratory investigation of programmer performance under on-line and off-line conditions. *IEEE Transactions on Human Factors in Electronics, 8*(1), 33–48.

Gray, W. D., John, B. E., & Atwood, M. E. (1993). Project Ernestine: Validating a GOMS analysis for predicting and explaining real-world task performance. *Human-Computer Interaction, 8*(3), 237–309.

Green, T. R. G., & Payne, S. J. (1984). Organization and learnability in computer languages. *International Journal of Man-Machine Studies, 21,* 7–18.

Grudin, J. (1989). The case against user interface consistency. *Communications of the ACM, 32*(10), 1,164–1,173.

Grupe, F. H. (1991). *Beginning Lotus 1-2-3, Version 3.0.* Dubuque, IA: W. C. Brown Publishers.

Guindon, R., Krasner, H., & Curtis, B. (1987). Breakdowns and processes during the early activities of software design by professionals. In F. M. Olson, C. Sheppard, & E. Soloway (Eds.), *Empirical Studies of Programmers: Second Workshop 1987,* Norwood, NJ: Ablex Publishing, 65–82.

Halasz, F., & Moran, T. P. (1982). Analogy considered harmful. In *Proceedings of the 1982 Conference on Human Factors in Computer Systems 1982,* New York: ACM Press, 383–386.

Hartson, H. R., Siochi, A. C., & Hix, D. (1990). The UAN: A user-oriented representation for direct manipulation interface designs. *ACM Transactions on Information Systems, 8*(3), 181–203.

Hayes, P. J., & Reddy, D. R. (1983). Steps toward graceful interaction in spoken and written man-machine communication. *International Journal of Man-machine Studies, 19*(3), 231–284.

Heckel, P., & Clanton, C. (1991). Roses and cabbages: Familiarizing and transporting user interface metaphors. In P. Heckel (Ed.), *The Elements of Friendly Software Design* (2nd ed.), Chapter 11. San Francisco: SYBEX.

Hewett, T. T., Baecker, R., Card, S., Carey, T., Gasen, J., Mantei, M., Perlman, G., Strong, G., & Verplank, W. (1992, 1996). *ACM SIGCHI Curricula for Human-Computer Interaction, Chapter 2: Human-Computer Interaction.* Retrieved July 5, 2006, from http://www.sigchi.org/cdg/cdg2.html

Hirsh-Pasek, K., Nudelman, S., & Schneider, M. L. (1982). An experimental evaluation of abbreviation schemes in limited lexicons. *Behaviour and Information Technology, 1*(4), 359–369.

Hix, D. (1990). Generations of user-interface management systems. *IEEE Software, 7*(5), 77–87.

Hix, D., & Hartson, H. R. (1993). *Developing User Interfaces: Ensuring Usability Through Product and Process*. New York: John Wiley and Sons.

Horton, W. (1995). Top ten blunders of visual designers. *ACM SIGRAPH Computer Graphics, 29*(4), 20–24.

Hudson, W. (2001). Toward unified models in user-centered and object-oriented design. In M. van Harmelen (Ed.), *Object Modeling and User Interface Design: Designing Interactive Systems*, Boston: Addison-Wesley, 313–362.

Humphrey, W. S. (1994, December). A personal commitment to software quality. *Yourdon's American Programmer.* Retrieved July 5, 2006, at http://www.sei.cmu.edu/publications/documents/95. reports/95.ar. psp.qual.html

Hutchins, E., Hollan, J., & Norman, D. A. (1986). Direct manipulation interfaces. In D. A. Norman, & S. W. Draper (Eds.), *User Centered System Design: New Perspectives on Human-Computer Interaction*, Hillsdale, NJ: Lawrence Erlbaum Associates, 87–124.

IBM Corporation. (1990). *System Application Architecture, Common User Access, Advanced Interface Design Guide, Document SC26–4582-0*. New York: IBM.

———. (1992). *Object-Oriented Interface Design: IBM Common User Access Guidelines*. Carmel, IN: Que.

Instone, K., Brown, E., Leventhal, L., & Teasley, B. (1993). The challenge of effectively integrating graphics into hypertext. In L. J. Bass, J. Gornostaev, & C. Unger (Eds.), *Human-Computer Interaction: Third International Conference, EWHCI'93, Lecture Notes in Computer Science,* vol. 753, Berlin: Springer, 290–297.

Instone, K., Teasley, B., & Leventhal, L. M. (1993). Empirically-based re-design of a hypertext encyclopedia. In S. Ashlund, K. Mullet, A. Henderson, E. Hollnagel, & T. White (Eds.), *Proceedings of the SIGCHI Conference on Human Factors in Computing Systems 1993*, New York: ACM Press, 277–284.

International Standards Organization. (1993). *ISO/IEC 11172–2: 1993, Information technology—Coding of moving pictures and associated audio for digital storage media at up to about 1.5 Mbps—Part2: Video.* Retrieved on July 6, 2005, at http://www.iso.org/iso/en/CatalogueDetailPage.CatalogueDetail? CSNUM-BER=22411

———. (1995). *ISO/IEC 13818-2: 1995 (E) Recommendation ITU-T H.262.* Retrieved July 5, 2006, from le-hacker.org/hacks/mpeg-drafts/is138182.pdf

———. (2000). *ISO/IEC 13818-2: 2000, Information technology—generic coding of moving pictures and associated audio information: Video.* Retrieved July 5, 2006, at http://www.iso.org/iso/en/CatalogueDe-tailPage.CatalogueDetail?CSNUMBER=35006

Jackson, M. A. (1975). *Principles of Program Design*. New York: Academic Press, Inc.

Jacob, R. J. K. (1990). What you look at is what you get: Eye movement-based interaction techniques. In J. J. Chew, & J. Whiteside (Eds.), *Proceedings of the SIGCHI Conference on Human Factors in Computer Systems: Empowering People 1990*, New York: ACM Press, 11–18.

Jacobson, I., Booch, G., & Rumbaugh, J. (1999). *The Unified Software Development Process*. Reading, MA: Addison-Wesley.

Jacobson, I., Christerson, M., Jonsson, P., & Övergaard, G. (1992). *Object-Oriented Software Engineering: A Use Case Driven Approach*. Reading, MA: Addison-Wesley.

Jaffe, S-C., & Winter, R. (Producers), & Meyer, N. (Director). (1991). *Star Trek IV: The Undiscovered Country* [Motion picture]. United States: Paramount Pictures.

Jaffee, S. (2000). Personal Communication.

James, W. (1890). *The Principles of Psychology* (2 vols.). New York: Henry Holt. Reprinted New York: Dover Publications, 1950.

Jeffries, R., Miller, J. R., Wharton, C., & Uyeda, K. (1991). User interface evaluation in the real world: A comparison of four techniques. In *Proceedings of the SIGCHI Conference on Human Factors in Computing Systems: Reaching through Technology,* New York: ACM Press, 119–124.

Jeffries, R., Turner, A., Polson, P. G., & Atwood, M. E. (1981). The processes involved in designing software. In J. R. Anderson (Ed.), *Cognitive Skills and Their Acquisition,* Hillsdale, NJ: Lawrence Erlbaum Associates, 255–283.

Jeong, W., & Gluck, M. (2003). Multimodal geographic information systems: Adding haptic and auditory display. *Journal of the American Society for Information Science and Technology, 54*(3). 229–242.

John, B. E. (1990). Extensions of GOMS analyses to expert performance requiring perception of dynamic visual and auditory information. In J. J. Chew, & J. Whiteside (Eds.), *Proceedings of the SIGCHI Conference on Human Factors in Computer Systems: Empowering People 1990,* New York: ACM Press, 107–116.

John, B. E., & Kieras, D. E. (1996a). Using GOMS for user interface design and evaluation: Which technique? *ACM Transactions on Computer-Human Interaction, 3*(4), 287–319.

————. (1996b). The GOMS family of user interface analysis techniques: Comparison and contrast. *ACM Transactions on Computer-Human Interaction, 3*(4), 320–351.

Johnson, J. (2000). *GUI Bloopers: Don'ts and Do's for Software Developers and Web Designers.* San Francisco: Morgan Kaufmann Publishers.

Johnson, J., Roberts, T. L., Verplank, W., Smith, D. C., Irby, C., Beard, M., & Mackey, K. (1989). The Xerox Star: A Retrospective. *IEEE Computer, 22*(9), 11–30.

Joint Task Force on Computing Curricula. (2001). *Computing Curricula 2001, Computer Science. Final Report. December 15, 2001.* IEEE Computer Society and Association of Computing Machinery. Retrieved July 5, 2006, from http://www.computer.org/portal/cms_docs_ieeecs/news/education/cc2001/cc2001.pdf

Jorge, J., Heller, R., & Guedj, R. (Eds.) (2001). *2001 EC/NSF Workshop on Universal Accessibility of Ubiquitous Computing: Providing for the Elderly.* New York: ACM Press.

Kaplan, S., & Kaplan, R. (1982). *Cognition and Environment: Functioning in an Uncertain World.* New York: Praeger.

Karat, C-M., Campbell, R., & Fiegel, T. (1992). Comparison of empirical testing and walkthrough methods in user interface evaluation. In P. Bauersfeld, J. Bennett, & G. Lynch (Eds.), *Proceedings of the SIGCHI Conference on Human Factors in Computing Systems 1992,* New York: ACM Press, 397–404.

Katz, I. R., Petre, M., & Leventhal, L. (2001). Editorial: Empirical studies of programmers. *International Journal of Human-Computer Interaction, 54*(2), 185–188.

Kieras, D. (n.d.). *GOMS Models: An Approach to Rapid Usability Evaluation.* Retrieved July 5, 2006, from http://www.eecs.umich.edu/~kieras/goms.html

Kieras, D. E. (1988). Towards a practical GOMS model methodology for user interface design. In M. Helander (Ed.), *Handbook of Human-Computer Interaction,* New York: Elsevier Science, 135–157.

Kiger, J. I. (1984). The depth/breadth trade-off in the design of menu-driven user interfaces. *International Journal of Man-Machine Studies, 20*(2), 201–213.

Kleiman, G. (1998, January). The E-rate is here! *Leadership and the New Technologies News & Reports.* Education Development Center, Inc. Retrieved July 5, 2006, from http://www2.edc.org/LNT/news/Issue1/e-rate.htm

Koenen, R. (Ed.). (2002) *MPEG-4 Overview (V.21—Jeju Version).* Retrieved July 21, 2006, from http://www.chiariglione.org/mpeg/standards.html

Kokjer, K. J. (1987). The information capacity of the human fingertip. *IEEE Transactions on Systems, Man, and Cybernetics, 17*(1), 100–102.

Kruchten, P., Ahlqvist, S., & Bylund, S. (2001). User interface design in the Rational Unified Process. In M. van Harmelen (Ed.), *Object Modeling and User Interface Design: Designing Interactive Systems,* Boston: Addison-Wesley, 161–196.

Kubeck, J. E., Miller-Albrecht, S. A., & Murphy, M. D. (1999). Finding information on the World Wide Web: Exploring older adults' exploration. *Educational Gerontology, 25*(2), 167–183.

Landauer, T. K., & Nachbar, D.W. (1985). Selection from alphabetic and numeric menu trees using a touch screen: Breadth, depth, and width. In *Proceedings of the SIGCHI Conference on Human Factors in Computing Systems 1985,* New York: ACM Press, 73–78.

Landauer, T. K., Galotti, K. M., & Hartwell, S. (1983). Natural command names and initial learning: A study of text-editing terms. *Communications of the ACM, 26*(7), 495–503.

Leavitt, H. J. (1951). Some effects of certain communication patterns on group performance. *Journal of Abnormal and Social Psychology, 46*(1), 38–50.

Lepper, M. R., & Malone, T. W. (1987). Intrinsic motivation and instruction effectiveness in computer-based-education. In R. E. Snow, & J. F. Marshall (Eds.), *Aptitude, Learning, and Instruction: Conative and Affective Process Analyses,* Hillsdale, NJ: Lawrence Erlbaum Associates, 255–286.

LeRoy, M. (Producer), & Fleming, V. (Director). (1939). *The Wizard of Oz* [Motion Picture]. United States: Metro-Goldwyn-Mayer Studios Inc.

Leventhal, L. (2001). Delivering instructions for inherently-3D construction tasks: Lessons and questions for universal accessibility. In J. Jorge, R. Heller, & R. Guedj (Eds.), *2001 EC/NSF Workshop on Universal Accessibility of Ubiquitous Computing: Providing for the Elderly,* New York: ACM Press, 51–55.

Leventhal, L., Teasley, B., Blumenthal, B., Instone, K., Stone, D., & Donskoy, M. (1996). Assessing user interfaces for diverse user groups: Evaluation strategies and defining characteristics. *Behavior and Information Technology, 15*(3), 127–137.

Leventhal, L. M., Barnes, J., & Chao, J. (2004). Term project user interface specifications in a usability engineering course: Challenges and suggestions. In *Proceedings of the 35th SIGCSE Technical Symposium on Computer Science Education,* New York: ACM Press, 41–45.

Leventhal, L. M., & Mynatt, B. T. (1991). *Breaking with Tradition: Using Rapid Prototyping in the Software Engineering Course.* BGSU Technical Report 91-Mar-01.

Liebelt, L. S., MacDonald, J. E., Stone, J. D., & Karat, J. (1983). The effect of organization on learning menu access. In *Proceedings of the Human Factors Society, 26th Annual Meeting,* Santa Monica, CA: Human Factors Society, 546–550.

Lindsay, P. H., & Norman, D. A. (1972). *Human Information Processing: An Introduction to Psychology.* New York: Academic Press.

Luqi. (1989). Software evolution through rapid prototyping. *IEEE Computer, 22*(5), 13–25.

Malone, T. W. (1981). Toward a theory of intrinsically motivating instruction. *Cognitive Science, 4,* 333–369.

Mandel, T. (1997). *The Elements of User Interface Design.* New York: John Wiley & Sons.

Marcus, A. (1993). Human communication issues in advanced UIs. *Communications of the ACM, 36*(4), 101–109.

Martin, J. (1973). *Design of Man-Computer Dialogues.* Englewood Cliffs, NJ: Prentice-Hall.

Maulsby, D., Greenberg, S., & Mander, R. (1993). Prototyping an intelligent agent through Wizard of Oz. In S. Ashlund, K. Mullet, A. Henderson, E. Hollnagel, & T. White (Eds.), *Proceedings of the SIGCHI Conference on Human Factors in Computing Systems 1993,* New York: ACM Press, 277–284.

Mayer, R. E. (1989). Models for understanding. *Review of Educational Research, 59*(1), 43–64.

———. (2001). *Multimedia Learning.* New York: Cambridge University Press.

Mayhew, D. J. (1992). *Principles and Guidelines in Software User Interface Design.* Englewood Cliffs, NJ: Prentice-Hall.

———. (1999). *The Usability Engineering Lifecycle: A Practitioner's Handbook for User Interface Design.* San Francisco: Morgan Kaufmann Publishers, Inc.

Maynes-Aminzade, D. (2005). Edible bits: Seamless interfaces between people, data and food. In *CHI 2005 Extended Abstracts (alt.chi),* 2,207–2,210.

McCracken, D. D., & Wolfe, R. J. (2003). *User-Centered Web Site Development: A Human-Computer Interaction Approach.* Upper Saddle River, NJ: Pearson Education, Inc.

McCue, G. M. (1978). IBM's Santa Teresa Laboratory—Architectural design for program development. *IBM Systems Journal, 17*(1), 4–25.

McLean, A. (2003). 130 years ago: Hunt and peck (in This Month in History). *Smithsonian Magazine, 14*(2), 19.

Meyer, J. (2001). Age: 2000, Census 2000 Brief. United States Census 2000. U.S. Census Bureau. U.S. Department of Commerce. Economics and Statistics Administration. Retrieved December 28, 2006, from http://www.census.gov/prod/2001pubs/c2kbro1-12.pdf

Microsoft Corporation. (1992). *The Windows Interface: An Application Design Guide.* Redmond, WA: Microsoft Press.

———. (1993). *The GUI Guide: International Terminology for the Windows Interface.* Redmond, WA: Microsoft Press.

———. (1994). *Microsoft Windows 95 User Interface Design Guide: Preliminary Draft 5.00.* Redmond, WA: Microsoft Press.

———. (1995). *The Windows Interface Guidelines for Software Design.* Redmond, WA: Microsoft Press.

———. (1999). *Microsoft Windows User Experience: Microsoft Professional Editions.* Redmond, WA: Microsoft Press.

———. (2003). *Microsoft Visual Basic.NET.* Retrieved April 16, 2003, from http://msdn.microsoft.com/ vbasic

Mieder, W. (1990). "A picture is worth a thousand words": From advertising slogan to American proverb. *Southern Folklore, 47,* 207–225.

Miller, D. P. (1981). The depth/breadth tradeoff in hierarchical computer menus. In *Proceedings of the Human Factors Society 25th Annual Meeting,* Santa Monica, CA: Human Factors Society, 296–300.

Miller, G. A. (1956). The magical number seven, plus or minus two. *The Psychological Review, 63,* 81–97.

Mullet, K., & Sano, D. (1995). *Designing Visual Interfaces: Communications Oriented Techniques.* Englewood Cliffs, NJ: SunSoft Press.

Myers, B. A. (1988). A taxonomy of window manager user interfaces. *IEEE Computer Graphics and Applications, 8*(5), 65–84.

———. (1989). User-interface tools: Introduction and survey. *IEEE Software, 6*(1), 15–23.

———. (1994). Challenges of HCI design and implementation. *interactions, 1*(1), 73–83.

———. (1998). A brief history of human-computer interaction technology. *interactions, 5*(2), 44–54.

Myers, B., Hudson, S. E., & Pausch, R. (2000). Past, present, and future of user interface software tools. *ACM Transactions on Computer-Human Interaction, 7*(1), 3–28.

Myers, D. G. (1998). *Psychology* (5th ed.). New York: Worth Publishers.

Myers, G. J. (1979). *The Art of Software Testing.* New York: John Wiley and Sons.

Mynatt, B. T. (1990). *Software Engineering with Student Project Guidance.* Englewood Cliffs, NJ: Prentice-Hall.

Mynatt, B. T., Leventhal, L. M., Instone, K., Farhat, J., & Rohlman, D. S. (1992). Hypertext or book: Which is better for answering questions? In P. Bauersfeld, J. Bennett, & G. Lynch (Eds.), *Proceedings of the SIGCHI Conference on Human Factors in Computing Systems 1992,* New York: ACM Press, 373–380.

Mynatt, C. R., & Doherty, M. E. (2002). *Understanding Human Behavior* (2nd ed.). Boston: Allyn & Bacon.

National Research Council. (1999). *Funding a Revolution: Government Support for Computing Research, Chapter 4, The Organization of Federal Support: A Historical Review.* The National Academies Press. Retrieved July 5, 2006, from http://www.nap.edu/readingroom/books/far/ch4_b1.html

National Telecommunications and Information Administration, U.S. Department of Commerce (1999). *Falling Through the Net: Defining the Digital Divide.* Retrieved July 5, 2006, from http://www.ntia.doc.gov/NTIAHOME/FTTN99/contents.html

Neal, L. (1990). Implications of computer games for system design. In D. Diaper, D. Gilmore, G. Cockton, & B. Shackel (Eds.), *Proceedings of IFIP INTERACT'90: Human-Computer Interaction 1990,* Amsterdam: Elsevier Science Publishers, 93–99.

Newell, A., & Rosenbloom, P. S. (1981). Mechanisms of skill acquisition and the law of practice. In J. R. Anderson (Ed.), *Cognitive Skills and Their Acquisition,* Hillsdale, NJ: Lawrence Erlbaum Associates, 1–55.

Newell, A., & Simon, H. A. (1972). *Human Problem Solving.* Englewood Cliffs, NJ: Prentice-Hall.

Nielsen, J. (1990). Paper versus computer implementations as mockup scenarios for heuristic evaluation. In D. Diaper, D. Gilmore, G. Cockton, & B. Shackel (Eds.), *Proceedings of IFIP INTERACT'90: Human-Computer Interaction 1990,* Amsterdam: Elsevier Science Publishers, 315–320.

Nielsen, J. (1993a). *Usability Engineering.* Boston: Academic Press.

———. (1993b). Iterative user-interface design. *IEEE Computer, 26*(11), 32–41.

———. (1994). Heuristic evaluation. In J. Nielsen, & R. L. Mack (Eds.), *Usability Inspection Methods,* New York: John Wiley & Sons, 25–62.

———. (1995). *Multimedia and Hypertext: The Internet and Beyond.* Boston: Academic Press Professional.

———. (2006a). *How to Conduct a Heuristic Evaluation.* Retrieved July 5, 2006, from http://www.useit.com/papers/heuristic/heuristic_evaluation.html

———. (2006b). *Ten Usability Heuristics.* Retrieved July 5, 2006, from http://www.useit.com/papers/heuristic/heuristic_list.html

Nielsen, J., & Molich, R. (1990). Heuristic evaluation of user interfaces. In J. J. Chew, & J. Whiteside (Eds.), *Proceedings of the SIGCHI Conference on Human Factors in Computer Systems: Empowering People 1990,* New York: ACM Press, 249–256.

Norman, D. A. (1988). *The Psychology of Everyday Things.* New York: Basic Books.

———. (1995). Designing the future. *Scientific American, September 1995,* 194, 198.

Norman, D. A., & Draper, S. W. (Eds.) (1986). *User Centered System Design: New Perspectives on Human-Computer Interaction.* Hillsdale, NJ: Lawrence Erlbaum Associates.

Open Group, The. (1995–2006). *The Open Group: Making Standards Work: The UNIX® System.* Retrieved July 5, 2006, from http://www.unix.org (UNIX® is a registered trademark of The Open Group).

Oviatt, S. (1999). Ten myths of multimodal interaction. *Communications of the ACM, 42*(11), 74–81.

———. (2001). Designing robust multimodal systems for universal access. In J. Jorge, R. Heller, & R. Guedj (Eds.), *2001 EC/NSF Workshop on Universal Accessibility of Ubiquitous Computing: Providing for the Elderly,* New York: ACM Press, 71–74.

Oviatt, S., & Cohen, P. (2000). Perceptual user interfaces: Multimodal interfaces that process what comes naturally. *Communications of the ACM, 43*(3), 45–53.

Pace, B. J. (1984). Color combinations and contrast reversals on visual display units. In M. J. Alluisi, S. deGroot, & E. A. Alluisi (Eds.), *Proceedings of the Human Factors Society 28th Annual Meeting,* Santa Monica, CA: Human Factors Society, 326–330.

Page-Jones, M. (1999). *Fundamentals of Object-Oriented Design in UML.* Reading, MA: Addison-Wesley.

Pausch, R., Proffitt, D., & Williams, G. (1997). Quantifying immersion in virtual reality. In *Proceedings of the 24th Annual Conference on Computer Graphics and Interactive Techniques,* New York: ACM Press, 13–18.

Pfleeger, S. L. (2001). *Software Engineering: Theory and Practice* (2nd ed.). Upper Saddle River, NJ: Prentice Hall.

Polson, P. G., Lewis, C., Rieman, J., & Wharton, C. (1992). Cognitive walkthroughs: A method for theory-based evaluation of user interfaces. *International Journal of Man-Machine Studies, 36*(5), 741–773.

Porter, L. W., & Lawler, E. E. (1965). Properties of organizational structure in relation to job attitudes and job behavior. *Psychological Bulletin, 64,* 23–51.

Powell, J. E. (1990). *Designing User Interfaces.* San Marcos, CA: Microtrend Books.

Pressman, R. S. (1992). *Software Engineering: A Practitioner's Approach* (3rd ed.). New York: McGraw-Hill, Inc.

———. (2001). *Software Engineering: A Practitioner's Approach* (5th ed.). New York: McGraw-Hill, Inc.

Puerta, A. R., Cheng, E., Ou, T., & Min, J. (1999). MOBILE: User-centered interface building. In *Proceedings of the SIGCHI Conference on Human Factors in Computing Systems: The CHI is the Limit 1999,* New York: ACM Press, 426–433.

Quatrani, T. (2000). *Visual Modeling with Rational Rose 2000 and UML.* Reading, MA: Addison-Wesley Publishing Company.

Reason, J. T. (1990). *Human Error.* New York: Cambridge University Press.

Rittel, H. J., & Webber, M. M. (1984). Planning problems are wicked problems. In N. Cross (Ed.), *Developments in Design Methodology,* New York: John Wiley & Sons, 135–144.

Robertson, G., Czerwinski, M., & van Dantzich, M. (1997). Immersion in desktop virtual reality. In *Proceedings of the 10th Annual ACM Symposium on User Interface Software and Technology 1997,* New York: ACM Press, 13–18.

Rohde, D. (1998, July 16). Should universal service be scrapped? *Network World.* Retrieved July 5, 2006, from http://www.cnn.com/TECH/computing/9807/16/universal.idg

Rosenfeld, R., Olsen, D., & Rudnicky, A. (2001). Universal speech interfaces. *interactions, 8*(6), 34–44.

Rosson, M. B. (1983). Patterns of experience in text editing. In A. Janda (Ed.), *Proceedings of the SIGCHI Conference on Human Factors in Computing Systems 1983,* New York: ACM Press, 171–175.

Rosson, M. B., & Carroll, J. M. (2002). *Usability Engineering: Scenario-Based Development of Human-Computer Interaction.* San Francisco: Morgan Kaufmann/Academic Press.

Rosson, M. B., Carroll, J. M., & Rodi, C. M. (2004). Case studies for teaching usability engineering. In *Proceedings of the 35th SIGCSE Technical Symposium on Computer Science Education,* New York: ACM Press, 36–40.

Royce, W. W. (1987). Managing the development of large software systems: Concepts and techniques. In *Proceedings of the 9th International Conference on Software Engineering,* Los Alamitos, CA: IEEE Computer Society Press, 328–338.

Rudd, J., Stern, K., & Isensee, S. (1996). Low vs. high-fidelity prototyping debate. *interactions, 3*(1), 76–85.

Rumbaugh, J. R., Blaha, M. R., Lorensen, W., Eddy, F., & Premerlani, W. (1991). *Object-Oriented Modeling and Design.* Englewood Cliffs, NJ: Prentice-Hall.

Rumbaugh, J., Jacobson, I., & Booch, G. (1999). *The Unified Modeling Language Reference Manual.* Reading, MA: Addison-Wesley.

San Diego Computer Museum. (2006). *Apple LISA 1983 Model 2-10.* Retrieved July 5, 2006, from http://www.computer-museum.org/main/collections/apple_lisa.shtml

Scharer, L. L. (1983). User training: Less is more. *Datamation, July 1983,* 175–182.

Schmuller, J. (2002). *SAMS Teach Yourself UML in 24 Hours* (2nd ed.). Indianapolis, IN: SAMS.

Schühlein, F. (2005). Talmud. *The Catholic Encyclopedia,* Vol. XV, Online Edition. Retrieved July 5, 2006, from http://www.newadvent.org/cathen/14435b.htm

Scriven, M. (1967). The methodology of evaluation. In R. Tyler, R. Gagne, & M. Scriven (Eds.), *Perspectives of Curriculum Evaluation,* Chicago: Rand McNally, 39–83.

————. (1991). Beyond formative and summative evaluation. In M. W. McLaughlin, & E. D. C. Phillips (Eds.), *Evaluation and Education: A Quarter Century,* Chicago: University of Chicago Press, 19–64.

Serco, Ltd. (2001). *Cost-effective User Centred Design, TRUMP Project.* Retrieved July 5, 2006, from http://www.usabilitynet.org/trump/index.htm

Shackel, B. (1986). Ergonomics in design for usability. In M. D. Harrison, & A. F. Monk (Eds.), *People and computers: Designing for usability, Proceedings of the HCI'86 Conference on People and Computers II 1986,* Cambridge, UK: Cambridge University Press, 44–64.

Shakespeare, W. (n.d.). The Tragedy of Hamlet, Prince of Denmark. *The Complete Works of William Shakespeare.* Retrieved July 5, 2006, from http://www-tech.mit.edu/Shakespeare/hamlet/index.html

Shaw, M. E. (1971). *Group Dynamics: The Psychology of Small Group Behavior.* New York: McGraw-Hill.

Shneiderman, B. (1980). *Software Psychology: Human Factors in Computer and Information Systems.* Cambridge, MA: Winthrop Publishers.

————. (1982). The future of interactive systems and the emergence of direct manipulation. *Behaviour and Information Technology, 1*(3), 237–256.

————. (1992). *Designing the User Interface: Strategies for Effective Human-Computer Interaction, second edition.* Reading, MA: Addison Wesley.

————. (1998). *Designing the User Interface: Strategies for Effective Human-Computer Interaction* (3rd ed.). Reading, MA: Addison Wesley.

————. (2000). Universal usability. *Communications of the ACM, 43*(5), 84–91.

————. (2001). CUU: Bridging the digital divide with universal usability. *interactions, 8*(2), 11–15.

Shneiderman, B., & Plaisant, C. (2005). *Designing the User Interface: Strategies for Effective Human-Computer Interaction,* (4th ed.). Boston: Pearson Education.

Smith, S. L., & Mosier, J. N. (1986). *Guidelines for designing user interface software. Report ESD-TR-86-278.* Bedford, MA: The MITRE Corporation.

Snyder, C. (2003). *Paper Prototyping: The Fast and Easy Way to Design and Refine User Interfaces.* San Francisco: Morgan Kaufmann.

Sommerville, I. (2000). *Software Engineering* (6th ed.). Harlow UK: Addison-Wesley.

Stanton, N. A., Taylor, R. G., & Tweedie, L. A. (1992). Maps as navigational aids in hypertext environments: An empirical evaluation. *Journal of Educational Multimedia and Hypermedia, 1*(4), 431–444.

Stevens, G. C. (1983). User-friendly computer systems? A critical examination of the concept. *Behaviour and Information Technology, 2*(1), 3–16.

Stevens, W., Myers, G., & Constantine, L. (1974). Structured design. *IBM Systems Journal, 13*(2), 115–139.

Stewart, T. (n.d.). *System Concepts.* Retrieved July 5, 2006, from http://www.system-concepts.com

Stiller, E., & LeBlanc, C. (2002). *Project-Based Software Engineering: An Object-Oriented Approach.* Boston: Addison Wesley.

Sun Microsystems, Inc. (1989a). *OPEN LOOK Graphical User Interface Application Style Guidelines.* Reading, MA: Addison-Wesley.

————. (1989b). *OPEN LOOK Graphical User Interface Functional Specification.* Reading, MA: Addison-Wesley.

————. (1994–2005). *Solaris 2.4 Software Developer AnswerBook: Standards Conformance Reference Manual: UNIX System V Release 4-Based (SVR4) Specifications.* Retrieved July 5, 2006, from http://docs.sun.com/app/docs/doc/801-6735/6i13eq5ed?a=view

Sutherland, I. E. (1963). Sketchpad: A man-machine graphical communication system. In *Proceedings of AFIPS Spring Joint Computer Conference,* Detroit, MI 329–346.

Teasley, B. E., Leventhal, L. M., Mynatt, C. R., & Rohlman, D. S. (1994). Why software testing is sometimes ineffective: Two applied studies of positive test strategy. *Journal of Applied Psychology, 79*(1), 142–155.

Teasley, B., Instone, K., Leventhal, L. M., & Brown, E. (1997). Effective illustrations in interactive media: What works? In S. Howard, J. Hammond, & G. Lindgaard (Eds.), *Proceedings of IFIP INTERACT'97: Human-Computer Interaction 1997,* New York: Chapman and Hall, 197–204.

Teasley, B., Leventhal, L. M., Instone, K., & Schertler-Rohlman, D. M. (1991). Longitudinal studies of the relation of programmer expertise and role-expressiveness to program comprehension. In *Proceedings NATO Advanced Research Workshop on User-Centered Requirements for Software Engineering Environments, NATO Advanced Science Institutes Series—Computer Science,* vol. 123, Springer.

TechTarget. (2004–2006). *Virtual Reality, searchSMB.com.* Retrieved August 4, 2006, from http://searchSMB.techtarget.com/sDefinition/0,,sid44_gci213303,00.html

Teitelbaum, R. C., & Granda, R. E. (1983). The effects of positional constancy on searching menus for information. In A. Janda (Ed.), *Proceedings of the SIGCHI Conference on Human Factors in Computing Systems 1983,* New York: ACM Press, 150–153.

Tetzlaff, L., & Schwartz, D. R. (1991). The use of guidelines in interface design. In S. P. Robertson, G. M. Olson, & J. S. Olson (Eds.), *Proceedings of the SIGCHI Conference on Human Factors in Computer Systems: Reaching Through Technology,* New York: ACM Press, 329–333.

Trace R & D Center. (2003). *Designing a more usable world—for all.* College of Engineering, University of Wisconsin-Madison. Retrieved July 5, 2006, from http://trace.wisc.edu

Trumbly, J. E., Arnett, K. P., & Martin, M. P. (1993). Performance effect of matching computer interface characteristics and user skill level. *International Journal of Man-Machine Studies, 38*(4), 713–724.

Tullis, T. S. (1983). The formatting of alphanumeric displays: A review and analysis. *Human Factors, 25*(6), 657–682.

U.S. Access Board. (2000). *Board Issues Standards for Electronic and Information Technology (12/21/00).* Retrieved March 30, 2003, from http://www.access-board.gov/news/508-final.htm

U.S. Access Board. (n.d.b). *Section 508 Homepage: Electronic and Information Technology.* Retrieved July 5, 2006, from http://www.access-board.gov/508.htm

U.S. Access Board. (n.d.a). *The Access Board: A Federal Agency Committed to Accessible Design.* Retrieved July 5, 2006, from http://www.access-board.gov

U.S. Department of Commerce. (2000). *Falling Through the Net: Toward Digital Inclusion. A Report on American's Access to Technology Tools. October 2000.* Retrieved July 5, 2006, from http://www.ntia.doc.gov/ntiahome/fttn00/contents00.html

U.S. Department of Defense. (1989). *Military Standard: Human Engineering Design Criteria for Military Systems, Equipment and Facilities. MIL-STD-1472D.* Washington, DC: U.S. Government Printing Office.

U.S. Department of Justice, Civil Rights Division, Disability Rights Section. (2005). *A Guide to Disability Rights Laws. September 2005.* Retrieved July 5, 2006, from http://www.usdoj.gov/crt/ada/ cguide.htm# anchor62335

U.S. Department of Justice. (2006). *ADA Homepage: Information and Technical Assistance on the Americans with Disabilities Act.* Retrieved July 5, 2006, from http://www.usdoj.gov/crt/ada/adahom1.htm

Waldrop, M. M. (2001). Origins of personal computing. *Scientific American,* December 2001, 84–91.

Wegweiser, E. (1996–2005). *Gallery of the Absurd,* v2.0. Retrieved July 5, 2006, from http://www.ichizen.com/goat/goat_ergonomics

Weinberg, G. M. (1971). *The Psychology of Computer Programming.* New York: Van Nostrand Reinhold.

Weinschenk, S., Jamar, P., & Yeo, S. C. (1997). *GUI Design Essentials.* New York: John Wiley & Sons.

Wharton, C., Rieman, J., Lewis, C., & Polson, P. (1994). The cognitive walkthrough method: A practitioner's guide. In J. Nielsen, & R. L. Mack (Eds.), *Usability Inspection Methods,* New York: John Wiley & Sons, 105–140.

WhatIs.com. (2004–2006). *Virtual Reality, searchSMS.com.* Retrieved August 4, 2006, from http://searchSMB.techtarget.com/sDefinition/0,,sid44_gci213303,00.html

Winter, D. (1996–1999). *Atari PONG—The first steps.* Retrieved July 5, 2006, from http://www.pong-story.com/atpong1.htm

Wozny, L. A. (1989). The application of metaphor, analogy, and conceptual models in computer systems. *Interacting with Computers, 1*(3), 273–283.

Yankelovich, N., Levow, G-A., & Marx, M. (1995). Designing SpeechActs: Issues in speech user interfaces. In I. R. Katz, R. Mack, L. Marks, M. B. Rosson, & J. Nielsen (Eds.), *Proceedings of the SIGCHI Conference on Human Factors in Computing Systems 1995,* New York: ACM Press, 369–376.

Yourdan, E., & Constantine, L. L. (1979). *Structured Design: Fundamentals of a Discipline of Computer Program and Systems Design.* Englewood Cliffs, NJ: Prentice-Hall.

Zimmerman, G., Barnes, J., & Leventhal, L. M. (2001). Building user-controlled 3D models and animations for inherently-3D construction tasks. *Proceedings of the 8th IFIP International Conference on Engineering for Human-Computer Interaction, Lecture Notes in Computer Science,* Vol. 2254, London: Springer-Verlag, 193–206.

# Index